CW01072793

ENFORCEMENT AGENCY PRACTICE IN EUROPE

ENFORCEMENT AGENCY PRACTICE IN EUROPE

Editors

MADS ANDENAS, BURKHARD HESS and
PAUL OBERHAMMER

Assistant Editor
Hugo Warner

With a Foreword by
Sir Jonathan Mance
and
an Introduction by
Professor Dr Peter Schlosser

BIICL
BRITISH INSTITUTE OF
INTERNATIONAL AND
COMPARATIVE LAW
www.biicl.org

Published and Distributed by
The British Institute of International and Comparative Law
Charles Clore House, 17 Russell Square, London WC1B 5JP

© The British Institute of International and Comparative Law 2005

British Library Cataloguing in Publication Data
A Catalogue record of this book is available from the British Library

ISBN 0–903067–69–2

Typeset by Cambrian Typesetters
Frimley, Surrey
Printed in Great Britain by Biddles Ltd
King's Lynn

Foreword by the Right Honourable Lord Justice Mance

One of the achievements of Lord Goff of Chieveley's chairmanship of the British Institute of International and Comparative Law was the choice of procedure as the main unifying theme of its research programme. With rare exceptions, procedure has not in the English legal tradition had the academic attention that it deserves. But procedure is fundamental to efficient justice. As judicial exchanges with other European jurisdictions regularly confirm, differences in procedure rather than in substantive outcome constitute the most significant distinctions between European legal systems. Lord Diplock once famously described the common law as a maze, not a motorway. Today, the metaphor brings a sense of unease and a hope that common law reasoning focuses rather on underlying principle than dogma and precedent. But it is still apposite at the international procedural level, while the need for clearer signposts marking easier paths to justice increases with the internationalization of life, commerce and law.

The Council of Europe strives in the wider European context to give reality to the principles of article 6 of the ECHR elucidated by the European Court of Human Rights. The European Union aims to improve coordination and where appropriate harmonize procedure. The Woolf reforms, with their emphasis on case management and cultural change, have had international resonance. So procedure merits academic attention; and there is, with the wave of fundamental reforms throughout European jurisdictions, a rich comparative material upon which to draw. The proliferation and increasing importance of international courts and tribunals points also to the need for procedural studies at their level. Many of the new courts are in the process of establishing procedural rules, and there is discussion about further reforms or developments of the preliminary reference procedure which is at the heart of the work of the European Court of Justice. Comparative study can assist to devise solutions where the wholesale adoption of a single national model would not be possible or practicable. Studies in the field of comparative procedure are thus timely and appropriate.

In the last five years, the British Institute of International and Comparative Law has undertaken several major research projects in the field. Under the direction of the Public International Law Section of the Institute's Advisory Board, chaired by Dame Rosalyn Higgins DBE QC, the Institute has completed the first stage of a project on 'Evidence in International Courts and Tribunals'. A seminar series on civil procedure has been organized in memory of Sir Jack Jacob QC, doyen of procedural practice and pioneer in its academic study. Professor Vaughan Lowe has been involved with a successful programme on 'Parallel Proceedings before International Courts and Tribunals'.

Among these many research activities are projects under the direction of the Comparative Law Section of the Institute's Advisory Board. These have recently included the publication, with the American Law Institute and UNIDROIT based in Rome, of *The Future of Transnational Civil Litigation: English Responses to the ALI/UNIDROIT Principles and Rules of Transnational Civil Procedure* (BIICL London 2004) edited by M Andenas, N Andrews, and R Nazzini, following a seminar opened by Lord Goff.

The present book is the outcome of another research project on civil procedure. Its subject is the practice of enforcement agencies in Europe. Research and harmonization at European Union level have so far aimed primarily at jurisdiction and recognition of judgments pursuant to the Brussels regime, which started as a Convention and is now for most purposes to be found in Council Regulation (EC) No 44/2001. The present project focuses on the next stage: What happens when you have a judgment that is recognized? [How] do you in practice get your money?

National law and practice tends in this field toward the impenetrable, even within any single jurisdiction. To understand and use other jurisdictions' procedures is yet more difficult. Although practical enforcement is obviously critical to the ability and willingness of users of any jurisdiction to achieve justice, there has as yet been no harmonization in EU directives or regulations in the whole field of enforcement falling beyond the scope of the Brussels regime.

The Institute's enforcement agencies project is funded by the European Commission. It has been directed by the Institute's Director, Mads Andenas. The present book is co-edited with two leading European civil proceduralists, Professor Burkhard Hess from the University of Heidelberg, and Professor Paul Oberhammer from Austria who has held chairs at German universities and is now Professor of Swiss and International Civil Procedure at Zurich University. Its preparation has depended upon the creation of a wide network of European proceduralists, who have since continued to cooperate in other fields—in particular with a project on concurrent civil, administrative and criminal proceedings, and in a colloquium in Uppsala, Sweden the proceedings of which will be published in 2005. Professor Peter Schlosser of the University of Munich, author of the initial report on the Brussels Convention, was introduced to the British Institute by Lord Goff, and has provided support throughout the project, as well as agreeing to write the introduction to this book.

The study of enforcement practices covers the following European jurisdictions: Austria, England and Wales, France, Germany, the Netherlands,

Spain, and Sweden. The analysis concentrates on the enforcement of civil judgments relating to money claims by the execution of movable assets. This was chosen as the core case of enforcement, and as requiring urgent attention at a European level.

The book sets out the Community law background of the comparative analysis. It focuses on the new provisions in Title IV of the EC Treaty, inserted by the Treaty of Amsterdam of 1997. The country reports, drafted by national experts, each address seven main questions: (1) the legal basis of law enforcement; (2) the structure behind the enforcement agencies; (3) the conditions for execution; (4) specific enforcement methods; (5) disclosure of information on the debtor and his or her assets; (6) remedies against wrongful execution; and (7) the efficiency of the proceedings.

The aim has been not merely to describe, but to assess the comparative efficiency of different enforcement systems and to suggest best enforcement practices. The study ends by drawing some conclusions about the possible directions which harmonization of enforcement law could take in the European Union. Its contents will I believe persuade even the most ardent defenders of national traditions that there is important practical work to be done at a European level in the field of enforcement practices!

JONATHAN MANCE
Chair of Advisory Board of the Institute's
Comparative Law Section

Editors' Preface

This book is the outcome of a project funded by the European Commission.

The European Union's long-term goal, stated at the Tampere Summit in 1999, is to create an area of free 'movement' of judgments in the same way that there is free movement of goods, persons, services and capital within the EU. Just as the free movement of goods has required the harmonization of standards relating to the manufacture and distribution of goods, the free movement of judgments will require the harmonization of procedural standards and the creation of new interfaces between the national systems. The result should be lower transaction costs for businesses and consumers, and more confidence that agreements will be honoured. The differences between the systems of civil procedure in the European Member States are deep-seated and relate in particular to different approaches to judicial organization. These approaches are underpinned by different policies and expectations. The development of appropriate rules for the European Judicial Area (EJA) is a complex task. Misunderstandings are commonplace and inhibit the design of suitable interfaces and the removal of obstacles to judicial cooperation. Practitioners typically do not have the time or the incentive to explore the reasons for the difficulties they face in cross-border disputes. Policy-makers lack input from practitioners into the policy-making process. It is essential that a framework be created within which detailed comparative information can be provided on subjects of interest to policy-makers so that structural differences can be properly taken into account.

Enforcement proceedings is a new subject in comparative research. Legislation and procedural cultures have remained separated along national lines. Cross-border interaction has been limited as in the traditional view enforcement measures are strictly limited by the principle of territoriality. Private international law does not traditionally address enforcement proceedings. International conventions only regulate the recognition of foreign judgments. The execution of the title after its recognition remains a purely national matter, and is not affected by the Brussels Convention. The current fragmentation hampers transborder debt collection. Creditors are confronted with different legal systems, language barriers, additional costs and delay and sometimes with a reluctance on the part of national authorities to enforce foreign but enforceable judgments. Different enforcement structures effectively divide up markets along national borders. Access to justice in the European Judicial Area in enforcement matters is not available. The question is, as Sir Jonathan Mance elegantly puts in it in his forword: [How] do you get your money? One reply is, business often gives up enforcing their claims abroad and write them off.

Enforcement proceedings have increasingly become a subject of comparative research and of legislation in the Member States and the European Union. All Member States have recently adopted extensive reforms in order to improve enforcement. The Storme Group published in 1993 a 'Draft of a Directive on the Approximation of Civil Procedures in Europe'. The Draft suggested extensive European harmonization of enforcement proceedings. There was some reluctance expressed by Member States and in the academic literature. In the Commission's 1997 'Communication on the Free Movement of Judgments', under a 'sectoral' approach the interfaces between national enforcement procedures and the Brussels' Convention were to be harmonized, especially concerning provisional and protective measures, and the transparency of the debtor's assets, and the possibilities explored for an exchange of information between enforcement authorities. The European Council at the Tampere Summit adopted the proposed strategy. Article 65 (c) of the Amsterdam Treaty (1997) entrusts the Community to 'adopt measures in the field of judicial cooperation in civil matters having cross-border implications'. This competence includes cross-border enforcement. In 2003, a group of legal experts under Professor Hess's direction completed a study on the transparency of debtor's assets, garnishments and provisional enforcement and protective measures, see Study JAI A3/02/2002 'on making more efficient the enforcement of judicial decisions within the European Union'. The legal and practical situation in 16 national jurisdictions was described and evaluated on the basis of questionnaires, best practices were identified and several proposals for Community measures were presented. The results of this study (now extended to cover the new EU Member States) will provide the basis for proposals in a Commission Green Paper on Enforcement in the European Judicial Area.

The Enforcement Agencies project and this book examine the structure, status and procedures of selected Member States' enforcement agencies and the implications for individuals and companies in seeking to enforce a judgment in the EJA. The project is part of a more ambitious programme. It constitutes one starting point for a long-running effort to make a substantial contribution to the development of the EJA.

The British Institute of International and Comparative Law has promoted the European Research Interchange (ERI), a network of academics expert in the problems of the EJA and cross-border enforcement. The ERI is a network of academics from institutions of eight Member States. The participants in the ERI work together, sharing information and research outcomes, and cooperating closely with one another with the view to establishing a European Area of Freedom and Justice. Most of the participants in the ERI and in the Enforcement Agencies project have contributed to this book. Throughout it has had the good fortune of receiving external revision and advice from Professor Dr Peter Schlosser, University of

Munich, the leading European, German and comparative civil procedural-ist who most English readers will recognize as the author of the *Schlosser Report on the 1st Treaty on Accession to the European Treaty on Jurisdiction and the Enforcement of Judicial Decisions* (OJ C 71, 1979). Dr Wendy Kennet, an expert on European enforcement issues, has also provided important assistance to the project. The editors would also like to express their gratitude to Sir Jonathan Mance for writing the foreword.

The topic chosen for research, and which attracted funding from the European Commission, that of Enforcement Agencies, has provided an interesting, shorter-term focus for the ERI; Professor Hess's project on transparency of debtor's assets, garnishments and provisional enforcement and protective measures, another focus. ERI is here to stay. Additional funding will be sought by the institutions involved in this project so that wider and more ambitious projects can be pursued. The flexibility of the ERI, with its low maintenance costs and an ability to expand, is its main strength, combined with the profile of the participants. This is already demonstrated by the cooperation that will be undertaken in the context of yet other initiatives funded by the Commission.

Parts III–V of the book are based in part on proceedings from the final meeting for this project held at the British Institute of International and Comparative Law in London on 23 April 2004 and entitled *Enforcement Agency Practice in Europe: Cooperation or Harmonization?*

We would like to thank Renato Nazzini and Wendy Kennett for their role in getting this project started. John Adam, Timothy Bowe, Tanja Domej, Jaime Gallego-Pow, Brian Romanzo, Lydia Sweeney, Marcus Mack, Mayte Cruz Ventura, and Eduardo Barrachina have assisted at different stages of the Enforcement Agencies Project. Hugo Warner has been involved the project from its inception, in the final phase also as Assistant Editor for this book. We would also like to express our gratitude to Chris Bell and Eral Knight at the Department of Constitutional Affairs.

Special thanks are owed to Jérôme Carriat, Henrik Nielsen and Mario Tenreiro of the European Commission. The Commission has not only provided the funding but has been much involved in the different activities.

MADS ANDENAS, BURKHARD HESS, AND PAUL OBERHAMMER
London, Heidelberg, and Zurich

Contents

List of Contributors

Professor Mads Andenas PhD (Cambridge) MA DPhil (Oxford). Director, British Institute of International and Comparative Law; Professor of Law, University of Leicester and Fellow, Institute of European and Comparative Law, University of Oxford.

Professor Torbjörn Andersson Jur Dr (Uppsala), Professor of Procedural Law, Juridiska institutionen, Uppsala University, Sweden.

Professor Juan Pablo Correa Delcasso Doctor of Law, Advocate and Professor of Law, University of Barcelona.

Andrew Dickinson Solicitor Advocate; Consultant to Clifford Chance LLP; Visiting Fellow in Private International Law, British Institute of International and Comparative Law.

Hugo Fridén University Lecturer in Procedure, Juridiska institutionen, Uppsala University.

Professor Burkhard Hess Ruprecht-Karls-University Heidelberg. Director, Institut für ausländisches und internationales Privat- und Wirtschaftsrecht.

Professor Ton Jongbloed Professor of the Law of Enforcement and Seizure, Molengraaff Institute for Private Law, University of Utrecht, The Netherlands. Deputy Justice Court of Appeal, Leeuwarden, The Netherlands.

Dr Georg E Kodek Judge of the Vienna Court of Appeals, LLM, Dr iur., Privat-Dozent in Civil Procedure, University of Vienna.

John Kruse Civil Enforcement Consultant, England and Wales.

Dr Sabine Lacassagne Centre de Droit Civil des Affaires et du Contentieux Economique, Université Paris X-Nanterre.

Marcus Mack Wissenschaftlicher Assistant, Ruprecht-Karls-University Heidelberg.

The Right Honourable Lord Justice (Sir Jonathan) Mance Lord Justice of Appeal, Court of Appeal for England and Wales.

Dr Renato Nazzini PhD (Milan) PhD (Lond). Solicitor. Visiting Fellow, British Institute of International and Comparative Law.

Professor Marie-Laure Niboyet Centre de Droit Civil des Affaires et du Contentieux Economique, Université Paris X-Nanterre.

Professor Paul Oberhammer Dr iur (Wien). Professor of Swiss and International Civil Procedure, Enforcement, Insolvency, Civil and Business Law, Zurich University.

Professor Peter Schlosser Professor *emeritus*, Institut für Bürgerliches Recht und Zivilprozeßrecht, Faculty of Law, University of Munich.

Hugo Warner LLB (Edinburgh). Research Fellow at the British Institute of International and Comparative Law.

Table of Cases

I International Tribunals

European Commission of Human Rights

European Court of Human Rights

European Court of Justice

II National Courts

Austria

France

Germany

United Kingdom (England)

United Kingdom (Scotland)

Table of Legislation

List of Abbreviations

All ER	All England Law Reports
BAG	Bundesarbeitsgericht (Federal Labour Court)
BGBl	Bundesgesetzblatt (Federal Law Gazette)
BGH	Bundesgerichtshof (Federal Court of Justice)
BRAGO	Bundesrechtsanwaltsgebührenordnung
Bull civ	Bulletin des arrêts de la Cour de Cassation: chambres civiles (publication of decisions of the French court of cassation)
BVerfGE	Entscheidungen des Bundesverfassungsgerichtes (German Federal Constitutional Court Reporter)
CA	Court of Appeal
CJJA	Civil Jurisdiction and Judgements Act 1982
CJPr	Code of Judicial Procedure (Sweden)
CLC	Commercial Law Cases
CMLR	Common Market Law Reports
CNJH	Chambre National des Huissiers de Justice (French National Chamber of Bailiffs)
COM	Commission documents (European Commission)
CPR	Civil Procedure Rules (England & Wales)
CP	Rep Civil Procedure Reports
EBR	European Business Register
EC	European Communities
ECHR	European Court of Human Rights
ECJ	European Court of Justice
ECJH	European Convention of Human Rights
ECR	European Court Reports
EEC	European Economic Community
EG InO	*Einführungsgesetz zur Insolvenzordnung* (Introductory Law of the German Insolvency Law)
EO	Exekutionsordnung (Austrian Enforcement Code)
EU	European Union
EuGH	*Europäischer Gerichtshof* (European Court of Justice)
EuGVÜ	Übereinkommen über die gerichtliche Zuständigkeit und die Vollstreckung gerichtlicher Entscheidung in Zivil- und Handelssachen (Convention of 27 September 1968 on Jurisdiction and theEnforcement of Judgments in Civil and Commercial Matters)
EuJL	European Journal of Law Reform
GVGA	Geschäftsanweisung für Gerichtsvollzieher (Procedural and Administrative Directive for Bailiffs in Germany)

GVKostG	Gerichtsvollzieherkostengesetz
HCEO	High Court Enforcement Officer
HGB	Handelsgesetzbuch (German Commercial Code)
HL	House of Lords
ICLQ	International and Comparative Law Quarterly
IECL	International Encyclopaedia of Comparative Law
ILA	International Law Association
ILPr	International Litigation Procedure
IPrax	Praxis des internationalen Privat-und Verfahrensrechtes
JC	Judgment Creditor
JCP	Jurisclasseur periodique
JD	Judgment Debtor
JEX	Juge de l'execution
JZ	Juristenzeitung
KB	Law Reports, King´s Bench Division
LEC	Ley de Enjuiciamiento Civil (Spanish Code of Civil Procedure)
NCPC	Nouveau Code de Procedure Civile (French Code of Civil Procedure)
NJW	Neue Juristische Wochenschrift
OGH	Oberster Gerichtshof (Austrian Supreme Court)
OJC	Official Journal of the European Communities containing Information and Notices
OJ L	Official Journal of the European Communities containing Legislation
PD	Law Reports, Probate Division (1875—1890)
PER	Protected Earning Rate
QB	Law Reports, Queen´s Bench Division (1952-)
RabelsZ	Rabels Zeitschrift für ausländisches und internationales Privatrecht
RBerG	Rechtsberatungsgesetz
RCDI	Revue International de Droit Comparé
RdC	Recueil des Cours de l'Academie de la Haye (Collected Courses of the Hague Academy of International Law)
RGZ	Entscheidungen des Reichsgerichtes in Zivilsachen (Reporter of the Federal Supreme Civil Court of the former German Reich)
RIW	Recht der Internationalen Wirtschaft
RSC	Ord Rules of the Supreme Court
Rv	Rechtsvordering (Dutch Code of Civil Procedure)
SCHUFA	Schutzgemeinschaft für allgemeine Kreditsicherung
TPDO	Third Party Debt Order

UIHJ	Union internationale des Huissiers de Justice (International Union of Bailiffs)
UKHL	House of Lords of the United Kingdom
VAT	Value Added Tax
WLR	Weekly Law Reports (1953–)
ZEuP	Zeitschrift für Europäisches Privatrecht
ZPO	Zivilprozessordnung (German Code of Civil Procedure)
ZRHO	Rechtshilfeordnung in Zivil- und Handelssachen (Law of judicial assistance in civil and trade matters)
ZZP	Zeitschrift für den Zivilprozess

CHAPTER 1

INTRODUCTION

Peter Schlosser[1]

It is true that an introduction to a book dealing with research in legal science should not be an anticipated review. Nevertheless, it is a welcome opportunity to express the gratitude of the anonymous collective of scholars and practitioners interested in this field. It is an expression of gratitude for this extremely timely volume.

Primarily, this is a classical work of analytical comparative legal research. In a well-defined but rather broad field, the isolated and inconsistent developments of multiple domestic legal systems have been analysed and put in a categorized order. The volume also includes essays of individual authors on interesting subjects related to the focus of the research programme. These essays stem from seminars and conferences made possible by the European Commission's generous award to the British Institute of International and Comparative Law. This award did not fall out of the blue.

Therefore, the first achievement to be grateful for is the proper identification of the research programme. Until recently, scholarly endeavour in the field of international civil procedure was almost exclusively restricted to jurisdiction and recognition of judgments. But even in this respect, the coming into force of the Brussels Convention had to be realized in order for our minds to be opened up to the neighbouring legal systems. The issue is the practical outcome of recognition and enforcement of judgments in another state. This has for a long time remained outside the interests of legal scholars, even though it has been evident that the topic is of utmost impact in practice. As late as 1996, Konstantinos Kerameus was still able to commence his seminal course *Enforcement in the International Context* in The Hague Academy by saying: 'Some years ago, it would have appeared strange to propose a course on enforcement proceedings in the framework of an international law programme.'[2]

This course and the publication of the tenth chapter of volume 16

---

[1] Institut für Bürgerliches Recht und Zivilprozeßrecht, Faculty of Law, University of Munich.

[2] *Académie de Droit International de la Haye/Hague Academy of International Law Recueil des Cours, Collected Courses* vol 264 (1997).

('Enforcement Proceedings') of the International Encyclopaedia of Comparative Law[3] by the same academic in 2002, were, in civil matters, the first pioneering publications on comparative law of enforcement procedures. Some other works succeeded, such as those referred to in chapter 3 of this book by Burkhard Hess. All of them achieved the height of what a single scholar is able to perform in his or her research.

Yet this is still far from being a reliable and sufficiently substantiated basis for the efforts of the European Community to bring the enforcement proceedings of its Member States into line with each other. This field of law is, more than any other branch of private law, characterized by an impenetrable mixture of legal and administrative rules as well as customary practice, the knowledge of which is to a great extent exclusive to the staff to whom enforcement is entrusted. Consequently, for the single outside observer, it is in many respects impossible to acquire the necessary knowledge, all the more so where there is a divergence between legal scholarship and practice.

Much gratitude is due to Directorate C ('Civil Justice and Citizenship') of the Justice and Home Affairs Directorate General of the European Commission. It immediately realized that the research of the British Institute of International and Comparative Law was directed precisely at forming the proper basis for its policy and legislative activities. Therefore the Commission granted an award to the Institute, reaching the very upper limit of what its practice of awarding funds had been. Even though the contributing scholars were not personally paid for their work out of Brussels funds, the research would not have been possible without promotion and support from Brussels.

Furthermore, the broad horizon of the project's supporters in Brussels is demonstrated by the fact that they did not limit their support to collecting materials and organizing meetings of the scholars involved for the purpose of integrating their respective findings into a suitable system of comparative yardsticks. Rather, they have extended their support to supplementary seminars and conferences on subjects relevant to the research programme. Parts II–IV of this volume are the fruits of such events. Professor Mads Andenas has been immensely successful in finding eminent authors for these sections.

In the same way as enforcement proceedings, provisional and protective measures were absent in comparative law research prior to the groundbreaking course by Sir Lawrence Collins—now a judge of the English High Court—given in 1992 to the Hague Academy of International law entitled

---

[3] KD Kerameus *Enforcement Proceedings* ch 10 vol 16 (2002); *International Encyclopedia of Comparative Law* K. Zweigert and U. Drobnig (eds) JCB F Mohr Siebeck (Tübingen/Martinus Nijhoff Leiden Boston).

Provisional and Protective Measures in International Litigation.[4] Nevertheless, in the context of cross-border protective measures, many difficulties remain. The European Court of Justice has taken a less than consistent approach and the Court's case law has given rise to many new problems. It follows that the Commission is well advised to promote further research in this field.

It is almost self-evident that in the matter of enforcement, the European Convention on Human Rights must, by necessity, have a major impact. Unfortunately, in some countries, such as Germany, the case law of the European Court of Human Rights has only occasionally found its way into standard publications such as popular legal reviews, practitioners' handbooks and commentaries on respective domestic legislation. The fact that the official languages of the Council of Europe are only English and French has not been the only barrier. Lawyers are also sometimes in principle reluctant to accept the intrusion of a foreign court into their legal world. It is true that the European Community is not as such a party to the European Convention on Human Rights, let alone the European Union. Nevertheless, the substantive provisions of the European Convention have been integrated by the European Court of Justice into the legal framework of the Community. Formally, this will be changed once the European Constitution comes into force, because it will set out its own list of fundamental rights. One would, however, be narrow-minded not to anticipate that the case law of the European Court of Human Rights will become the case law of the European Constitution. The Commission should be encouraged further to promote the idea—with all proper diplomatic delicacy—that the European Convention on Human Rights, soon being integrated into the European Constitution, will to a large degree replace domestic constitutional law.

Last but not least, thanks must be extended to the scholars participating in the research programme. They have developed working practices and an idealism far beyond their duties. They were not satisfied in juxtaposing pieces of information and logically deriving 'principles'. In procedural law, the test is one of efficiency (including efficiency in protecting the defendant from ill-treatment) rather than the effective application of 'principles'. In procedural law in general, and in enforcement law in particular, it is important for an outside observer to learn how things are organized in practice (even when they are poorly organized). Experience shows that, for this purpose, it does not suffice to invite practitioners of a series of given domestic legal systems to tell how things occur in their home states. Apparently, in a very early phase of their research, the participating scholars found out that an appropriate device by which to achieve insight into other enforcement systems was a series of comparative case studies on unlawful enforcement

---

[4] 'Provisional and Protective Measures in International Litigation' 234 *RdC* (1992).

(see the Appendix). In his comparative chapter on these, Paul Oberhammer discloses with mild amusement that time and again national reporters confessed 'not to fully understand' the questions in the respective questionnaire. The authors of this volume made every effort to overcome these barriers to mutual understanding, finding a way through their hidden causes and clearly to identify differences and similarities.

Finally, overall thanks must be given to the British Institute of International and Comparative law, personified by its Director, Professor Mads Andenas and his collaborators, for having organized the research project admirably. Someone who has never been involved in basic comparative law research cannot appreciate the amount of organizational work and imagination demanded to avoid a superficial and, hence, misleading analysis of a rather broad field of socio-legal activities. Normally, a single law school is not sufficiently equipped to carry out such research. Nor is temporary support, such as was awarded in this case by the Commission, a proper substitute for the necessary permanent infrastructure.

May the sponsors of this Institute keep their minds open!

PART I

EUROPEAN AND NATIONAL MODELS

CHAPTER 2

NATIONAL PARADIGMS OF CIVIL ENFORCEMENT: MUTUAL RECOGNITION OR HARMONIZATION IN EUROPE?

Mads Andenas[1]

I. COMPARATIVE AND EUROPEAN PROCEDURAL LAW

Lord Justice Bingham stated in the early 1990s that '[p]rocedural idiosyncrasy is not (like national costume or regional cuisine) to be nurtured for its own sake.'[2] Civil enforcement is an area that bears out this point very well. Having very different national regimes increases cost and can make it impractical to enforce a claim. The national legal systems are resistant to harmonization. The impact of European Union law has been limited. Civil enforcement is an area where the law has not followed the development of the Internal Market.

Comparative civil procedure has an important role to play here. It can contribute to the very active domestic legal reform, and also in developing European understanding and concepts. 'Judicial cooperation' can only develop and function if the actors in the different national systems can communicate.

Comparative civil procedure can also assist in the assessment of the need for procedural harmonization, and of how much harmonization is required before different systems can manage to communicate. In this context, Lord Justice Bingham's statement is interesting. It points to a more realistic appreciation of the intrinsic value of maintaining all the features of different procedural systems, and perhaps even of maintaining different procedural systems as such.

---

[1] I would like to acknowledge the assistance of Timothy Bowe in the drafting of this chapter.

[2] *Dresser UK Ltd v Falcongate Ltd* [1992] QB 502, 522.

II. NATIONAL PARADIGMS OF CIVIL ENFORCEMENT: MUTUAL RECOGNITION OR
HARMONIZATION IN EUROPE?

Harmonization of civil procedure is not a new issue in European law. European Union law is however still at the 'judicial cooperation' stage rather than moving towards any procedural unification. The purpose of this chapter is to ask, when looking at the paradigms of civil enforcement procedure in the selected States as is done in this book, what is the most practical method for improving the movement of judgments within the European Judicial Area. The benefit of harmonization is clear but is that attainable through European legislation? Can much the same be achieved through a process of improved communication and increased understanding of different civil paradigms, or are other alternatives available?

Regulatory and procedural diversity may be seen to create an enforcement deficit. In the recent debate some authors have returned to the embrace of regulatory and procedural diversity. Constitutional problems and also efficiency grounds and the lack of necessity provide a basis for their argument.[3] The alternative model of reflexive harmonization has been held out as preserving and promoting legal diversity and experimentation across the European Union steering the process of domestic evolution in the light of the general principles of EU law.[4]

This book provides interesting material for such discussion. The balancing between the efficiency of EU law and national autonomy has lead to the formulation of a principle of procedural autonomy. Can the Internal Market function with the present degree of reliance on the different national paradigms? This question requires painstaking analysis, based on empirical study, both on a normative and at a quantitative level. It is also a question of values, and it is in particular here that it is important to maintain a realistic appreciation of the intrinsic value of maintaining different procedural systems.[5]

III. CIVIL ENFORCEMENT

Civil enforcement of judgments currently requires a judgment creditor to negotiate the complicated structures of a process particular to each Member

---

[3] See M Dougan *National Remedies Before The Court of Justice* (Hart Publishing Oxford 2004) 171.

[4] Op cit 187–9 and S Deakin 'Regulatory Competition Versus Harmonization in European Company Law' in D Esty and D Gerardin (eds) *Regulatory Competition and Economic Integration: Comparative Perspectives* (OUP Oxford 2001).

[5] See the discussion of similar issues in M Andenas (ed) *English Public Law and the Common Law of Europe* (Key Haven Publishing London 1998).

State within the European Union. No one civil procedure is the same. Judgment creditors are usually confronted with similar difficulties when subject to the exequatur procedure. Enforcement of judgments are delayed, costly and often rendered ineffective in a Member State different to that in which judgment was issued. It is clear that the system is coloured by misunderstanding between Member States when a judgment becomes subject to transboundary movement. The result is an unbalanced and unequal treatment of creditors within the European Union through territorial prejudice.

Following the accession of the ten new Member States[6] on 1 May 2004, ineffective enforcement is more than unsatisfactory; it is hindering the positive cohesion of an enlarged European Community.

This book offers an analysis of the current difficulties facing judgment creditors and goes some way to provide tenable solutions to the challenges they face. It provides an analysis of the structure, status and procedures of selected Member States' enforcement agency and the implications for individuals and companies in seeking to enforce judgment in the European Judicial Area.[7]

The contents of this book correspond to the threefold structure of analysis adopted by the British Institute of International and Comparative Law that culminated in a conference in 2004.[8] That conference, which was attended by the contributing authors, addressed 'The Future of Enforcement Agency in Practice in Europe Cooperation or Harmonization.' The Institute's initiative was to examine the differences of national enforcement procedures and, through a collaborative effort of comparative analysis, identify tenable solutions to improve equality for judgment creditors across the Community. The project was generously supported by the European Commission, and took place within a framework of a network of academics working in the discipline of civil procedure.

There were three stages to this project. First, each contributing author submitted a national report detailing enforcement agency practices in their Member States. These reports occupy Part I of this publication and provide substantial information about enforcement agency essential for effective comparative analysis. Professor Dr Burkhard Hess provides an illuminating opening chapter that draws these reports together into a cohesive introductory explanation of the civil procedure rules operating across the Community. Professor Juan Pablo Correa Delcasso concludes this first

---

[6] The new Member States are Cyprus, Czech Republic, Estonia, Hungary, Latvia, Lithuania, Malta, Poland, Slovakia, and Slovenia.

[7] Austria, England and Wales, France, Germany, The Netherlands, Spain, and Sweden.

[8] See Sir Jonathan Mance's foreword to this book about the work of the British Institute in the field of civil procedure and also other BIICL publications based on previous projects; M Andenas, N Andrews, and R Nazzini (eds) *The Future of Trans-National Commercial Litigation: English Responses to the ALI/UNIDROIT Principles and Rules of Trans-National Civil Procedure* (BIICL London 2004).

section by moving the discussion towards an appreciation of how competing methods of civil procedure effect efficient enforcement. It is his opinion that the real question of efficiency lies not in identifying the authority responsible for enforcement but rather in the transparency of the debtor's assets.

Secondly, Parts III, IV, and V contain the analytical chapters presented by each contributor at the conference. Having passed through the comparative analysis stage of the project, these sections comprise the main body of the text and attempt to suggest whether judgment creditors would be better protected and equally treated through harmonization or improved understanding. In answering this question, which forms the focus of this opening chapter, a range of subjects were thrown into relief. Professor Ton Jongbloed questioned whether there should be a European Bailiff operating within the Community, whereas Professor Burkhard Hess and Andrew Dickinson delivered their opinions about the provisional and protective measures that would be necessary under a harmonized system in the European Judicial Area. Dr Georg Kodek and John Kruse lifted the discussion away from practical measures and towards legal principles by sharing their understanding about how the European Convention on Human Rights impacts on enforcement practices.

Finally, the annex contains the Member State responses to a series of questions designed to examine how each selected State remedies unlawful execution of a judgment.

While the focus of this project is to examine the over-arching practical elements and legal principles that facilitate or hinder enforcement agency in the Community, a parallel study was conducted by Professor Burkhard Hess on a more specific area of enforcement procedure. This study related to the transparency of a debtor's assets, provisional enforcement and protective measures as well as attachment of bank accounts. Garnishment proceedings are integral to any discussion concerning methods of enforcement and so, although the terms of reference for Professor Hess's study is different from that which preoccupies this book, there are discrete similarities between the two studies which will provide invaluable cross-fertilization of ideas and solutions when assessing the concept of mutual recognition or harmonization in Europe. To this extent, Professor Hess's study will be more fully addressed below.

So, the purpose of this chapter is to ask, when looking at the paradigms of civil enforcement procedure in the selected States, what is the most practical method for improving the movement of judgments within the European Judicial Area? The benefit of harmonization is the establishment of a common core but is that attainable through European legislation? Is the legal purpose of enforcement procedures better achieved, and more politically palatable, through a process of improved communication and increased understanding of different civil paradigms, or does that only create a diluted form of recognition and overburden functioning systems whilst allowing poor systems to get worse? The traditional internal market solution is to have a combined framework predicated on the principles of mutual recognition but supplemented by a network of complementary Community legislation.

Before tackling these questions it is useful to understand the background from which this project stems and the problems it was hoping to counter.

IV. BACKGROUND TO THE PROJECT

The Tampere Summit, held in 1999, made a bold step towards reorganizing the recognition of judicial proceeding across the European Community. The European Council determined that its long-term goal would be to create a an area of free movement of judgments in the same way that there is free movement of goods, persons, services, service, and capital within the European Union. The cornerstone of effective cooperation between Member States in the enforcement of judgments is mutual recognition of judicial decisions.

The two specific objectives set by the Tampere Council were better access to justice and mutual recognition of judgments, both of which call for improved enforcement procedures of monetary judgments, especially in consumer matters and debt collection. The practical effect of these objectives is a certainty for the litigant who, when issued with a judgment in their favour, will know that it will be declared enforceable by the courts of other Members States and will be effectively enforced.

At present, judicial decisions taken in one Member State are not automatically recognized in another Member State. For that decision to be valid, the judgment creditor must enter into exequatur, intermediate, proceedings. This procedure obstructs the free movement of judgments and renders decisions subject to a territorial notion of justice which is inappropriate in a Community environment.

The first of the Tampere Council's two objectives was defined by the European Commission as 'A genuine area of justice that must ensure that individuals and businesses can approach courts and authorities in any Member States as easily as in their own and not be prevented or discouraged from exercising their rights by the complexity of the legal and administrative systems in the Member States.' This is particularly relevant when enforcing judgment. The shared sense of justice of the public would be undermined if a final judgment of the court of one Member State had varying prospects of successful enforcement depending on the Member State in which enforcement must take place. The concept of access to justice cannot therefore be limited to the provision of financial aid to litigants who are unable to afford the costs of litigation.

Access to justice also means that the legal system must be able to provide effective protection of the rights of European citizens, which includes the effective enforcement of judgments. If there is no mechanism in place to enable a judgment creditor to enforce his decision then the difficulty he faces becomes a denial of justice, especially for consumers or small and medium commercial concerns.

As for recognition of judgments, Member States' enforcement procedures in relation to enforcement agencies and redress against unfair enforcement decisions are an aspect of procedural law on which a common understanding is necessary in order to facilitate the application of the principle of mutual recognition and enforcement of judgments within the Union. The preferred method for promoting mutual recognition, whether through harmonization or increased communication about systems, is a point for discussion.

The four fundamental freedoms are facilitated by European legislation designed to create a set a common standard of operation throughout Member States in matters involving a transboundary element. It is unsurprising therefore that commentators would draw upon the notion of harmonizing procedural standards in order to create a space within the European Judicial Area that would enable the free movement of judgments, the concomitant effect of which would be lower transaction costs for businesses and consumers and increased confidence that agreements would be honoured.

Harmonization is however one interpretation of 'mutual recognition' across the Community. Certainly, if all Member States were reading from the same rules when confronted with a request to enforce an 'external' judgment, then the result for the judgment creditor is likely to be the same. But mutual recognition can also be interpreted to mean understanding of Member State civil procedure for enforcement. This approach would not result in the same level of hegemony that would come from harmonization, but it would focus attention on those systems that unnecessarily obstruct enforcement of foreign judgments and encourage improvement. Of course it could also result in pressure being placed on efficient systems.

The differences between the systems of civil procedure in the European Member States are deep-seated and relate in particular to different approaches to judicial organization. These policies are underpinned by different policies and expectations (which may have rather an incidental or arbitrary historical origin) making the development of appropriate rules for the European Judicial Area a difficult task. Domestic reform is based on national traditions and responses to European initiatives closely linked to the national path. Path-dependency is a fact, no matter how weak the justifications for a rule in a national tradition. Misunderstandings are common place and inhibit the removal of obstacles to judicial cooperation.

Practitioners rarely have the time or the incentive to explore the reasons for the difficulties they face in cross-border disputes and policy makers lack input from practitioners into the policy making process.

It is against this background that the aims of the Tampere Summit are to be realized. They can only be realized by altering the current fractured process of enforcement within the Community into a coherent system. Then judicial decisions can move freely within the European Judicial Area.

V. COMMUNITY LEGISLATION

The principle of mutual recognition across the European Community is not new. The 1968 Brussels Convention ('the Brussels Convention') established rules on the jurisdiction, recognition and enforcement of judgments in civil and commercial matters. However, the Convention confines itself to 'governing the procedure for obtaining authorization for enforcement and does not contain provisions concerning enforcement so properly called'.[9] A second convention was adopted in 1998 dealing with the jurisdiction, recognition and enforcement of judgments in matrimonial matters, yet this convention never entered into force, but was transformed into a Council Regulation that was adopted following the adoption of the Treaty of Amsterdam in May 1999. The advent of that treaty altered the complexion of judicial cooperation in civil matters within the Community. It granted the European Community competence in judicial and domestic issues of the Member States prompting a revision of the Brussels Convention and a Council Regulation.

Of the three Council Regulations[10] that have been adopted to aid mutual recognition of judicial decisions in civil matters, one is important for the analytical focus of this book. Council Regulation (EC) 44/2001 ('the Brussels I Regulation') replaces, with the exception of Denmark, the

---

[9] *P Capelloni et F Aquilini v C J Pelkmans* [1985] ECR 3147 at 16.

[10] Council Regulation (EC) No 44/2001 of 22 Dec 2000 on jurisdiction and the recognition and enforcement of judgments in civil and commercial matters (Official Journal L 12 of 16 Jan 2001) (the 'Brussels I' Regulation); Council Regulation (EC) No 1347/2000 of 29 May 2000 on jurisdiction and the recognition and enforcement of judgments in matrimonial matters and in matters of parental responsibility for children of both spouses (Official Journal L 160 of 30.6.2000) (the 'Brussels II' Regulation); Regulation (EC) No 1346/2000 relating to insolvency proceedings(Official Journal L160, 30 June 2000). On 3 May 2002 the Commission a Proposal for a Council Regulation concerning jurisdiction and the recognition and enforcement of judgments in matrimonial matters and in matters of parental responsibility repealing Regulation (EC) No 1347/2000 and amending Regulation (EC) No 44/2001 in matters relating to maintenance (COM (2002) 222). This Proposal brings together Council Regulation (EC) No 1347/2000, the Commission proposal on parental responsibility presented in September 2001 (OJ C 332 of 27 Nov 2001) and the French initiative on rights of access presented in July 2000 (OJ C 234 of 15 Aug 2000).

Brussels Convention. The Regulation establishes common standards on jurisdiction and the enforcement of judgments in civil and commercial matters, and contains provisions relating to contracts concluded by consumers through on-line transactions.[11]

The Brussels I Regulation addressed mutual trust, stating at part 17 of the preamble:

By virtue of the [...] principle of mutual trust, the procedure for making enforceable in one Member State a judgment given in another must be efficient and rapid. To that end, the declaration that a judgment is enforceable should be issued virtually automatically after purely formal checks of the documents supplied, without there being any possibility for the court to raise of its own motion any of the grounds for non-enforcement provided for by this Regulation.

The Regulation therefore does not foresee the need for a continued use of the exequatur procedure yet it does maintain the rights of appeal. Part 18 of the preamble continues:

However, respect for the rights of the defence means that the defendant should be able to appeal in an adversarial procedure, against the declaration of enforceability, if he considers one of the grounds for non-enforcement to be present. Redress procedures should also be available to the claimant where his application for a declaration of enforceability has been rejected.

So, whilst mutual recognition is understood to facilitate the enforcement of judgments in disputes involving cross-border pecuniary claims, the Regulation does not introduce a harmonized civil code to enable execution of the judgment. However, significant advances have been made in several areas, including bankruptcy and the service of judicial and extra-judicial documents.[12]

A number of measures ancillary to, but complementing, mutual recognition have been adopted in order to implement the principle of mutual recognition, one of the most significant of which being the European Enforcement Order. This Order aims to remove the need for authorization for enforcement but will not provide specific provisions on enforcement procedure. Consequently national procedures will continue to be relied upon. However, this might cause difficulty in judgment enforcement between Member States and would not be in keeping with the scheme of a European Judicial Area and free movement of judgments.

---

[11] The European Council and European Commission issued a joint declaration concerning Arts 15 and 73 to improve understanding of the provisions dealing with on-line transactions.
[12] Regulation (EC) No 1346/2000 relates to insolvency proceedings (Official Journal L160, 30 June 2000) and came into force on 31 May 2002. Regulation No 1348/2000 concerns the service in Member States of judicial and extrajudicial documents in civil or commercial matters.

The Tampere European Council asked the Council and the Commission to initiate work on those aspects of procedural law for which common minimum standards are considered necessary to facilitate the application of the principle of mutual recognition, respecting the fundamental legal principles of Member States. The European Council advanced the practical development of this principle by inviting the Council and the Commission to prepare new procedural legislation in cross-border cases, in particular those elements which are instrumental to smooth judicial cooperation and to enhanced access to law, for example provisional measures, the taking of evidence, orders for money payment and time limits.

Consequently, the Council Programme of Measures for Implementation of the Principle of Mutual Recognition of Decisions in Civil and Commercial Matters[13] proposed to adopt measures ancillary to mutual recognition such as minimum standards for certain aspects of civil procedure, to increase the efficiency of measure providing for improved enforcement of decisions and to improve judicial cooperation on civil matters in general. The development of efficient methods of execution of 'external' decision is a point developed by Professor Juan Pablo Correa Delcasso in part I of this book. In response to this programme, the Council adopted Regulation (EC) No 1206/2001 on Cooperation between the Courts of the Member States in the Taking of Evidence in Civil or Commercial Matters[14] with the intention of improving, simplifying and accelerating the cooperation between courts when taking evidence.

Furthermore, the Council has adopted Council Decision 2001/470/EC[15] which formally establishes a European Judicial Network in Civil and Commercial Matters and launched a consultation on a preliminary draft proposal for a Council regulation concerning applicable law for non-contractual obligations. Part of the broader debate concerning the Commission's activities within the field of mutual recognition within the sphere of judicial cooperation, includes a number wide-ranging consultations to identify tenable solutions designed to simplify the working process for those citizens of the Community confronted with cross-border litigation. This involves participation in the work of international organizations such as the United Nations, the Hague Conference on Private International Law and the Council of Europe.[16] These developments fit within Regulation (EC) No 743/2002 that establishes a general framework for

---

[13] 30 Nov 2000 (OJC 12, 15 Jan 2001, 1).
[14] 30 Nov 2000 (OJC 12, 15 Jan 2001, 1).
[15] OJL 174, 27 June 2001, 25.
[16] Listing these activities by public international organizations, mention could be made of the work of other organizations such as the American Law Institute, see Andenas, Andrews, and Nazzini (eds), op cit.

Community activities to facilitate the implementation of judicial cooperation in civil matters for the period 2002–6.[17]

It is clear that the institutions of the European Community are engaged
in developing reasonable solutions to enhance the principle of mutual
recognition of judicial decisions across the Union, yet no specific decision
has been made about how that can be most appropriately achieved. The
contributions of our authors in this volume therefore, provide a timely
analysis of the problems confronting an exercise of this size. The collaborative effort of this volume reflects the pan-European approach adopted by
the European Union during its consultative stages and provides a varied
perspective to a common problem.

The European Constitution will give a clearer status to harmonization of
European civil procedure. The basis in Article 65 EC will be complemented
by the incorporation of the conclusions of Tampere and introduces the
possibility of taking measures guaranteeing wider access to the courts.
Further harmonization of the law of European civil procedure is expressly
mentioned.

VI. WHICH WAY NOW?

So, mutual recognition is understood to be essential to judicial cooperation
and enforcement of judgments across the European Union, but there is a
space between the theoretical implications and the practical application of
that concept. The focus of this study was to explore whether national paradigms of national civil procedure were most susceptible to a system of
mutual recognition based upon shared information and mutual understanding or a harmonized civil code for enforcement directed by European
legislation.

The project pursued this analysis through a number of specific objections
which are documented in this book. First, the British Institute of
International and Comparative Law sought to collect, analyse and dissem-
inate accurate information concerning the practices of enforcement agencies
in selected European countries. The purpose of this initial stage was to
move beyond the wording of the civil code and get an understanding of
how enforcement actually operates in each country, allowing the Institute
and contributing authors to work on a solid foundation of comparative
analysis.

Secondly, working with that material, the structures and practices of

---

[17] See the very helpful overview and discussion in M Freudenthal 'The Future of European
Civil Procedure' (2003) 7/5 Electronic Journal of Comparative Law <http://www.
ejcl.org/ejcl/75/art75-6.html>.

enforcement agency in Europe were compared in order to identify the better features of each system as well as the drawbacks of functioning in a particular way. As Parts II–IV in this book illustrate, this data was used as the basis for a comparative analysis and discussion seminar in London on 23 April 2004, the aim of which was to improve understanding between European actors and generate solutions and possible reforms.

Finally, it is intended that the information shared and the ideas coming from a comparative analysis of this sort would enhance the cooperation of enforcement agencies in Europe. If implemented by the European Commission, it is anticipated that this project will increase awareness of the of the procedure governing enforcement agency practice in the European Union, as well as provide workable solutions for the creation of effective cross border enforcement procedures and prompt further research into methods for developing and approximating enforcement procedures of the Member States.

The Institute's project is therefore a relatively broad brush-stroke analysis of the current enforcement practices operating in selected Member States, which aims to understand national civil paradigms, identify areas for change and communicate ideas for reform to practitioners and policy makers in order to arrive at a tenable method for practically applying the concept of mutual recognition to cross-border enforcement.

The direct and indirect beneficiaries of this project illustrate the ambitious, global approach of the Institute's study. Policy-makers at the European and domestic level will benefit from having valuable and accurate information on enforcement practices in Europe which is relevant to policy and law making. A detailed appreciation of the powers available to enforcement agencies when accessing data about the debtor's assets is also essential when formulating efficient legislation in this area and might prompt Member States to improve and/or change their enforcement practices of their enforcement agencies.

Smaller commercial organizations and consumers will also benefit from the analysis contained in this book. Practical consideration of delay and cost must always thread through any civil procedure and enforcement is no different. The exequatur procedure obstructs the execution of a judgment but in a way that is actively detrimental to the judgment creditor who can be faced with added expense of renewed proceeding and delay.

All judgment creditors, whether industrial or private within the European Community, are entitled to an expeditious, efficient and predictable process when seeking to enforce a judgment in another Member State. Such a system should be based on the principle of mutual recognition and take steps towards a free movement of judgments within the European Union.

VII. THE HEIDELBERG PROJECT ON GARNISHMENT ORDERS

This project does not operate in a vacuum. It complements and is complemented by similar projects throughout Europe, each operating under the
Grotius programme and investigating a number of factors that determine
the efficiency of different enforcement agency models. Important questions
include whether enforcement agencies operate within the public or private
sphere, how heavily the state intervenes and regulates enforcement procedure, and whether enforcement agents administer any other function
attached to their office? These are question which are addressed by
Professors Hess, Delcasso, and Jongbloed as well as Andrew Dickinson in
this volume. However, an important factor pertinent to the discussions
contained in this edition is to what extent enforcement agents can access
data about the debtor's assets.

    Professor Hess, Director of the Institute of Comparative and Private
International Law at the University of Heidelberg directed a project in 2002
that investigated how the transparency of a debtor's assets, the attachment
of bank accounts and provisional enforcement and protective measures
contributed to the efficiency of enforcement of judicial decisions within the
European Union ('the Heidelberg project').[18]

    There are important and clear similarities between the project from
which this book comes and that of Professor Hess. The Heidelberg project,
like the Institute's, provides a comparative analysis of enforcement proceedings in the European Union but extends that analysis to examine the 'interfaces' between the Brussels I Regulation and the national enforcement laws.
The general objective of the Heidelberg project was to improve cross-
border enforcement of pecuniary claims in the European Judicial Area by
arriving at a number of policy considerations for garnishment proceedings.
The comparative analysis of the project was structured around four questionnaires, each addressing a specific topic concerning access to debtor
information. These were: transparency of debtors' assets, garnishment of
bank accounts, provisional enforcement and protective measures. These
questionnaires were answered by national reporters of (at that time) the 15
Member States.

    As in the Institute's project, Professor Hess emphasized the need to move
beyond a mere description of enforcement codes and conduct a comparative analysis using material which is provided in response to specific questions about how enforcement procedure is executed within selected

---

[18] Study No JAI/A3/2002/02 on making more efficient the enforcement of judicial decisions
within the European Union: Transparency of a Debtor's Assets, Attachment of a Debtor's Bank
Accounts, Provisional Enforcement and Protective Measures. Version of 18 Feb 2004.

Member States.[19] Although interest at a Community level has increased concerning the free movement of judgments, information on such proceedings are mainly recorded in a form intended for use by practitioners rather than for use in academic research,[20] the reason for which Professor Hess ascribes to the principle of territoriality. According to this approach, enforcement measures are sovereign acts of the states making them territorial in scope. The effect is that enforcement measures carrying a transborder effect are considered an infringement of the territorial sovereignty of the affected state, and, therefore, are excluded.[21] Although this is not an absolute paradigm, for instance it has been replaced by the principle of universality in insolvency proceedings,[22] it is an aspect of comparative study that Professor Hess cites as impairing cross-border information about enforcement systems in Member States.

The structure of the Heidelberg project follows a clear analysis of its three designated areas of interest beginning with the transparency of debtors' assets before addressing attachment of bank accounts and concluding with provisional enforceability and protective measures.

Looking first at the transparency of a debtor's assets, Professor Hess is in no doubt that cross-border recovery of judgments is impaired by the differences between the national legal systems, causing creditors in Europe to be treated unequally. The Heidelberg project recommends that all sources of information (including registers and debtors' declaration and disclosure by garnishees) should be available in all national jurisdictions. Equal access to the same sources of information guarantees equal treatment of creditors and debtors in the European Judicial Area.[23]

Secondly, in terms of the transparency of debtors' assets, Professor Hess considers the situation in Europe to be unsatisfactory. In some Member States (especially Germany, Austria and Greece), transborder garnishment is permitted, while others (the majority) rely strictly on territoriality (Belgium, Denmark, Finland, Ireland, Italy, Luxembourg, The Netherlands, Portugal, Scotland, and Sweden). The result is that garnishors, as with many other types of cross-border judgment creditors within the European Judicial Area, are treated differently. While this result might be acceptable as a consequence of the differences between non-harmonized national systems, the current fragmentation does not meet the needs of commercial actors within the single market. A direct consequence of the current state of affairs might be 'garnishment shopping' within the European Judicial Area.[24] This would result in efficient enforcement

---

[19] ibid 9.   [20] ibid.   [21] ibid 10.
[22] According to the concept of universality, bankruptcy orders are recognized and enforced in other States, ibid 11.
[23] ibid 48.   [24] ibid 89.

systems being burdened with 'external' judgments while inefficient systems would be left to worsen.

The most ambitious remedy to this problem recommended in the Heidelberg project is a European instrument designed to unify garnishment proceedings. A similar, if more modest proposal, put forward is to permit cross-border garnishment generally and establish a set of minimum standards to regulate European garnishment; however, harmonization of such a procedure would be difficult given that the current practice across Europe is deeply embedded in the structures of national civil codes. A European instrument of that sort would need to apply not only to cross-border garnishment but also to domestic proceedings making its effective utility difficult to ensure.[25]

It is precisely this type of point which illustrates the difficulty of giving practical effect to the principle of mutual recognition. As a concept, mutual recognition between Member States is theoretically desirable when coordinating enforcement proceedings but, the different domestic and European procedures that such an instrument would be required to contain, would limit its practical effect. As Professor Hess states in the Heidelberg project,

From a theoretical perspective the proposed European Garnishment order is mainly based on the guiding principles of mutual recognition [...] and 'universality', because a cross-border validity of a garnishment order would be explicitly allowed. However, the application of these principles is restricted to the first stage of enforcement proceedings (ie the seizure of the account). Therefore, the second stage of garnishment proceedings (collection, distribution of the claim, and protection of the debtor as well as the decision on the objections of the garnishee) remains completely subject to the enforcement laws of the Member State where the garnishment is effected. In a literal sense the 'European Enforcement Order' operates as a 'door opener' allowing a creditor to institute enforcement proceedings immediately abroad which are, however, conducted according to the applicable laws at the place of enforcement.

The final area of analysis in the Heidelberg project was provisional and protective measures. All Member States provide for provisional and protective measures to secure creditor's claims in cases of urgency, the consensus across Member States being that provisional measures are aimed at protecting the future enforcement of a judgment.[26] Provisional and protective measures secure the creditor's claim by preventing the debtor from evading his legal responsibilities in payment of that debt. The provisional remedies available in each Member State are mostly similar and, for the purposes of comparative research, national reporters in the Heidelberg project agree they can be broadly categorised as those aimed at reserving a future enforcement such as preliminary attachments or freezing order; provisional

---

[25] ibid 91.   [26] ibid 118.

measures designed to regulate the status quo of the parties; and measures that protect future specific performance, especially interim payments.

However, some differences do exist between the national measures, even though the impact of cross border provisional relief has been enhanced within the European Union through cooperation between national courts within the context of Articles 31 and 32 of the Brussels' Regulation.[27] Professor Hess recommends, in line with the consensus among Member States, that Article 31 of the Brussels I Regulation should be clarified concerning the limitations of the judicial competences for (ancillary) provisional measures. There is currently confusion about whether interim payments are 'provisional measures' in the sense of Article 31 even though there are, according to Professor Hess, compelling reasons to exclude them from that provision. The main reason for this being that it is the function of these remedies not only to protect the creditor for future realization of the judgment in the main proceedings but to replace lengthy main proceedings themselves.[28] In many Member States, these remedies are not considered to be 'provisional measures' but a form of summary proceedings, therefore interim payments should be linked to other summary proceedings.

To aid clarification of Article 31, Professor Hess suggests that a second paragraph be inserted containing the following definition of provisional measures: 'For the purposes of the first paragraph, provisional, including protective measures are measures to maintain the status quo pending determination of the issues at trial; or measures to secure assets out of which an ultimate judgment may be satisfied.' Accompanying this should be clarification concerning the jurisdiction of the court to grant provisional and protective measures which should be in keeping with the case law of the ECJ and provide that the principle responsibility lies with the court deemed competent according to the Regulation to determine the main proceedings in the case under Article 2-25.[29] Consequently, Article 31 should be clarified so as to apply to any provisional measure (with the exception of an interim payment) which is sought in order to block the defendant's assets or to preserve the status quo pending a final decision on the merits.[30]

A European Protective Order for cross border garnishment of bank accounts would also go some way to supplementing the legal protection of creditors contained in the Brussels Convention. The Heidelberg project suggests that such an instrument would need to be based on the principle of mutual trust in the judicial systems of the Member States and should provide for comprehensive responsibility of the court exercising jurisdiction in the matter. The court would also be empowered to grant provisional and protective measures which are automatically enforced in all other Member

---

[27] ibid 120.   [28] ibid 139.
[29] ibid 140.   [30] ibid 141.

States, on the basis of a form.[31] The Europe Protective Order should then be served on the debtor and the debtor should be obliged to disclose the whereabouts of his assets on the basis of the European Assets Declaration. Ancillary measures could be ordered and strictly confined to the assets located in that Member State, yet the effectiveness of these measures relies, as with all policy recommendations in this area, upon cooperation and trust between Member States.[32]

VIII. THE CHOICE BETWEEN PARADIGMS

What is then the most practical method for improving the movement of judgments within the European Judicial Area? The benefit of harmonization is the establishment of a common core but how far is that attainable through European legislation? Is the legal purpose of enforcement procedures better achieved, and more politically palatable, through a process of improved communication and increased understanding of different civil paradigms, or does that only create a diluted form of recognition and overburden functioning systems whilst allowing poor systems to get worse? The typical internal market solution is to have a combined framework predicated on the principles of mutual recognition but supplemented by a network of complementary Community legislation.

First of all further study is required in order to understand national civil procedure paradigms, and to identify areas for change and communicate ideas for reform to practitioners and policy makers in order to arrive at a tenable method for practically applying the concept of mutual recognition to cross border enforcement. But this study does demonstrate the need for further action. The starting point must be that that all judgment creditors within the European Community are entitled to an expeditious, efficient and predictable process when seeking to enforce a judgment in another Member State. Another starting point is that such a system needs to be based on the principle of mutual recognition. The question is then what further steps need to be taken toward a free movement of judgments within the European Union.

The further action will need to include some form of convergence in the institutional and procedural enforcement law. It is difficult to see how this can develop in any organized way without an EU initiative for further harmonization. The extent and form of such harmonization will depend on the outcome of further study. The harmonization will best take place in regulations to ensure its uniformity in this practical area where uniformity is so important, The Heidelberg study on garnishment proceedings show

---

[31] ibid.　　　　[32] ibid 142.

the way forward in providing a model that can be applied at a more general level.

There is also an important challenge to scholarship. Legal scholarship still grapples with the general concepts that can be developed from the needs based and very practical development of European civil procedure. The development and clarification of basic concepts is required in order to realize a European procedural system whichever paradigms one chooses. One discussion is whether one already has the emergence of an independent European law of civil procedure, distinguishing itself from national civil procedure as well as from international civil procedure.[33] European Union law, with the different measures in EU legislation, the case law in the European Court of Justice and national courts on their interpretation, forms a large body of legal material. Then there is the application of general doctrines of EU law, with the principles of effectiveness of EU law and of national procedural autonomy having an increasingly practically very important impact. The European Convention on Human Rights sets other requirements to national (and EU) civil courts and procedures at several levels and through the case law of the European Court of Human Rights, with an increasing degree of detail.

One also needs the contribution from comparative civil procedure in the assessment of how much harmonization is required before different systems can manage to communicate. It may also assist in challenging the defence of the national systems solutions as natural law. Here we can return to the beginning, to Lord Justice Bingham's statement. Scholarship can provide further support for a more realistic appreciation of the intrinsic value of maintaining all the features of different procedural systems. It may also have something to say about the value of maintaining different procedural systems in general in Europe, seen from the point of view of civil procedure. This can assist in giving procedural diversity the appropriate weight in the general constitutional discussion.

---

[33] See also here the very helpful overview and discussion in M Freudenthal 'The Future of European Civil Procedure' (2003) 7/5 Electronic Journal Of Comparative Law <http://www.ejcl.org/ejcl/75/art75-6.html>. and the emerging literature addressing these issues: M Storme (ed) *Procedural Laws in Europe* (Maklu Antwerpen 2003); B Hess 'Der Binnenmarktprozess' JZ 1998 1021–32; id 'Aktuelle Perspektiven der europäischen Prozessrechtsangleichung' JZ 2001, 573–83. KD Kerameus 'Angleichung des Zivilprozessrechts in Europa' (2002) 66 RabelsZ 5; CH van Rhee 'Civil Procedure: A European Ius Commune?' ERPL, 2000 589–611; M. Storme (ed) *Approximation of Judiciary Law in the European Union* (Nijhoff Dordrecht 1994); M Freudenthal and FJA van der Velden, `Europees procesrecht van het Verdrag van Amsterdam' in E.H. Hondius et al (eds) *Van Nederlands naar Europees Procesrecht? Liber Amicorum Paul Meijknecht* (Kluwer Dordrecht 2000) 81–98.

CHAPTER 3

COMPARATIVE ANALYSIS OF THE NATIONAL REPORTS

Burkhard Hess

I. THE 'EUROPEANIZATION' OF ENFORCEMENT LAWS

A. *Enforcement in the European Judicial Area (Article 65 EC Treaty)*

Only recently have enforcement proceedings become the subject of comparative research. In this field, legislation and procedural cultures have remained distinctly separated along national lines. Cross-border interaction has not appeared, because, according to the traditional view, enforcement measures are strictly limited by the principle of territoriality.[1] Neither did private international law address enforcement proceedings. As a matter of principle, international conventions only regulate the recognition of foreign judgments and other enforceable instruments. The execution of the title after its recognition remains a purely national matter of the requested state. In Europe, the Brussels Convention[2] clearly 'respected' this external frontier of national enforcement proceedings.[3]

The current, fragmented, situation is hampering transborder debt collection. In the Internal Market creditors are confronted with different legal systems, language barriers, additional costs and delay and—sometimes—with a reluctance on the part of national authorities to enforce foreign enforceable titles. From the perspective of creditors, different enforcement structures may have a similar effect to borders between states. For many creditors, efficient access to justice in the European Judicial Area

---

[1] This view was recently stressed by the House of Lords in *Societé Eram Shipping Co Ltd v Compagnie Internationale de Navigation and others* ILPr 2003, 468; [2003] 3 WLR 21 (HL) ; it corresponds to the French doctrine Cf E Guinchard 'Les procédures civiles d'exécution en droit international privé' in *Droit et Pratique des Voies d'Exécution* 2004/2005, 1711.04 : 'principe directeur'.

[2] Brussels Convention of 27 Sept 1968, [1978] OJ L-304/77.

[3] In the case 148/84 [1985] ECR 1981, *Deutsche Genossenschaftsbank v Brasserie du Pécheur*, the ECJ expressly held: 'The [Brussels] Convention merely regulates the procedure for obtaining an order for the enforcement of foreign enforceable instruments and does not deal with the execution itself, which continues to be governed by the domestic law of the court in which execution is sought' (emphasis added). This legal situation remained unchanged under Regulation EC 44/01.

in enforcement matters is not available. As a result, enterprises—especially small and medium-sized—do not seek to enforce their debts abroad, but simply write them off.[4]

A result of the fragmented legal situation and the insufficient cooperation among national authorities is the encouragement of unilateral actions by the Member State relating to the transborder debt collection. Some national legal systems have created extra-territorial instruments such as 'worldwide freezing injunctions and search orders',[5] others allow cross-border garnishment against third parties situated abroad,[6] particularly where banks with Europe-wide operations are involved.[7] These new developments show that there is a need for harmonization or at least approximation of the enforcement systems in the European Judicial Area.

Since the 1990s enforcement proceedings have increasingly become a subject of comparative research and of legislative challenge in the Member States and by the Community.[8] Almost all of the Member States adopted extensive reforms in order to improve enforcement.[9] In 1993, the Storme Group published the 'Draft of a Directive on the Approximation

---

[4] W Kennett 'General Report: Enforcement' in M Storme (ed) *Procedural Laws in Europe, towards harmonization* (2003) at 81.

[5] B Hess Study JAI A3/02/2002 on making more efficient the enforcement of judicial decisions within the European Union: *Transparency of a Debtor's Assets, Attachment of Bank Accounts, Provisional Enforcement and Protective Measures.* the study is available at <http://europa.eu.int/comm/justice_home/doc_centre/civil/studies/doc/enforcement_judicial_d ecisions_180204_en.pdf> at 76.

[6] A similar decision (allowing the cross-border effect of garnishment) is Cour de Cassation 30 May 1985, Revue Critique 1986, 329, although this decision only set out an obligation *in personam* to furnish information across boarders, Cf annotation of Battifol. Cf Hess, Study JAI A3/02/2002, p.79 with further references

[7] Since the 1990s, a broad consensus has been reached that debtors and third parties are obliged to provide information of the assets located abroad, Cf Hess, Study JAI A3/02/2002, 35 with further references.

[8] See especially W Kennett *The Enforcement of Judgments in Europe* (OUP, Oxford, 2000), 61-98; KD Kerameus 'Enforcement in the International Context', 264 RdC, 215 (1997). Comparative research on enforcement was provided for by HF Gaul 'Das Rechtsbehelfssystem der Zwangsvollstreckung—Möglichkeiten und Grenzen einer Vereinfachung', ZZP 85 (1972) 251, 279 (describing remedies in several European jurisdictions). A useful guide from the practitioner's perspective is provided by H Weißmann and E Riedel *Handbuch der internationalen Zwangsvollstreckung* (looseleaf edition). P Kaye (ed) *Methods of Execution of Orders and Judgments in Europe* (1996). Important comparative research was undertaken in several seminars organized by the Union Internationale des Huissiers de Justice, M Caupain and G de Leval (eds) *L'efficacité de la justice civile en Europe* (1999); A Verbeke and M Caupain (ed) *La Transparence patrimoniale—Condition nécessaire et insuffisante du titre conservatoire européen?* (2000) ; J Isnard and J Normand (ed) *Nouveaux droits dans un nouvel espace européen de justice : Le droit processuel et le droit de l'exécution* (2002); J Isnard and J Normand (eds) *L'aménagement du droit de l'exécution dans l'espace communautaire—bientôt les premiers instruments* (2003).

[9] B Hess Study JAI A3/02/2002, 12.

of Civil Procedures in Europe'.[10] This Proposal addressed (for the first time) enforcement proceedings as a matter for European harmonization. Although the proposals were met with reluctance by the Member States and in the legal literature,[11] the Commission took up some of these ideas and published in 1997 a 'Communication on the Free Movement of Judgments'.[12] The Communication contained a 'sectoral' approach and proposed to harmonize the interfaces between national enforcement procedures and the Brussels Convention, especially provisional and protective measures, the transparency of the debtor's assets and to explore possibilities for an exchange of information between enforcement authorities.[13]

Although these proposals were met with scepticism in the legal literature, the European Council at the Tampere Summit adopted the proposed strategy.[14] This summit took place against the backdrop of Article 65(c) of the Amsterdam Treaty of the European Union (1997) which entrusts the Community to 'adopt measures in the field of judicial cooperation in civil matters having cross-border implications'. This competence includes cross-border enforcement.[15] Some months later, the European Council adopted an Action Plan[16] which contains a Working Programme for the implementation of the new competence.[17] This programme envisages measures in the field of enforcement which had formerly been proposed by the Commission's Communication.

At present, the basis for legislative activity by the Community is being prepared by comparative research. Last year, a group of legal experts under my direction completed a study on the transparency of debtor's assets, garnishments and provisional enforcement and protective measures.[18] The legal and practical situation in 16 national jurisdictions was described and evaluated on the basis of questionnaires, best practices were identified and

[10] M Storme (ed) *L'approchement du Droit Judiciaire de l'Union Européenne* (1994), 185–219.

[11] See especially the discussions of the German Association of Procedural Law (Zivilprozessrechtslehrervereinigung) in 1996 in *Lenken, Zeitschrift für den Zivilprozess* 106 (1996), 337 .

[12] Cf Communication to the Council and the Parliament on the free movement of judgments and avenues to be explored for an improvement of the administration of justice in the European Union of 26 November 1997, COM(97) 609 final, OJC 33, 31 Jan 1998.

[13] Communication of 26 Nov 1997 COM(97) 609 final, paras 42–60.

[14] Conclusion of the Presidency, paras 29–39, especially para 36. W Kennett *Enforcement* (OUP, Oxford, 2000) 52–8; B Hess, IPRax 2001, 389.

[15] B Hess Study JAI A3/02/2002, 12.

[16] Action Plan of 30 Nov 2000, OJC-12, 15 Jan 2001.

[17] B Hess 'Aktuelle Perspektiven der europäischen Prozessrechtsangleichung', *Juristenzeitung* 2001, 573 ; M Fallon and Meeussen, 'Private International Law in the European Union and the Exception of Mutual Recognition' [2003] YB Private Int'l L 38

[18] Study No JAI/A3/2002/02.

several proposals for Community measures were presented.[19] The results of
this study (which is being extended to cover the new EU Member States)
will be integrated in a Green Paper on Enforcement in the European Judicial
Area. Today, legislative action of the European Union in the field of
enforcement seems imminent.

B. Enforcement and Debt Collection

The Community's activities in enforcement matters are not confined to article 65 EC Treaty. There is also a broader approach which generally includes
all forms of collecting debts within and outside from formal enforcement
procedures (*inkasso*). From this perspective, cross-border debt collection is
considered a service which is, as a matter of principle, protected by Article
49 and 50 EC Treaty. This approach is not a new one. In 1995, the ECJ was
asked in a preliminary ruling whether Germany violated Articles 49 and 50
of the EC Treaty, because German legislation (*Rechtsberatungsgesetz*)[20]
reserved debt collection to attorneys and excluded businessmen of other
Member States from the German market.[21] The Court held that cross-
border debt collection was covered by Articles 49 and 50 of the EC Treaty.
However, the ECJ decided that these provisions had not been violated
because the aim of protecting consumers against any unlawful and non-
professional debt collection was considered a legitimate and proportionate
ground for excluding non-lawyers from this business.

This case law may change in the near future. On 5 March 2004, the
Commission published a Proposal for a General Directive on Services in
the Internal Market which shall apply to all cross-border services which
are not governed by specific Community legislation.[22] The proposal is
based on the principles of mutual recognition and the country of origin.[23]
Article 16 states that a provider of services who has been admitted in one
Member State may practise freely in all Member States and shall be

[19] The study proposes to adopt a Community Regulation on Enforcement which should
contain a European Assets Declaration, a European Third Debtor Declaration; a European
Garnishment Order (for cross-border garnishments and, finally, a European Protective Order.
The new instruments shall supplement the existing national procedures in the Member States,
not supplement existing instruments. Cf Study JAI A3 02/2002, 145.
[20] The *Rechtsberatungsgesetz* is explained in the German Report at 25–6.
[21] ECJ Case C-3/95, ECJ Reports 1996 I-6511, para 38.
[22] Proposal of 3 Mar 2004, COM(2004)2 final. The directive shall implement the results of
the Lisbon European Council with the view of making the EU the most competitive and
dynamic knowledge-based economy in the world by 2010.
[23] This application of these principles in European Private and Procedural Law is not undis-
puted, see W Kennett *General Report Enforcement* in M Storme (ed) *Procedural Laws in
Europe* (Maklu, Antwerpen, 2003), 81 ; M Fallon and J Meeusen 'Private International Law
in the European Union and the Exception of Mutual Recognition' (2000) 4 Yb Private Int'lL
37, 40.

subject only to the provisions of the Member State of origin. According to Article 18, the Directive shall not apply to 'the judicial recovery of debts' during a transitory period which shall cease (at the latest) on 1 January 2010.

Cross-border debt collection in Europe will be liberalised by 2010 if the Member States and the Parliament accept this proposal. The Commission intends to start complementary harmonization in this field immediately after the adoption of the Services Directive.[24] However, the Draft does not provide for a clear definition of 'judiciary recovery of debts'. It seems that the Commission intends to liberalize all forms of debt collection activities. However, the activities are currently exercised in some Member States as a general business, while other Member States reserve this activity to lawyers or bailiffs. Against the backdrop of Articles 55 and 45 EC Treaty which except the exercise of official authority from the freedom of services, it seems to be necessary to define a clear borderline between enforcement proceedings which form an inherent part of the judiciary of the Member States and general debt collection activities.[25] Nevertheless, there is no doubt that the liberalization of debt collection will deeply influence the enforcement structures in the Member States. Accordingly, the 'free choice' of Member States between a public or a (more or less regulated) private system of debt collection will be influenced and partly replaced by the Community's regulation of cross-border services.

C. Constitutional Requirements Pertaining to Enforcement

The third area where national enforcement systems are increasingly 'Europeanized' is the constitutional underpinnings of enforcement.[26] Since 1997, the European Court of Human Rights has applied Article 6 of the ECHR (access to justice) to enforcement proceedings.[27] The application of Article 6 implies that the creditor can claim a right not only to recovery within reasonable time, but also that the procedures for recovery and seizure should be efficient.[28] As all EU Member States are bound by the European Convention on Human Rights, they must, under Article 6 ECHR,

[24] Cf Art 40(1)(c) of the Draft Directive.

[25] Only the latter activities should be covered by the principle of origin.

[26] Constitutional mandates for enforcement are described by KD Kerameus, IECL 10–17 [2003]; Fricéro 'La libre exécution des jugements dans l'espace judiciare européen, un principe émergent?' (2003) Mél Normand 173

[27] Similar constitutional guarantees are contained in Art 47 EU Charta of Human Rights; Cf B Hess 'EMRK, Grundrechte-Charta und Europäisches Zivilverfahrensrecht' *liber amicorum Eric Jayme* vol I (2004) 339.

[28] A Verbeke 'Execution Officers as a Balance Wheel in Insolvency Cases' [2001] 9 Tilburg Foreign Law Review 7, 9

provide fair and efficient enforcement structures and procedures.[29] In this context, it is interesting to note that the influence of the ECHR is broader than the impact of Community law. While Article 65 EC Treaty is confined to 'proceedings' and must therefore respect the existing enforcement structures in the Member States, Article 6 ECHR does not know such limits.[30] Therefore the Contracting Parties to the Convention must also adapt their (internal) enforcement organization to the constitutional requirements. Accordingly, the Council of Europe elaborated several Recommendations on the efficiency of enforcement structures and proceedings.[31] These recommendations contain proposals for best practices in enforcement matters and include the organization of enforcement.[32] Minimum standards for an efficient organization of enforcement agencies are currently defined by the ECHR.

It should be noted that not only the creditors', but also the debtors', rights are protected by constitutional guarantees. Their human dignity and privacy are protected by Article 8 ECHR.[33] An important guiding principle, which is inherent to enforcement proceedings, is proportionality.[34] Proportionality is relevant to 'balancing' the competing rights and interests of the parties. According to this principle, enforcement measures should not unnecessarily infringe upon the debtor and third parties; disproportionate or vexatious measures are not allowed.

[29] European Court of Human Rights, 19 Mar 1997, *Hornsby v Greece*, ECHR Reports 1997 II 495; 11 Jan 2001, *Lunari v Italy*, ECHR Reports 2001. Fricéro 'Le droit européen à l'exécution des jugments'; (2002) Revue des Hussissiers de Justice, 6 ; P Yessiou-Faltsi 'Le droit de l'exécution selon la jurisprudence de la Cour Européenne des Droits de l'Homme: Analyse et Prospective' in J Normand and J Isnard, *Le droit processuel et le droit de l'exécution* (2002), 195.

[30] It remains to be seen how the parallel provision of Art II/47 of the European Constitution will be interpreted in the context of Community law ('ie the principle of defined and limited competencies).

[31] Working Party on the Efficiency of Justice, Recommendation of the Committee of Ministers to Member States on Enforcement Rec (2003) 17, adopted on 9 Sept 2003, especially Part IV (Enforcement Agents).

[32] Cf Recommendation no 3 of the 24th Conference of European Ministers of Justice, Oct 2001, Moscow.

[33] Leroy 'L'efficacité des procédures judiciaires au sein de l'Union européenne et les garanties des droits de la défense, la transparence patrimoniale' in M Caupain and J de Leval *L'efficacité de la justice en Europe* (1999) 273, 275–96.

[34] In some Member States, the principle of proportionality is expressly stated in their procedural codes, for instance see 803(1) ZPO: 'Execution effected on movable property takes place by way of an attachment. It may not be extended beyond what is necessary for the satisfaction of the creditor and for covering the costs of execution.'

It is a matter of fact that a close relationship exists between enforcement organization and enforcement proceedings. However, while enforcement proceedings are based upon similar structures, there exist considerable differences between enforcement agencies. In particular, enforcement agents are differently qualified. Accordingly, any harmonization of enforcement proceedings presupposes that the European instruments are drafted so as to be workable under the existing structures. Therefore, harmonization of enforcement proceedings seems to be much more complicated than the harmonization of judicial procedures which are (as a rule) applied by (highly qualified) judges and lawyers.

However, at present, not much knowledge relating to the enforcement structures in the Member States is available.[35] This was why in 2002 the British Institute of International and Comparative Law initiated a comparative study on the organization of enforcement agencies in different European Member States. This study covers the following national systems: Austria, England and Wales, France, Germany, the Netherlands, Spain, and Sweden. The aim of this study is to explore the relationship between the organization of enforcement agencies and the efficiency of the national systems.[36] From its beginning, the Research Interchange was closely linked with the parallel study on *Making More Efficient the Enforcement of Judicial Decisions within the European Union*.[37] Many of its members also prepared national reports for this parallel study.

III. DIFFERENT STRUCTURES OF ENFORCEMENT ORGANIZATIONS

A. *Centralized and Decentralized Systems*

The national reports reveal divergences relating to the organization of enforcement agencies. A key distinction relates to the uniform or segregated organization of enforcement organs and procedures. Some national systems provide for a comprehensive enforcement structure where the execution of monetary claims against the debtor's assets (with the exception of enforce-

---

[35] First comparative studies were presented by W Kennett *Enforcement Agents in Europe* (2002) and by KD Kerameus 'Enforcement' IECL vol XVI, ch 10 (2002) para 10–16.

[36] The Institute coordinated six national studies which were originally based on a uniform questionnaire. In addition, the Research Interchange met three times over the duration of the project; two meetings were held in London and one in Heidelberg.

[37] JAI A3 02/2002.

ment against land) is carried out by one single organ. The most striking example is Sweden (Finland recently adopted a similar model) where the National Enforcement Agency is in charge of the execution of court judgments, administrative decisions, arbitral awards and other *titres exécutoires*.

However, 'centralized' systems do not presuppose an administrative structure of enforcement organs. In Austria and in Spain, the courts are responsible for all enforcement proceedings.[38] This does not preclude the possibility that different persons within the Court's organization might be responsible for the different procedures. Therefore, in these jurisdictions court officers directly contact the debtor, effect seizures and collect the money at his home. The progress of the enforcement proceedings is controlled by the Court, the residual responsibility lies with the judge. A centralized structure also exists in the Netherlands (and in Belgium), where enforcement is comprehensively carried out by bailiffs who are liberal professionals and (since 2001) have been subject to competition.[39]

The situation in France is to some extent different: As a matter of principle, the bailiffs (*huissiers de justice*) are in charge of enforcement proceedings. However, the attachment of salaries, which is in practice one of the most important modes of enforcement, is carried out by the president of the local courts (*tribunal d'instance*). In Germany, the enforcement structure is much more fragmented. Several enforcement organs are in charge for (more or less) different methods of enforcement. Garnishments are effected by the local courts, while the seizure of movables is carried out by bailiffs. The German system relies on the initiative of the judgment creditor (and of his counsel). It is up to the creditor to apply directly to the bailiff or to the local court when seeking enforcement measures; the creditors control the enforcement strategy.[40] The most decentralized enforcement structure was found in England and Wales, where the competence of enforcement organs depended on the kind of judgments which were enforced. Garnishments (which are now called Third Party Debt Orders) are ordered by the court which gave the judgment.[41] The attachment of earnings is made by the

[38] However, there is a great divergence between Spain and Austria: while in Spain the court which renders the judgment is also responsible for its enforcement, enforcement in Austria is carried out by the local courts where assets of the debtor are located.

[39] Such bailiffs are also in charge for the collection of public taxes and dues. Nevertheless, there exists a second system which is carried out by state-employed enforcement agents. However, sometimes some of this work is now offered by tender to the bailiffs. This is explained futher in the Dutch national report.

[40] The enforcement system is largely based upon the idea that the creditor should control enforcement proceedings and the enforcement strategy. Therefore the creditor's choice of the competent organ was the legislator's motivation for the adoption of the decentralized system, HF Gaul 'Zur Struktur der Zwangsvollstreckung' *Der Deutsche Rechtspfleger* (1971) 81.

[41] CPR 70; English Report para 26.

county courts.[42] Seizures of goods which are based on judgments of the High Court of London are enforced by the High Sheriffs, Under Sheriffs and Sheriffs' Officers. At the county court level, judgments are enforced by court bailiffs who are employed by the court service. In addition, private bailiffs offered their services. Public bodies wanting to enforce their actions, such as the inland revenue and local council authorities, either employ their own agents or contract out to private bailiffs.[43] Recently, the English system has been changed.[44]

B. *Different Enforcement Organs*

A second, considerable difference between the national systems relates to the competent organs: at the European level, at least four different systems must be distinguished. The main reasons for this fragmentation are historical and related to the cultural development of the national systems. Originally, the enforcement of judgments was considered in most countries as a part of the judicial proceedings and, therefore, the judge who rendered the judgment was also in charge of its enforcement and enforcement procedures were dealt with as a kind of (second) adjudication of the matter.[45] This concept still exists in Spain[46] and to some extent in England and Wales.[47] In Germany, the responsibility of the judge for the enforcement of his judgments was given up when the Code of Civil Procedure was adopted.[48] Germany partly adopted the French model, where bailiffs act outside the court system. Today, a clear separation between judicial and enforcement proceedings seems to be a common feature of most of the jurisdictions.[49] However, this separation does not mean that the constitutional procedural guarantees do not apply to enforcement. Quite the

---

[42] Attachment of Earnings Act 1971, English Report, paras 40–9, 13–17.

[43] In addition, major state courts also employ their own agents or contract out to private bailiffs in order to collect debts owed to the public sector, namely council tax debt or criminal charges As will be seen, the current, fragmented situation is currently undergoing substantial reforms.

[44] United Kingdom Department for Constitutional Affairs, *White Paper on Effective Enforcement*, March 2003, Cm 5744 HMSO, available at <http://www.dca.gov.uk/enforcement/agents02.htm>. The reform entered into force in April 2004.

[45] HF Gaul Zeitschrift für den Zivilprozess 85 (1972) 251, 270; The historical developments in Germany are described by L Rosenberg, HF Gaul, and E Schilken *Zwangsvollstreckungsrecht* (10th edn 1987) §5 II, 35.

[46] Since 1978, it is guaranteed by Art 117 of the Spanish Constitution, Spanish Report, 1.

[47] English Report para 26 ; CPR 70, Practice Directions in CPR 72 taking legal effect from March 2002.

[48] According to the Motives the task of the judges was to decide the case and not to enforce the judgment, Hahn, Materialien zur CPO, 137, 220; Gaul, *Der deutsche Rechtspfleger* (1971) 81.

[49] Exceptions: Spain, Denmark, and—to some degree—England and Ireland.

contrary: at the constitutional level, judicial and enforcement proceedings remain closely interconnected.[50]

1. Bailiff-oriented Systems

In France, Benelux, and Scotland (as well as in many Eastern European countries and in Portugal), enforcement is carried out by enforcement agents (*huissiers de justice*) who act as officers appointed by the State, but outside the court system. In the Netherlands, a reform in 2001 deregulated the status of the bailiffs who now act as independent professionals in a competitive system.[51] Bailiffs are remunerated by (considerable) fees and,[52] apart from enforcement, they are responsible for wide-ranging tasks which also include the service of documents, the documentation of a given situation and (especially) pre-litigation debt collection.[53] In France, bailiffs are also organized as public officers acting outside of the courts. Judicial intervention (and help) can be obtained by the 'judge of enforcement' (who is the president of the local court/*tribunal de grande instance*). In these jurisdictions, the social and economic standing of bailiffs is very high.[54]

2. Court-oriented Systems

Court-oriented systems are found in Austria, Spain and also in Denmark. Compared in detail, the organization of court-oriented enforcement is very different from country to country. In Austria the local courts at the domicile of the debtor are responsible for the enforcement proceedings, which are regularly carried out by the court clerk (*Rechtspfleger*)[55] in a completely separate procedure. In Spain the judge who made the judgment is also responsible for its enforcement. Accordingly, the competence of the Spanish court is not determined by the debtor's domicile or the location of his assets but by the general heads of jurisdiction. Therefore, the Spanish system relies on judicial cooperation between different courts.[56] In Spain, the judge is

---

[50] European Court of Human Rights, 19 Mar 1997, *Hornsby v Greece*, ECHR Reports 1997 II 495; 11 Jan 2001, *Lunari v Italy*, ECHR Reports 2001. VN Fricéro 'Le droit européen à l'exécution des jugments' (2002) Revue des Husissiers de Justice 6.

[51] Dutch Report 8.

[52] But they may also conclude price agreements with their clients, which also allow contingency fees, Dutch Report 8.

[53] Accordingly, a good remuneration of other services may allow some 'cross-financing' of enforcement.

[54] At present, 3271 *huissiers* de justice are appointed; 987 are acting individually; 2,284 are associates (*huissier de justice en qualité d'associé*), Senat Français *Réforme du statut de certaines professions judiciaires* <htttp://www.senat.fr./rap/102-222/102-22617.html>, visited at 27 April 2004.

[55] Austrian Report 16.

[56] It seems conceivable that the Spanish enforcement system may influence a creditor's choice to sue the debtor at home and not in a specific head of jurisdiction.

primarily responsible for the enforcement of the judgments and this judge regularly orders—on application by the creditor—the garnishment of the debtor's assets.[57]

In court-oriented systems, the seizure of movable property is effected by bailiffs or *agentes judiciales* who are civil servants employed by the court. These persons are in direct contact with the debtor and may even—under the supervision of the court—negotiate an amicable settlement of the debt.[58] However, their activities are strictly controlled by the court.

3. Mixed Systems

Mixed systems exist in Germany and in England. In these countries, enforcement proceedings are partly carried out by bailiffs or sheriffs (especially the seizure of movable property), while garnishments are ordered by the court. However, there are great differences between the systems. In Germany, bailiffs act as court officers, but they run their own offices outside the court and are under its supervision (cf section 766 ZPO). Their remuneration is mainly covered by salary and only partially complimented by fees.[59] Garnishments are effected by the court officers (Rechtspfleger)[60] in a written procedure without a hearing of the debtor (Section 834 ZPO). The claim is usually assigned to the creditor who collects the money from the third-party debtor (without any further involvement of the enforcement court).[61] The Rechtspfleger are responsible for a wide range of quasi-judicial and administrative functions in relation to enforcement, the land registry and insolvency proceedings. They are also civil servants (of a higher rank than bailiffs) acting wholly within the court's purview. They are remunerated only by salary.[62]

In England, third-party debt orders are granted by the judge of the court which gave the judgment. The attachment of debts is effected in a two-stage procedure: on application of the creditor, the judge grants an interim Third Party Debt Order and fixes a date for a hearing. In the hearing, the judgment

---

[57] The need of requesting the assistance of the judge at the debtor's domicile or at the location of his assets leads to considerable delays within the Spanish system, Cf W Kennett, in M Storme (ed) *Procedural laws in Europe* (Maklu, Antwerp, 2003), 81, 98; Spanish Report 12–13.

[58] In Austria, recent reforms enlarged the powers of the bailiff of negotiating a payment on instalment or to rearch an amicable settlement on behalf of the debtor, see W Jakusch 'Die EO-Novelle 2003', *Österreichiche Juristenzeitung* (2004) 201.

[59] German Report 22.

[60] The seizure and auctioning of real estates apply also within the competency of the court clerks (Rechtspfleger). A comparative study on the legal status of court clarks has been presented by the Council of Europe, G Oberto, *Recrutement et formation des magistrats en Europe* (Council of Europe, Strasbourg, 2003).

[61] Section 835 ZPO.

[62] German Report 11.

debtor and the third-party debtor may object to the order, the debtor may also apply for his protection (of maintenance needs); the court will decide all issues and make a final order. Therefore, according to English law, garnishments are effected in a (simplified) ordinary court proceeding.[63] The actual payment of the money seized to the creditor requires a second decision of the court which is granted after a hearing where the judgment debtor and/or third party debtor may contest the order.[64] The seizure of movable property is carried out by high court and county sheriffs (who are civil servants) and—on the choice of the creditor—by private bailiffs.[65] The fragmented structure of enforcement agents has been replaced by a uniform system provided for 'enforcement agents' who are regulated, licensed and qualified professionals. The regulatory body which licenses all enforcement agents is the Security Industry Authority (SIA). It is expected to publish a code of conduct for enforcement agents in the near future.[66] At first sight, the free competition between the enforcement agents is an additional feature of the English system.

4. Administrative Systems

A completely different enforcement organization is found in Sweden and Finland. In these countries, enforcement is carried out by an administrative body which is operating completely outside the courts. The Swedish authority is organized as an administrative body under the supervision of the Ministry of Finance and divided into 10 regional agencies which themselves are split between 84 offices. The competencies of the Enforcement Authority also relate to summary proceedings, reconstruction of bad debts, supervision of bankruptcies, etc. In Sweden, the enforcement strategy is mainly controlled by the Enforcement Agency. As a matter of principle, there is no room for private enforcement of judgment debts.[67] Recently, the structure of the Enforcement Authority was changed and the collection of taxes is now transferred to the National Tax Board.[68]The new structure will remove any priority accorded to public debts.

C. Regulation and qualification of enforcement agents

Finally, the national reports show considerable differences relating to the

---

[63] English Report paras 26–32.
[64] ibid 9–11 and 13–15.
[65] In practice, the large majority of warrants is executed by private bailiffs, ibid 4.
[66] ibid para 17, 4–5.
[67] This does not exclude activities of inkasso agencies which collect debts on a voluntary basis before enforcement proceedings are initiated, Swedish Report 2.
[68] Swedish Report 4.

personal status and the professional qualification of enforcement agents. Bailiff-oriented systems (France, Netherlands) provide for highly qualified agents (with a university degree). As a rule, they operate within a regulated profession and are remunerated by fees. The typical structure is a civil partnership.[69] The reputation of bailiffs is very high—comparable to the reputation of other public officers such as notaries or even judges.[70]

The qualification of the agents working within the Swedish and Finnish Enforcement agencies is equally high. They are specialised lawyers with a university degree. However, being public servants they are remunerated by the State. In addition, the Enforcement Agency is also staffed by civil servants who do not have a university degree and who are trained and educated by in-house courses.[71] However, the responsibility of a highly qualified and specialised officer in each individual proceeding is clear.

The qualification of the personnel in court-oriented and mixed systems is different. In these systems, with the exception of Spain (where the judge who gave the judgment is responsible for its enforcement)[72] enforcement measures are mainly carried out by court officers or bailiffs who do not need to possess a university degree nor a secondary school certificate, they are trained 'in-house' for the needs of their profession.[73] A striking example is Germany, where the bailiffs are not highly qualified. Accordingly, enforcement proceedings are organized so as not to overstrain the enforcement personnel. German enforcement law is based on a so-called guiding principle of 'formality'. According to this principle, enforcement organs are not empowered to undertake any substantive investigation relating to the enforceable instrument and are not competent to decide any issue of substantive law. They are simply bound by the enforceable title.[74] Any substantive determination related with enforcement is, as a matter of principle, to be made by the civil courts.

The Austrian system does not know any similar separation, as the judge in the enforcement court closely controls the enforcement proceedings. While the overwhelming majority of enforcement matters are dealt with by

---

[69] In France, the *huissiers* act in the form of a société civile professionelle, Law of 29 Nov 1966, Cf W Kennett *Enforcement Agents* (2002) 109.

[70] French Report 1.

[71] Swedish Report 5.

[72] In England, a clear difference exists between garnishment (third party debt order) which is effected by the judge of the court who gave the judgment) and the seizure of movable property which is effected by sheriffs or (private, non certificated) bailiffs who often do not dispose of any qualification, English Report, paras 14–16.

[73] The Federal States Bavaria and North Rhine Westphalia maintain 'Schools for the Judiciary Staff' (Juristenschule) where young bailiffs are trained by judges and experienced colleagues.

[74] Accordingly, these systems do not allow for any enforcement of a simple invoice or a promissory note, because the enforcement of such titles presupposes an substantive check of the prerequisites of enforcement which are not documented by an enforceable title.

court officers (Rechtspfleger), the judge can always intervene and reserve those matters to himself which he considers as difficult or of fundamental importance.[75] The legal position of the German *Rechtspfleger* is different, because legislation recently conferred the control of the *Rechtspfleger*'s activities to the superior court.[76] Accordingly, the judges of the enforcement court are only competent for the supervision of the bailiffs and are not involved in garnishment proceedings which are carried out by the Rechtspfleger.[77]

VI. CORRELATIONS BETWEEN ENFORCEMENT STRUCTURE AND PROCEDURE—
SOME EXAMPLES

The last remarks illustrate that enforcement structures and procedures are closely interrelated. Further examples of the relationship are given here.

A. *The prerequisites of enforcement*

A higher level of qualification of enforcement agents and the centralized organization of enforcement allows a wider range of enforceable instruments, because the enforcement agent may check their reliability before ordering enforcement measures. Accordingly, the Dutch system provides for enforcement proceedings which are based on bills of exchange[78] while, in Germany, the creditor must first sue the debtor in expedited proceedings. Enforcement is subject to the judgment given in those proceedings.[79]

Court-oriented systems often provide for a kind of enforcement process which is sometimes carried out by the court.[80] In Austria, enforcement proceedings are initiated by a procedure for granting a warrant for execution (*Bewilligungsverfahren*). In theory, the debtor must present an enforceable instrument with an application for a warrant of execution. Both prerequisites should be checked by the court. In practice, the number of cases where the examination by the court led to the denial of the application was extremely small. In 1995, legislation introduced a simplified

[75] Austrian Report 10.   [76] German Report 13.
[77] ibid 13.
[78] The legal situation in France is identical, T Moussa and S Guinchard *Droit et Pratique des Voies d'Exécution* (2004/2005) 125.11.
[79] In this context, it is interesting to note that the European instruments on enforcement closely follow the German model: the free movement of enforceable titles within the scope of the Regulation 44/01/EC is limited to judgments, court settlement and notarial documents. Cf Arts 32, 57 and 58 Reg. EC 44/01, generally KD Kerameus IECL XVI, paras 10–22.
[80] Historically, enforcement proceedings were initiated by a formal law suit of the creditor, HF Gaul ZZP 85 (1972), 251, 269; GW Wetzell *System des ordentlichen Civilprozesses* (3rd edn 1878) 514.

procedure which is mainly based on electronic data exchange (section 54a EO, vereinfachtes Bewilligungsverfahren): According to the new procedure, the creditor may apply online for a warrant of execution (electronic forms are available at the website of the Federal Ministry of Justice); the presentation of an enforceable title is not required. The debtor is protected by a specific remedy against the warrant of execution within two weeks after its service (Einspruch, s 54c EO).[81] As a result, the Austrian legislation replaced the former opening procedure by a simple electronic application which is regularly granted without any examination.[82] Today, Austria is the only EU Member State where enforcement proceedings are initiated without any formal presentation of the enforceable title by the creditor.

B. The challenging issue: The gathering of information for enforcement purposes

A close correlation between enforcement structures and available procedures exists in relation to the entitlement to information about the location of the debtor's assets. At present, the European systems provide for two different methods for obtaining information about the debtor's assets. The first is to oblige the debtor (and in garnishment proceedings the third debtor) to disclose the whereabouts of his assets to the creditor or the enforcement agent. The second is to grant enforcement agents qualified access to non-public registers.[83]

The main problem with the debtor's declaration lies in the fact that the declaration must be given personally.[84] If the debtor refuses to disclose his assets, the enforcement organs (with the help of the police) may exercise physical coercion and arrest him.[85] The making of an incorrect or false declaration by the debtor is treated as a criminal offence. Therefore, in some Member States, the declaration is sworn under oath as an affidavit.[86]

However, there exists a second, more efficient, method of obtaining the required information. Modern enforcement laws grant qualified organs

---

[81] The debtor can only oppose that the application did not correspond to the enforceable title, Austrian Report 7.

[82] The efficiency of the proceedings has been considerably improved. However, this procedure seems acceptable as enforcement proceedings are centralised and closely supervised by the enforcement court.

[83] B Hess Study JAI A3/02/2002, 35.

[84] HF Gaul *Neukonzeption der Sachaufklärung in der Zwangsvollstreckung* 108 ZZP 1, 8 [1995].

[85] In England and Wales, the failure to comply with a court order will be sanctioned by a contempt of court, English Report, para 66.

[86] Example s 807, 478–83 ZPO. In 1991 an amendment of the Austrian Enforcement Code introduced a new procedure where the declaration is provided without oath. However, the criminal sanction remained unchanged, cf Study JAI A3/02/2002, Austrian Report Transparency, 51-52.

access to non-public files. In Austria, and in Spain especially, the enforcement courts may request information about the debtor's employment from social insurance registers. In Spain and in Sweden, the enforcement organs may also directly request information from fiscal records.[87] In the Netherlands[88] and in Belgium,[89] bailiffs can get information about the debtor's address and employment from social security records. In Luxembourg, a creditor may ask the *juge de paix* to contact the social security register in order to find out the debtor's address and employment.[90] In France, the legal situation was more complicated as the *huissiers de justice* were not allowed to access directly administrative and fiscal records, but had to request the help of the *Procureur de la République*. In practice, this cooperation did not work efficiently.[91] The legal situation has been considerably changed: Since February 2004, the French bailiffs can immediately access the tax administration in order to obtain information about the debtor's bank account. In addition, the Procureur de la République must support the bailiffs' search for the debtor's address and employer.[92] All in all, the opening of access to such information has considerably improved the efficiency of enforcement proceedings (especially garnishments).

However, in decentralized systems, direct access of creditors to (non-public) registers is excluded by data protection. In these Member States, creditors face serious problems when seeking to enforce their claims. One example is Germany where the creditor's choice of the enforcement organ largely depends on the location of the debtor's assets. At present, a creditor who does not dispose of any information of the financial situation of his debtor may request the competent bailiff at the debtor's domicile for enforcement measures. If the bailiff fails to contact the debtor, the debtor may be summoned for giving his assets declaration.[93] On the basis of the information given by the debtor, the creditor may start enforcement

---

[87] Spanish Report 7; Swedish Report on Transparency of Assets (Study JAI A3/02/2002) 4–5.

[88] Kennett *Enforcement of Judgments* 102.

[89] Study JAI A3/02/2002: National Report Belgium Transparency, 4 (bailiffs may directly contact Société Carrefour which indicates the employer of the debtor), A Verbeke 'L'information sur le patrimoine. Nécessité d'un droit d'exécution équilibré' in Chambre Nationale des *Huissiers* de Justice (eds) *Le rôle social et économique de l'huissier de justice* (Brussels 2000), 165, 187.

[90] Study JAI A3/02/2002: Luxembourg Report Transparency, 2 and 6. The creditor must not present an enforceable title.

[91] Additionally, the *huissiers* are prohibited from using the information obtained for purposes other than the enforcement of the title held by the creditor.This prohibition corresponds to general principles of the protection of data transfer, see Art 7 Directive 95/46/EC.

[92] Act of 11 Feb 2004, Journal Officiel of 12 Feb 2004, 2854. However, French legislation did not allow any full access of the bailiffs to all sources of information which might be useful for enforcement purposes.

[93] As this declaration entails serious disadvantages for the debtor (the inscription in the debtors' list), most debtors will pay in order to avoid this procedure, German Report 8.

proceedings again. However, contrary to the situation in many neighbour states such as Austria, neither the bailiffs nor the Rechtspfleger in the enforcement courts are empowered to access directly the social security registers, which also exist in Germany.[94]Therefore, the creditors lose time (and often money), the working capacity of bailiffs is unnecessarily spent and, finally, the debtor's declaration might not be very helpful to the creditor. This example shows the advantages of a 'centralised system' where a specialised and qualified enforcement agent is entitled to access restricted information directly.

C. Remedies and control of enforcement agents

Different enforcement structures entail different review proceedings. In jurisdictions where enforcement is carried out by enforcement agents in the private sector, the control of the bailiffs operates in a twofold way. In France and in the Netherlands there are specific remedies against the bailiffs' actions which are decided by the enforcement courts.[95] In addition, as bailiffs are regulated professionals, they are subject to the supervision of their professional bodies which may impose disciplinary sanctions. The behaviour of regulated professionals is often stipulated comprehensively in codes of conduct which are issued by the professional bodies and subject to the approval of the competent authorities.[96] In the Netherlands, bailiffs are subject to a comprehensive regulatory framework on recording and accounting which is supervised by the Financial Supervision Office once a year.[97] A similar control shall be introduced in England.

The control of enforcement agents in court-oriented and mixed systems is mainly exercised by the enforcement court. All national systems provide for specific remedies against unlawful behaviour of the enforcement organs.[98] The decisions of the enforcement judges are subject to general remedies. In court-oriented systems, the judge of the enforcement court may also decide on objections against enforcement measures which are based on substantive law.[99] All objections (by the debtor and the third-party debtor) against the seizure and/or the enforceable title are heard immediately by the

---

[94] In maintenance proceedings, direct access to these registers is now opened to the courts, see s 643 ZPO (1998), Hess 'National Report: Germany' in A Verbeke and M Caupain (eds) *La transparence patrimoniale* (Paris, 1999), 47–50; 300–17.

[95] Anquetil *Compétence d'attribution du juge de l'exécution* in S Guinchard and G Moussa (eds) *Droit et Pratique des Voies d'Exécution* (2004/05) 212.60

[96] National Report Netherlands 8.

[97] ibid 13.

[98] Austrian Report 21; German Report 12.

[99] Generally HF Gaul *Das Rechtsbehelfssystem der Zwangsvollstreckung* ZZP 85 (1972), 251, 267.

enforcement court.[100] Decentralized systems allocate these objections to the civil courts where ordinary proceedings must be instituted.[101]

The legal situation in the Scandinavian systems is similar. In Sweden, supervision of the Enforcement Agency is exercised by the ordinary courts. However, according to the practice of the Enforcement Agency, a (non-formal) self-correction of enforcement measures (on simple application of the affected party) often takes place.[102] Objections based on substantive law are heard by the civil courts.

V. THE IMPACT OF ENFORCEMENT CULTURES

A. *Different concepts of enforcement: debt collection or mediation?*

An important influence on the form of enforcement structures relates to the different policy objectives behind execution. Enforcement can be regarded as a 'mechanism' for securing an efficient payment by the debtor and, accordingly, enforcement agents act as debt collectors. However, modern systems consider enforcement agents as 'balance wheels' between the creditors and the debtors who shall promote amicable settlements between the parties.[103] From this perspective, enforcement agents may also prevent 'social exclusion' of debtors and bankruptcy proceedings.[104]

There is a general trend indicating that modern systems consider enforcement to be more than single debt collection. Austria and Germany recently adopted some (minor) legal reforms which empower the bailiffs to encourage the parties to agree on payments by instalment.[105] In France, the attachment of earnings is automatically preceded by an attempt at conciliation.[106] Conciliation is also often attempted in Spain (and in the Netherlands). Once again, a centralised system may facilitate conciliation, because the enforcement organ gets a comprehensive picture of the financial situation of the debtor. Consequently, enforcement agents should be empowered to

---

[100] A similar situation exists in France where the juge d'exécution (JEX) immediately decides on objections of the third-party debtor against the garnishment.

[101] Example Germany, s 767(1) ZPO: 'Objections which concern the claim determined by the judgment shall be asserted by the debtor by way of an action before the trial court of first instance.'

[102] Swedish Report 8–9.

[103] Perrot 'Le rôle économique et social des *huissiers* de justice' in Chambre Nationale des *Huissiers* de Justice (ed) (2000) 199, 202.

[104] White Paper on Enforcement 17 (stressing the United Kingdom government's committment of 'tackling over indebtedness and addressing concerns about increased levels of consumer debt').

[105] Germany: ss 806 b; 900 (3) ZPO; Austria: ss 25–25d, 45a EO (as amended by 1 Jan 2004), W Jakusch ÖJZ (2004) 201, 205.

[106] French Report 4.

promote such settlements. From a structural perspective, settlement attempts seem to be mostly successful if they are negotiated 'on the spot' by the enforcement agent at the home of the debtor. In garnishment proceedings, the situation is different: Any attempt at settlement must take place in a hearing after the seizure. However, such a hearing does not take place in all jurisdictions.[107]

B. The Role of the Creditor and the Enforcement Organ

While in all jurisdictions the creditor initiates and terminates the enforcement proceedings, there exist considerable differences in the control of enforcement proceedings and strategy. In decentralized systems, the creditor initiates and chooses the method of enforcement by approaching the competent organ. Accordingly, the progress of the proceeding depends to a large extent on the creditor's strategy. In centralized systems, the enforcement organ may be empowered to control the enforcement proceedings comprehensively and to decide upon the enforcement strategy.[108] However, most of the national systems expressly state that the creditor may choose the assets targeted by the execution.[109]

One additional point relates to the factual relationship between enforcement agents and creditors. If an enforcement agent is completely financed by the creditor on a—perhaps insufficient—fee system), a factual dependency by the bailiff on certain (powerful) creditors might emerge. Therefore, the capacity of an enforcement agent to resist such pressure depends on factors such as professional solidarity and financial independence.[110] In Germany, the fee system was finally introduced in the early 1960s, because the divergent level of income between bailiffs sometimes led to abuse.[111]

---

[107] In Germany, garnishments are effected without any (formal) opportunity for a settlement. However, the court clark may, on application of the debtor, order a (partial) release of the seizure of an account, for protecting the debtor's maintenance needs. This decision is regularly taken in a written procedure where also the creditor is heard (s 850 h ZPO). It seems to be possible that the court clark (Rechtspfleger) proposes a settlement to the parties in these proceedings.

[108] In some jurisdictions, the progress of the proceedings is determined by a *gradus executionis* which orders a priority of certain methods of enforcement, cf on this question Austrian Report 11–12; French Report 4 (on the sale of movable property).

[109] Example: France, Art L 22-1, French Report 2; Sweden, National Report 7.

[110] W Kennett 'General Report Enforcement' in Storme (ed), *Procedural Laws in Europe* (Maklu, Antwerp, 2003) 81, 104.

[111] HF Gaul *Zur Struktur der Zwangsvollstreckung*, Der deutsche Rechtspfleger (1971) 81, 82–3.

C. Incentives for speeding up enforcement proceedings

Many national enforcement systems are currently inefficient; the personnel and technological support are often lacking, and the procedures are too lengthy and complicated.[112]

The most efficient incentive for speeding up enforcement is to open it to market forces. The recent reforms in the Netherlands and in England clearly move in this direction. In these countries, open competition between different bailiffs is allowed nationwide; bailiffs may arrive at fee arrangements with (specific) creditors. As a balancing mechanism, supervision and discipline have been tightened considerably.[113] Other systems (especially France, Belgium and Portugal) do not provide for the same degree of competition between bailiffs who act as regulated agents in the public rather than private sector. Competition takes place in the service of documents.[114]

In those Member States where enforcement is considered a function integral to the judiciary, competition seems to be excluded. For example, in Germany, each bailiff has a monopoly within a defined area of territorial competence (Bezirk).[115]However, even a conception of enforcement as a judicial activity does not exclude the financing of bailiffs to some extent by a payment according to the result-based scheme.[116]

Therefore, improvement of enforcement proceedings does not presuppose any outsourcing of the enforcement organs from the judiciary. The question was discussed in Austria, but the legislature decided not to change the existing system, mainly because additional changes of the enforcement law would have been necessary. Finally, as the Austrian Report correctly states, the outsourcing of bailiffs from the judicial system in a private structure still requires the maintenance of some fundamental functions in the enforcement courts. Constitutional law requires that any search of the debtor's premises (without his consent) can only be carried out with a court order.[117] However, even this situation might be solved according to the French model, where the enforcement is mainly the task of the bailiff, but

[112] Germany is one example for a national system, where procedural and institutional reforms are needed. The introduction of the French (or Dutch) bailiff system has been recently proposed by the Federal State Baden-Württemberg, German Report 24.
[113] Dutch Report 7–8; W Kennett 'Enforcement: General Report' in *Procedural Laws in Europe* (Maklu, Antwerp), 81, 101.
[114] Kennett, *Enforcement Agents in Europe* 96.
[115] This system was introduced in the 1960s, the former experience was, that bailiffs had their own territorial districts, but they were paid solely by the fees they received from their activities. Accordingly, bailiffs in rural districts were in a very bad situation while bailiffs in urban areas were privileged. These inequalities led to bad practices which encouraged the legislation to change the system and to finance the bailiffs mainly by salary.
[116] Austrian Report 19; in Germany a small pArt of the bailiffs' fees is paid out to the bailiffs.
[117] Austrian Report 20; for Germany see ss 758 a and 901 ZPO, Arts 13 and 104 of the German Constitution.

a specialised enforcement judge may always intervene when specific difficulties arise or constitutional needs require his intervention.

There is no doubt that privatization of the enforcement agents can be beneficial, but there are also some dangers: where an enforcement agent acts for creditor clients, the structure of enforcement—and the incentives offered to enforcement agents—must be such as to ensure that those agents continue to respect the rights of the debtors. Therefore, close supervision by professional bodies is necessary. In addition, the debtor must have a powerful remedy against any abuse of enforcement.[118] Even in systems where bailiffs act in the private debt collection sector, they should always act as neutral and independent judicial officers keeping an equal distance from both parties (debtor and creditor).[119]

VI. CONCLUSION

When this comparative study was initiated, the participants in the Research Interchange expected to detect considerable differences between the national systems. The national reports demonstrate that this expectation was correct. Creditors within the European Judicial Area are confronted with very different enforcement structures which may hamper an efficient debt collection. As a consequence, creditors must regularly consult a practising lawyer in the Member State where enforcement is sought. However, a better information of the structure of enforcement systems may improve the current situation.[120]

Finally, I would like to address a fundamental issue: Would it be possible to identify structures of an ideal enforcement organization which would correspond to the needs of cross-border debt collecting? While a clear answer is not possible, some advantages of the different structures can be ascertained: Centralised systems (conferring the enforcement of monetary claims to one enforcement organ)[121] seem to be more efficient than decentralized ones. The advantages of centralised systems have several causes; the creditor may immediately initiate the proceedings without any inquiry of the competent organ; an enforcement agent with comprehensive powers may inquire into the financial situation of the debtor and access to non-public registers; parallel enforcement is largely excluded; attempts at settlements

---

[118] W Kennett General Report in Storme *Procedural Laws in Europe*, 81, 100.

[119] It remains to be seen whether the new Dutch enforcement system meets these fundamental requirements. On the social role of the bailiffs see de G Leval, 'Le rôle social de l'huisser de justice', in: Chambre Nationale des Huissers de Justice (ed), *Le rôle social et économique de l'huisser de justice*, 5.

[120] For instance, this information should be made available at the website of the European Judicial Network.

[121] With the exception of enforcement against immovables.

may be better coordinated. Finally, cross-border cooperation between national enforcement organs (which exists on an informal basis between bailiffs in France, Belgium and the Netherlands and which will be formally regulated by a Convention of the Nordic States) presupposes comprehensive responsibility of enforcement organs for the proceedings.

However, it seems impossible to come to a similar conclusion in relation to the different enforcement systems. Bailiff-oriented, court-oriented and administrative systems perform quite well, at least if they are sufficiently equipped and financed. From the political perspective, the bailiff system might be preferred, as the costs of enforcement are mainly borne by the interested parties and not by the public sector. Such an increase of the costs must be borne by the judgment debtor—this may amount to a heavy burden. The experience in France and the Benelux shows that the costs of enforcement are relatively high and that the competencies of the bailiffs relate to additional tasks which also finance their business.[122]

The Austrian court-oriented system also performs quite well, especially due to the efficient utilization of electronic data processing and information technology. However, there exists a definite risk that additional competencies in enforcement proceedings are transferred from the (expensive) judges to the less qualified and less expensive court officers (Rechtspfleger). This development, which has taken place in Germany, might also happen in Austria.[123] If so, the well-functioning Austrian system might be impaired.

Finally, the Swedish Enforcement Agency performs extremely well, with an average of 3 months in all enforcement proceedings. However, the Nordic administrative structure seems to be rather unique in Europe,[124] as most EU Member States still consider enforcement proceedings as a judicial and not an administrative function.[125]

To sum up, it can be stated that that those three different types of enforcement structures which are deeply embedded in the legal and historical cultures of the Member States seem equally able to guarantee efficient enforcement as guaranteed by Article 6 ECHR. The functioning of the enforcement agency in Europe depends, as does the functioning of the judiciary as a whole, mainly on the willingness and ability of the Member States to finance sufficiently their judicial institutions. However, if adequate financing by the Member States can no longer be afforded, the 'privatization' of enforcement agencies through the introduction of a professional, but highly regulated, bailiff system would be a workable, and therefore, preferable alternative.

[122] These activities might, to some extent, also finance the enforcement of judgments and other titles.
[123] Austrian Report, 19.
[124] A similar administrative structure exists, however, also in Switzerland.
[125] Cf Kerameus, IECL XVI, Chap 10–15.

CHAPTER 4

EFFICIENCY IN THE METHODS OF ENFORCEMENT OF JUDGMENTS: PUBLIC VS PRIVATE SYSTEMS[1]

Juan Pablo Correa Delcasso[2]

The efficient enforcement of judgments is, without doubt, one of the most important issues affecting the execution of judicial resolutions. Without an efficient system of enforcement, the purpose of the creditor's litigation is frustrated, rendering it difficult for the creditor to recover the amount owed by the debtor or obtain specific performance of the debt.

In order to address this point, I have read the reports of each of the participating Member States and noticed that fundamental differences exist between the countries that are taking part in this project. By drawing upon these accounts, and by using my Spanish experience in this matter, my first conclusion concerning the problem of efficiency in the methods of enforcement of judgments is that the obstruction lies, most likely, not in the opposition of public and private systems, but rather in the efficiency and speed of each internal jurisdiction to execute a judgment. The most important problem however is the level of transparency that can be reached on the patrimony of the debtor.

In Germany, for example, a country which, like Austria or Spain, has a public system, Burkhard Hess and Markus Mack write that a creditor has to wait about six months for any activity by the bailiff, and attribute the main cause of these delays to the insufficient number of bailiffs. That is why the Government of the Land of Baden-Württemberg proposed reform at the federal level to introduce a system of bailiffs that would operate on a private basis, comparable to the *huissiers* in France. At the same time, German law does not allow enforcement agents to have access to any special information (which explains why, in practice, some private

---

[1] Translated by Mayte Cruz Ventura, Ribalta Abogados, Barcelona; this chapter is based on proceedings from the final meeting for this project held at the British Institute of International and Comparative Law in London on 23 April 2004 and entitled *Enforcement Agency Practice in Europe: Cooperation or Harmonization?*
[2] Doctor of Law, Advocate and Professor, University of Barcelona.

investigators provide information about the location and the financial situation of the debtor); however, the bailiff does have a statement of the debtor's assets which provides an incentive for the debtor to voluntarily pay the amount due rather than have the bailiff disclose his assets.

In Austria, which has a strong court-oriented system, Paul Oberhammer writes that the enforcement court order is issued through an expeditious process (only formal requirements for the enforcement are to be checked). That is why, in his opinion, 'there's hardly any reason to consider sourcing out of the court system another method of privatization', although this does not mean that it could not, at some point, be necessary to change some methods of execution in order to provide a more efficient system. If I have understood, an important number of provisions nowadays try to change the old legal method of enforcement against movable assets in favour of the execution of monetary claims, and in particular attachment of earnings. With regard to execution upon monetary claims, the court can request, within a limited period of time, the Central Association of Austrian Social Insurance Associations to disclose the debtor's employer and, in consequence, to disclose one of the most important parts of the debtor's assets: his salary.

England and Wales have a mixed system (some of the enforcement agents are private). The conclusions of such a system are:

First, that the system is inefficient because of difficulties in gathering information: the system is out of date and not in line with the demands of the modern world and commercial practice. In addition, the current system relies on the creditor obtaining information about the debtor.

Secondly, it is an expensive system; if one uses orders to obtain information about the debtor, processing time is longer and more expensive; that is why a Government White Paper recommends modifications in the current system in order to obtain information about the debtor from other sources and improve the existing fee structure by introducing an upfront fee payable by the creditor before any enforcement action is taken. This last recommendation is particular to the English system and cannot be taken as a common problem in the methods of enforcement in the rest of Europe.

And finally, France, the Netherlands and Sweden have private systems of execution in civil cases, with France and the Netherlands permitting differing degrees of intervention and supervision by the court, and Sweden functioning without court intervention.

In this sense, it is important to notice that the private system is not always a synonym for efficiency, especially in France, where the *huissier* must file a request—in order to collect information—with the department of the public prosecutor, the only authority empowered to give information about the debtor. On this point, Marie-Laure Niboyet and Sabine Lacassagne write that the system is not very efficient, because this department has a very heavy work load. Information is therefore provided much later than would be possible by other private organizations (eg private detectives) such as in Germany where information is given about the debtor's assets. Also, the huissier can only obtain the debtor's address, the address of the debtor's employer and the debtor's bank account details from this department, and not other precious information such as his revenues or the taxes he has paid to the State. An additional question for consideration is the cost of all the different measures taken by the *huissier de justice* in the pursuit of enforcing judgment.

In the Netherlands, Ton Jongbloed says that creditors are in general satisfied with the current system. Sweden has an absolute administrative system that seems very efficient; as Torbjörn Andersson and Hugo Fridén said in their report, around 75–80 per cent of the private claims are handled in less than three months, just half of the time that a creditor needs to start the execution with a Bailiff (*Gericthsvollzieher*) in Germany.

And what about Spain? In our country, like in Austria or Germany, the execution of judgments is an activity wholly reserved to the courts, which must 'pass judgment and enforce that which has been decided', as set out in Article 117 of the Constitution. Enforcement of judicial decisions was traditionally one of the worst areas of the Spanish procedural system because the old procedural code, dating from 1881, was issued in a liberal context preoccupied with the needs of a rural society. Consequently, it was not suitable for the demands of the modern world and commercial practice.

In particular, it was impossible to obtain information of the debtor's assets; the public auction was inefficient with assets being sold for ridiculous prices, or the enforcement could take months, perhaps years, only to obtain an uncertain result, which was sometimes bad for the creditor.

This situation was remedied with the institution of the new code of civil procedure which came into force on 1 January 2001. The code introduced new institutions such as the debtor's statement of his assets; the sale of his assets (movable or immovable) through specialist institutions; or the obliged cooperation of public entities and third-party debtors in order to locate the debtor's assets.

The system remained a public system, because, inter alia, the legislator could never privatise enforcement—unlike in Sweden, for example, that has the opposite system to Spain—without entering into conflict with the Spanish legal system, and especially with Article 117 of our Constitution.

The law now allows the court to obtain all kinds of information about the debtor's assets (in particular from the tax and social administration). It establishes the compulsory cooperation of third-party debtors in order to locate his assets. By this the situation has radically changed. In most cases the debtor pays before a seizure can be decided by the court in order to avoid the complicated effects of a seizure, in particular when it refers to bank accounts to avoid the disposal of the seized amount after it is increased by 30 per cent interest and expenditure costs.

Like in Germany, the court may penalize non-compliance with the order to provide a list of sufficient assets to cover the debt, and may also penalise third-party debtors who are unwilling to give the required information by fining them. Even if this is a relatively infrequent practice, in the three cases I have found of non-compliance with the order the different courts have penalized the debtor or the third debtor, which clearly shows that courts wish, on the one hand, to ensure that legal provisions are fulfilled and, on the other, are prepared to remove the permissive legal culture that allowed judgments to be executed in a way that was not satisfactory for the creditor.

Finally, it is worth noting that the tax authority, in order to assist the court in the disclosure of debtor's assets, has created, in each large city, the *Oficinas de Averiguación Patrimonial* which provides tax information about the debtor within two or three weeks of a request. The social security authorities cooperate with the judge, providing him with information of the debtor's salary, pensions or any other income received, as well as any other public registers to which the creditor normally has access.

In conclusion, having read the different national reports and by drawing on my own experience of the Spanish legal landscape in this area, the complexion of which has been marked over the last four years following the important reforms realized by the code of civil procedure (2000), it is my opinion that the answer to the important issue of efficiency in the methods of enforcement of judgments must be found in the transparency of the debtor's assets more than in the nature of the authority responsible for enforcement. Countries in which the enforcement of judgments are directed by a judicial authority (Germany or Austria, for instance), are highly efficient as far as actual enforcement is concerned. Their legal system sets forth coercive measures against the debtor which are efficient enough to achieve enforcement (such as the debtor's statement regarding his assets) or require the collaboration of the administration in order to gather information about the employment and salary of the debtor. Conversely, a system which lacks the communication about the details of the debtor, such as that of the French, is paralysed because the main agent of the enforcement, the *huissier de justice*, does not have the sufficient means to know the assets of the debtor.

Other factors are important and should be kept in mind, such as the celerity of the judicial body or the private agent who has to enforce the judgment (on this point I recently read in the 'Revue des Huissiers de Justice' how the Portuguese agent—the *solicitador*—had, in contradistinction to the French system, modern facilities at his disposal which enable him to quickly seize a motor vehicle or a bank account or even property), or finally, the costs incurred within an enforcement procedure itself, which are so high that they prevent the creditor using all of the mechanisms at his disposal. In England and Wales, but not in Spain, where Justice was completely free until very recently (except the fees of the *procurador* and the lawyers) and, since 1 April 2003, only the firms whose turnover exceed 6 million euros have to pay fixed judicial costs, in accordance with the legislation in force in consideration with the amount claimed. The rest of the creditors, and in particular, individuals, may dispose of all the means available within the judicial system to enforce a judgment, and, as such, do not pay any judicial fee.

CHAPTER 5

MARKET INTEGRATION, THE HARMONIZATION PROCESS, AND ENFORCEMENT PRACTICES IN THE EU MEMBER STATES

Mads Andenas[1] *and Renato Nazzini*[2]

I. INTRODUCTION

This chapter will present an overview of enforcement practices in the following EU Member States: the Republic of Austria, England and Wales, the French Republic, the Federal Republic of Germany, the Kingdom of the Netherlands, the Kingdom of Spain and the Kingdom of Sweden. The analysis will focus on the enforcement of civil judgments relating to money claims by the execution of movable assets, as these aspects appear to cover the most common issues in enforcement practice and need urgent consideration on a European level. Therefore deliberately excluded are issues relating to public claims against private individuals, criminal prosecution, claims for specific performance, and claims for the return of an object or the giving of a statement. Also excluded are the fields of tax and alimony as they deserve a study of their own.

The chapter is structured as follows. First, it sets out the Community law background of the comparative analysis. It focuses on the new provisions in Title IV of the EC Treaty, inserted by the Treaty of Amsterdam. Secondly, the chapter summarises the country by country reports as drafted by the national experts as found at the Annex. The analysis is structured in eight parts—each part corresponds to a different jurisdiction. Within each jurisdiction there are seven main questions. These are: (1) the legal basis of law enforcement; (2) the structure behind the enforcement agencies; (3) the conditions for execution; (4) specific enforcement methods; (5) disclosure of

---

[1] PhD (Cambridge) MA DPhil (Oxford). Director, British Institute of International and Comparative Law.
[2] PhD (Milan) PhD (Lond). Visiting Fellow, British Institute of International and Comparative Law.

information on the debtor and his or her assets; (6) remedies against wrongful execution; and (7) the efficiency of the proceedings. The comparative analysis provides indications as to the degrees of efficiency of the different enforcement systems and best enforcement practices. Finally, the chapter provides a general outlook and conclusion on the harmonization of enforcement law in the European Union.

II. THE COMMUNITY COMPETENCE IN THE AREA OF THE ENFORCEMENT OF JUDGMENTS

The Treaty of Amsterdam inserts a new Title IV into the European Community Treaty. This brings about a dramatic change in the area of the Community competences in the area of civil procedure and enforcement of judgments. Article 65 EC provides that measures in the field of judicial cooperation in civil matters having cross-border implications, to be taken in accordance with Article 67 and so far as necessary for the proper functioning of the internal market, shall include the following: (a) improving and simplifying the system for cross-border service of judicial and extrajudicial documents; cooperation in the taking of evidence; and the recognition and enforcement of decisions in civil and commercial cases, including decisions in extrajudicial cases; (b) promoting the compatibility of the rules applicable in the Member States concerning the conflict of laws and of jurisdiction; (c) eliminating obstacles to the good functioning of civil proceedings, if necessary by promoting the compatibility of the rules on civil procedure applicable in the Member States. Section (c) is particularly relevant to the question of the internal rules on enforcement of judgments. There is established a Community competence for the adoption of measures aiming at promoting compatibility in the civil procedure rules in the Member States.

The question arises as to whether the rules on enforcement of judgments fall within this competence. The point of construction is whether rules on enforcement are 'rules on civil procedure' applicable in the Member States. In some Member States the enforcement system is largely 'privatized' and enforcement takes place though procedures that would fall outside the scope of a narrow meaning of 'civil procedure'.[3] In other Member States the enforcement of judgments is effected through a court procedure governed by the principles that apply to civil procedure and administered by the same judges that hear contentious civil matters.[4] In yet other Member states

---

[3] In England and Wales the enforcement of judgments can be carried out by private bailiffs whose acts are governed by private law.

[4] In Austria, the enforcement of judgments is commenced by application to the court. The entire procedure is a court procedure.

enforcement has been entrusted to administrative agents or bodies.[5] The characterization of the enforcement rules in the Member States could be in terms of civil procedural law, private law, or administrative law.

In the face of such diversity of enforcement agencies and practices, the question of whether internal enforcement procedures may fall within the Community competence relating to civil procedure must be solved by going back to first principle. Civil procedure is adjectival law. It regulates the process of doing justice between the parties. This process is not only concerned with reaching a decision that determines the parties' civil rights and liabilities. Such a decision would be moot if the successful party were unable to obtain full and actual satisfaction of its rights as determined in the judgment. The enforcement of civil judgments is, therefore, an essential constituent of the civil justice system. Because of the practical nature of most of the steps required in the execution process, the enforcement of judgments has historically been seen as a discreet function entrusted to administrative or private bodies rather than to the courts themselves. However, the courts have always played a fundamental role in the enforcement of judgments. It is the relationship between the courts and the enforcement agencies that is relative to different legal systems and different stages of the historical development of the civil justice systems. In some systems the courts have taken over all the tasks relating to enforcement while in other systems some tasks are, or can be, performed by persons outside the court system. The analysis of the structure and function of the enforcement agencies in the Member States that have been the subject of this study clearly demonstrates the relativity of the characterization of enforcement activity into the categories of private law, administrative law, or civil procedure. This further demonstrates that the Community competence must be interpreted functionally and not formally. Enforcement falls within Article 65 EC because it is an integral part of the civil justice system of the Member States without which the very purpose of civil litigation would be meaningless.

III. THE STRUCTURE OF THE ENFORCEMENT AGENCIES

The question arises as to the competence of the Community in relation to the structure of the enforcement agencies. If the enforcement rules are a fundamental component of the civil justice systems of the Member States,

---

[5] In France, the *huissiers de justice* act under the supervision of the courts and must apply to the court or the department of the public prosecutor in order to be authorized to carry out certain enforcement activities. However, they are not part of the court structure. They are public officers and perform functions that are often ancillary or complementary to the exercise of jurisdiction by the courts. However, it would appear that their office is not judicial but rather administrative.

it is less obvious that the Community competence extends to the structure of the enforcement agencies. The structure of the enforcement agencies varies considerably amongst the Member States. In Sweden, the enforcement of judgments is the task of a specialist administrative body while in Austria the courts have the exclusive power to enforce civil judgments. In other Member States, the task of enforcing civil judgments has been entrusted to *huissiers de justice*, bailiffs, and other professionals, whose status, qualifications, and legal characterization vary to a significant degree from officers of the court to public officers outside the court structure to private practitioners exercising a regulated profession. How far can Community law impact on these apparently internal matters? The answer to this question lies in the undisputable fact that the structure of the enforcement agency determines the enforcement procedure and the enforcement procedure ultimately determines whether the judgment creditor will be able to obtain satisfaction of his credit.

It is one of the main conclusions of this study that the structure of the enforcement agencies determines the efficiency of the enforcement process. However, it is clear that if this is the basis for the Community competence in this field, Community measures should be limited to what is necessary to ensure that differences in enforcement systems do not have a negative impact on trade between Member States by discouraging investment and trade in countries where inefficient enforcement structures and procedures make it comparatively more difficult and expensive to obtain satisfaction of judgment credits. It is difficult to imagine that the relevant differences among Member States will by replaced by a harmonized system. The path towards harmonization must be based on the principle of efficiency and equivalence of the enforcement systems of the Member States. Community law should have as its primary objective in this area that the enforcement systems of the Member States should all be equivalently efficient for those involved in cross-border activities. This will avoid distortions in the common market and secure a level playing field throughout the Community.

IV. THE COMPARATIVE METHODOLOGY

This comparative report identifies best enforcement practices in the Member States whose systems have been analysed. Best practices are discussed in terms of efficiency of the system as a whole. This exercise allows for the application of three dichotomies that prove to be particularly useful in identifying the features of an efficient system and the best enforcement practices conducive to expedient enforcement of civil judgments in the Community. These dichotomies are the following: (a) 'public' vs 'private' systems; (b) monolithic vs pluralistic systems; (c) non-competitive vs competitive systems.

The dichotomy 'public vs private systems' relates to the nature of the enforcement agency. It is not relevant, for the purposes of this analysis, whether the enforcement agency is a court or other public body. The necessary and sufficient conditions of a public system is that enforcement is entrusted to a public body and the costs of enforcement are, at least in part, borne by the general public through general taxation. Private systems are those where enforcement is entrusted to professionals or other persons that are not public authorities.

The dichotomy 'monolithic vs pluralistic systems' relates to the presence of enforcement agencies of a different nature. If the enforcement of judgment is entrusted to one agency or category of agents only, the system is monolithic. If there is more than one enforcement agency bearing responsibility for enforcing civil judgments, the system is pluralistic.

The dichotomy 'non-competitive vs competitive systems' relates to the degree of competition among two or more enforcement agencies of different nature or among enforcement agents of the same nature. Competition must occur at the same level. Therefore, a system is not competitive if it is a pluralistic system, ie there is more than one enforcement agency, but different agencies have been entrusted with different and non-overlapping enforcement tasks.

V. ENFORCEMENT PRACTICES IN SELECTED MEMBER STATES

A. Austria

1. The legal basis of law enforcement

The legal sources of law enforcement are the *Exekutionsordnung* (Execution Code) of 27 May 1896, the *Zivilprozessordnung* (Civil Procedure Code) and its corresponding secondary legislation. Generally speaking the enforcement of judicial decisions is laid down in t he *Exekutionsordnung*, and secondary legislation only adds technical provisions. In addition, the *Zivilprozessordnung* provides general provisions (for example on parties, proceedings, oral hearing, evidence, judicial orders and directions as well as appeals by way of *Rekurs* (recourse)).

2. Structure of the enforcement agencies

Law enforcement is a public concern and this has resulted in the Austrian enforcement process being characterized by the strong involvement of the court. There are almost no provisions for the involvement of agents which are not part of the state court system.

(a) Courts

The enforcement of judgments is exclusively within the competence of the *Bezirksgerichte* (district courts), these being the lowest courts in the court system. It is only the *Bezirksgerichte* that have the competence to grant warrants of execution. The court that passed the judgment and issued the instrument to be enforced is no longer involved in the enforcement process.

Austrian enforcement procedure is therefore dominated by the role of the courts.

(b) The Rechtspfleger *(Court Clerk)*

The courts' responsibilities in enforcement proceedings are in practice mainly performed by *Rechtspfleger* (Court Clerks). A court clerk is delegated the task of levying the execution upon movable assets and earnings although he is still an officer of the court and bound by the competent judge's directions. The judge can always reserve matters to himself if he wishes within these areas, and the law has reserved the enforcement of international matters and the execution of immovable property *ab initio* to the judge. However, the majority of enforcement matters are dealt with by the *Rechtspfleger*.

(c) Gerichtsvollzieher *(Bailiff)*

A *Gerichtsvollzieher* is a civil servant who carries out acts of enforcement on behalf of the court. In practice, the focus of his work is on the attachment of assets on the basis of very generally drafted warrants of execution, and on the sale of such attached assets through various means.

3. Conditions for execution

Under Austrian law, enforcement requires a court order for a warrant of execution (*Exekutionsbewilligungsbeschluss*). In general, the judgment creditor has to submit the judicially enforceable instrument with the application for a warrant of execution. The court has to examine whether the instrument and the application correspond to each other. The court then issues the warrant of execution without hearing the debtor.

In addition, there is a simplified procedure for granting a warrant of execution (*vereinfachtes Bewilligungsverfahren*). The simplified procedure removes the requirement to present the judicially enforceable instrument with the application for enforcement. It is applied to the enforcement of monetary claims up to EUR10,000 (excluded however for execution upon immovable property). The simplified procedure became feasible due to the integration of information technology in the court process.

4. Methods of enforcement

Execution can be served upon immovable and movable property, upon earnings and 'other assets' such as, for example, commercial enterprises (by placing the business under receivership). It is up to the creditor to choose the asset upon which execution is levied and the method of execution.

(a) Immovable property

Upon immovable property, there are three methods of execution, the *Zwangshypothek* (compulsory mortgage), the *Zwangsverwaltung* (compulsory administration) and the *Zwangsversteigerung* (compulsory sale). With the compulsory mortgage, the creditor is not satisfied but his debt is secured by means of a mortgage registration with the land registry in his favour. The *Zwangsverwaltung* and *Zwangsversteigerung* lead to the creditor's direct material satisfaction.

(b) Movable property

As regards execution upon movable property, the property is first attached by the *Gerichtsvollzieher* (bailiff) following the issue of a warrant of execution drafted in general terms. Generally, the property is then sold by the *Gerichtsvollzieher* either 'on the spot', in the court auction house or through private auctioneers.

In order to encourage the debtor to make voluntary payment, the bailiff has the power to collect payments from the debtor and to suspend the realization of attached assets

(c) Attachment of earnings

As for attachments of earnings, these need to be ordered by the court. In the application for an attachment order, the creditor only has to claim that the debtor is entitled to income which can be attached; in addition, s/he only has to give the debtor's date of birth. On this basis, the court can request the *Hauptverband der österreichischen Sozialversicherungsträger* (Federation of Austrian Social Insurance Institutions) to disclose who the debtor's employer is. The communication between the court and the *Hauptverband* is computer-based and therefore relatively prompt. The attachment is served without the creditor having to file any further request.

(d) Business under receivership

A business may be placed under receivership to manage the debtor's company and to pay any profit earned to the creditor.

5. Information about the debtor

The attempts of enforcement agencies to support the creditor in the pursuit of his or her rights could be futile if there is not sufficient information on the debtor and his or her assets.

As already mentioned, it is up to the creditor to find the asset to be executed and to choose the asset that is to be executed if there are several. If this fails, the debtor may be required to present a list of assets to the bailiff under penalty of fine or imprisonment.

The *Hauptverband der österreichischen Sozialversicherungsträger* (Federation of Austrian Social Insurance Institutions) as referred to above under Question d.(c) is also an important source of information for the creditor.

6. *The Debtor's Remedies*

(a) Remedies during the Execution Proceedings
During the execution proceedings themselves, the debtor has essentially two remedies together with a possibility to apply for interim measures.

(i)   The *Rekurs* (recourse) is an appeal to the *Landesgericht* (Regional Court). In the recourse proceeding, the debtor is not allowed to bring forth new facts or evidence, and the court assesses the correct application of the law to the facts.

(ii)   The debtor may apply for termination of execution (*Einstellung*) on various specified grounds. These include the following: if the judgment being executed has been set aside; if the execution is levied upon property exempt from execution; if the execution has been declared unlawful by a court; if creditor has withdrawn his or her application for execution; if execution appears not to exceed the costs; if the confirmation of enforceability has been reversed; if execution not covered by an enforceable instrument; if the debtor claims he has satisfied the creditor or the creditor has granted him extra time to make payment or has waived enforcement.

(iii) The debtor has various interim measures available to him to avoid execution while either a recourse or an application for termination for execution is being processed. This includes an interruption *(Innehaltung)* and a suspension *(Aufschiebung)*.

(b) Ordinary Remedies
If the debtor wishes to oppose the execution but did not have grounds to do so under the remedies available to him during the execution proceedings, he must file ordinary proceedings different from the execution proceedings. The debtor may here have either objections against the claim itself (for example if additional time for payment has been granted after the enforceable judgment was issued) or against the warrant of execution (if for example a prerequisite for execution is missing).

In addition, third parties can also file a remedy. Such would be the case if the third party wanted to assert that the execution is levied upon property to which he/she also has a right.

7. Efficiency of the legal system

The Austrian system is a public, monolithic, non-competitive system. The most efficient method of enforcement is considered to be the attachment of earnings. The efficiency of this method of enforcement is due to the availability of up-to-date information about the debtor's employment from the Federation of Austrian Social Insurance Institutions. All persons in employment are registered with the Federation. This makes attachment of earnings a speedy and effective enforcement method.

The use of technology is also one of the strengths of the system. In the enforcement of money claims, the *Mahnverfahren* (*ex parte* order for payment) can be granted in a procedure which is commenced with an online application for a payment order against the debtor. If the debtor does not defend him- or herself in due time, the payment order becomes enforceable. The creditor can also apply online for enforcement.

It seems that the system is overall efficient. In general terms, a characteristic of the Austrian system is that it is not possible to have recourse to enforcement agencies outside the court structure. Therefore, no competition between enforcement agencies exists. The efficiency on the system lies in the efficient administration of justice organized by the State through resources largely drawn from general taxation. This feature is not dependent on the enforcement system being a fully integrated element of the court system. The same features in terms of efficiency, simplicity, absence of competition among enforcement agencies, and financing, at least in part, through general taxation, are shared with systems based on enforcement carried out by administrative bodies.

B. England and Wales

1. The legal basis of law enforcement

Enforcement law in England and Wales has its basis in statute and case law. The main statutes in this area are the Charging Orders Act 1979 and the Attachment of Earnings Act 1971. These are complemented by the Civil Procedure Rules (CPR), the Rules of the Supreme Court (RSC), the County Court Rules (CCR), and Practice Directions (PD). A White Paper published by the Department for Constitutional Affairs envisages the passing of new legislation to modernize and simplify the law of enforcement as a part of a wide-ranging enforcement review.

2. Structure of the enforcement agencies

Different enforcement agents coming from both the public and private sectors undertake the enforcement of judgments in England and Wales. At High Court level, there are High Sheriffs, Under Sheriffs, and Sheriff's Officers. At County Court level, there are court bailiffs who are employed by the Court Service. Public bodies such as the Inland Revenue and Local Council Authorities either employ their own agents or contract out the enforcement of their credit to private bailiffs. In addition, Magistrates' Courts employ their own agents or again contract out to private bailiffs in order to recover debts owed to the public sector, including council tax debts and criminal fines.

(a) High Court Sheriffs and Officers
Statutory provisions applying to the High Court enforcement personnel are contained in the Sheriffs Act 1887.

(i) High Sheriff
The High Sheriff is the principal executive officer of the Crown. It is the oldest continuous Crown appointment and has existed for more than 1,000 years. A High Sheriff is appointed to each county for a period of no more than one year, has virtually no involvement in enforcement and does not receive an income from it. The actual duties are traditional and symbolic and include responsibility for attending to the High Court judges.

(ii) Under Sheriff
The High Court judgment enforcement process is very complex. As High Sheriffs only remain in office for one year, s/he is obliged to appoint Under Sheriffs who carry out the actual enforcement work. Under Sheriffs are usually solicitors and often partners in a law firm. Even though they are responsible for carrying out the High Sheriff's daily duties, they are not part of the Court Service. Their conduct is governed by the Law Society.

(iii) Sheriff's Officer
The Under Sheriff gives day-to-day instructions to the Sheriff's Officer. The Sheriff's Officer is a private bailiff but he is also an officer of the Supreme Court. Under Sheriffs are appointed by the High Sheriff and either employed by the Under Sheriff or self-employed.

(b) Bailiffs
(i) County Court bailiffs
County court bailiffs are employed by the Court Service and are therefore civil servants who are subject to the Civil Service rules on recruitment and

monitoring. There are approximately 634 county court bailiffs in England and Wales. Bailiffs are appointed to assist the District Judge who sits in the county court. County court bailiffs cannot enforce judgments in excess of £5,000 except those arising out of an agreement regulated by the Consumer Credit Act 1974. If the amount of the judgment is between £600 and £5,000 the creditor can choose between enforcement at High Court or county court level. Empirical evidence suggests that county court bailiffs tend to deal with low value non-business debts.

(c) Certificated Private Bailiffs

The work undertaken by Sheriffs and county court bailiffs represents only a small proportion of the total volume of warrants enforced nationally, the majority being enforced by private bailiffs in pursuit of public sector debts.

Some private bailiffs belong to the Certificated Bailiff Association (CBA) or the Association of Civil Enforcement Agencies. Bailiffs undertaking the enforcement of certain debts, namely in the areas of distress for rent, road traffic penalties, and council tax, must be certificated.

Although they are not employed by the Court Service, certificated private bailiffs are seen as court representatives as they act under a certificate issued by the court. The court therefore exercises a certain amount of control over their conduct. There is, however, no formal regulatory control of certificated bailiffs and no monitoring or auditing of bailiff practices. If a certificated bailiff is guilty of misconduct, he may be subject to disciplinary action by the Certificated Bailiff Association.

(d) Non-certificated Private Bailiffs

Some private bailiffs are neither sheriffs nor certificated bailiffs. They enforce debts where enforcement is not statutorily confined to the authority of county court bailiffs, sheriffs, or certificated bailiffs. There are no qualification requirements to become a non-certificated private bailiff. Private bailiffs often belong to private companies or act on behalf of local authorities, for instance in the recovery of council tax or on behalf of magistrates' courts in the recovery of fines. Private bailiffs are not regulated and therefore their behaviour is not subject to scrutiny.

3. Conditions for execution

The conditions for execution in England and Wales depend on the execution method chosen by the creditor. Generally, the creditor needs a warrant of execution (issued by the County Court) or a writ of fi-fa (*fieri facias*; issued by the High Court) in order to start enforcement. For the most common method—the recovery through the sale of the debtor's goods—a warrant of execution or a writ of fi-fa is sufficient. For garnishee proceedings, the creditor needs in addition a third party debt order by the court. In order to place a charge on the debtor's property (land, securities, funds in court, beneficial interest under a trust), the creditor must secure a charging order by the court. The attachment of earnings cannot be executed without an attachment of earnings order by the court.

If the creditor decides to enforce his or her county court judgment using the Sheriff, which s/he is entitled to choose if the judgment is between £600 and £5000 (normally the Sheriff deals with High Court judgments, and the county court judgments are dealt with by a bailiff), the creditor must obtain a certificate of judgment in the county court, register the judgment as a High Court judgment, and issue a writ of fi-fa in the High Court, which will then be passed to the Under Sheriff.

4. Methods of enforcement

The following court-based methods are those currently available to a judgment creditor who wishes to enforce a judgment: Third Party Debt Orders (previously 'garnishee proceedings'), placing a charge, attaching earnings, and selling goods of the debtor to the value of the outstanding debt in public auctions.

The judgment creditor can use any available method to enforce the judgment and can use more than one method, either at the same time or one after another (CPR 70.2 (2)). However, the judgment creditor can only be paid once in respect of the satisfaction of the same credit. Therefore, especially when more than one method is used at the same time, the judgment creditor must inform the court—or the sheriff in case of High Court writ of execution—in writing of any payment received between the date of issue of the enforcement process and the execution.[6]

(a) Third party debt orders

Third Party Debt Orders (TPDOs) have been introduced by the Civil Procedure Rules as from March 2002. Part 72 and supplementary Practice Directions replace the old rules relating to garnishee proceedings with clearer and more straightforward provisions. TPDOs are used when the judgment creditor wishes to be paid by a third party who owes money to the judgment debtor. The third party is, in most cases, a bank or building society which holds money in a bank account for the judgment debtor. Clearly the judgment creditor will have the current account details of the judgment debtor, be it through Part 71 proceedings (discussed below) or by other means.

---

[6] PD 70, para 7.

The judgment creditor can apply[7] for a TPDO before a judge without the need to give notice[8] to the third party. If the judge grants an interim TPDO *ex parte*, he will then appoint a date for a hearing in order to decide whether to make a final TPDO.[9] Copies of the interim TPDO, the application notice (form), and any documents in support of it, must then be served[10] on the third party not less than 21 days before the fixed date for the hearing. The judgment debtor is also entitled to service of the above mentioned items not less than seven days after they have been served on the third party and not less than seven days before the date appointed for the hearing.[11]

The main effect of the interim TPDO is to prevent the third party from making any payments that would reduce the amount it holds for the judgment debtor to below the amount due to the judgment creditor and the fixed costs[12] of the application.[13] If this causes hardship to the judgment debtor, he can apply for a hardship payment order under CPR 72.7. If the third party is a bank or building society, the interim TPDO also imposes duties upon it to be performed within seven days of being served with the interim TPDO: (1) to carry out a search and identify all accounts held with it by the judgment debtor; (2) to disclose the account details and balance to the court and the judgment creditor within 7 days of being served with the interim TPDO; and (3) if no account is held or the bank or building society is unable to comply with the order for any other reason, to inform the court and the judgment creditor of that fact.[14] A third party other than a bank or building society has to inform the court and the judgment creditor in writing within seven days of being served with the interim TPDO if he claims not to owe any money to the judgment debtor or to owe less than the amount specified in the order.[15]

The third party is advised that no payment should be made to the judgment creditor at this stage. The third party should wait for a final TPDO to avoid the risk of having to pay twice if the TPDO is not made final.[16] If the third party or the judgment debtor objects to the order being made final, he must file and serve written evidence stating the grounds for his objections on the other parties not less than three days before the hearing.[17]

---

[7] CPR 72 PD 1 gives detailed rules regarding the form of application and the information that should be contained therein are in CPR 72 PD 1.

[8] CPR 72.3. It is clear that, in such proceedings, urgency is of the essence. Further, giving notice would create the risk of the money 'disappearing'.

[9] CPR 72.4.

[10] CPR 72.5. For rules relating to service, see CPR Part 6.   [11] Ibid.

[12] See CPR 45.6   [13] Ibid.

[14] CPR 72.6 (1)–(3).   [15] CPR 72.6 (4)

[16] See *Crantrave Ltd v Lloyds Bank plc* [2000] QB 917.

[17] CPR 72.8

(b) Charging orders

The Charging Orders Act 1979 and the procedural rules under RSC, Ord 50 and CCR, Ord 31 apply to this type of enforcement. A charging order allows a judgment to be enforced by placing a charge to the debtor's land, securities, funds in court, and beneficial interest under a trust.

The charge enables the creditor to secure payment of money owing under the judgment. The creditor obtains a charge over a particular asset but this does not guarantee payment. The fee for a charging order is £50

(c) Attachment of earnings

This enforcement method is only available in the county court. It is an effective enforcement method where the debtor has continuous employment. The authority to make attachment of earnings orders is created by the Attachment of Earnings Act 1971. An application to the county court in the district in which the debtor resides should be made.

Section 3 of the 1971 Act sets out the conditions which apply to the granting of the order. The conditions are as follows: (a) the debtor has failed to pay at least one of the payments due; (b) any order or warrant for the debtor's committal under the Debtors Act 1869 must have been discharged before an attachment of earnings order may be made; (c) the debtor should have an identifiable employer from whom he received earnings.

The employer must comply with the terms of the order and money deducted from the debtor's earnings belongs to the creditor from date of payment into court, assuming that no petition in bankruptcy has been filed against the debtor.

The order will lapse if the debtor leaves the employment of the employer to whom the order was sent. However, the employer must give notice of this cessation of employment to the court and the order can be revived if redirected to a new employer.

The fee to issue is £50.

(d) Execution by warrant of execution or by writ of fi-fa (fieri facias)

This is still the most commonly used form of execution. Under this method, an application must be made to the county court or the High Court for the grant of a warrant of execution or a writ of fi-fa. On the authority of the warrant or writ, the county court bailiff, or the High Court Sheriff, will attempt to recover goods to the value of the outstanding debt from the judgment debtor. The goods will then be sold at public auction if the judgment debtor does not pay his debt.

5. Information about the debtor

The Government proposes the introduction of a new court procedure called the data disclosure order (DDO) to assist with the enforcement of judgments. The DDO will be an order of the court applied for by the creditor or by a licensed enforcement agent acting on the creditor's behalf. To apply for a DDO the creditor will need to complete the relevant application form with the correct fee. Once received by the court a copy of the form will be sent to third parties from whom information is sought. When the form is returned to the court by all third parties, the designated court service officer will assess the information received. They will not release the information directly to the creditor; this is to limit the improper use of the data and respect the principles set out in the Data Protection Act 1998. However, a notice of the result, indicating which enforcement options could be facilitated by the DDO should the creditor wish to apply for them, would be sent to the creditor or the licensed enforcement agent.

6. *The debtor's remedies*

The confrontational nature of enforcement means that grievances will be common and therefore a simple remedial structure is necessary. The Government plans to have irregular (including excessive) action by enforcement agencies dealt with by the Complaints Board of the Authority exercising the regulatory and supervisory function. However, illegal action including wrongful execution will continue to be dealt with by the courts. Whereas there is currently a distinction between distraint and execution, the proposal would remove this distinction and the remedy would be simple damages up to the value of the goods plus any relevant special damages.

The Government also wishes to introduce a provision to the effect that interpleader action should be limited to claims of full ownership, and that therefore 'if on application made within seven days after the date of execution of the warrant by the debtor or any other person who owns a seized article the judge is satisfied that the article is exempt from distress, an order releasing the article from the distress shall be made.'

Furthermore the Government proposes to abolish the ancient and little used remedy of replevin as they consider that the remedies for illegalities and irregularities will be sufficient. There appears to be no need for a separate remedy for illegal seizure of goods.

7. *Efficiency of the system*

(a) *Inefficiency due to difficulties in gathering information*
It is widely acknowledged that the existing system of judgment enforcement is ineffective primarily because it is an out-of-date system that has not evolved in line with the demands of the modern world and modern commercial practice. It is for this reason that the present Government has

undertaken a complete review of the system and recently issued a White Paper in relation to reforming it.

Court service statistics show that, in relation to warrants of execution, which make up approximately 85 per cent of all enforcement action, about 35 per cent of warrants actually issued are paid. This figure would rise to 75 per cent if 'unenforceable' warrants were excluded. Unenforceable means those that are not legally enforceable by reason of an incorrect address or for some other reason such as that the debtor is bankrupt.

The high volume of warrants of execution in comparison to the other enforcement methods can perhaps be partly attributed to the tradition of this enforcement method dating back hundreds of years but it may also be said that it is indicative of the fact that judgment creditors have little information about the debtor on which they are able to take an informed decision. All that is required to issue a warrant of execution is the debtor's name and address. In contrast, an attachment of earnings order requires the debtor's earnings, their expenditure and their employer's details. As the current system relies on the creditor obtaining information from the debtor, it is not surprising that the judgment creditor opts for methods which require as little information as possible but prove not to be the most successful enforcement method. If, on the other hand, more information was readily available for the creditor, then he would be more likely to choose a method that produced results.

There are of course means of obtaining information about the debtor, such as an oral examination procedure (CCR Ord 25, rr 3 and 4). However, such a procedure takes time and more money.

It is for this reason that one of the recommendations put forward by the Lord Chancellor's Review has been that information about the debtor be made available from other sources in order that delay in enforcement is reduced and that the information (come from an independent source and therefore by its very nature) be more reliable. This recommendation has been adopted by the Government in its White Paper in the form of a Data Disclosure Order.

(b) Inefficiency due to the current fee structure
The current fee system is governed by the principle that the debtor should bear the costs if s/he delays payment of the debt. The problem is that the creditor obtains debt recovery services from the public and private sector but does not pay for them. Creditors therefore have no interest in what the service costs. On the other hand, the system is not favourable to the creditor either. The more the judgment debtor has to pay in costs, the less the creditor recovers. Attachment of earnings would therefore often be more beneficial to both debtor and creditor; however, it is the warrant that is most often resorted to.

The Government proposes a major change to the existing fee structure by introducing an upfront fee payable by the creditor before any enforcement action is taken. This represents a radical departure from the current principle that the debtor should bear all the costs. The Government's economic analysis identified this up-front fee, in conjunction with better access to information, as a key element in the profitability and probability of enforcement. It is suggested that an upfront fee will encourage the creditor to improve the quality of the information that s/he has to provide to the enforcement agent. The Government's preferred option is a negotiable fee within a band with a fixed floor and a ceiling for debts below a value threshold to be determined by regulation—the floor providing a minimum return for the enforcement agent and a ceiling protecting the debtor, the fee being recoverable when enforcement is successful.

Currently problems are caused if the debtor offers to repay the debt directly to the creditor after the warrant has been handed to the enforcement agent, as the agent may have undertaken work for which he may charge a legitimate fee. If, however, the creditor does accept payment from the debtor after issuing the warrant, they should be able to recover the amount of the up-front fee (which they will already have paid to the enforcement agent) in addition to the judgment debt. The enforcement agent will retain the fee and the fee will be recoverable from the amount owed by the debtor to the creditor.

(c) Overall assessment of the system

The enforcement system in England and Wales is fragmented. It is not easy to apply to it the three dichotomies 'public vs private', 'monolithic vs pluralistic', and 'non-competitive vs competitive'. On balance, however, it can be said that the systems edges towards a private, pluralistic, and competitive model. This will particularly be the case if and when the Government plans to modernize enforcement law are carried into effect. It is worth expanding on this point.

At present, to a foreign creditor faced with the problem of enforcing a judgment credit, the system may well appear confused and inefficient. The Government has undertaken a major review of enforcement law that will lead to simplified and more efficient enforcement structures and procedures. However, the English system has its advantages. Because of its historical development and the absence of major comprehensive reforms in recent times, several enforcement agencies are entrusted with the responsibility of enforcing judgment credits. This creates competition in two ways. The first clearly relates to competition in respect of the enforcement of the same type of judgment credits. The second relates to competition in respect of the comparative efficiency of different structures that, though not necessarily performing the same tasks as regards the same categories of judgment credits, perform the same function and can, therefore, be compared in terms of efficiency of processes and outcomes. The model is, however, not one of competition in real terms because the systems of incentives and disincentives for the user of the service, being the judgment creditor, and the provider of the service, being the enforcement agent, is not based on the elements of supply, demand, and price. The system can be defined as being in a state of evolving pluralism that may lead, aided by appropriate legislative and regulatory reforms, to a pluralistic competitive privatized model under the supervision of the courts. The advantages of such a system would be those of competition based on appropriate incentives and disincentives for the service users and the service providers. However, a clear disadvantage of the system would be that international cooperation would be more difficult since cooperation is facilitated by the existence of a centralized public law-based structure bearing the responsibility for enforcing all the judgments. Furthermore, a system that places emphasis on the judgment creditor as the user of the service may be more appropriate when significant amounts of money are at stake and, as a consequence, a serious degree of involvement of the creditor should be expected. It may be less appropriate for small or uncontested debts where a creditor faced with difficult choices as to which enforcement agency to resort to and bearing the financial risks of the failure to enforce the judgment may well consider it more convenient to give up his right altogether. There must clearly be safeguards built into the system to ensure that small judgment debts can be efficiently and effectively enforced.

C. France

1. The legal basis of enforcement

Various pieces of legislation are applicable to the enforcement of judgments depending on the assets against which the judgment is to be enforced as well as the particular enforcement measures.

Enforcement of judicial decisions in France is principally governed by a statute dated 9 July 1991 and its implementation decree of 31 December 1992. The scope of this statute however only concerns enforcement on movable property and protective measures.

The execution upon immovable property is regulated in articles 673 to 779 of the *Code de Procédure Civile* (1806).

Some other enforcement procedures are codified in special codes. For these measures, the statutory law of 1991 represents what could be considered the general law on enforcement proceedings.

2. Structure of the enforcement agencies

Enforcement of judgments is considered to be a prerogative of the State in that it falls within the realm of the State's *imperium*. In the vast majority of instances it is carried out by public officers known as *huissiers de justice*.

(a) Huissiers de justice

The *huissier* is often responsible for the entire enforcement procedure, although should he encounter any difficulties he may submit them to the *juge de l'execution* (JEX) or the *Ministère Public* (the Department of the Public Prosecutor) for consideration and for the appropriate measures to be taken. The JEX is a judge with general authority to deal with all difficulties arising from the enforcement of judgments.

The *huissier* may only undertake the enforcement procedure upon request of a creditor residing within the area of his territorial authority (upon delivery of the *titre exécutoire*—this normally being a final judgment against the debtor). It is also the creditor who chooses the measure to be directed against the debtor by the *huissier* as well as the asset against which execution is to be directed.

The *huissiers* are independent and private agents of law enforcement who run their own business and can hire clerks. Their remuneration comes exclusively from the fees paid by the creditors or debtors, and such fees are determined by reference to the value of the claim. They are financially independent from the State. Nevertheless, the fees are regulated for those duties which are within their exclusive authority. For other duties that are not of their exclusive authority (for example drafting private documents, assistance, representation), the *huissier* can freely determine the fee.

Even though they are financially independent, the huissiers are '*officiers ministériels*' (public officers) (ie their documents have notarial value). It is the *huissier*'s competence to issue writs and lead the procedures within the district of the *tribunal d'instance* (district court level) of their residence. The *huissier* can also be appointed to undertake investigations.

The professional 'guild' of the *huissiers* is supervised by the Ministry of Justice, and a *huissier* can be prosecuted by the Public Prosecutor (*Procureur de la République*) if a complaint is filed against him. The departmental chambers of the *huissiers* control their members, conduct investigations, and audit the accounts of the *huissiers*.

(b) Other enforcement agents

Beside the *huissiers* there are four other types of enforcement agents with specialised duties.

(i)   The auctioneer (*commissaire-priseur*) is also a public officer and has the monopoly on judicially ordered auction sales of movable property.

(ii) In addition, the *tribunal de commerce* (commercial court) can engage a goods broker (*courtier en merchandise*) to sell on auction the wholesale goods that have been the subject of an attachment.

(iii) As regards attachment of earnings, it is the *greffier du tribunal d'in-stance* (the court clerk of the *tribunal d'instance*) that has an important role in the attachment of a debtor's earnings.

(iv) Fourthly and lastly, notaries and solicitors play a residual role in enforcement procedure. They can register judicial securities (*nantissement de fond de commerce, hypothèque*) and can also issue the order for attachment of immovable property (*les saisies immobilière*) to the *huissier*.

3. Conditions for execution

The *titre exécutoire* is the order delivered in the name of the State that gives the creditors the power to obtain enforcement of the judicial decision. The executory character of the order is established by the '*formule exécutoire*' which is inserted in the judgment. Ordinarily a *titre exécutoire* will only be given if the decision is final (ie there is no possibility of appeal) although the judge may allow for interim execution.

4. Methods of enforcement

Under French law, the general principle is that all the debtor's assets are liable to execution to discharge any debt owed to his creditors. The creditor chooses: (1) the assets on which execution is to be levied; (2) the enforcement measure that appears most suitable to him. There is no order of priority of enforcement measures except in relation to the execution of immovable property.

As for movable assets, the four main methods of execution are judicial sale, attachment of cars, attachment of earnings, and third party debt orders.

(a) Judicial Sale (saisie-vente d'un bien corporel)
The judicial sale targets movable property of the debtor that is either in the debtor's or a third party's possession. The attachment of the movable property is carried out by the *huissier*. The attachment consists of a formal prohibition to the debtor to dispose of the property in question. The attached property remains in the debtor's possession. Following a one-month period, the attached property can be sold at a public auction.

Some assets fall within the category of non-attachable property. Non-attachable property comprises basic household equipment of the debtor and his or her equipment necessary to perform his or her profession, as well as items vital for the care of a disabled or ill person.

(b) The attachment of motor vehicles (saisie de véhicule terrestre à moteur)
The attachment of motor vehicles can take place by one of two methods:

(a) by registration of the seizure with the *préfecture* (police headquarter), thereby rendering impossible any transaction on the vehicle; the debtor is notified within eight days after the registration, and the freezing effect of the measure lasts for two years; (b) the vehicle is physically immobilised; the *huissier* indicates his or her details on the vehicle, and after notification the debtor has one month to challenge the measure or to pay. If the debtor does not react, the vehicle can either be sold (and the sales revenue passed on to the creditor) or become the property of the creditor.

(c) The attachment of earnings (saisie de rémunérations)
The debtor's salary is divided into three parts. To provide a minimum amount for the debtor's living expenses, the minimum wage is not attachable. A second part of the salary is only attachable to alimony creditors. The third part is attachable by all creditors. The competence to order attachments of earnings rests solely with the *tribunal d'instance* (county court level). The attachment is preceded by a procedure of conciliation between debtor and creditor. If the conciliation fails, the *greffier du tribunal* (the court clerk) proceeds to the attachment procedure within eight days after the failed settlement attempt. S/he notifies the employer and the debtor. The employer has 15 days to inform the court about the legal position of the employee and then deduct from the employee's monthly salary the maximum amount permitted under law to be paid to the *greffier* of the court who is responsible for the distribution of the money among the creditors.

*(d) Third party debt orders or garnishment (*saisie-attribution des créances de somme d'argent)

This method of enforcement allows the creditor to prevent a third party against whom the debtor is judicially enforcing a debt from paying the debtor and to obtain from such third party direct satisfaction of his debt.

As soon as the garnishment is notified to the third party, the creditor becomes owner of the third party money up to the amount of his debt. Third parties must inform the *huissier* about the extent of their debt to the debtor. The *huissier* notifies the debtor within 8 days of the garnishment, and if the measure has not been challenged by the debtor after a month, the creditor is entitled to be paid. If insolvency proceedings have been started against the debtor, the creditor remains protected if the notification took place before the beginning of the insolvency procedure.

If the third-party debtor is a bank, the bank must inform the *huissier* about all the accounts of the debtor and their balance. On a strict reading of the law, a garnishment would have a freezing effect on all bank accounts, even if the debt amounts to less. To avoid the economic paralysis of the

debtor, banks place the amount seized in a special bank account and in relation to the remaining amounts ask the debtor to subscribe to other guarantees to protect the bank as well as other debtors. This practice, however,
depends on the agreement of all parties and/or the intervention of the JEX.

5. *Information about the debtor*

Investigations into the debtor's financial situation might contravene the
principle of privacy, banking secrecy, and data protection legislation. It
seems, however, intolerable that the enforcement of a court judgment may
be stultified due to a lack of information about the debtor's assets. The solution adopted in French law is as follows. The *huissier* can ask the department of the public prosecutor (*Procureur de la République*) for assistance
in order to obtain the debtor's personal data. Enquiries relating to the
private affairs and financial situation of the debtor are strictly controlled by
law. The department of the public prosecutor is the only authority empowered to enquire into the debtor's personal data. The *huissier* him or her self
does not have direct access to the information. He must ask the *Procureur
de la République* for the information s/he needs. The *Procureur de la
République* will then make the appropriate enquiry. The information that
the department of the public prosecutor can disclose to the *huissier* consists
of the debtor's address, the address of the debtor's employer, and the details
of the debtor's bank account. The use of the information provided by the
department of the public prosecutor is limited to the specified judgment
being enforced. The unauthorised use of the information other than for the
purpose of the execution of the specified judgment for which it was
requested is a criminal offence. However, empirical evidence suggests that
the effectiveness of the criminal sanctions is doubtful other than in the cases
of *flagrante delicto*.

This system for disclosure of information about the debtor is not very
successful given the work overload of the department of the public prosecutor. Enquiries about the debtor's affairs and financial situation take time.
Generally, the information, once obtained, is outdated when the department of the public prosecutor finally communicates the data to the *huissier*.
As a consequence, private organizations providing investigative services
have emerged.

6. *The debtor's remedies*

The debtor does not have a remedy against the *titre exécutoire* .

Remedies against irregular and illegal enforcement of judgments are
remedies against the *huissier*'s action. There are three responsibilities: civil,
disciplinary, and criminal. The *huissier*'s criminal liability will not be

further discussed in this context as it does not provide a direct remedy to the debtor.

The *huissier* is responsible to the debtor and the third parties in tort (*faute délictuelle*). On this basis, the debtor can sue on four grounds: a) lack of information; b) lack of advice; c) irregular measures; d) illegal measures. The *JEX* is competent to hear an action in tort relating to the responsibility of the *huissier* if his conduct has caused a loss to the debtor during the enforcement proceedings. The *Tribunal de Grand Instance* has jurisdiction in all other cases, such as for example nullity of the writ.

In addition, the debtor can obtain the stay of execution or the withdrawal of the enforcement measure. The *JEX* is competent to rule on this claim as well as to decide on the responsibility of the *huissier* and creditor for loss incurred due to unjustified or irregular execution.

As regards disciplinary responsibility, the *huissier* can be prosecuted by the *Procureur de la République* (who represents the Ministry of Justice) when s/he does not comply with the professional requirements of probity, honour, and tact. The breach of disciplinary rules needs to be intentional in order to lead to sanctions. Negligence might however engage civil responsibility. The departmental chambers and the *tribunal de grand instance* (high court level) are competent to investigate and apply the sanction of temporary or permanent interdiction from office.

7. The efficiency of the system

The French enforcement system is private, monolithic, and competitive. The *huissiers de justice* are public officers when they exercise enforcement functions but they are also members of a regulated profession which they exercise for profit by organizing their own practice, hiring employees, and competing with other *huissiers* for business. Therefore, although there are public officers, their enforcement activity is not financed through general taxation and their nature is closer to that of a professional in private practice than to that of a public body. Furthermore, the system is based on a competitive model although competition takes place among independent enforcement agents that are members of the same profession rather than among different enforcement agencies. The analysis of the French system shows that a competitive model does not necessarily presuppose a fully privatized system. It also shows that the concepts of the private as opposed to the public nature of the enforcement agent are relative. The *huissiers de justice* are public officers but exercise a profession for profit and are organized in firms on a private law basis. Their characterization as public officers, therefore, follows from the exercise of a public function rather than from the nature of the agent. Furthermore, the system of remedies against illegal and irregular execution is modelled on the law of tort and the *huissier*'s liability in tort for unlawful conduct causing a loss to the debtor. This model clearly points to the private law nature of the enforcement system. However, the supervision by the JEX over the entire enforcement process seems to point in the different direction.

The main problem in the French system is perceived to be the difficulty in obtaining information about the debtor's assets. This is due to the fact that the *huissier* does not have direct access to information on the debtor's assets. Nor is there any provision for the *huissier* or the creditor to apply to the court for assistance in this matter. The necessary involvement of the department of the public prosecutor is the cause of the inefficiency. The *Procurer de la République* is generally overloaded with work and does not have, and is unable to obtain, updated information on the debtor's assets. This has led to a very rare use of the powers of the public prosecutor to obtain information about the debtor's assets and to an increasing use of private investigative agencies.

A feature of the system which is considered to be very effective is the use of periodic penalties (*astreinte*) that may be applied in order to persuade the debtor to comply with the judgment as soon as possible. This seems to be particularly effective, however, in cases of orders for specific performance rather than in cases of enforcement of money judgments.

Other areas are more difficult to assess. The ambivalent role of the *huissier de justice*, who owes duties to the creditor and the debtor at the same time, is a good example. The *huissier* may succeed in building a new direct link between creditor and debtor, which may lead to the case being settled. Furthermore, if the *huissier* can secure the debtor's cooperation, including as regards disclosure of his assets, he can more efficiently advise the creditor on the method and timing of the enforcement. On the other hand, the duties of the *huissier* to inform and advise the debtor may be in conflict with his duties to enforce the judgment on behalf of the creditor. Overall, however, the ambivalent role of the enforcement agent under French law can be regarded as adding to the efficiency of the enforcement system as one single person unites two interests and is familiar with both parties of the enforcement proceeding.

The principles on recoverability of costs in enforcement proceedings also lead to inefficiencies. *Huissiers* charge fees for their work that are set by State regulation in relation to the value of the claim. The *huissier*'s fees are paid by the creditor initially, and are then recoverable from the debtor. However, legal fees incurred after the date of execution and fees of any private detectives are not recoverable. These can be substantially higher than the fees charged by the *huissier*. As a consequence, the creditor bears part of the costs of the enforcement proceedings which erodes part of the credit.

D. Germany

1. The legal basis of enforcement

German enforcement law for civil claims is codified in Chapter 8 (paragraphs 704–945) of the Code of Civil Procedure, *Zivilprozessordnung* (*ZPO*). Additional provisions relating to execution of immovable property are to be found in the Code regulating sequestration and public sale (*Gesetz über die Zwangsversteigerung und Zwangsverwaltung, ZVG*). The organization of the courts as well as the status of the bailiffs and court officers is governed by the Act on the Organization of the Civil Courts, *Gerichtsverfassungsgesetz* (*GVG*) and by the Act on Court Officers, *Rechtspflegergesetz* (*RPflG*).

2. Structure of the enforcement agencies

(a) General

In Germany, enforcement proceedings are considered to be an essential function of the State which is exclusively exercised by State organs according to binding legal provisions. Therefore, apart from the rare and limited exception of distress, any kind of 'law enforcement' carried out other than through the prescribed procedures and by the appointed bodies is strictly forbidden. The Federation and the Federal States must provide for efficient enforcement agencies and procedures, because, according to the case law of the German Constitutional Court, the constitutional guarantee of access to justice also includes efficient enforcement proceedings.

(b) Courts

Enforcement is carried out by the enforcement courts (*Vollstreckungsgerichte*), these normally being within the local courts (*Amtsgericht*) where the property to be seized or attached is located. The *Vollstreckungsgerichte* has competence in relation to the following:

- Enforcement of monetary claims through garnishment proceedings (for example bank accounts) or other attachments of property rights;
- Execution on immovable property of the debtor by way of the registration of an enforcement mortgage, or by the forced sale or forced administration of the real estate;
- Imposition of fines for the debtor's refusal to disclose assets under oath;
- Grant of required authorization in respect of certain enforcement activities. For instance, while bailiffs are responsible for the execution of movable property, some of their tasks, such as searching a home without the owner's consent, are subject to the prior authorization of the

enforcement court. The judge's intervention is required by the German Constitution.[18]

Most of the functions conferred on the enforcement court are actually performed by the court clerk (*Rechtspfleger*). His responsibilities include garnishment proceedings and enforcement measures relating to real estates. However, in difficult cases, especially matters involving the constitutionality of a legal provision or the application of foreign law, the court clerk must refer the case to the judge.

Court clerks are civil servants. Therefore, they are fully subject to disciplinary control, which includes their working hours, and their income derives fully from a fixed salary. However, paragraph 9 of the *Rechtspflegergesetz* grants them independence in their judicial and administrative activities (*sachliche Unabhängigkeit*) in a way which is similar to judicial independence. As a consequence, they are not directly subject to the directions of the enforcement judges. Their decisions may be appealed to the district court. The supervision of the court clerks does not at all correspond to the close supervision of bailiffs by the enforcement judge.

In practice, the court clerks (*Rechtspfleger*) are the most important enforcement agents, as they carry out most forms of seizure, especially garnishments. Additionally, the number of garnishments is much higher than the number of seizures of movable property.

(c) Bailiffs (Gerichtsvollzieher)

Bailiffs are responsible for the execution on movable property (including negotiable instruments) by way of seizure and public sale, for the delivery or recovery of assets, and for evictions. Bailiffs are also responsible for the service of documents relating to other forms of seizure. In 1998, German legislation conferred on the bailiffs the additional responsibility of obtaining a declaration of the debtor's assets.

Bailiffs are mainly remunerated by salary, although part of their income derives from fees charged to the creditor for performance of enforcement tasks. Such fees are subject to caps. The costs incurred by the creditor in the enforcement of a judgment are recoverable from the debtor.

Normally, several bailiffs are appointed to the local courts. Judgment creditors may directly apply to the general court office which will help them to identify the competent bailiff. The competence of the responsible bailiff is determined by reference to the domicile of the debtor or the location of the assets to be seized.

While in the 19th and early 20th centuries, a competitive system was in

---

[18]   Art 13(2) of the Constitution.

place, nowadays bailiffs have a monopoly in a defined area of territorial competence (*Bezirkssystem*, district system). Therefore, the earnings of a bailiff depend to some extent on the kind of district s/he is responsible for. The rules on territorial competence exclude any form of competition.

Bailiffs act under the supervision of the enforcement judge although they maintain an office under their own responsibility and at their own expense. The judgment creditor and the debtor, as well as any affected third person, may challenge the legality of any action of the bailiff before the enforcement court.

If the bailiff neglects the duties set out in the regulations by gross negligence, he will be held personally liable to the State for damages occurring to debtors or creditors.

Additionally, the federal state employing the bailiff is liable for his simple negligence under the terms of State responsibility.

(d) Judges

The main competence of the judges in enforcement matters relates to the control of the bailiff's actions. The bailiff's actions can be challenged before the enforcement judge. Additionally, the intervention of the judge is also necessary if enforcement measures infringe upon certain constitutional rights of the debtor, for example if the bailiff intends to search the home of the debtor without his consent[19] or if the creditor applies for an arrest (imprisonment) of the debtor.[20]

Some of the court clerk's actions may be challenged before the enforcement judge. Additionally, the enforcement judge will become involved if the enforcement procedure is complex, for instance if the constitutionality of a legal provision is questioned, or the application of foreign law is in issue.

As a result of the constitutional guarantee of judicial independence, judicial activity is only subject to the judicial review exercised by the superior courts.

(e) Debt recovery agencies

The monopoly on enforcement possessed by the State and the interdiction of any kind of enforcement activity carried out outside the prescribed legal framework does not exclude the existence of private services for the recovery of debts. There are many such services in Germany, most of them organized by attorneys. However, no debt recovery service may achieve the satisfaction of the credit regardless of the debtor's cooperation.

---

[19] Art 13 of the Constitution.   [20] Art 104 of the Constitution.

3. Conditions for execution

Enforceable instruments are mainly judgments which have become *res judicata* and provisionally enforceable judgments. Paragraph 794 ZPO contains an additional list of enforceable instruments such as court settlements *(Prozessvergleiche)*, court cost orders *(Kostenfestsetzungsbeschlüsse)*, enforceable default summons (*Vollstreckungsbescheide*, based on orders for payment *(Mahnbescheide)*), decisions granting the *exequatur* on arbitral awards and enforceable instruments of public notaries *(Notarielle Urkunden)*.

4. Methods of enforcement

(a) General

The German system relies on the creditor's initiative: it is up to the creditor to gather the necessary information and to decide on the method of enforcement by applying directly to the competent organ. The competent organ then carries out the enforcement, although it is up to the creditor to choose a different method if the selected measure fails.

German law distinguishes between the enforcement of monetary claims (paragraphs 803–82a ZPO) and of non-monetary claims (paragraphs 883–98 ZPO).

The following methods of enforcement are available depending on whether the claim is monetary or not:

* Execution on movable property: this may involve the seizure of property at the debtor's home; the movable property is then sold by public sale;
* Third party debt order (garnishment): this method may be used for monetary debts and non-monetary debts;
* Execution on immovable property: this includes the registration of a mortgage in the creditor's favour, forced sale, and forced administration;
* Fines or even imprisonment: this is a method of enforcement used where the action is to force a person to refrain from doing an act.

(b) Provisional measures

Provisional execution may be allowed before the judgment is final. This may be avoided by the debtor if security is provided. Provisional measures are designed to secure future enforcement of either monetary claims or non-monetary claims.

An arrest is aimed to protect monetary claims. It provisionally attaches assets (including third-party debts) by merely freezing them. If these measures are unlikely to succeed, imprisonment of the debtor may be ordered.

An injunction may be ordered with respect to a particular object of litigation. Restraining orders or interim payments may also be granted.

5. Information about the debtor

It is the creditor's task to gather information on the debtor's location and to find out the whereabouts of suitable assets on which execution can be levied. Normally, the enforcement agents do not conduct investigations to uncover debtors' assets. German law does not allow enforcement agents special access to information. The current situation is very burdensome for the judgment creditors and their legal representatives. In practice, private investigators provide information about the location and the financial situation of the debtor.

If it is clear to the bailiff when undertaking a seizure of property that the property subject to the seizure will not suffice to satisfy the creditor's debt, he can question the debtor about any claims he holds against third parties, and can then pass on this information to the judgment creditor. He can also ask any person in the debtor's household about the debtor's employer and pass this information on to the creditor. Third parties are not, however, obliged to respond to these questions, and the bailiff must inform them about their right to refuse to answer.

Only if attempts at seizure have been or are likely to be unsuccessful can the judgment creditor request the bailiff to summon the debtor to disclose all his assets on solemn declaration. The debtor is required to attend a hearing and to provide the required information on solemn affirmation. If the debtor contests his obligation, the enforcement court, in the person of the court clerk, will hear the case. On the creditor's request, the same court, but this time with a judge presiding, may even order the imprisonment, for a term of up to six months, of a debtor who refuses to give the solemn declaration. If the debtor makes the required declaration at the hearing, the bailiff normally files the declaration (which is delivered on a standard form) at the enforcement register and sends a copy to the creditor. During a period of three years following the hearing, the debtor must give an additional declaration, if a creditor (in possession of a *titre exécutoire*) shows that there are reasons to believe that the debtor disposes of a new source of income. Registration lapses after three years, but the debtor can also get his name removed from the register if he satisfies the judgment creditor in the interim.

In practice, the main function of the debtor's declaration is not to disclose his assets but to provide an incentive to the debtor to pay voluntarily. The declaration of assets is registered on the 'debtor's register' which is maintained by the enforcement court and available to any creditor seeking information about the financial situation of the debtor (some local courts even offer electronic registers accessible via internet). The debtor's creditworthiness is thus a matter of public record, and in practice a person who is on such a record will find it very difficult to obtain credit.

6. The debtor's remedies

The German system of legal remedies is particularly complicated and confusing. Generally, the remedies can be divided into two groups according to the nature of the defect complained of. The first group deals with procedural irregularities. The second group refers to objections and complaints derived from substantial law (*Vollstreckungsgegenklage*) and to third-party complaints in opposition (*Drittwiderspruchsklage*).

Remedies relating to procedural irregularities vary depending on whether the act complained of has been performed by the bailiff or by the court clerk. If the act complained of has been performed by a bailiff, the main remedy in this respect is the execution complaint (*Vollstreckungserinnerung*). This complaint is heard by the judge of the enforcement court competent for the territory where the bailiff's conduct (*Gerichtsvollzieher*) took place.

As far as the conduct of the court officer (*Rechtspfleger*) is concerned, the situation in relation to the execution complaint is more complicated. If an *ex parte* measure has been ordered, the affected party may challenge the legality of the enforcement measure by a 'modified complaint' which is first reviewed by the *Rechtspfleger* himself. His decision is subject to a review by either the district court (*Erinnerung, Durchgriffsbeschwerde*) or the enforcement judge himself depending on the circumstances. If a measure is ordered where both parties have been heard, the court officer's decision is again subject to review by either the district court judge or the enforcement judge depending on the circumstances.

In relation to objections based on substantive law, only those objections which arose after the end of the last hearing of the case on the merits are admitted. Any decision of the enforcement court can be appealed and a second appeal is available to the Federal Supreme Court if the case relates to a question of general importance.

7. The efficiency of the system

The German system is public, monolithic, and non-competitive. As regards the monolithic nature of the system, it is true that there are three different enforcement agencies: a) courts; b) court clerks; c) bailiffs. However, they seem to be integrated in the same overall judicial structure. Court clerks are officers of the court. Bailiffs maintain their own office and are partly remunerated by fees paid in respect of the performance of enforcement activity.

However, they are appointed to the court, act under the supervision of the court, and their acts can be challenged before the enforcement court. Functionally, at the very least, they act within the realm of public law.

The principal defects of the German system are perceived to be the following: (1) the difficulty in obtaining information on the debtor's assets; (2) the small number of bailiffs; (3) the lack of competition between enforcement agencies; (4) the complexity of the system of remedies.

As regards disclosure of information about the debtor's assets, the German system does not confer on the enforcement agents powers to obtain disclosure from the debtor outright or access to publicly-held information. In practice, and unless it can be shown that there is no reasonable prospect of recovery on the judgment, it is a precondition for the procedure to summon the debtor to render a declaration that enforcement steps must have been taken and have been unsuccessful. Furthermore, the number of bailiffs is very low. Their insufficient number results in a delay of around six months before s/he takes any action upon a creditor's request. If no assets are to be found and a declaration of assets is to be taken from the debtor, the period of time before the creditor recovers on the judgment can be excessively long.

The German system is characterized by the absence of competition between different enforcement agencies. *Rechtspfleger* are court clerks while bailiffs are fully integrated in the court system, act under the supervision of the court, and have a defined territorial competence. There is no competition between court clerks and bailiffs because their powers are different in respect of the different methods of enforcement. The costs and fees system is very rigid too.

With respect to the efficiency of the debtor's remedies, these are considered to be particularly complicated and confusing. This may give rise to unnecessary litigation and requires highly specialized legal advice even in relatively small and simple cases.

E. Netherlands

1. The legal basis of enforcement

Dutch enforcement law is codified in Book 2 and Book 3, Title 4 of the *Wetboek van Burgerlijke Rechtsvordering* (Code of Civil Procedure) and thus regulated together with civil procedural law. Book 3 deals, inter alia, with provisional enforcement measures and the *exequatur* procedure. Book 2 contains rules on the enforcement of judgments and other enforceable instruments such as monetary awards by the criminal courts or administrative authorities. In addition to the Code, secondary legislation contains technical provisions on enforcement law.

2. *The structure of the enforcement agencies*

Court clerks do not have any special function in the enforcement proceedings, and special enforcement officers like the *Rechtspfleger* in Germany simply do not exist.

Three different kinds of professionals deal with execution in the Netherlands: (1) the *gerechtsdeurwaarder* (court bailiff); (2) state-employed enforcement agents; (3) notaries.

(a) *The* gerechtsdeurwaarder *(bailiff)*

The bailiff has an independent and central position in the Dutch legal system. Currently, there are 325 bailiffs and 225 deputy bailiffs in The Netherlands. The bailiff is responsible for administrative tasks such as serving processes, serving judgments, carrying out preventive attachments, attachments of assets, evictions, and supervising public auctions. The bailiff is also allowed to undertake non-administrative practices. Since the entrance into force of the Act on Bailiffs (2001), bailiffs not only act independently, but also act in much freer competition with each other. This has been achieved by relaxing the requirements to start a practice, giving more freedom in relation to fee arrangements with clients, and increasing the degree of regulation and supervision of the profession through the Royal Professional Organization of Bailiffs and the Chamber of Bailiffs.

The rules of practice are as follows. A candidate bailiff must attain adequate training and qualifications. He has to present a business plan for approval by the regulatory authority. After the approval of the business plan, he can be appointed at the location where he wishes to set up his practice. In the course of his practice, the bailiff has to comply with statutory disciplinary rules, codes of conduct, and professional codes. The bailiffs and deputy bailiffs are responsible for their duties and for complying with the professional and ethical standards of their profession. In first instance, the Chamber of Bailiffs examines disciplinary cases.

The *Koninklijke Beroepsorganizatie van Gerechtsdeurwaarders* (Royal Professional Organization of Bailiffs) is the umbrella organization for all bailiffs in the Netherlands. Every bailiff is required to be a member of this organization. The organization consists of a central board, the national council of bailiffs, and the general assembly of bailiffs. The board runs the general management of the organization and is entrusted with the promotion of proper professional conduct. The council of bailiffs decides on the general policy of the organization, adopts bylaws, and appoints and supervises the board. The general assembly advises the council about the professional codes.

(b) State-employed enforcement agents

State-employed enforcement agents are only responsible for the collection of public taxes and dues. However, this work can now be offered, by tender, to the court bailiffs.

(c) The notary

The notary is the holder of a public office. He is only involved if the execution regards the sale of immovable property. The notary performs all the activities relating to the sale.

3. The conditions for execution

In the Netherlands, it is not necessary to apply to the court for a warrant of execution as a precondition for starting enforcement proceedings. Enforcement can be commenced if the instrument to be enforced is one that is defined in article 430 of the *Wetboek van Burgerlijke Rechtsvordering*. These include not only decisions of civil courts and arbitral tribunals but also decisions on monetary claims by criminal courts, administrative authorities, social insurance institutions, and enforceable notarial instruments. Thus, it is not necessary to obtain a special writ of enforcement.

4. Methods of enforcement

In the Netherlands, a distinction is generally made between direct and indirect enforcement. Direct enforcement procures the satisfaction of the creditor's rights through a procedure aiming at the final result of transferring money to the creditor regardless of the cooperation of the debtor. Indirect enforcement procures the cooperation of the debtor through the imposition on him of penalties for non-performance of his obligations under the judgment.

Methods of direct enforcement include the following: (1) seizure for the enforcement of money debts with respect to movable property, shares, immovable property, ships, and airplanes; (2) garnishment orders. In the Netherlands, however, there is a general perception that traditional methods of enforcement are not as effective as the recently introduced system of periodic penalties.

In addition to the direct enforcement procedures, the indirect method of the *dwangsom* (*astreinte*) is considered to be very successful. This method consists of an order to the debtor to pay his creditor a sum of money without any connection to the damage the creditor suffered or will suffer in case of non-performance or overdue performance of the principal obligation. This order puts the debtor under pressure to fulfil his or her main obligation. The *astreinte* is regularly calculated per each day by which the performance (of the judicial decision) is delayed or per individual violation of the judicial decision. The range of court orders to which an *astreinte* can be applied is remarkably broad and there is wide judicial discretion. The creditor must apply to the court for an order to be made but the judge is not bound by any specific amount indicated by the claimant as to the appropriate level of the periodic penalty.

5. Information about the debtor

Information concerning the debtor can be obtained electronically by a bailiff (not by other persons) from official (parish) registers. Arrangements are in place to ensure that bailiffs can obtain confirmation of the correct information about a party's name, address, or place of residence. Such information is also readily available through commercially-provided databases and other information sources. Dutch bailiffs have no access to registers connected with the social security system or the tax authorities. Neither is there an official register of places of employment.

6. The debtor's remedies

The debtor, the creditor, and third parties can file complaints in respect of the enforcement procedure with the court having jurisdiction according to the provisions of the *Rechtsvordering*. The complaint gives rise to a special summary proceeding before the president of the District Court.

Particular remedies and safeguards apply when the court makes orders for periodic penalty payments. If it appears—after the court had imposed an *astreinte*—that the main obligation (which shall be secured by the *astreinte*) is difficult or impossible to perform, the debtor can request the judge who ordered the *astreinte* to lower or revoke the *astreinte*. Furthermore, once an *astreinte* is due, the collection of the amounts can take place only within a period of six months. The time limit tries to prevent situations occurring where a mere passive attitude of the debtor will result in excessive debts accruing.

Disciplinary remedies can also be sought against the bailiff and the deputy bailiff for misconduct.

7. Efficiency of the system

The Dutch system is private, monolithic, and based on competition. Enforcement is mainly carried out by bailiffs exercising a regulated profession. There is no competition among enforcement agencies of different kinds but bailiffs are in competition with each other. This is clearly conducive to efficiency in that bailiffs have an incentive to provide the best service on the most attractive terms.

The problems with the Dutch system follow from the ineffectiveness of the traditional methods of enforcement. This is due, at least in part, to the lack of access by bailiffs and creditor to comprehensive and updated information about the debtor's assets. Bailiffs have access to parish registers but the information they can obtain is very limited. As a result, the enforcement process is commenced without a clear picture of the debtor's financial situation. On the other hand, a factor that contributes to the efficiency of the system is the possibility of indirect enforcement. The *astreinte* is considered to be an effective way to provide powerful incentives to the debtor to comply with his obligations. This method is frequently employed in the Netherlands. However, it would appear that a system which relies too heavily on indirect enforcement as a consequence of the perceived inefficiency of the traditional methods of execution does not strike the right balance. In particular, and perhaps paradoxically, indirect enforcement relying on periodic penalty payments may be more effective if used against wealthy debtors who are more inclined to weigh the financial benefits and disadvantages of non-payment of the judgment debt. Furthermore, if the debtor does not pay up his debt, the accrual of the additional debt resulting from the periodic penalty payment may lead to bankruptcy or insolvency thus damaging all the creditors without necessarily benefiting the judgment creditor for whose benefit the periodic payment was initially imposed. Therefore, it would appear that while a system of *astreintes* contributes to efficient enforcement, an enforcement process too heavily reliant on the *astreintes* and not complemented by efficient methods of direct enforcement would be imbalanced and inefficient as a whole.

F. Spain

1. The legal basis of enforcement

The enforcement of judicial decisions is governed by articles 538 et seq. of the *Ley de Enjuiciamiento Civil* (LEC), which provides for a unified regime for the enforcement of all sorts of civil claims, both judicial and extrajudicial.

2. The structure of the enforcement agencies

Law enforcement lies within the exclusive competence of the courts which must 'determine and enforce that which has been decided' as prescribed in the Spanish Constitution (article 117). Once the relevant court has delivered the *titre exécutoire*, the judgment creditor may petition the *juzgado de primera instancia* (the district court) to start enforcement proceedings and order the appropriate type of enforcement.

The *Agentes Judiciales* (court clerks) carry out seizures. They have police authority in order to perform their tasks.

3. The conditions for execution

The creditor (through an advocate or *procurador* if the sum exceeds Euro 900) must request enforcement from the *juzgado de primera instancia* (district court) that originally heard the case within five years from the date on which the final judgment was given. In the request for enforcement the creditor has to specify:

The *titre exécutoire* on which the applicant is relying in order to request enforcement. Final judgments and arbitral awards are *titres exécutoire*.

The method of enforcement sought, together with the amount claimed plus interest and costs (which must not exceed 30 per cent of the principal obligation).

A description of the assets that can be seized, together with a statement as to whether the debtor considers them sufficient to cover the debt.

If the creditor has indicated that he does not have knowledge of debtor's assets that would be sufficient to cover the debt, the creditor may ask the court to carry out enquiries of financial institutions, public entities, public registers, and individual and legal persons that the creditor himself indicates. The court will not carry out such investigations if the creditor is able to obtain the information himself or through his representative.

The debtor's identity together with the identity of any other person who may be liable for the debt.

A *titre exécutoire* must be final. There are specific rules for provisional enforcement.

On application by the creditor, containing the information indicated above, the *juzgado de primera instancia* issues the enforcement order. The enforcement order is not subject to appeal.

The enforcement order must contain the names of the persons to be served with the enforcement order, the amount sought, the means to identify and find the debtor and his or her property which have been approved by the court, the methods that the court will apply to seize the debtor's assets, and the debtor's previous summons if the matter relates to an extra-judicial claim.

4. The methods of enforcement

The law on the enforcement of money claims (*ejecución dineraria*) is regulated in 133 articles. The main relevant principles are the following.

(a) Seizure of movable assets

The seizure of assets must always be proportionate, ie the creditor must never seize a greater value than the amount fixed in the enforcement order, unless there are no less valuable assets to seize. The enforcement procedure must always be suspended (if an appeal has been filed) or annulled (if no appeal is filed) if the debtor pays the amount required by the enforcement order. The amount of money deposited by the debtor is delivered to the creditor, unless the enforcement order has been opposed. In the absence of a specific agreement between creditor and debtor, the court will seize the assets that are easiest to sell and whose sale is least onerous for the debtor. If the application of such criteria is difficult or impossible, then the court will seize assets in the following order: the debtor's bank account; shares and other marketable securities; jewellery and works of art; revenues of a certain value; movable property (including shares that are not marketable); immovable property; wages and pensions; and, finally, investments, credits, and rights realisable in the medium- to long- term. A business may also be seized if the court decides it is appropriate.

(b) Seizure of salaries and pensions

The seizure of salaries, pensions, or other monetary revenues is carried out by court order addressed to the appropriate entity or person. The addressee of the order is obliged to transfer the amount indicated to a specified account.

(c) Seizure of bank accounts

The seizure of a bank account is fairly simple. The court will order the financial institution to retain a certain amount within the debtor's bank account, and the debtor may freely dispose of anything other than that amount.

(d) Seizure of immovable property

The seizure of immovable property is carried out by a provisional inscription in the public land registry. The inscription is the first procedural step in the process. The seizure of immovable property brings about the satisfaction of the credit through the sale of the asset.

(e) Unseizeable assets

Some assets cannot be seized by law. Such is the case of household goods, or the debtor's clothes and the debtor's books and instruments that are necessary for him to exercise his profession. Income equivalent to the minimum wage is also unable to be seized, whether received by wage, pension, or other form payment. For amounts above the minimum wage, there is a

sliding scale on the amounts that can be seized (ie up to double the minimum wage only 30 per cent of such amount can be seized, up to triple the
amount of the minimum wage only 50 per cent of such amount can be
seized etc.). Such a sliding scale does not apply if the enforcement relates to
the payment of alimony.

(f) Sale of the assets
In some cases, there is no sale as such or the process is very straightforward.
Any cash seized will be handed over to the creditor. Any marketable securities shall be sold by the court on the appropriate market, and the proceeds
handed over to the creditor.

The court is also responsible for the sale of all other assets. The three
general methods of sale are:

(1) Through the parties themselves by an agreement between them which
    needs to be approved by the court;
(2) By a specialist person or establishment under the control of the court;
(3) At a court auction. The sale at court auctions was formerly the only
    way to turn the assets into money. The new *Ley de Enjuiciamiento Civil*
    now provides that the sale by a specialist establishment and by the
    parties themselves must be preferred to the more burdensome court
    auction procedure.

If the parties have not agreed a value for the assets, they will be valued by
an expert appointed by the court. The expert valuer will value the assets
within 8 days.

If the creditor requests it, or if the debtor requests it and the creditor
consents, the court may agree the sale of the assets by a specialist person or
entity that specializes in the sale of such type of assets. If the parties have
not agreed otherwise, the specialist cannot sell the asset for less than 50 per
cent of the value given to such asset by the valuer (70 per cent of the value
if it is an immovable asset). The specialist will pay the proceeds from the
sale (less fees and disbursements) into a designated bank account. The
specialist has six months in which to sell the asset(s), after which his
mandate will be revoked. He may be granted a further six months to sell
the asset(s) if he was not able to sell them due to circumstances beyond his
control.

If there has been no agreement to sell, and there has been no request for
sale by a specialist, the assets will be sold at a public auction. The creditor
can participate in the public auction.

Should an asset belonging to a third party be seized, such seizure and its
ulterior sale shall be valid. However, a third party has a special remedy to
protect his right to the property (and to prevent its sale). Such a remedy
must be invoked before the sale of such asset (*tercería de dominio*). If after

the sale of an asset it is established that it belonged to a third party, the third party will only have an action for damages against the debtor (Article 594 LEC).

(g) Administration of the seized assets by the creditor

Upon the creditor's request, the court may authorize the administration of certain or all the assets that have been seized, so that the revenues that they may produce may be used to pay off the debt owed plus interest and costs.

(h) Provisional enforcement

Provisional enforcement may only be granted at the claimant's request. Provisional enforcement may not entail the nullity of titles relating to industrial property or the inscription (registration) of title to property on public registers. The claimant is no longer required to provide a security for the amount being executed. The defendant cannot oppose provisional enforcement of money claims, but may oppose the particular method of enforcement used if it is to cause damages that are impossible to restore or compensate if the judgment is overturned. He may also avoid provisional enforcement of a money claim if he makes a payment into court for the amount for which he is liable, including interest and costs.

In the case of monetary claims, should the judgment be overturned once provisional enforcement has begun or been completed, the execution will cease, the original creditor will return any amounts received, together with any costs resulting from enforcement that the debtor has been obliged to satisfy, and the creditor will be liable for the debtor's damages.

Foreign judgments that are not final may not be enforced in Spain unless otherwise specified by Treaty.

5. Information about the debtor

The sources of information about the debtor's assets are the creditor, the debtor, and third parties or public bodies under a court order.

First, the court will rely on the creditor to provide any information on the debtor's assets.

Should the creditor not be able to provide such information, the debtor will be required by the court to provide a list of sufficient assets to cover the debt. The court may punish non-compliance with such an order with fines or even imprisonment.

The creditor may also ask the court to require financial institutions, public registers, public bodies, and individual and legal persons indicated by the creditor, to provide the court with a list of the assets belonging to the debtor of which they have a record. The creditor must specify the reasons why such entity or person has the information required. The court will not require any information from any entity or person if the creditor can obtain such information himself or through his representative (*procurador*). All persons and entities are obliged to cooperate to the fullest extent (and the court may impose fines for non-cooperation) save if cooperation infringes human rights.

6. *The Debtor's remedies*

The enforcement order is not subject to appeal. However, the debtor may oppose enforcement on different grounds.

First, the debtor may allege excess (*pluspetición*), this being a claim that the court has granted the enforcement order for a higher amount than the actual claim. A very simple procedure applies to determine the exact sum. Despite this procedure, there is no stay of the enforcement proceedings unless the debtor pays the amount owed into court.

Secondly, the debtor may oppose the enforcement order on the grounds of form or procedure. The court has discretion to stay the enforcement proceedings.

Thirdly, the debtor may oppose the enforcement on substantive grounds. The judge may appoint a hearing in which both the debtor and the creditor will be heard if the parties have requested it. Substantive grounds include: (1) payment of the debt or performance of the other obligation required by the judgment; (2) expiry of the limitation period applicable to the enforcement action. Enforcement must be sought within five years of the judgment; (3) settlement out of court. Opposition to enforcement based on these grounds will not suspend enforcement.

The debtor may wish to oppose not the enforcement itself, but a particular act of enforcement. He may do this on two grounds: (1) the rules applicable to the enforcement procedure have been infringed; (2) the court has not acted in accordance with the judgment. In this event the aggrieved party can be the creditor as well as the debtor.

Finally, if after the trial new facts or acts come to light that cannot be used to oppose enforcement by way of the above mentioned remedies, the debtor may rely on any such facts or acts in ordinary court proceedings.[21]

7. *Efficiency of the system*

The Spanish system is public, monolithic, and allowing no competition among enforcement agencies. This generates inefficiency. The inefficiency derives not from the involvement of the courts as such but from the fact that the courts have a heavy docket not confined to enforcement proceed-

---

[21] Art 564 LEC.

ings. As a result, enforcement of judgments is slow and inefficient. The solution advocated by Spanish scholars has generally been in the direction of 'outsourcing' the enforcement of judgments. One notable measure that has been taken is the 'outsourcing' of the sale to specialized bodies or even permitting it to be arranged by agreement of the parties approved by the court. The clear policy behind these provisions is revealed by the fact that the sale at the court auction, which involves use of court resources and is a slow and burdensome process, is residual and can only be ordered if the other two methods cannot be deployed. The new provisions on obtaining information about the debtor's assets are also considered to benefit the efficiency of the system. However, these reforms are too limited in scope and have not brought about significant improvements in terms of efficiency.

It is interesting to compare the Spanish system with the Swedish system. The former is considered to be rather inefficient while the latter is generally deemed very efficient. Both systems are monolithic, based on the exclusive enforcement jurisdiction of public bodies, and not allowing any competition between enforcement agencies. The most notable difference in the model is that the Spanish system is court-based while the Swedish system relies on the exclusive enforcement jurisdiction of a specialized agency. It is submitted that this is the key factor. In Spain, enforcement proceedings are conducted by the courts and court officers. The same body combines several functions, including adjudication and enforcement. This leads to a lesser degree of specialization and heavier workload. It is also possible that in the prioritization and allocation of work within the judicial system, the objective of efficient and effective enforcement of civil judgment must be pursued together with other objectives, such as the administration of criminal and civil justice. In Sweden, on the other hand, the high degree of efficiency in the system is largely due to the existence of a specialized body whose main task is enforcement, including, prominently, the enforcement of civil judgments. The comparative analysis is important because it seems to suggest that the efficiency of the system is not determined by competition between enforcement agencies as opposed to monolithic systems or by the private as opposed to the public nature of the enforcement agencies. What matters, in the first place, is the specialization and dedication of the enforcement agencies. If the same agency carries out heterogeneous tasks that may conflict with each other in terms of prioritization and resource allocation, this clearly affects the efficiency of the enforcement of civil judgments. Furthermore, the heterogeneous nature of the tasks entrusted to the same agency entails a lower degree of specialization.

G. Sweden

1. The legal basis of enforcement

Swedish enforcement law is codified in the Code of Execution (*Utsökningsbalken*) and the Ordinance on Execution. Both were enacted in the early 1980s. The *Utsökningsbalken* sets out the rules for enforcement agents and the enforcement of direct monetary obligations and other obligations.

2. The structure of the enforcement agencies

In Sweden, the enforcement of judgments is entrusted to the Enforcement Authority. This is a public body in charge of the execution of court judgments, administrative decisions, arbitral awards, and other *titres exécutoires*. The Swedish Enforcement Authority (*Kronofogdemyndigheten*) and the National Tax Board (*Riksskatteverket*) are independent from the courts and bear the responsibility for enforcing judgments and debts owed to the State.

The Authority is divided into 10 regional agencies which themselves are organized in 84 offices. There is no room for enforcement of judgment debts by the creditor himself or by private organizations.

The National Tax Board is an agency of the Ministry of Finance. In each specific case, the National Tax Board confers competence on a Crown Inspector (*Kronoinspektören*) to carry out executive tasks such as seizure or eviction. The Crown Inspector is a public officer.

Apart from the enforcement of *titres exécutoires*, the Enforcement Authority also acts as claimant in public cases. This role of the Authority however is being reviewed; the alternative would be to confer this role to the Tax Authorities as representatives of the State.

The Enforcement Authority employs lawyers, executive civil servants (with a university degree), administrative, and educational staff.

There is no judicial control of the Authority's activities prior to commencement of enforcement proceedings. Coercive measures are decided by the Authority alone. Although these decisions may be appealed to a court, the measures of coercion are not suspended unless the court issues an order on interim relief. The very decision to carry out enforcement in a particular case may be subject to appeal to a court. The appeal as such, however, does not bring about a stay of the enforcement. Such stay must be specifically applied for and lies with the court's discretion.

3. The conditions for execution

Enforcement is initiated by a written or oral application for execution. The application must be founded upon a *titre exécutoire*. A *titre exécutoire* can be a court judgment, other court decisions, arbitration awards, and administrative decisions. These *titres* may be enforced immediately, ie before the time limit for appeal has lapsed. However, the enforcement may not be completed before the time limit ends and the judgment is final. For example, seizure of an asset may be made in respect of a debt founded upon a judgment by a county court (district court), notwithstanding that the time limit for appeal is still running. However, the Enforcement Authority must not sell the seized item before the time limit has expired.

In order to halt a commenced enforcement procedure, the debtor, or a third party, must appeal against the *titre exécutoire* and concurrently apply to the court for interim relief against the enforcement. The concurrent application for interim relief is necessary since the appeal as such does not stay the enforcement proceeding.

4. *The methods of enforcement*

The Enforcement Agency has very wide-ranging powers of enforcement. Among the methods of enforcement we may find both direct and indirect methods. It is important to note that it is for the Enforcement Authority to decide what kinds of assets are to be seized, and priority is given to property upon which execution is less costly and inconvenient for the debtor.

(a) Attachment of earnings
Attachment of earnings is carried out by an order addressed to the debtor's employer to pay a certain amount of the debtor's salary to the Enforcement Agency. The attachment may not extend to the entire salary on the grounds that the debtor must be able to pay for his living expenses and those of his family.

(b) Seizure of movable and immovable assets
As a result of the Enforcement Agency's wide ranging powers, it may seize any of the assets of the debtor, even by forcing entry into the debtor's home. In addition, two presumptions work in the creditor's favour. First, any movable property in the debtor's possession is presumed to be owned by the debtor unless proved otherwise. Secondly, any immovable property registered on public records is presumed to be owned by the person in favour of whom it is registered.

(c) Fines
In order to make debtors fulfil their duty of disclosure, the Enforcement Authority has the power to impose periodic penalty payments and detention.

5. Information about the debtor

The Enforcement Authority is responsible for making inquires into the debtor's assets following application for enforcement. The creditor can apply for the inquiry into the debtor's assets. S/he may either apply for a complete or a limited inquiry. The application must have as its legal basis an executable enforcement order. Every single authority is competent to make inquiries in the whole Swedish territory. The Enforcement Authority is competent to require the debtor to disclose—under oath if deemed necessary—a list of his or her assets. To force debtors to fulfil their duty of disclosure, the Authority has the power to impose sanctions for non-compliance in the form of periodic penalty payments and detention. Third parties are also required to provide information to the Enforcement Authority if legally requested to do so.

As regards the inquiries that may be carried out, the Enforcement Authority has far-reaching access to public records and computer databases. Among the records that prove to be most useful for the Authority are tax records, records and registers of share-holding in public companies, registers recording the ownership of cars, ships, weapons, real estates, and race horses, social insurance records. Powers to obtain information and identify assets suitable for execution are also exercised in the course of the subsequent steps of the enforcement procedure. The Authority may carry out a search of the debtor's home. During the search, the officers of the Authority may request the debtor to provide information about his assets and may apply coercive measures in case of non-cooperation. The officers carrying out the search may also use coercive measures to gain entry into the premises and search for assets. It goes without saying that the creditor may draw the attention of the Enforcement Authority to the existence of some particular asset.

6. The debtor's remedies

The Enforcement Authority can withdraw or modify any order and any other steps made in the enforcement proceedings. It may do so of its own motion or on application by the debtor or a third party. The procedure for the application is laid down in the Code of Execution (*Utsökningsbalken*).

In addition, the Authority's decisions can be appealed to the District Courts. Decisions by District Courts may themselves be subject to appeal to the Courts of Appeal and the Supreme Court. The grounds for appeal are: (1) third-party rights on the assets on which execution is levied; (2) procedural irregularities in the enforcement process; 3) certain substantive issues such as the fact that the debtor has paid the debt.

7. *Efficiency of the system*

The Swedish system is a monolithic, administrative-based model that allows no competition among enforcement agencies. The system is efficient. Around 75–80 per cent of civil enforcement matters are completed in less than three months and the costs seem reasonable. The efficiency of the system may follow from the following factors:

A formal time limit of one year has been established in order to complete the enforcement of civil judgments. In addition, enforcement can commence before the judgment is final.

The Enforcement Agency has a duty to obtain information about the debtor's assets. This duty is complemented by the nationwide access to public records that give a fairly accurate picture of the debtor's assets. Furthermore, the Agency has the power to require the debtor to make a declaration in respect of his assets.

There are legal presumptions that favour effective and speedy enforcement. In particular, any movable assets in the debtor's possession are presumed to be in his ownership and any asset entered in a public register is presumed to be in the ownership of the registered owner.

The Enforcement Agency is a public authority, thereby making the costs to the creditor reasonable. Costs vary depending on the likely outcome for the creditor. However, it may be argued that funding recovery on civil judgment mainly through general taxation is not efficient and excessively biased in favour of the creditor, who does not bear the risk of non-recovery of the costs of the execution, and the debtor, who does not have to pay the full loss that his non-compliance has caused to society. The bias in favour of the creditor and debtor can create wrong incentives.

The provisions applicable in case the debtor or a third party wishes to challenge a particular measure are particularly efficient. If the debtor or a third party wants to challenge any measure, there is provision not only for appeal at court level but also for an application directly to the Enforcement Agency. The administrative procedure is much more expedient than court proceedings and is a very efficient way of dealing with grievances by the third party or the debtor in clear-cut cases.

VI. CONCLUSION: BEST PRACTICES AS THE BASIS FOR CONVERGENCE

The comparative study outlined efficiencies and inefficiencies of the enforcement systems of the selected Member States. By and large, it appears that the efficiency of a system does not depend on it being based on competition between enforcement agencies or it being more or less privatized. One of the most efficient systems appears to be the Swedish system, which is

public, monolithic, and uncompetitive. Another system which is rather efficient is the Austrian system, which is, again, public, monolithic, and non-
competitive. On the other hand, the French system, which is private,
monolithic, and competitive, is not fully efficient given the difficulties in
obtaining accurate information about the debtor's assets.

If the categories of *public vs private* and *competitive vs non-competitive*
have not produced the expected results in terms of higher efficiency of
private, pluralistic, and competitive systems, the analysis of the category of
monolithic vs pluralistic systems has shown that monolithic systems are
generally more efficient. Furthermore, the categories of *public vs private*
and *competitive vs non-competitive* have also proven to be useful in focusing the analysis on the nature of the enforcement agency and the structure
of the system as a whole. As a result of the comparative analysis, a number
of best practices in the selected Member States have been identified that
may serve as basis for convergence. These are set out in the following paragraphs.

The problem of obtaining information about the debtor's assets is
perceived as a key issue in all the selected Member States. Best enforcement
practices rely on specialized bodies, whose main responsibility is the
enforcement of judgments, being able to rely on publicly held up-to-date
information about the debtor's assets or employment. Systems that rely on
compelled declarations by the debtors, such as the English and the German,
are generally not considered to be efficient. This is because the procedure to
compel the debtor to make a declaration as to his assets is surrounded with
safeguards and burdensome, and non-compliance with the duty to render
the declaration may be difficult to enforce. It is much more efficient to
obtain reliable information at the very early stages of the enforcement
proceedings regardless of the voluntary or compelled cooperation of the
debtor.

Equally inefficient seems to be the French system. In France, the task of
conducting an investigation about the debtor's assets has been entrusted to
the *Procureur de la République*, a public authority whose primary function
is not to secure the enforcement of judgments. The workload of the office
of the public prosecutor impairs a speedy and effective enquiry about
debtor's assets. Another significant element generating inefficiency is that
there is no comprehensive and readily available information in possession
of public authorities that can be used for the purposes of enforcement. By
contrast, efficient systems such as the Swedish and the Austrian rely on
publicly-held information such as tax records in Sweden and details of the
debtor's employer held by the *Hauptverband der österreichischen
Sozialversicherungsträger* in Austria. Therefore, it appears that best practices in obtaining information about the debtor's assets must also rely on
existing public and private databases that are not regulated by enforcement

law and only become relevant to enforcement indirectly when the data in question are needed to identify assets suitable for execution. This is a potential problem in the process of harmonization or convergence of enforcement law in this area since harmonization or convergence depend, to a significant degree, on factors extraneous to the enforcement process.

The *astreinte*, the periodic penalty payment aimed to pressurize the debtor to pay his debt in order to avoid incurring even greater financial penalties, is a particularly effective enforcement method. The analysis of the French and Dutch system shows that a power of the enforcement agency to impose periodic penalty payments is a useful complement of the system. However, it must be stressed that an efficient enforcement system must include the *astreinte* in the panoply of enforcement methods but should not rely on the *astreinte* as its principal enforcement method. The *astreinte* is particularly appropriate: for the enforcement of non-monetary judgments, including orders for specific performance. The *astreinte* in these circumstances is key to ensuring that the legal system is efficient. If the judgment orders the debtor to behave in a certain way that cannot be enforced regardless of its active cooperation, there is no other way to secure enforcement of the specific performance than putting pressure on the debtor by threatening a consequence for non-performance that outweighs its perceived benefits. In some circumstances, it may not be sufficient to substitute the monetary value of the non-performance or of the creditor's loss for the obligation of specific performance. In this is the case, it appears that the *astreinte* is a necessary complement of the system. As regards the enforcement of monetary judgment, the *astreinte* may be particularly effective against wealthy debtors willing to carry out a balancing exercise weighing the benefits and adverse consequences of non-performance. If the debtor has insufficient assets, the *astreinte* may not be appropriate and even counterproductive.

It is not easy to identify, in terms of best practices, absolute or relative advantages of *monolithic v pluralistic* systems and of *competitive v non-competitive* systems. The results of the study, however, seem to suggest that monolithic systems perform better than pluralistic systems. There are advantages in a public, monolithic, non-competitive system such as the Swedish regime or in a private, monolithic, competitive system such as the French model, over a pluralistic system such as the English system. A monolithic system is more focused in terms of expertise and resources. Furthermore, it is more user-friendly and conducive to cooperation with enforcement agencies of other Member States.

As regards *competitive vs non-competitive* systems, it is not possible to identify the superior model. The Swedish model, which is non-competitive, performs at least as well as the French model, which is competitive. Furthermore, where inefficiencies have been identified in competitive systems, such inefficiencies do not relate to the lack of competition. For instance, in the French model, a major problem is the difficulty in obtaining information about the debtor's assets. This is not caused by the competitive nature of the system but rather by the inefficiency of the public authority entrusted with the task of conducting investigations about the debtor's assets.

The dichotomy *public v private* does not produce a clear outcome in terms of efficiencies and best practices. In particular, some public systems perform well, such as the Swedish model, while others, such as the Spanish one, do not. This could be explained by the degree of specialization of the enforcement agency. When the enforcement agency has as its main task the enforcement of judgments, this allows focusing resources, building up expertise, and prioritizing effectively enforcement proceedings according to factors endogenous to the enforcement process. This is clearly the case in Sweden, where the Swedish Enforcement Authority performs well because its main focus is the enforcement of judgments, orders, and other decisions. The problem with entrusting the enforcement of judgment to the courts is that courts in the EU Member States generally have a very heavy workload which includes matters other than enforcement. The prioritization of enforcement proceedings will be made according to factors that are largely exogenous to the enforcement process. Furthermore, the enforcement of civil judgments may not be the main focus of the administration of justice that is often concerned with criminal and civil cases perceived by the Government departments responsible for judicial affairs, the judiciary, and the public opinion to be more important than the enforcement of civil judgments. In terms of training, specialization, allocation of resources, and prioritization, the enforcement of civil judgments is generally not the key concern. This may be one of the reasons why the German and the Spanish court-based systems do not perform in a way that is perceived to be adequately efficient. Therefore, it would appear that, regardless of the dichotomy *public v private*, a system performs better if enforcement is entrusted to agencies that specialize in enforcement and whose main task is the enforcement of judgments.

Finally, in relation to remedies, the comparative study reveals a tendency of debtor's and third party's remedies towards excessive complexity and fragmentation. Convergence in this area would appear to be extremely difficult although simplification of the law in this area at national level based on some common principles would have clear benefits. The analysis of the enforcement practices in the selected Member States points to best practices that may be adopted as a basis for common principles in the area of remedies. A particularly interesting area for consideration may be the introduction of an expeditious procedure in the form of an administrative complaint to deal with straightforward cases out of court. Many Member

States provide for a procedure which is meant to be 'summary' or 'expedited' to deal with certain enforcement disputes in respect of which the application of the ordinary rules of procedure would appear to be too burdensome. However, the comparative analysis and empirical evidence shows that court procedure is rarely really 'summary' or 'expedited'. The very fact that the procedure is before the court generates complexities and costs. The existence of an out-of-court procedure would appear a pre-requisite for real expedition and cost-savings to be achieved. The function of such a procedure would be to avoid unnecessary or dilatory litigation of simple cases. Because civil rights or obligations are affected in enforcement proceedings, proceedings before the courts may not be excluded or unduly delayed. However, several options remain open: (1) an informal administrative, arbitral, or ADR procedure by agreement of the parties; (2) informal administrative, arbitral, or ADR procedure, compliance with which is not strictly mandatory but can be sanctioned by the judge in court proceedings at his discretion when giving case management directions or awarding costs; (3) an informal administrative, arbitral, or ADR procedure, compliance with which is by law a condition of admissibility of court proceedings relating to the same matters.

In conclusion, the comparative analysis has shown that there is little common ground in the EU Member States when it comes to enforcement law. Paradoxically, this can be seen as a clear advantage at this early stage of EU approximation and harmonization. Each jurisdiction offers very different approaches of law enforcement. Thus, the European Union inherits a great number of conceivable possibilities to help the judgment creditor to his or her rights and at the same time to prevent the debtor from undue constraints. On the other hand, the fragmentation leads to losses of efficiency and may lead to distortions in the common market. The comparative study demonstrates that there is no superiority of private, pluralistic, and competitive systems over public, monolithic, and non-competitive systems. However, monolithic systems, competitive and non-competitive, perform better than pluralistic systems and non court-based systems, whether public or private, perform better than court systems owing to factors relating to specialization, resources, and prioritization. The study has identified best practices that are suitable as a basis for convergence or harmonization. It is suggested that harmonization could take place as regards well-defined problem-areas that are crucial to the efficiency of the systems and whose inefficiency risks creating significant distortions in the common market. The comparative analysis points to three areas that could be suitable and where best practices can be identified as a basis for harmonization: (1) disclosure of debtor's assets; (2) *astreintes*; (3) common principles in the field of remedies for the debtor as discussed under heading (6) in the seven country sections.

PART II

NATIONAL REPORTS

CHAPTER 6

AUSTRIA

Professor Paul Oberhammer[1]

I. INTRODUCTION

A. *The* Exekutionsordnung

Austrian enforcement law[2] is codified in the *Exekutionsordnung* (Execution Code) of 27th May 1896,[3] hereinafter referred to as the *EO*. It deals with the enforcement of the instruments stipulated in §1 of the *EO*. These include not only the decisions of civil courts and arbitral tribunals but also certain decisions on monetary claims of criminal courts, administrative authorities, social insurance institutions as well as enforceable notarial instruments. Therefore, unlike in German law, civil procedure and enforcement are not jointly governed in one Act. However, the *Zivilprozessordnung* (Code of Civil Procedure) was drafted and enacted together with the *EO*. These two Acts are linked in that pursuant to §78 of the *EO* the general provisions of the Code of Civil Procedure governing parties, proceedings and oral hearings, evidence, the taking of evidence and the individual means of evidence, judicial orders and directions and appeals by way of *Rekurs* (recourse) apply even in enforcement law. According to case law it is also possible to apply some other provisions of the Code of Civil Procedure to enforcement matters analogously.[4] Enforcement law is

---

[1] Professor of Swiss and International Civil Procedure, Enforcement, Insolvency, Civil and Business Law, Zurich University, Switzerland.

[2] As is the case in many small countries, there is not very much literature in Austria about enforcement law. The *Kommentar zur Exekutionsordnug* (2000) P Angst (ed) offers an extensive commentary which is up-to-date; another commentary on the *EO*, edited by A Burgstaller and A Deixler-Hübner, is currently published in separate instalments. Otherwise there are currently only two textbooks which are up-to-date: M Neumayr *Exekutionsrecht* (2004) and W Rechberger and P Oberhammer *Exekutionsrecht* (2002). Note should also be taken of the slightly older textbooks by *Holzhammer*, Österreichisches Zwangsvollstreckungsrecht[4] (1993) and W Rechberger and D Simotta *Exekutionsverfahren* (1992). Furthermore, an overview of court decisions can be gleaned from PP Angst, W Jakusch, and *Pimmer, Exekutionsordnung samt Einführungsgesetz, Nebengesetzen und sonstigen einschlägigen Vorschriften* (1995) and E Feil *Exekutionsordnung* (1997). There does not appear to be any non-German literature on the topic.

[3] RGBl 1896/79.

[4] Cf, eg, the Oberster Gerichtshof (Supreme Court), EvBl 1994/60 = JBl 1994, 478.

governed almost exclusively by the *EO*; in addition a few provisions of enforcement law are found in secondary legislation, but these are not relevant for this article since they are nearly all more technical in nature.[5]

The *EO* governs two fundamentally different areas of law, on the one hand enforcement law (§§1–377 of the *EO*) and on the other hand the law of injunctions (§§378–404 of the *EO*). The section on enforcement law is divided into three parts: 'General Provisions' (§§1–86 of the *EO*), 'The Enforcement of Money Debts' (§§ 87–345 of the *EO*) and 'Enforcement to Compel an Act or Restraint' (§§346–69 of the *EO*). The section on 'Security' (§§370–404 of the *EO*) governs not only injunctions but also the levying of execution as security for money debts (§§370–7 of the *EO*). This levying of execution as security for money debts actually falls under enforcement law; these provisions must be seen against the background that Austrian law does not recognize the concept of the provisional enforceability of judgments or instruments (as recognized under German law). §§370 of the *EO* therefore provides a possibility of enforcing certain judgments or instruments (which have not yet become executable) until the creditor has obtained security (but not payment).[6]

The general part of the *EO* also contains provisions on the recognition of foreign judgments and their endorsement as being enforceable. The reason for this is that, until the *EO* was amended in 1995,[7] Austrian law did not recognize a specific (separate) *exequatur* procedure. Rather, there was a particular procedure for granting a warrant of execution[8] (as part of the enforcement procedure itself) in the case of foreign judgments or instruments, which (put simply) also had the function of endorsing the judgment or instrument as being enforceable. An separate *exequatur* procedure was introduced by the 1995 *EO* amending statute because of Austria's accession to the Lugano Convention and the consequent necessary amendments to Austrian law to bring it in line with European civil procedure. When this was done, the tradition was maintained of taking up the provisions on recognition and the endorsement of enforceability of foreign judgments in the law of enforcement, which is where, until then, the special provisions

---

[5] Cf the overview on this in W Rechberger and P Oberhammer *Exekutionsrecht* (2002), margin no 9.

[6] The fact that Austrian enforcement law does not know the concept of provisional enforceability is sometimes seen as showing a significant difference between German and Austrian law. In practice, however, the legal consequences of provisional enforceability under German law and execution for security under Austrian law are very often identical. The main difference is that under Austrian law it is possible to levy execution upon an instrument which has not yet become finally and absolutely enforceable only in order to secure money debts; if one considers that there is, however, also the possibility of an injunction for securing the satisfaction of other claims, the practical consequence is that the differences are levelled out even further.

[7] Cf I.C.1. below.

[8] Cf III.A.below.

governing the actual procedure for enforcing foreign judgments were to be found.

B. *Substantive foundations of and models for the legislation*

When the *EO* entered into force on 1 January 1898 it superseded the provisions on enforcement contained in the *Allgemeine Gerichtsordnung* (General Judicature Code) of 1781.[9] The latter was by then already completely outdated and, moreover, only fragmentary. The substantive sources which the legislator drew upon at the time were largely those upon which the whole of Austrian civil procedure was based. First, of course, the hitherto legal status and legal practice were used as a basis. As was the case with civil procedural law as a whole—which was completely re-codified at the time—the entry into force of the *EO* was a significant turning point in the Austrian procedural system, based primarily on the reception of the German Code of Civil Procedure and the individual influence of *Franz Klein*, the 'father' of Austrian legislation on civil procedure. Although it was *Klein's* philosophy, based on economic efficiency and social balance (and also most clearly influenced by the ideology of a 'strong state'), which helped him to achieve a breakthrough on a number of issues, also concerning enforcement law,[10] one should not underestimate the influence which German law had. Nevertheless, German and Austrian law are not as similar in the field of enforcement law as they are for example in commercial and company law, where often it is only the detail which differs. In enforcement law the differences begin with the very structure of the procedure which is different from German enforcement proceedings due to the fact that under Austrian law every enforcement first requires a warrant of execution to be ordered by the court (*Exekutionsbewilligungsbeschluss*).[11] This gives rise to numerous fundamental differences, for example differences in the function of the *Gerichtsvollzieher* (court bailiff)[12] or the remedies available in the enforcement procedure.[13] In Austrian enforcement practice references to German cases or German literature are therefore rare; this is of course different in academic literature and in the legislation, where German law is frequently drawn upon or used as a model.

---

[9] Cf W Rechberger 'Franz Klein und das Exekutionsrecht' in H Hofmeister (ed) *Forschungsband Franz Klein* (1988) 119; A Konecny 'Die *Exekutionsordnung* nach 100 Jahren' in G Mayr (ed) *100 Jahre österreichische Zivilprozeßgesetze* (1998) 95.

[10] For a detailed commentary on this cf W Rechberger 'Franz Klein und Exekutionsrecht' 119.

[11] Cf III.A. below.

[12] Cf II.C. below.

[13] Cf III below.

C. Recent Reforms

1. General

The basic structure of Austrian enforcement law has not changed since the *EO* entered into force on 1 January 1898, despite the fact that the *EO* was, of course, amended numerous times, especially in 1991,[14] 1995,[15] 2000,[16] and 2003[17] when numerous aspects were reformed. This must be seen against the background that the Austrian legislature has chosen to take a substantially 'evolutionary' approach in this field over the last decades. At the centre of the legal-political reform the debate was largely how to improve existing law (within the given system) with a great number of solutions concentrating on details and which were derived mainly from reports from practice, but there was no attempt to change the system itself with regard to any fundamental issues. This approach is typical for the legislature in the field of procedural law over the last few decades. Also in the field of civil trial proceedings and insolvency law there have been numerous individual amending statutes, each of which mainly tried to implement insight gained from practical experience by making changes to details.

By contrast there has been a 'revolutionary' development in the Austrian civil judicature in the last two decades brought about by the immense use of modern information technology. The Austrian legislature has often correctly assumed that increased efficiency in court proceedings can be achieved especially by using information technology for dealing with matters which arise *en masse* in the same form. The integration of such technical innovations in the court process has, of course, meant that numerous adjustments have had to be made at statute level. In the context of enforcement law, particular mention of the simplified procedure for granting a warrant of execution (*vereinfachtes Bewilligungsverfahren*), introduced by the 1995 *EO* amending statute,[18] should be made. In connection with enforcement law, a further major development in trial procedural law should be noted. The majority of civil judicially enforceable instruments derive from payment orders in *Mahnverfahren*[19] (*ex parte* orders for payment) aided by automated technology. This instrument created within the framework of the 1983 civil procedure amending statute and the legislation based on that (in particular the Ordinance on Electronic Transactions[20] and the 1995 *EO* amending statute) ensured that in the great majority of payment claims the creditors can initially apply online for

---

[14] BGBl 1991/628.
[16] BGBl I 2000/59.
[18] Cf I.C.3.
[19] Cf J Bosina and M Schneider *Das neue Mahnverfahren und die ADV-Drittschuldneranfrage* (1987).
[20] BGBl 1995/559.

[15] BGBl 1995/519.
[17] BGBl I 2003/31.

a payment order to be issued against the debtor. In the event that the debtor does not appeal against the payment order within the time limit, the payment order becomes enforceable. Following this, the creditor can again apply online for enforcement, whereby the warrant of execution (*Exekutionsbewilligung*) is granted without hearing the debtor. This development has contributed towards the efficiency of debt collection under Austrian law to a much greater extent than can be explained in an article about its legal basis.

2. The reform of execution upon money claims

At the centre of the 1991 *EO* amending statute was the legal reform of the execution upon money claims.[21] This amending statute must be seen against the background that major parts of the most important means of this type of enforcement—namely the attachment of earnings—had been governed by a separate statute (enacted during the German occupation of Austria) since 1940.[22] In 1991 the provisions on this subject were re-integrated into the *EO*. The strong influence which German law had on the substantive content was, however, maintained, whilst at the same time new developments in Germany were also absorbed. Accordingly, it is precisely the 'social' provisions on the protection against attachment in proceedings for the attachment of earnings which are today still almost the same as the German provisions.[23] A particular aim of the reform was also to curb the attachment of movable property in favour of the attachment of earnings.

A change in this type of enforcement which was of particular practical significance was already brought about by the civil procedure amendments

---

[21] Cf O Hagen 'Zur Reform der Lohnpfändung' *DRdA* 1991, 329; F Mohr 'Die neue Lohnpfändung', *EO-Novelle 1991* (1991); G Mayr *Die Exekutionsordnungs-Novelle 1991* (1992); H Fink and A Schmidt *Handbuch zur Lohnpfändung* (1995). In the course of this amending statute the provisions on the consequences of futile enforcement measures were amended. Until then the archaic institution of an *Offenbarungseid* (oath of disclosure) still existed, where, if enforcement measures for delivery up of a thing failed or the attachment of movable property failed or the enforcement upon a money debt failed the debtor had to swear to a list of his assets (or in practice often to the fact that he had no assets) in an oral hearing before the judge. This oath has been replaced by a list of assets certified on a form presented to the debtor by the court bailiff; this declaration can be compelled by a prison sentence, false statements can render the debtor liable to prosecution. In practice, though, the enforcement of such measures is hardly ever necessary; it almost never occurs that a debtor does not fill out the form presented to him by the court bailiff.

[22] The provisions governing protection from execution originally contained in the *EO* were substituted by the *Lohnpfändungsverordnung* (Ordinance on the Attachment of Wages) in 1940; after the Second World War ended these continued to apply (with several changes) in Austria and were not replaced until the *Lohnpfändungsgesetz* (Act on the Attachment of Wages) in 1955 (BGBl 1955/51).

[23] Cf the detailed commentary by P Oberhammer in P Angst (ed) *Kommentar zur Exekutionsordnung* (2000), commentary on §§290 of the *EO*.

of 1986.[24] A problem which is typical when the creditor is seeking the attachment of earnings is the fact that the creditor does not know who the debtor's employer is. Already when civil procedure was reformed in 1983[25] the possibility of filing an application for attachment without naming the debtor's employer was created. The debtor was then asked to disclose who his employer was. However, this measure did not succeed. In only about 6 per cent of cases did the debtor actually disclose the name of his employer.[26] The 1986 amendment created a model which has functioned successfully until the present day. In his application for an attachment order, the creditor only has to claim that the debtor is entitled to income which can be attached; in addition he must state the debtor's date of birth. On this basis the court then requests the *Hauptverband der österreichischen Sozialversicherungsträger* (Central Association of Austrian Social Insurance Institutions) to disclose who the debtor's employer is; the communication between the court and the *Hauptverband* is computer-aided and is therefore relatively quick.[27] Once the court has received the information about the debtor's employment, his income out of that employment is attached automatically without the creditor having to file any further request. This possibility has meant that, provided one is in legal employment, it is no longer possible in Austria to avoid enforcement; as a consequence it is no longer necessary for the creditor to obtain information 'privately'.[28] This has not caused any constitutional concerns in Austria with regard to the basic right of the protection of personal data.[29]

3. Simplified grant of a warrant of execution

The 1995 *EO* amending statute first introduced substantial changes to the procedure for granting a warrant of execution (*Exekutionsbewilligungsverfahren*). This must be understood against the background that in Austria every enforcement action requires a court order for a warrant of execution.[30] Until the 1995 *EO* amending statute (and even today if the value of the

---

[24] BGBl 1986/71.   [25] BGBl 1983/135.

[26] J Bosina and M Schneider *Das neue Mahnverfahren und die ADV-Drittschuldneranfrage* (1987) 231.

[27] Cf F Mohr 'Anfrage an den Hauptverband bei Gehaltsexekution' *RdW* 1988, 91.

[28] This model must be seen against the background that every employee in Austria is obliged to be insured with certain social insurance institutions and as a consequence these social insurance institutions have data about every employment relationship. In addition, anyone who lives in Austria is subject to a statutory duty to register with the authorities; pursuant to §294(3) of the *EO* the registration authorities are under an obligation to inform anyone who presents them with a judicially enforceable instrument of the debtor's date of birth as stated in the register.

[29] Cf D Simotta, 'Einige Probleme des Datenschutzes im Zivilverfahrensrecht' *ÖJZ* 1993, 842 .

[30] Cf III.A.

matter in dispute is more than EUR 10,000) it was necessary to submit the judicially enforceable instrument with the application for a warrant of execution. The court competent for enforcement matters (usually therefore the *Rechtspfleger*)[31] then had to examine whether the judicially enforceable instrument and the application for enforcement corresponded with one another. This process gave rise to two fundamental practical problems. First, the number of cases in which the outcome of this examination of the judicially enforceable instrument was that the application had to be denied, either in whole or part, was extremely small. A study carried out by the Federal Ministry of Justice found that it was only 1.04 per cent of all cases.[32] Examination of the judicially enforceable instrument, which was usually futile, tied up significant amounts of working capacity. Secondly, the duty to present the judicially enforceable instrument was also an obstacle to the possibility which was planned at the time (and which is already reality today) of filing applications for enforcement online. The new simplified procedure for granting a warrant of execution introduced by the 1995 *EO* amending statute removed the requirement to present the judicially enforceable instrument with the application for enforcement in certain cases. The simplified procedure for granting a warrant of execution can be applied in particular to all cases in which the creditor is enforcing a monetary claim where the debt to be collected does not exceed EUR 10,000; execution upon immovable property is excluded (§54b of the *EO*); this new regulation therefore covers the great majority of enforcement procedures. The debtor is given an opportunity pursuant to §54c of the *EO* to raise a specific remedy (the so-called *Einspruch*) against the warrant of execution within 14 days of its service. This new remedy, introduced by the 1995 *EO* amending statute, can only be exercised on the ground that there is no judicially enforceable instrument corresponding with the warrant of execution or if the judicially enforceable instrument does not correspond with the details stated in the application for the warrant of execution. Such an examination of compatibility between the judicially enforceable instrument and the application for enforcement therefore now only takes place if a debtor appeals. This simplified procedure has proved to be excellent in practice; nowadays the percentage of such remedies based on the non-compatibility of the enforceable instrument and the warrant of execution is less than 1 per cent of all cases.[33] The possibility thereby created of making applications for execution online and of granting such applications in a computer-aided process has meant substantial simplification and less work for the parties as well as the courts.[34]

---

[31] Cf II.B.
[32] Bundesministerium für Justiz (ed) *ADV-Exekutionsverfahren* (1995) 417.
[33] Cf A Konecny *Die Exekutionsordnung nach 100 Jahren* 115.
[34] This new change is particularly based on extensive preparatory scientific work by A

4. The reform of execution upon movable property

The legislator of the *EO* paid particular attention to the levying of execution upon immovable property in the section of enforcement law containing the special provisions; already when the *EO* entered into force the criticism was made that it was too focused on the interests of rural land owners and not enough by the interests of the urban population.[35] By contrast the execution upon movable property (as a method of enforcing money claims) was governed only rather cursorily; two weak points were particularly criticized. First, the attachment of movable goods was governed only very superficially, the *EO* hardly mentioning what powers the *Gerichtsvollzieher* (court bailiff) had in the preliminary stage of attachment (in particular his powers to trace attachable assets). Secondly, the provisions on realising proceeds from attached movable assets were not very satisfactory; in principle, attached goods had to be sold 'on the spot' (ie at the debtor's place of residence or business), which, in the course of time, was, on the one hand, considered unreasonable hardship for the debtor and, on the other hand, had negative consequences on the value realized.[36]

With the 'trace and seizure process' (*Auffindungs- und Zugriffs-verfahren*) introduced by the 1995 *EO* amending statute the powers of the court bailiff with regard to the attachment of movable goods were significantly extended. Until then numerous actions by the court bailiff, necessary for successful execution upon movable goods, required an application and the court bailiff was only permitted to act upon a corresponding order of the court. Since then the court bailiff must (to put it simply) himself try to attach goods successfully on the basis of very 'generally' drafted warrants of execution.[37] At the same time the court bailiff has been given greater powers for collecting payments from debtors. In order to encourage the debtor to make voluntary payments a possibility was created whereby the realization of attached goods could be suspended if corresponding payments were made; the court bailiff was also given power to make

Konecny: cf A Konecny 'Automationsunterstützte Datenverarbeitung im Exekutionsverfahren' in *Bundesministerium für Justiz* (ed) ADV-Exekutionsverfahren (1995) 65; on the introduction of the simplified procedure for the grant of a warrant of execution cf T Klicka and I Albrecht *Die EO-Novelle 1995—Änderungen im allgemeinen Teil, ecolex* 1995, 707; F Mohr 'Vereinfachtes Bewilligungsverfahren und andere am 1.10.1995 in Kraft getretene Bestimmungen der EO-Novelle 1995', *ÖJZ* 1995, 889; B Kloiber 'Die Exekutionsordnung-Novelle 1995. Ein Überblick über die mit 1.10.1995 in Kraft getretenen Änderungen' *ÖA* 1996, 2.

[35] Cf W Rechberger *Franz Klein und das Exekutionsrecht* 127.

[36] Cf A Konecny, *Die Exekutionsordnung nach 100 Jahren* 105; of course the introduction of so-called auction houses—where the courts, through the court bailiff, sold the attached goods—had brought some improvement in this regard earlier on; Cf H Kollroß, 'Zur mangelnden Wirksamkeit der Fahrnizexekution' *GZ* 1929, 137.

[37] Cf B Kloiber 'Das Auffindungs- und Zugriffsverfahren' *ZIK* 1996, 80.

arrangements for payment in instalments to be agreed between the creditor and the debtor.[38] These new provisions have led to a substantial increase in the payments made by debtors to the court bailiffs.[39]

The powers of the court bailiff were also extended with regard to the sale of attached goods; it is now up to him to decide where the sale should take place; in so doing, more and more responsibilities have been outsourced to private auction houses.[40] This has enhanced the efficiency of enforcement, as generally the profits from the sale in such auction houses are much higher than those attained in sales on the spot.

The *Exekutionsordnungs-Novelle* 2003 (2003 *EO* amending statute) incorporates these provisions on the 'new' powers of the court bailiff into the general part of the *EO*. Therefore, these powers are no longer restricted to the enforcement upon movable property. Therefore, the 'trace and seizure process' can henceforth also take place in enforcement procedures concerning the surrender of movable assets.[41]

5. The reform of execution upon immovable assets

Finally, the 2000 *EO* amending statute introduced (in addition to a radical reform of the *exequatur* procedure for foreign judicially enforceable instruments, which had only been introduced by the 1995 *EO* amending statute) numerous amendments regarding the execution upon immovable assets. These were mainly simplifications of this extremely complex method of execution brought about by modifying details. These detailed changes could only be explained if the reader had a sound understanding of this method of execution and the rules governing it prior to the amending statute.[42]

D. The methods of execution for enforcing money debts

1. Overview of the methods of execution

The catalogue of the methods of enforcement and assets upon which

---

[38] Cf P Oberhammer 'Fahrnisverwertung nach der EO-Novelle 1995: Grundsätzliche Neuerungen im Verwertungsverfahren' *ZIK* 1996, 84.

[39] According to E Schneider and H Roth 'Eine Leistungsschau des österreichischen Zivilprozesses anhand der Zahlen des Jahres 1996' in Bundesministerium für Justiz, P Lewisch and W Rechberger (eds) *100 Jahre ZPO. Ökonomische Analyse des Zivilprozesses* (1998) 18.

[40] Cf P Oberhammer 'Die Fahrnisverwertung nach der EO-Novelle 1995: Das Verkaufsverfahren von der Bestimmung des Versteigerungstermines bis zur Ausfolgung des Erlöses' *ZIK* 1996, 121.

[41] Cf W Jakusch Die EO-Novelle 2003, ÖJZ 2004, 201 (203).

[42] Cf F Mohr 'Zwangsversteigerung einer Liegenschaft' in *Festschrift für Robert Dittrich* (2000) 493; F Mohr *Die neue Zwangsversteigerung. EO-Novelle 2000* (2000); F Mohr *Exekutionsordnungs*-Novelle 2000, ecolex 2000, 641; F Mohr 'Die Zwangsversteigerung einer Liegenschaft nach der *Exekutionsordnung*-Novelle 2000', Immolex 2000, 275.

execution can be levied is regulated in the section on the enforcement of money debts (§§87–345 of the *EO*) such that execution can be levied upon practically every exploitable asset.

There are three methods of execution upon immovable property. With the *Zwangshypothek* (compulsory mortgage) the creditor is not satisfied but is secured by means of a *Hypothek* (mortgage) entered in the land register in his favour. He is thus granted priority over other creditors (not yet secured by a prior right *in rem*) in any subsequent execution proceedings; this method of execution is completed with the entry of the mortgage in the land register. By contrast, the *Zwangsverwaltung* (compulsory administration) and *Zwangsversteigerung* (compulsory sale) of real property do lead to the creditor being satisfied.

When execution is levied upon movable property, the movable property is first attached by the *Gerichtsvollzieher* (court bailiff). The property is then sold at auction or either by the court bailiff 'on the spot', but much more frequently in the court auction house or through private auctioneers; in special cases it is possible to realize the proceeds by some different method, for instance by private contract by the court bailiff or by the sale of securities through a bank authorised by the court bailiff. When execution is levied upon money claims, attachment is ordered by the court. By this order, the garnishee is thereby prohibited from making payment to the debtor and the debtor is restrained from making any disposal. Such receivables are then usually realized in practice by transferring the receivable to the creditor for collection. The creditor can then demand payment from the garnishee, whereby the garnishee—for instance the debtor's employer—has to calculate himself how much of the receivable is attachable. There are analogous provisions for levying execution upon claims for the surrender of movable and immovable tangible assets.

Compared internationally, there are particularly detailed provisions on the 'levying of execution upon other assets'. These provisions (§§330–45 of the *EO*) are catch-all clauses for assets which are not covered by the above-mentioned methods of enforcement. A provision which is peculiar to Austrian enforcement law is §341 of the *EO* which provides for execution to be levied by means of a business being placed under receivership. In this context the court has power to appoint a receiver—outside insolvency—to manage the debtor company. The receiver then pays the profit earned to the creditor.[43]

---

[43] The *EO* legislator had high expectations from introducing this, at the time 'modern', method of execution, as it was of the opinion that this method would achieve higher proceeds than breaking up the business in levying execution upon individual business assets (and would at the same time satisfy the concept of giving debtors greater protection). In practice, however, this method of execution has proved to be a futile instrument in most especially because the legislator's expectations have, by and large, proved to be unrealistic from an economic point of view. Cf P Oberhammer, 'Unternehmen, Gesamtsache, Unternehmenszubehör- und Pfändung', in *Festschrift für Heinz Krejci* (2001) 281.

2. *Relationship between the various methods of enforcement*

In principle, when enforcing money claims, it is a matter for the creditor to choose the property upon which execution is levied and the method of execution. The concept of a *gradus executionis* (a statutorily prescribed sequence of methods of execution) is basically unknown to Austrian law. Nevertheless, certain elements of this concept have been introduced into the *EO*:

Until the *EO* entered into force in 1898 execution upon money claims was effected by auctioning the claim. This wholly inefficient method of execution is now only of residual use, in those cases where it is not possible to transfer the claim to the creditor (cf. §319 of the *EO*); in practice this method of execution no longer plays a role. In addition there are some other provisions under Austrian law, ordering such a sequence of the methods of execution when money claims are enforced. The warrant of execution can, for a start, be restricted to certain methods of execution, if the application for execution clearly shows that one or more of the methods of execution applied for will suffice to satisfy the creditor according to §14 (1) of the *EO*. Upon the application of the debtor the compulsory sale of real property, which has been applied for and in respect of which a warrant has been granted, can be suspended and instead receivership can be ordered, if the average annual excess of proceeds from administrating the real property to be auctioned is sufficient to satisfy the creditor (§201 of the *EO*). This provision, which appeared to be particularly important to *Franz Klein*,[44] is, in practice, of little importance nowadays; though it does have a preventative character in terms of 'arbitrary' applications for execution because of petty claims and this preventative character should not be underestimated.

A number of provisions nowadays try to curb execution upon movable assets in favour of execution upon money claims (in particular the attachment of earnings). The thinking behind these provisions is that the attachment of earnings is usually the 'milder' method and, moreover, that one can usually expect greater proceeds from this method of enforcement.[45] In

---

[44] Cf W Rechberger *Franz Klein und das Exekutionsrecht* 123.

[45] This notion, which was particularly emphasized by the legislator of the 1991 *EO* amending statute, is in some aspects questionable: It proceeds from the fact that attachment of earnings are usually significantly higher than proceeds from execution levied upon movable assets; it might also be true that the attachment of movable assets in the debtor's home is felt to be 'more severe' than mere monthly deductions from the debtor's salary. However, on the one hand there is a certain tendency for employers to dismiss employees whose salaries are attached; on the other hand, practice shows that execution levied upon movable assets has not been curbed to the extent hoped by the legislator. One should realize that execution levied upon movable assets also exerts pressure, which should not be underestimated, on the debtor to satisfy the creditor voluntarily. Cf A Konecny *Die Exekutionsordnung nach 100 Jahren* 117; P Oberhammer 'Fahrnisverwertung nach der EO-Novelle 1995: Grundsätzliche Neuerungen im Verwertungsverfahren' ZIK 1996, 84.

detail, the *EO* has the following provisions in this connection. The attachment of earnings pursuant to §294 a of the *EO*—that is, in cases where the creditor does not know who the employer is[46]—cannot be applied for after a warrant of execution has been granted for execution upon movable assets until one year has elapsed since the warrant of execution was issued, or until the creditor provides prima facie evidence that he learned of the existence of recurring money claims only after he had applied for a warrant of execution upon movable assets (§14 (3) of the *EO*). If the creditor levies execution upon movable assets and money claims at the same time and because of the same debt, the sale of the attached goods must be suspended *ex officio*, if the proceeds from the execution upon the money claims will, in all probability, lead to the creditor being completely satisfied within one year (§264 a of the *EO*). In the event that execution upon a salary claim, or other existing periodic money claim, is pending, a warrant of execution upon movable assets in order to collect the same debt may be granted, but executed only if execution pursuant to §294 a of the *EO* (ie attachment of earnings in cases where the employer is not known) has failed because the *Hauptverband der Sozialversicherungsträger* (Central Association of Social Insurance Institutions) was unable to give a positive answer to the request about a possible employer, or if the employer (who is under an obligation to provide the creditor with information) does not acknowledge the debt as justified or fails to give a declaration or if the creditor applies for execution to be levied upon the movable property after receiving the employer's declaration (§14(2) of the *EO*).

3. Enforcement Agents

(a) The Court/Judge

Compared internationally, the Austrian enforcement procedure is structured in a very 'court-oriented' way. An indication of this is especially that every execution procedure has to be instituted by a court order—the order of a warrant of execution *(Exekutionsbewilligungsbeschluss)*.[47] Unlike in the German procedure for the grant of a court's certificate of enforceability *(Vollstreckungsklausel)*, this order is concerned not (only) with the enforceability of the instrument, but rather with commencing the actual enforcement procedure. Ever since the 1995 *EO* amending statute only the *Bezirksgerichte* (district courts), being the courts competent for enforcement matters, have had the competence to grant warrants of execution; these are the lowest courts in the court system. The court which passed the judgment or issued the instrument to be enforced therefore no longer has any competence in the execution proceedings. The district courts are also

---

[46] Cf C.2. above.   [47] Cf III.A. below.

competent for every other order in the execution process. This concentration of the execution process on the district courts should not, however, be misunderstood as being a 'centralization' of enforcement measures. In particular, several courts out of the 147 Austrian *Bezirksgerichte* (district courts) acting in enforcement matters[48] can be competent for enforcing the same judicially enforceable instrument if various methods of execution are applied for (cf §18 of the *EO*).

In 2003, there are 222 judges acting in enforcement matters in Austrian *Bezirksgerichte* (district courts). Most of these judges do not act exclusively in enforcement matters; altogether there are only 47.28 *Vollzeitkapazitäten* ('full-time capacities'—the measuring unit for state personnel, which is the equivalent for one person working full-time) of enforcement judges.[49]

Training and appointment of judges are regulated in the *Richterdienstgesetz* (Judicial Service Act).[50] The first and basic requirement for appointment as a judge is a university degree in law (*Magister iuris*). In addition to this, the candidate must complete a practice period of altogether four years and nine months, mostly at different courts, and then pass the judicial exam (*Richteramtsprüfung*). The first phase of the training process is the so-called court traineeship (*Gerichtspraxis*),[51] lasting nine months. At the end of this traineeship the trainees who qualify for appointment as *Richteramtsanwärter* (judge candidates) are selected. According to the *Richterdienstgesetz* (Judicial Service Act), prerequisites for appointment as a judge candidate are (apart from the already mentioned law degree and court traineeship) Austrian citizenship and full legal capacity. The candidate must be personally, mentally, professionally and physically suited for the judicial profession. The methods of selection include a psychological test, a written exam and interviews (usually with the president of the *Oberlandesgericht*).[52] The judge candidates are appointed by the Federal Minister of Justice on the basis of (non-binding) proposals by the president of the *Oberlandesgericht* (Higher Regional Court). Only a very small percentage of all aspirants is appointed. The practice period of judge candidates lasts at least four years, the greater part of which is spent at courts. It is obligatory for all candidates to spend a certain period of time at a *Bezirksgericht* (district court), at a *Landesgericht* (regional court), at a

---

[48] There are 150 *Bezirksgerichte* altogether; two of them are specialised in criminal matters and one in commercial matters; these three courts do not conduct enforcement proceedings.

[49] Particularly in smaller *Bezirksgerichte* (district courts) many judges do not have a single field of practice but rather have to deal with all matters in these courts' competence.

[50] BGBl 1961/305. The provisions on the training of judge candidates were fundamentally reformed by the 1988 *Richterdienstgesetz* amending statute (BGBl 1988/230).

[51] The court traineeship is regulated in the *Rechtspraktikantengesetz* (Court Trainees Act), BGBl 1987/644.

[52] For a short survey of how the selection process is carried through in practice, Cf J Schiller 'Auswahl des richterlichen Nachwuchses' *RZ* 1995, 156. .

public prosecutor's office, at a penal institution and with an attorney, a public notary or the *Finanzprokuratur.*[53] A certain part of the practice period may be spent at an *Oberlandesgericht* (Higher Regional Court), at the *Oberste Gerichtshof* (Supreme Court), at the Ministry of Justice or at a probation office. In addition to this practical training, judge candidates must also attend training courses. The practice period is concluded by the judicial exam (consisting of a written and an oral part).[54] Judges are appointed, as a rule, by the Federal Minister of Justice (only a few high-ranking judges are appointed by the Federal President). The first appointment of a young judge is usually at a *Bezirksgericht* (district court).

(b) The Rechtspfleger *(court clerk)*
The function of the district court as the competent court for execution matters must not detract from the reality of the enforcement process. In reality the majority of court responsibilities in enforcement proceedings are performed by a *Rechtspfleger* (court clerk). A court clerk is an officer of the court who has certain qualifications and must be distinguished from a *Gerichtsvollzieher* (court bailiff). There are 170.85 *Vollzeitkapazitäten* (full-time)[55] court clerks acting in enforcement matters.

The institution of the *Rechtspfleger* is provided for in Article 87a of the Austrian *Bundes-Verfassungsgesetz* (Federal Constitution), authorizing the legislator to transfer certain types of judicial tasks to specially trained federal officers. According to this constitutional provision, the competent judge can at any time reserve such matters to himself or take charge of them; the *Rechtspfleger* is bound by the competent judge's (and nobody else's) directions. This provision was included in the constitution by an amendment in 1962;[56] the institution of the *Rechtspfleger* (court clerk) had already existed for decades before that, though. The constitutional 'acknowledgement' of the *Rechtspfleger* (court clerk) removed all fears that it might be unconstitutional to transfer judicial tasks to 'non-judges'; the provision also grants the *Rechtspfleger* (court clerk) a certain degree of independence by stating that he is not bound by any orders but those of the competent judge.

The training, appointment, and competences of the *Rechtspfleger* (court clerk) are regulated in the *Rechtspflegergesetz* (Act governing Court Clerks).[57] There are four fields in which court clerks can act. The applicant must pass specialized training courses to be appointed as a court clerk for

---

[53] The *Finanzprokuratur* is a state office whose task is to give legal advice to public bodies and represent them in court proceedings.
[54] Cf G Mayr *Die österreichische Juristenausbildung* (1998) 193.
[55] These are performed by 244 'physical' *Rechtspfleger* (court clerks).
[56] BGBl 1962/162.
[57] BGBl 1985/560.

a certain field. Such fields are: (1) civil procedure, enforcement and insolvency matters; (2) non-adversary proceedings; (3) land and ship register matters; and (4) business register matters. All *Rechtspfleger* (court clerks), regardless for which field they are appointed, can act in the *Mahnverfahren* (*ex parte* order for payment procedure). The largest number of court clerks act in land register matters, followed by those appointed for enforcement matters. More than 70 per cent of all court clerks work in these two fields.[58]

In order to be appointed as a court clerk, the applicant must have passed the *Matura* (school-leaving examination qualifying for admission to a university) or the *Beamtenaufstiegsprüfung* (an exam public officials can take after several years of service in order to be promoted). The president of the *Oberlandesgericht* (Higher Regional Court) decides on the admission of candidates to court clerk training. Only applicants with at least two years' work experience in the *Gerichtskanzlei* (court office) who have passed the *Gerichtskanzleiprüfung* (court office exam) and the *Fachdienstprüfung* (skilled work exam) can be admitted. The three-year training period comprises practical and theoretical training. In the practical part, the candidate works in courts, preparing decisions in the field of practice for which he wants to be appointed. The theoretical part consists of two courses, a basic course *(Grundlehrgang)* that has to be taken by all candidates and a specialized course *(Aufbaulehrgang)* for the field of practice for which the candidate wishes to be appointed. There is an examination at the end of each of the two courses. After successfully passing the training and the examination, a *Rechtspflegerurkunde* (court clerk certificate) is issued to the candidate, authorizing him to work as a *Rechtspfleger* (court clerk) in the respective field of practice. The allocation of court clerks to the courts is conducted by the president of the *Oberlandesgericht* (Higher Regional Court).

The duties of a court clerk include, in particular, the entire levying of execution upon movable assets and the enforcement upon monetary claims. Consequently, the overwhelming majority of enforcement matters are dealt with by the *Rechtspfleger*. Only tasks that were considered to be too complicated or too important remained in the exclusive competence of the judge—especially 'international' matters and most enforcement acts concerning immovable property, but also the imposing of personal arrest.[59]

When carrying out his duties, a court clerk is bound by the directions of the competent judge; the judge can also reserve certain matters to himself and deal with them himself if he considers this expedient in view of the

---

[58] Cf Bundesministerium für Justiz (ed) *Die Organization der Rechtsberufe in Österreich* (2002) 27 (available at <http://www.justiz.gv.at/broschueren/download/rechtsberufe_09_2002.pdf>).
[59] Cf for details the provisions of the *Rechtspflegergesetz*, esp. §16 and §17.

actual or legal difficulty of the matter or the importance or implications of the decision. Conversely, a court clerk must present a matter to the judge if the judge has reserved it to himself or has taken charge of it, if the court clerk wishes to deviate from the judge's legal opinion, of which he is aware, or if, in dealing with the matter, legal or actual difficulties arise.[60]

In general, the remedies for the *Rechtspfleger*'s decisions are the same as if the decision had been passed by a judge. There is a peculiarity, though: the competent judge can grant the appellant's request himself; only if the judge thinks that the remedy against the *Rechtspfleger*'s decision should be (at least partly) dismissed does he have to present the matter to the higher court. Moreover, the *Rechtspflegergesetz* provides for a specific remedy for decisions of a *Rechtspfleger* if recourse would normally not be admissible on account of the value of the case being too small. In such cases a *Vorstellung* (presentation) to the competent judge is admissible; the judge then has to decide the case himself.

(c) The Gerichtsvollzieher (court bailiff)

Compared internationally, the *Gerichtsvollzieher* (court bailiff) has a relatively subordinate position in Austrian enforcement law. His duty is mainly to actually implement the act of enforcement in practice. However, the court bailiff is not responsible for imposing coercive measures on a person; instead, in order to combat any resistance against the execution, the court bailiff can, pursuant to §26(2) of the *EO*, request police intervention. Unlike in German law, an application for enforcement is always filed with the court and never with the court bailiff; the court bailiff therefore always acts upon a court order granting a warrant of execution.

A court bailiff is a civil servant (employed at the district court and fully integrated into its organization), who carries out acts of enforcement on behalf of the court. The focus of his work is, in practice, the levying of execution upon movable assets. In this context, as part of the 1995 *EO* amending statute, the position of the court bailiff was reformed to the effect that he can now work independently to a greater extent than until then;[61] the 2003 *EO* amending statute extended the field of application of these powers[62]—of course enforcement still requires a warrant of execution ordered by a court in every case (but no longer for every single action of the court bailiff). In addition the *Gerichtsvollzieher* becomes involved in enforcing the surrender of movable assets or the surrender of possession of property or premises.[63]

---

[60] Cf G Mayr Aufgaben des Rechtspflegers in Österreich' *DRpfl* 1991, 397.

[61] Cf I.C.4.

[62] Cf I.C.4.

[63] Cf for details W Rechberger and P Oberhammer *Exekutionsrecht* (2002) margin no 23.

There are 400 *Gerichtsvollzieher* (court bailiffs) in Austria, filling 380.14 *Vollzeitkapazitäten* (full-time). Becoming a *Gerichtsvollzieher* does not require the *Matura* (school-leaving examination qualifying for admission to a university); it is sufficient if the candidate has completed the nine years of compulsory school attendance. A court officer who wishes to become a *Gerichtsvollzieher* must take an exam consisting of a written and an oral part; this exam can be taken after six months' work experience.[64] Candidates who have passed this exam and worked as an associate *Gerichtsvollzieher* for three years can take the *Gerichtsvollzieherfachprüfung* (court bailiff specialization exam) after attending a training course of four to six months' duration (or an intensive course lasting eight weeks).[65]

E. 'Outsourcing' enforcement—a future perspective?

The Austrian enforcement process is therefore characterized to a great extent by the acts of state organs and a strong involvement of the court; unlike for example in French law, there are almost no provisions for organs which are not part of the state court system[66] to become involved and even the *Gerichtsvollzieher* (court bailiff) has only a 'minor' role (compared with the situation under German law). The court's dominating role (which in practice means the dominating role of the *Rechtspfleger*) in the enforcement procedure is sometimes criticised.[67] As has already been mentioned, the 1995 *EO* amending statute extended the powers of the *Gerichtsvollzieher* (court bailiff) regarding execution upon movable assets.[68] So far there has been little discussion about outsourcing any part of the enforcement system out of the state court apparatus.

Such thoughts were, however, expressed at the beginning of the last government's term of office in 2000. At the moment though it does not look as though these considerations have blossomed beyond the early stages; the

---

[64] Cf Dienstanweisung vom 26. Dezember 1923 über die Prüfung zur Erlangung eines Dienstpostens des Zwangsvollstreckungsdienstes (Gerichtsvollzieherprüfung) (Service instruction of 26th December 1923 on the exam for attaining a position in the enforcement service), JABl 1/1924; this service instruction will expire on 31 Dec 2004 (cf BGBl I 1999/191).

[65] Cf *Verordnung des Bundesministers für Justiz vom 24. September 1973, mit der die Ausbildung für die Gerichtsvollzieherfachprüfung und die Gerichtsvollzieherprüfung geregelt werden* (Regulation of the Minister of Justice on the preparation for the court bailiff specialization exam and the court bailiff exam), BGBl 1973/507.

[66] An exception is the role of private auctioneers in the public sale of attached movable property; Cf I.C.4. above. Private debt collection agencies (*Inkassobüros*) play a certain role in practice. These agencies are only allowed to collect non-contested debts by reminding the debtor to pay; they cannot represent creditors in court procedures and are not a part of the enforcement system.

[67] Cf W Rechberger and P Oberhammer *Exekutionsrecht* (2002) margin no. 19.

[68] Cf I.C.4.

2003 *EO* amending statute does not provide for any kind of outsourcing, although it concentrates on the role of the court bailiff (especially by improving the relevant fee system in order to stimulate efficiency with a 'payment according to results' scheme).[69] However, these attempts were the impetus for an internal business administration study about the job of the *Gerichtsvollzieher* (court bailiff) commissioned by the Federal Ministry of Justice and carried out by Swiss management consultants and presented in 2001. The subject of this study was the job of court bailiffs in levying execution upon movable assets. At the centre of the study were considerations about possible methods of increasing efficiency (and thus reducing costs) through organizational measures. The study offers two alternatives as suggested proposals. One alternative is a 'conventional approach to a solution' which rests mainly on organizational improvements without changing the system of execution; the other alternative is a 'model of outsourcing within the justice system', which is based on 'uncoupling the financial services of the court bailiff from the administration of justice by means of adjudication.' However, this solution does not contemplate 'privatizing' the execution system either and, naturally, does not offer any answers to any legal questions arising from any such outsourcing and thus to the question of what the practical problems would be of partly separating the execution system from the organization of the courts. It is also typical that here—as with some other debates about increasing the efficiency of the court procedure (not only, but also) in Austria—it is not clear whether the aim is to achieve better legal protection for the parties concerned or only savings for the national budget.

In my opinion, the no doubt 'modern' philosophy of outsourcing public responsibilities, also in the area of execution matters, calls for great care because the system today which is 'court-oriented' does not cause any serious problems: The court warrant of execution is issued in a process which is very expedient, in particular the defendant is not heard; put simply, only the sufficiency of the application to establish the prerequisites of enforcement (and not the factual allegations) are checked (and the judicially enforceable instrument and the application for execution are compared only when the simplified warrant procedure[70] does not apply, ie in exceptional cases). Conversely, the debtor could not, anyhow, be denied the possibility of filing a remedy against the instigated execution, in which case the court would then, in any event, be the competent body. With numerous methods of enforcement which are significant in practice (such as the levying of execution upon money claims or upon immovable assets), transferring the responsibilities to the court bailiff, let alone outsourcing or privatizing them, would conflict with the Austrian legal system in a number

---

[69] Cf W Jakusch, *ÖJZ* 2004, 201.   [70] Cf I.C.3.

of respects. Separating the execution system out of the organization of the courts, especially privatization, would not only mean that Austrian enforcement law would have to be completely 'restructured', but so too would large parts of substantive law and land registry law (and it would throw up numerous constitutional questions). Against this background there is hardly any reason to consider outsourcing such methods of execution out of the court system. Of course, more far-reaching delegation of judicial duties to the *Rechtspfleger* (court clerk) would be conceivable; in view of the fact that the *Rechtspfleger* (court clerk) is, even now, responsible for the majority of enforcement matters, any such delegation would, of course, not have any great rationalization effect. A true outsourcing of enforcement process responsibilities is basically only conceivable (with regard to those methods of enforcement which have quantitative significance) in the area of execution upon movable assets. In this connection, however, one must appreciate that, although outsourcing this area out of the justice organization would conceivably have a rationalization effect, it would also involve substantial problems of coordination between the court and the *Gerichtsvollzieher* (court bailiff). The way in which the court bailiff is currently integrated into the court organization means that the information processes are relatively simple. These would very probably be much more complicated if the execution service were outsourced. It should also be noted that numerous enforcement measures require a court decision also for constitutional reasons; for instance this is so when premises are searched without the debtor's consent, a case which is typical when execution is levied upon movable assets. Under Austrian constitutional law, such a search can be carried out only with a court order. It is doubtful whether any resulting 'juxtaposition' of the court and outsourced court bailiff would in fact lead to any notable increase in efficiency. In this connection it can be summarized that, although the Austrian enforcement system is very 'court-oriented', this does not cause any notable problems which call for a fundamental departure from this system.[71]

1. Remedies

(a) Brief overview of the enforcement procedure

In order for an instrument or judgment to be enforced, its enforceability must first be confirmed by the court which issued the instrument or judgment. This confirmation of enforceability *(Vollstreckbarkeitsbestätigung)* must not be confused with the enforceability clause *(Vollstreckungsklausel)* under German law. The purpose of the confirmation is only to officially certify that the instrument is enforceable, in particular because any

---

[71] See also A Konecny Die *Exekutionsordnung nach 100 Jahren* 110.

prescribed time to appeal, which would suspend enforcement, has expired. This process does not involve any other checks that any additional pre-conditions for enforcement are met; it is not part of the enforcement proceedings. The debtor can defend himself against this confirmation of enforceability with an application for the annulment of the confirmation.

As has already been mentioned, every Austrian execution process always begins with a court order for a warrant of execution (*Exekutions-bewilligungsbeschluss*). The warrant of execution (*Exekutionsbewilligung*) is granted without hearing the debtor.[72] The execution court therefore examines (in practice, on the grounds of particulars given by the creditor) whether the particular execution applied for is permissible; if it is, the execution is approved by court order. This approval is not 'general' in nature, ie its purpose is not to approve enforcement of the particular instrument or judgment 'in general,' rather it refers to the actual method of enforcement applied for by the creditor. How concretely the enforcement measures to be applied have to be described in the warrant of execution varies depending on the method of execution. In the case of execution upon movable assets, it is sufficient if the attachment and the sale of the movable assets in the debtor's possession are ordered;[73] for the attachment of bank accounts it is only necessary to state that the debtor's receivables from his account with a particular bank are attached.[74]

The warrant of execution must be served upon the debtor; the only exception to this is if the execution is levied upon movable assets which do not fall under the simplified warrant procedure;[75] in this case, the warrant of execution is not served until the assets are actually attached. Enforcement measures can be taken immediately on the basis of the warrant of execution.

In the event that it concerns a method of execution in which practical acts of law enforcement are required, the court issues a corresponding order to the *Gerichtsvollzieher* (court bailiff).[76] This is the context where the grown 'independence' of the court bailiff mentioned above (provided for in the 1995 and 2003 amendments)[77] is relevant; different from what was the law before 1995, only a 'general order' to levy execution on movable assets (and not a detailed order concerning specific activities of the bailiff) is required.

---

[72] For the rare exceptions when it is permissible to hear the debtor, see W Rechberger and P Oberhammer, *Exekutionsrecht* (2002) margin no 94.
[73] Cf W Jakusch in P Angst, *Kommentar zur Exekutionsordnung* §54 margin no. 27.
[74] Cf P Oberhammer in P Angst *Kommentar zur Exekutionsordnung* §294 margin no 37.
[75] Cf I.C.3.
[76] Cf F Mohr, remarks in P Angst *Kommentar zur Exekutionsordnung* §249 margin no s 10.
[77] See I. C. 4.

If the judicially enforceable instrument is still too indefinite (because, for instance, the date payment is due or the deadline for performance is not determined by the calendar or the judicially enforceable instrument contains a stable value clause different from the official consumer price index), or if a legal successor to the creditor wishes to enforce the instrument or if the instrument is to be enforced against a legal successor of the debtor, the judicially enforceable instrument needs to be 'supplemented'. If the relevant facts can be evidenced by means of public documents or officially certified documents, that is sufficient; it is then possible to add a 'simple supplement to the instrument' as part of the execution process (practically together with the warrant of execution). However, if there are no such documents available, the creditor must commence an action to have the judicially enforceable instrument supplemented (*Titelergänzungsklage*). This is decided in accordance with the provisions of the Code of Civil Procedure (that is to say in ordinary proceedings), not in execution proceedings.

The next steps in the process naturally depend on the method of enforcement chosen. If the enforcement measures taken are successful (ie if the creditor is thereby completely satisfied), the execution ends automatically. However, if the enforcement measures taken finally prove futile or if a remedy against the enforcement succeeds, the proceedings must be discharged by court order.

Unfortunately, there are no relevant statistical data on the efficiency of enforcement proceedings. This is due to the fact that the statistical data collected by the Ministry of Justice basically only relate to the number and duration of proceedings; these can be rather good indicators of the efficiency of litigation—matters are different, though, with enforcement proceedings the duration of which does not say much about their efficiency. However, practical experience shows that the process for the issue of the warrant of execution is very expedient;[78] if there are problems with the enforcement of claims, they are hardly due to the organization of the enforcement system but rather to the fact that there often simply are not any assets to be seized.

The costs of execution depend on the method of enforcement and on the assets upon which execution is levied; the costs are payable by the creditor and have to be reimbursed to him by the debtor. A case example is provided in the annex.

[78] See II.D.

2. The debtor's remedies

(a) General

The system of remedies under Austrian enforcement law[79] is not easy to understand from a foreign point of view. Basically, there are two groups of defence available to the debtor. The debtor can raise the defences within the first group in the execution proceedings; the defences within second group need to be raised by filing an action in (ordinary) court proceedings. In some cases there is also a possibility of cumulating more than one of the remedies explained below.

(b) Remedies in execution proceedings

First the debtor can defend himself against the order for a warrant of execution by means of a *Rekurs* (recourse). This recourse is an appeal to the higher *Landesgericht* (Regional Court), whereby the debtor claims that the warrant of execution was unlawful on the basis of the creditor's application. In this connection it should be noted that the debtor is strictly prohibited from raising any new facts or new evidence with his recourse. Since the debtor was not heard in the proceedings for granting the warrant of execution, the cognition of the recourse appeal court is, in practice, limited to reviewing whether the warrant should have been granted pursuant to the particulars stated by the creditor. As a practical consequence a recourse against the order granting the warrant of execution can only appeal against mistakes in the execution court's legal assessment. In certain cases, it is possible to appeal against the decision of the recourse court by way of *Revisionsrekurs* (an appeal on points of law) to the *Oberste Gerichtshof* (Supreme Court); this is only possible if the decisions of the first court and the recourse appeal court differed from one another.

In some cases the debtor can apply for execution to be suspended (*Aufschiebung*). This is especially possible if he has filed a remedy against the underlying judicially enforceable instrument or judgment or against execution itself; in some cases, however, such suspension is dependent on the provision of security by the applicant.

An interruption *(Innehaltung)* must be distinguished from suspension *(Aufschiebung)*. In these cases the *Gerichtsvollzieher* (court bailiff) can temporarily refrain from continuing the execution. This is permissible in cases where the debtor demonstrates to the court bailiff that he has in the meantime satisfied the creditor or that the creditor has granted him extra time for payment and the debtor can provide corresponding documents. The court bailiff must then report to the court that he has temporarily inter-

---

[79] See for details W Rechberger and P Oberhammer, *Exekutionsrecht* (2002) margin no s 170.

rupted the process; the debtor thus wins time to file a remedy. This must be distinguished from the possibility available to a court bailiff to interrupt the sale of attached movable property when execution is levied upon movable property, if it appears likely that the debtor will discharge the debt within four months.

§§39 and 40 of the *EO* contain a catalogue of grounds upon which a debtor can file an application with the execution court for the execution to be terminated (*Einstellung* of the enforcement proceedings). Pursuant to §39 of the *EO* this is possible if the underlying judicially enforceable instrument has been set aside, if execution is levied upon property which is exempt from execution, if the execution has been declared unlawful by a final decision of a trial court, if the creditor has withdrawn his application for execution, if there is no expectation that the proceeds resulting from levying or continuing with levying execution will exceed the costs, if the confirmation of enforceability which has been issued has been reversed or if the execution is not covered by a judicially enforceable instrument. In some of these cases execution must be terminated *ex officio*. At least in those cases where the court must establish facts in order to reach a decision to terminate execution, the creditor must be given an opportunity to make submissions.

§40 of the *EO* stipulates a special ground for a termination of execution. Pursuant to this provision a termination of execution can be applied for if the debtor claims that he has satisfied the creditor, or that the creditor has granted him extra time to make payment or has waived enforcement. If the debtor is able to provide reliable documentary evidence of such circumstances, the execution can be terminated by the execution court. In the event that the creditor, when heard, disputes that there is any justification in the debtor's objections, the matter is decided not in the execution proceedings, rather the debtor is referred to taking legal action. He can then raise his objections in an *Oppositionsklage* (opposition action) or *Impugnationsklage* (impugnment action).

If there is ground for terminating the execution only in respect of part of the execution or if the execution has been enforced to a greater extent than was necessary in order to fully satisfy the creditor, the execution must be restricted (*Einschränkung* according to §41 of the *EO*).

Pursuant to §68 of the *EO* there is a possibility of applying for judicial redress from the execution court for an unlawful act of execution, by means of filing a *Vollzugsbeschwerde* (a remedy against the way enforcement is levied). This appeal is structured much like §766 of the German Code of Civil Procedure. However, because of the fact that in Austria every execution requires a court order for a warrant of execution (which is subject to remedies itself), the scope of application of this provision is relatively small. In most cases of unlawful execution, the warrant of execution must be challenged with a *Rekurs* (recourse) or an *Einstellungsantrag* (application for termination) or an *Impugnationsklage* (impugnment action). A *Vollzugsbeschwerde* pursuant to §68 of the *EO* therefore only applies to actual acts of the *Gerichtsvollzieher* (court bailiff), such as an unlawful attachment of movable property; vice versa the creditor can also file a *Vollzugsbeschwerde*, for example if the court bailiff has failed to take certain appropriate enforcement steps.

(c) Court actions by the debtor
The legal remedies available to a debtor in execution proceedings are thus restricted in two ways. If he files a *Rekurs* (recourse) he cannot introduce any new facts or evidence, and if he files an *Einstellungsantrag* (application for a termination of execution) he can only claim the grounds stipulated in §§39 and 40 of the *EO*. A debtor must therefore file an action to commence ordinary proceedings according to the Code of Civil Procedure to assert any objections which he cannot raise in the execution proceedings. In this connection the *EO* provides for two types of action, namely the *Oppositionsklage* (opposition action) pursuant to §35 of the *EO* and the *Impugnationsklage* (impugnment action) pursuant to §36 of the *EO*.

With an *Oppositionsklage* (opposition action) the debtor asserts 'objections against the claim'. Typical grounds for an opposition action are that the enforceable claim has been discharged or that additional time for payment has been granted or that a settlement regarding the claim has been concluded. In any event, these objections must have arisen after the relevant point in time when the decision was reached in the proceedings which led to the judgment to be enforced.

The *Impugnationsklage* (impugnment action) is for raising 'objections against the warrant of execution'. §36 of the *EO* sets out some grounds for this; essentially these relate to the absence of a prerequisite for execution. The impugnment action is therefore—systematically seen—the 'general' legal remedy in the law of execution; apart from the cases stipulated in §36 of the *EO*, it is always applied if a prerequisite for execution is not given (and no other remedy is available to the debtor). In practice, however, this remedy plays a less important role in contrast to the *Einstellungsantrag* (application for a termination of execution) and *Oppositionsklage* (opposition action) which are of much more importance.

An *Oppositionsklage* (opposition action) and *Impugnationsklage* (impugnment action) are decided in ordinary proceedings pursuant to the Code of Civil Procedure. The only special rule is that in both cases the debtor must submit all of the facts and evidence in support of his objections already together with the statement of claim. (No such restriction applies elsewhere in Austrian procedural law.) If an opposition action or impugnment action is allowed by a final decision, the execution must be terminated by an order of the execution court.

F. Legal remedies available to third parties

Third parties affected by the execution can sometimes themselves become involved in the execution proceedings; for instance this is so for persons who have certain rights *in rem* on real property upon which execution is levied. In certain cases third parties can raise a *Vollzugsbeschwerde* pursuant to §68 of the *EO*. If a third party wishes to assert that he has a right to the property upon which execution is levied, which right prevents execution (for instance because he, not the debtor, is the owner of the attached property), he must assert this by way of legal action in order to commence ordinary proceedings pursuant to the Code of Civil Procedure; this action pursuant to §37 of the *EO* is called an *Exszindierungsklage* in Austria, but is sometimes also called a *Drittwiderspruchsklage* (third-party action against execution), which is the same term as that used in German legal terminology. Third parties who have a lien on movable property, upon which execution is levied, without being in the possession of that property also have the possibility of instituting a *Pfandvorrechtsklage* (an action asserting a prior right under a lien) pursuant to §258 of the *EO*. With such an action the third party does not assert that the execution is unlawful, rather he asserts his right to be satisfied with priority.

CHAPTER 7

ENGLAND AND WALES

Mads Andenas

I. INTRODUCTION AND TERMINOLOGY

A. *Introduction*

The current study will focus mainly on the enforcement of money judgments in civil proceedings in England and Wales.[1] It therefore will not deal with 'enforcement' by insolvency proceedings and the enforcement of judgments against states. The first part of this study will deal with the enforcement agents in England and Wales. It will then deal with the different methods of enforcement and, thereafter, indicate which orders can be obtained from from judgment debtors ('JDs'). The study will then proceed to deal with the remedies the JD can obtain against unlawful enforcement measures, and conclude with an examination of the efficiency of the enforcement system.

B. *Terminology*

(a) 'Enforcement': In the context of money judgments, the problem of enforcement arises when a money judgment or order for support has not been paid spontaneously so that measures have to be taken to ensure that the JD complies with the order of the court.

(b) 'Execution': The term 'execution' generally refers to the enforcement of civil court judgments, whether by charging order, 'garnishee' order etc. Technically, it is used to refer to the seizure of goods to recover judgment debts.[2]

---

[1] J Beatson *Independent Review of Bailiff Law* (University of Cambridge, Centre for Public Law, 2000); W Kennett 'The Enforcement Review: A Progress Report' (2001) 20 CJQ 36; Lord Chancellor's Department Green Paper *A Single Piece of Bailiff Law and a Regulatory Structure for Enforcement* (LCD, London, 2001) Annex C 'Information on Current Arrangements' at http://www.dca.gov.uk/enforcement/enfrevoi/repoc.htm; J Baldwin *Evaluating the Effectiveness of Enforcement Procedures in Undefended Claims in the Civil Courts* (LCD Research Series 3/03 2003).

[2] J Kruse *The Law of Seizure of Goods, Debtor's Rights and Remedies* (Barry Rose Law Publisher, Chichester, 2000).

II. SOURCES

The law relating to enforcement in England and Wales is found in statute and case law. The long list of relevant primary legislation includes the Charging Orders Act 1979, the Attachment of Earnings Act 1971, the County Court Act 1984, the Taxes Management Act 1970, the Courts Act 2003 and the Supreme Court Act 1981.[3] Secondary legislation pertaining to the enforcement of judgments in England and Wales can be found in the Civil Procedure Rules (CPR) and Practice Directions (PD), and the former Rules of the Supreme Court (RSC), and County Court Rules (CCR) as Schedules 1 and 2 to the CPR.

Enforcement law is currently undergoing substantial reform. Recently Parts 70 to 73 of the CPR came into force, modifying the terminology and procedures for some (but not all) methods of enforcement. The entire philosophy of the CPR and the Woolf Reforms, with its emphasis on efficiency, proportionality and case management, must therefore underscore the law even though most previous case law is still applicable. A White Paper published by the then Lord Chancellor's Department (now the Department for Constitutional Affairs) has proposed the creation of a single unified piece of enforcement legislation, a new regulatory regime for enforcement agents, a single simplified fee structure, changes to distress for rent, attachment of earnings orders and charging orders, and the introduction of data disclosure orders.

III. ENFORCEMENT AGENTS

In England and Wales the court does not automatically enforce its judgments.[4] It is for the judgment creditor (hereafter 'JC'), not the Court, to take steps to procure the enforcement of the judgment not the court, CPR 70.[5] There are several different types of enforcement agents belonging to both the public and private sectors. At High Court level, they are now cumulatively known as High Court Enforcement Officers (HCEOs). At County Court level, they are County Court bailiffs who are civil servants employed by the Court Service. Public bodies wanting to enforce claims, such as the Inland Revenue, Customs and Excise and Local Authorities either employ their own agents or contract out to private bailiffs.

[3] As we know from John Kruse's chapter in this book (Chapter 18), even this expanded list only covers the tip of the iceberg of statute law, secondary legislation and case law that is central to civil enforcement law.

[4] See J Beatson *Independent Review of Bailiff Law*, n 1 above.

[5] H Brooke (gen ed) *Civil Procedure* 'The White Book' (Sweet & Maxwell, London, 2004) CPR70.0.2; Vol I 1649.

Magistrates' Courts also employ their own agents or again contract out to private bailiffs in order to recoup debts of a public nature, such as council tax debt or criminal fines.

A. High Court Enforcement Officers

Statutory provisions for the High Court enforcement personnel were contained in the Sheriffs Act 1887. This has now largely been superseded by the Courts Act 2003.

1. High Sheriff

High Sheriffs have retained their position as the oldest continuous Crown appointment, and have existed for more than 1,000 years. A High Sheriff is appointed to each county for a period of no more than one year. Their obligations with regard to High Court enforcement have gradually been removed from them. The remaining duties are largely traditional and symbolic, or related to supporting community causes and charities.[6]

2. Under Sheriff

Even with the removal of their obligations for High Court enforcement, as High Sheriffs only remain in office for one year, they usually appoint Under Sheriffs to assist them in their remaining duties. Under Sheriffs are usually solicitors and often partners in a law firm and, as such, their conduct is governed by the Law Society.

3. High Court Enforcement Officers

Implementation of High Court enforcement orders is now carried out by HCEOs. They are appointed by the Lord Chancellor or his appointed delegate (in practice, this is done by his delegate, the Senior Master of the Queens Bench Division of the High Court). They are drawn mainly from the ranks of those who previously worked as Under Sheriffs or Sheriffs' Officers. To be appointed, they have to meet strict criteria regarding training, qualifications, financial probity and professional conduct.

---

[6] Cf <http://www.privy-council.org.uk/output/page29.asp>. Formerly the High Sheriff was the principal law enforcement officer in the county, but over time most of the responsibilities of the office have been transferred elsewhere or are obsolete, and the functions of the post are now almost entirely ceremonial or representational. They attend judges sitting in local courts and provide hospitality for them, and many are active in local and national schemes that reflect their historical functions.

B. Bailiffs

1. County Court Bailiffs

County Court bailiffs are employed by the Court Service and are therefore civil servants who are subject to the Civil Service rules regarding recruitment and monitoring. There are approximately 650 County Court bailiffs in England and Wales. Bailiffs are appointed to assist the District Judges who sit in the county court. County Court bailiffs cannot enforce judgments in excess of £5,000 except those arising out of an agreement regulated by the Consumer Credit Act 1974. If the amount of the judgment is between £600 and £5,000 the creditor can choose between enforcement at High Court or County Court level. Findings suggest that county court bailiffs tend to deal with low value non-business debts.

2. Certificated Private Bailiffs

The work undertaken by HCEOs and County Court bailiffs represents only a small proportion of the total volume of warrants enforced nationally, the majority being enforced by private bailiffs in pursuit of public sector debts.

Some private bailiffs belong to trade associations such as the Enforcement Services Association (ESA) or the Association of Civil Enforcement Agencies (ACEA). ESA tends to represent individual bailiffs whereas ACEA's membership tends to be made up of firms, partnerships and companies. Bailiffs undertaking distress for rent, road traffic penalties and council tax must be certificated.

Although they are not employed by the Court Service, they are seen as court representatives as they act under a certificate issued by the Court. The Court therefore exercises a certain amount of control over their conduct. There is, however, no formal regulatory control of certificated bailiffs and no monitoring or auditing of bailiff practices. A bailiff's misconduct may nevertheless be the subject of a complaint to the relevant trade association, or to the judge who issued the certificate.

3. Non-certificated Private Bailiffs

These are private bailiffs who are neither HCEOs nor certificated bailiffs. They enforce debts where enforcement is not statutorily confined to the authority of county court bailiffs, sheriffs or certificated bailiffs. Non-certificated bailiffs have limited powers. They cannot levy distress for rent, road traffic debts, council-tax or non-domestic rates or enforce the collection of money due under High Court and County Court orders.

There are no qualification requirements to become a non-certificated private bailiff. Private bailiffs often belong to private companies or act on behalf of local authorities, or on behalf of magistrates' courts in the recovery of fines. Private bailiffs are not regulated and therefore their behaviour is not subject to scrutiny. The only possibility of complaint a party has against the acts carried out by a non-certificated bailiff, is against the organization on whose behalf he acts, or through any trade association to which he or his employer may belong.

C. Reform

According to the White Paper *Effective Enforcement*[7] published in March 2003, the Government aims to do away with the distinctions that currently exist between all those employed in enforcement work. The new 'enforcement agents' will be regulated, licensed and qualified professionals. Enforcement procedure and practice have been in transition during the last few years and are still undergoing substantial reform. For example, under section 99 and Schedule 7 of the Courts Act 2003, High Sheriffs were relieved of their High Court execution responsibilities in April 2004. HCEOs and bailiffs will become 'enforcement agents' under the proposed unitary system of regulation, powers and fees. The regulatory body which will license all enforcement agents and investigate any complaints against them will be the Security Industry Authority (SIA). The SIA will also consider issuing a Code of Practice, which will build on the 'National Standards for Enforcement Agents'.[8] This document has been widely distributed, well received and supported by the enforcement industry.

IV. CONDITIONS FOR EXECUTION

The preconditions for execution will depend upon the method of enforcement chosen by the JC. The creditor needs a warrant of execution[9] (issued by the county court) or a writ of fi-fa[10] (*fieri facias*; issued by the High Court) in order to start execution against goods. In order to place a charge on the JD's property (land, securities, funds in court, beneficial interest under a trust), the court has to issue a charging order.[11] Attachment of earnings[12] cannot be executed without an attachment of earnings order by the court. For certain limited kinds of debt and in exceptional circumstances, it

---

[7] Cm 5744, HMSO. It is also available on the DCA's website. http://www.dca.gov.uk.
[8] May 2002. Available at <http://www.dca.gov.uk/enforcement/agents02.htm>.
[9] See para 52.   [10] See paras 50 and 51.
[11] See para 33.   [12] See para 40.

is still possible to commit the JD to prison.[13] If the JC wishes to attach money held in a bank or building society account, he will issue a Third Party Debt Order (TPDO). If the order is made final, the money which is owed by the defendant to the claimant is paid to the claimant from the account. The third party debt order can also be sent to anyone who owes the defendant money.[14] These measures will be examined below.

The functional and jurisdictional variety of enforcement measures and personal means that on occasion proceedings may need to be transferred between courts before enforcement can start. For example, if the creditor decides to enforce a County Court judgment using the services of a HCEO, as he is entitled to if the judgment is between £600 and £5000 (normally the sheriff deals with High Court judgments, and county court judgments are dealt with by a bailiff), he must obtain a certificate of judgment in the County Court, register the judgment as a High Court judgment and issue a writ of fi-fa in the High Court, which will then be passed to a HCEO. Where execution against goods is sought, High Court cases where the judgment debt is below £600 must be transferred to the County Court for enforcement;[15] and County Court cases where the debt exceeds £5,000 must be enforced in the High Court (except, as mentioned previously, for Consumer Credit Act regulated debts).[16] A High Court claim in which a charging order is sought and the judgment debt is below £5000 must be transferred to the county court.[17] A High Court claim in which an Attachment of Earnings order is sought must be transferred to the County Court.[18]

V. ENFORCEMENT OF FOREIGN JUDGMENTS OR ARBITRAL AWARDS

A. *Foreign Judgments*

Traditionally, a foreign money judgment could be enforced in England and Wales by bringing an English action for summary judgment claiming the

---

[13] PD70, para 1.2(1), Debtors' Act 1869 ss 4 and 5, Administration of Justice Act 1970, s 11.

[14] The organization or person that is holding the money is referred to as the 'third party'. A third party debt order will prevent the defendant having access to the money until the court makes a decision about whether or not the money should be paid to the claimant. In these proceedings the person who the money to the claimant is referred to as the 'judgment debtor'; the claimant is referred to as the 'judgment creditor'. The money held by the third party must be held solely for the debtor. The claimant cannot, for example, apply for a third party debt order against a joint bank account unless the judgment debt is owed by all the account holders. See <http://www.courtservice.gov.uk/you_courts/civil/enforcement/thirdparty/intro.htm>.

[15] High Court and County Courts Jurisdiction Order 1991 (SI 1991/724), Art 8(1)(b).

[16] ibid Art 8(1)(a).

[17] Charging Orders Act 1979, s 1(2).

[18] Attachment of Earnings Act 1971, s 1.

amount of the judgment as a debt. The foreign judgment given by a court of competent jurisdiction gives rise to an obligation to pay, which can be enforced in England at common law.[19] However, in these cases several conditions must be met, relating to the nature of the judgment and the jurisdiction of the court of origin.[20] A number of bilateral and multilateral conventions have been entered into which promote the reciprocal recognition and enforcement of judgments. Thus, a speedier procedure allows for judgments to be directly enforceable, avoiding the need for a second claim before an English court. The Administration of Justice Act 1920 (AJA) and the Foreign Judgments Act 1933 (FJA) implement such Conventions as have been entered into by the United Kingdom and a number of (mostly Commonwealth) sovereign states, but not, for example, the USA. Within the European Union, the Council Regulation (EC) No 44/2001 on Jurisdiction and the Recognition and Enforcement of Judgments in Civil and Commercial Matters (Jurisdiction Regulation) streamlines the procedure for registration in the United Kingdom of judgments of a court of EU member states.

B. Arbitral Awards

The enforcement and recognition of arbitral awards in England and Wales depends on the Convention under which the award was made. Relevant conventions are, for example, the 1961 Geneva Convention on International Commercial Arbitration, the 1958 New York Convention on the Recognition and Enforcement of Foreign Arbitral Awards and the 1965 Washington Convention on the Establishment of the International Centre for the Settlement of Investment Disputes (ICSID). Accordingly, the Arbitration Acts 1950 and 1996 provide for the recognition and enforcement of arbitration awards and implement the United Kingdom's obligations under the above-mentioned Conventions.

An arbitration award made under the New York Convention will be recognized and enforced as set out in the Arbitration Act 1996. While the Geneva Convention is implemented in the 1950 Arbitration Act. Generally, the 1996 Act will prevail over the 1950 Act. However, if a party is not party to the New York Convention, but to the Geneva Convention, the Arbitration Act 1996 preserves the position under the 1950 Act.

---

[19] *Grant v Easton* (1883) 13 QBD 302 *Schibsby v Westenholz* (1870) LR 6 QB 155, 159. This is the 'obligation' theory of recognition and enforcement of foreign judgments. See also *Adams v Cape Industries* [1990] Ch 4 at 457 (Scott J), 513, 552 (CA).

[20] See Sir L Collins et al (ed) *Dicey & Morris The Conflict of Laws* (13th edn Sweet & Maxwell London 2000) Rules 35 ff with commentary). C Clarkson and J Hill *Jaffey on the Conflict of Laws* (2nd ed Butterworths Lexis Nexis London 2002) 154 et seq.

The registration of procedures under the AJA and the FJA may also be used for the enforcement of arbitration awards which have already been registered for enforcement as judgments in their home country and certain special arbitration awards such as those of the Centre for International Investment Disputes. Where an award of arbitration has been made under the AJA or FJA and the award has already been made enforceable as a court judgment in that country, then the AJA/FJA procedures apply to the enforcement of the award.

An award made in a country which is outside the Commonwealth and which is not a party to either the Geneva or the New York Convention (this would include some important South American countries) can only be enforced by issuing court proceedings based on the award and applying for summary judgment.[21]

VI. METHODS OF ENFORCEMENT

The court-based methods available to a JC are: Third Party Debt Orders (formerly called 'garnishee orders'), charging orders, attachment of earnings and seizure and sale at public auction of goods belonging to the JD to the value of the outstanding debt in public auctions. The JC can use any available method to enforce the judgment and can use more than one method to enforce the judgment, either sequentially or simultaneously, but he can be paid only once.[22] However, the JC can be paid only once. Therefore, especially in cases where more than one method is used at the same time, the JC must inform the court in writing—or the sheriff in writing in the case of a High Court writ of execution—of any payment received between the date of issue of the enforcement process and the execution.[23]

A. *Third Party Debt Orders*

Third Party Debt Orders (TPDOs) have been introduced in the Civil Procedure Rules together with supplementary Practice Directions in Part 72 CPR, taking effect from March 2002. Part 72 replaces the old rules relating to garnishee orders. Generally, Part 72 provides for a clearer and more straightforward procedure, as, for example, an affidavit is no longer necessary.[24] TPDOs are used when the JC wishes to be paid by a third party who owes money to the JD. The third party is, in the majority of cases, a bank or building society which holds money in a bank account for the JD. The JC will have obtained the bank details of the JD, be it through Part 71 proceedings (discussed below) or by other means.

---

[21] See Dicey and Morris, *The Conflict of Laws*, Rules 59 et seq.
[22] CPR 70.2(2).   [23] PD 70, para 7.
[24] *Civil Procedure* ('The White Book') (Sweet & Maxwell London 2004) 1666.

The JC may apply[25] for a TPDO to a judge without the need to give notice[26] to the JD or the third party. If the judge grants an interim TPDO, a date will be fixed for a hearing in order to decide whether to make a final TPDO.[27] Copies of the interim TPDO, the application notice (form) and any documents filed in support must then be served[28] on the third party not less than 21 days before the fixed date for the hearing. Service must also be effected by the JD not less than seven days after service on the third party and not less than seven days before the date fixed for the hearing.[29]

The main effect of the interim TPDO is to prevent the third party from making any payments that would reduce the amount it holds for the JD to below the amount due to the JC including his costs[30] of the application.[31] If this causes hardship to the JD, for example by preventing him from paying his rent or buying food, the JD can apply for a hardship payment order under CPR 72.7, permitting him to make one or more payments out of the account. This seeks to achieve a balance between the rights of the JD and those of the creditor. If the third party is a bank or building society, the interim TPDO also imposes duties upon it which must be performed within seven days of service. The duties are: (1) to carry out a search and identify all accounts held by the JD; (2) to disclose the account details and balance to the court and the JC within seven days of being served with the interim TPDO; and (3) if no account is held or the bank or building society is unable to comply with the order for any other reason, to inform the court and the JC of that fact.[32] A third party other than a bank or building society has a duty to inform the court and the JC in writing within seven days of being served with the interim TPDO if he claims not to owe any money to the JD or to owe less than the amount specified in the order.[33]

The third party should make no payment to the JC at this stage. The third party should wait for a final TPDO to avoid the risk of having to pay twice if the TPDO is not made final.[34] The JD or any third party objecting to the final order, or who knows or believes someone else has a claim to the money, must file and serve written evidence stating the grounds of any objection or details of the other claim not less than three days before the hearing.[35] If another person has a claim to the money, the court will serve notice of the application and the hearing on that person.[36]

---

[25] CPR 72 PD 1 gives detailed rules regarding the form of application and the information that should be contained therein.

[26] CPR 72.3. It is clear that, in such proceedings, speed is of the essence. Further, giving notice would create the risk of the money or assets being dissipated or concealed.

[27] CPR 72.4.   [28] CPR 72.5. For rules relating to service, see CPR Part 6.

[29] ibid.   [30] See CPR 45.6.   [31] ibid.

[32] CPR 72.6 (1)–(3).   [33] CPR 72.6 (4).

[34] See *Crantrave Ltd v Lloyds Bank plc* [2000] QB 917 (CA).

[35] CPR 72.8.   [36] CPR 72.8(5).

At the hearing, the court may grant a final TPDO, discharge the interim TPDO, decide any issues or direct a trial of any issues that may arise.[37] The court has a discretion to refuse to make a final TPDO and it is up to the JD to show why it should not be granted. The court may refuse to issue a final TPDO if it would be inequitable to do so, as would be the case where there is a real risk that the third party may remain liable before a foreign court.[38] When the third party makes a payment under a TPDO, it should be discharged from its liability; thus the court will not grant a TPDO if the third party's debt is governed by English law and if the third party is located in a jurisdiction that will not recognize such a discharge.[39] If a JD is insolvent, the court may refuse to make a TPDO so that the JC is not preferred over the general body of creditors.[40] However, if a JC has obtained a TPDO in competition with other creditors who have been slower in taking action, that should not affect the court's discretion to make a final TPDO.[41]

A minimum debt of £50 is required in both the High Court and the County Court in order to commence Part 72 proceedings. The fee for such a proceeding is £50.[42] The creditor normally has to pay the costs of the TPDO proceedings out of the money recovered and in priority to the judgment debt, so if the amount recovered only covers the costs, it is the debt which is left outstanding. Determination of the costs are, however, at the court's discretion and the court may, therefore, make a costs order, in appropriate circumstances, against the JD even if the TPDO proceedings were unsuccessful.

The third party debt order may not be granted—upon discretion of the court—if it would be inequitable to grant it. It is for example inequitable if the JD has gone insolvent, as then the effect of the JD's insolvency may be to prefer the JC over the general body of creditors.[43] Another occasion to deny a TPDO is where the possibility of a party having to pay twice over exists as, for example, where the party would remain liable before a foreign

---

[37] CPR 72.8(6).

[38] *Deutsche Schachtbau- und Tiefbohr-Gesellschaft mbH v Ras Al Khaimah National Oil Co.* [1990] 1 AC 295 (HL); *Société Eram Shipping Co. Ltd v Compagnie Internationale de Navigation* [2001] 2 All ER (Comm) 721.

[39] *Société Eram Shipping Co. Ltd v Compagnie Internationale de Navigation* [2003] UKHL 30, [2003] 3 WLR 21 (HL); in *Kuwait Oil Tanker Co. SAK v Qabazard* [2003] UKHL 31, [2003] 3 WLR 14 (HL) the House of Lords characterized a bank account held by a Swiss bank as a foreign debt, and a TPDO as 'enforcement' of the judgment in rem against the debt, for the purposes of Art 16(5) of the Lugano Convention, which gives exclusive jurisdiction to the Court of the state where enforcement is sought. Their Lordships also stated that, were the matter merely one of discretion (that is, not one of jurisdiction), there would be very strong reasons for refusing to grant a TPDO in such circumstances: at [2]. See Dickinson (2004) 120 LQR 16.

[40] *Pritchard v Westminster Bank Limited* [1969] 1 WLR 547 (CA); *Roberts Petroleum Ltd v Bernard Kenny Ltd* [1983] 2 AC 192 (HL).

[41] *Reed v Oury* (2000) LTL 12 Feb 2001.   [42] County Court Fees Order 1999 Sch 1.

[43] *Roberts Petroleum Ltd v Bernard Kenny Ltd* [1983] 2 AC 192, HL.

court.[44] Other occasions may be a winding-up order petition, a petition which can only be made when the company is unable to pay its debts and if it is 'just and equitable that the company should be wound up'.[45]

B. Charging Orders

The Charging Orders Act 1979 and CPR Part 73 govern this type of enforcement. A charging order is defined by section 1(1) of the Charging Orders Act 1979 as an order 'imposing on any such property of the JD as may be specified in the order a charge for securing payment of any money due or to become due under [a] judgment or order'. Such a charge may be imposed on the JD's land, securities, beneficial interest under a trust and funds in court.[46] If the subject matter of the order is securities, such as shares the creditor may apply to the court for a 'stop order'[47] on the company in question to prevent any transfer of the shares occurring or a 'stop notice'[48] which prevents any such transfer without the company first giving the creditor notice of the proposed transfer.

The order enables the JC to secure payment of money owed in the sense that he obtains a charge over a particular asset but it does not guarantee payment. As such, it is an indirect method of enforcement. An order for sale of the charged asset may be applied for after the charging order is granted in order to enforce payment.[49] Application for a charging order may be made without notice and must, subject to certain exceptions, be issued in the court that made the judgment.[50] Charging orders are normally made by the County Court, as the jurisdiction of the High Court is more limited.[51] A single charging order may be applied for in respect of more than one judgment or order against the same JD.[52] Interest and costs are recoverable under a charging order, whether it expressly provides for them or not,[53] but interest falling due more than six years before the commencement of the proceedings will not be recoverable.

The procedure for this method of enforcement is similar to that for TPDOs in that there will be an interim charging order (formerly a charging order *nisi*) and a hearing to decide whether to make it final or not, the burden being on the JD to show why it should not be made.[54] The court has a discretion not to make the interim charging order, for example, in

---

[44] *Deutsche Schachtbau- und Tiefbohrgesellschaft mdH v Shell International Petroleum Co. Ltd* [1990] 1 AC 295, HL.

[45] Cf EC Regulation on insolvency proceedings. [46] Charging orders Act 1979, s 2.

[47] CPR 73.12. [48] CPR 73.17.

[49] CPR 73.10. This can only be done by using separate proceedings under CPR Part 8.

[50] CPR 73.3. [51] CPR 73.3 (3).

[52] Charging Orders Act 1979, s 1(2).

[53] *Ezekiel v Orakpo* [1997] 1 WLR 340 (CA). [54] CPR 73.4.

cases where it would be oppressive to the JD. Any evidence to prove that the JD is not willing to pay rather than cannot pay should be included in the JC's application.

The interim charging order, application notice and any supporting documents must be served on the JD, such other creditors as the court may direct (in particular, the JC must disclose any creditors of whom he is aware) and certain other specified persons, at least 21 days before the final hearing.[55] The effect of the interim charging order being served on these persons is to prevent them from disposing of any of the assets or interests that they might have in them until the final hearing and to allow other creditors to intervene.

The interim charging order should be registered[56] so that it is not defeated by sale to a bona fide purchaser for value without notice. If at the hearing it is decided that the charging order should be discharged rather than being made final, the registration must be immediately removed. Any person objecting to the order being made final must file and serve written evidence stating the grounds of his objections not less than seven days before the hearing.[57]

The principles governing the exercise of the court's discretion in deciding whether to make the order final are substantially identical for TPDOs and charging orders. Accordingly, the court must take into account all the relevant circumstances and the interests of all parties involved, including those of other unsecured creditors.[58] If the debt is small, then an application to make a charging order on an asset of substantial value should normally be refused.[59] Where a judgment debt is payable by instalments, the charging order may secure the whole of the debt and not merely arrears of instalments. The court fee for a charging order is £50.

To apply for the sale of charged property owned by the JD[60] separate proceedings must be brought under CPR Part 8. The court has a discretion and will take into account all circumstances before making such an order. An order for the sale of the JD's home would be an extreme sanction and might even have human rights implications.[61] However, it might be appropriate where the JD has persistently neglected or refused payment without any valid reason.

---

[55] CPR 73.5(1).

[56] Pursuant to Charging Orders Act 1979, s 3 If the charging order belongs to land, it will usually be registered as a pending action under the Land Registration Act 1925 or the Land Charges Act 1972 before it is served on the debtor. The Land Registration Act 1925 is now repealed by the Land Registration Act 2002 and COA 1979 s 3 amended accordingly.

[57] CPR 73.8(1).

[58] Charging Orders Act 1979, s 1(5); *Roberts Petroleum Ltd v Bernard Kenny Ltd* [1982] 1 WLR 301, CA.

[59] *Robinson v Bailey* [1942] Ch. 268 at 271, per Simmonds J.   [60] CPR 73.10.

[61] The court will have to consider Art 8 European Convention on Human Rights.

C. *Attachment of Earnings*

Attachments of earnings are an effective enforcement method where the JD has continuous employment and has sufficient earnings. An attachment of earnings order may be made to secure the payment of a judgment debt if the debt is not less than £50 or, for the amount remaining payable under a judgment, for a sum of not less than £50.[62] It involves ordering the JD's employer to make periodic deductions from the JD's earnings and to pay the deducted monies to a court officer until the debt is paid in full. There is a centralized system for the collection of payments. Jurisdiction to make attachment of earnings orders (AEOs) is wholly statutory, created by the Attachment of Earnings Act 1971. Most AEOs are made in the County Court as the County Court can make such orders to secure payments under both High Court or County Court maintenance orders, judgment debts and payments under administration orders, whereas the High Court can only grant an AEO in order to secure payments under a High Court maintenance order.[63]

The application should be made to the County Court in the district in which the JD resides.[64] The application may also be made to the court that gave the judgment the JC is seeking to enforce if the JD does not reside in England or Wales or the creditor does not know where he resides.[65] The application may be made by the JC, the JD or any creditor named in an administration order (an order issued by the county court to administer the JD's estate). Notice of the application must be served on the JD who must file a reply within eight days of service.[66]

The application must certify the amount of money remaining due under the judgment or order and that the whole or part of any instalment due remains unpaid. The JD must be served with a notice of the application and with a form for reply. The JD must then file his reply within eight days of service.[67] If the JD fails to reply to the court within eight days, a statement of the JD's earnings and any other information may still be obtained from anybody who appears to have the JD in his employment.[68]

For an AEO to be granted, it must appear to the court that the JD has failed to pay at least one of the payments due[69] unless the application is made by the JD himself. Any order or warrant for the JD's committal under the Debtors Act 1869 must have been discharged before an attachment of earnings order can be made for under section 3(7) of the Attachment of Earnings Act 1971, no AEO can be made to secure the payment of a judgment debt if there is in force such a warrant in respect of that debt. The

[62] CCR 27.7(9).
[63] Attachement of Earnings Act 1971, s 1.   [64] CCR 27.3(1).
[65] CCR 27.3(2).   [66] CCR 27.5(2).   [67] CCR 27.5(2).
[68] CCR 27.6.   [69] Attachment of Earnings Act 1971, s 3(3).

court may, however, discharge the order or warrant with a view to making an AEO instead. The court fee to issue an AEO is £50.[70]

The AEO is issued by 'the court' which may mean a court officer or by a district judge. If the court officer has sufficient information after receipt of the JD's reply, he may issue the order.[71] If an order is issued by the court officer, the JC or JD may, within 14 days and on giving reasons, apply for a hearing for the order to be reconsidered.[72] At the hearing, the district judge has the power to confirm the order or set it aside and issue a new order as he sees fit.[73] If the court officer does not issue the order, he will have to refer the application to the district judge.[74] If the latter considers he has sufficient information, he will determine the application. Otherwise, he must direct a day for a hearing of the application.[75] The question as to whether there is 'sufficient information' is left entirely to the court officer or the district judge, as the case may be, for determination.

The AEO is directed to the JD's employer[76] and it specifies the whole amount payable under the relevant adjudication including any relevant costs. In addition, the order specifies a reasonable 'normal deduction rate' and a 'protected earnings rate' (a reasonable minimum amount of earnings which will not be reduced, taking into account the JD's resources and needs).[77]

The employer must comply with the terms of the order[78] and money deducted from the JD's earnings belongs to the creditor from the date of payment into court, assuming that no petition in bankruptcy has been filed against the JD. On the making of a bankruptcy order, normally a creditor with a provable debt is not entitled to retain the benefit of an attachment unless it was completed or the sums paid before the commencement of the bankruptcy. The JC will be entitled to any monies paid into court between the petition date and the date of the bankruptcy order, unless he had received notice of the presentation of the petition.[79] The court may discharge the AEO on the making of a bankruptcy order.

The grant of an AEO has an effect on some of the other measures.[80] For instance, after an AEO has been issued no warrant of commitment can be issued in consequence of any proceedings for the enforcement of the debt started after the date of the AEO. Moreover, leave must be obtained from the County Court for the recovery of debt by execution against any prop-

---

[70] County Court Fees Order 1999 Sch 1.
[71] CCR 27.7 (1).
[72] CCR 27.7 (2).
[73] CCR 27.7 (7).
[74] CCR 27.7 (4).
[75] CCR 27.7 (5).CCR 27.7 (5).
[76] Attachment of Earnings Act 1971, s 6.
[77] ibid ss 6(4) and (5).
[78] ibid s 7(1)
[79] *Re Green (a bankrupt) ex parte the Official Receiver v Cutting* [1979] 1 All ER 832.
[80] Attachment of Earnings Act 1971, s 8.

erty of the JD.[81] If a warrant of commitment is made the AEO ceases to have effect[82] and the employer's liability will be terminated.

In any proceedings where the court has the power to make an AEO or where an AEO has already been made, the court may ask the JD or any person who appears to have the JD in his employment to give to the court a signed statement with particulars of the employment.[83]

The court may also issue an order to vary or discharge the existing AEO.[84] The AEO will lapse if the JD leaves the employment of the employer to whom the order was sent.[85] However, the employer must give notice of this cessation of employment to the court and the order can be revived if redirected to a new employer. The JD has an obligation to notify the court whenever he changes his employment and provide particulars of his new earnings and any new anticipated earnings.[86] It is to be noted that the Act does not impose any obligation on the JD to notify changes in his earnings while in the same job. In addition, section 15 imposes an obligation on any person who becomes the JD's employer and has knowledge of the existence of the AEO and by what court it was made, to notify the court in writing that he has become the JD's employer and include in his notification a statement of the JD's earnings and anticipated earnings. This obligation remains even if the JD has already informed the court about these changes.

Where there are two or more AEOs applied for against the JD or an AEO is already in force against the JD and a further AEO or consolidated AEO is applied for, the court may make a consolidated AEO.[87] Application for a consolidated AEO may be made either by the JD or by any person who has obtained or is entitled to apply for an AEO.[88] The court officer may also make a consolidated AEO on his own motion where there is already in force such an order against the JD, and an application is made for a further (non-consolidated) AEO. However, this can only be done after all the parties have been given an opportunity to submit written objections.[89]

D. Execution by Warrant of Execution or by Writ of fieri facias (fi-fa)[90]

Execution against goods through the warrant of execution in the County Court and the writ of fi-fa in the High Court is still the most commonly used means of enforcement. It enables the JC to recover the outstanding debt and costs of the execution through the seizure of the JD's goods of corresponding value belonging to the JD. If the JD does not pay up, the goods are sold at a public auction.

---

[81] Attachment of Earnings Act 1971, s 8(2).   [82] ibid s 8(4).
[83] ibid s 14.   [84] ibid s 9.   [85] ibid s 9(4).
[86] ibid s 15.
[87] CCR 27.18.   [88] CCR 27.19(1).   [89] CCR 27.20.
[90] A writ ordering a levy on the belongings of a debtor to satisfy the debt.

The writ of fi-fa is issued by the High Court and is enforced by a HCEO. The JC must pay a fee and produce a draft writ of fi-fa, *a praecipe*[91] and the judgment for the writ to be issued. The writ is issued by being sealed[92] and is expressed in the general form of a royal direction. Addressed to a HCEO, it directs the HCEO to seize such goods from the JD as may be sufficient to satisfy the amount of the judgment, interest and costs of the execution, including the officer's costs and charges. It also directs the officer to pay the JC the amount levied, excluding his costs and charges.

Its equivalent in the County Court is the warrant of execution, which is enforced by the County Court's bailiffs. The procedure in the County Court requires the JC to file a request for the issue of a warrant of execution to the court, upon which the court informs its bailiffs.

All judgments that are below £600 must be enforced in the County Court. Judgments that are above £600 (except those regulated by the Consumer Credit Act 1984) may be enforced in the High Court. Any judgment for £5,000 and above must be enforced in the High Court (again, except for those regulated by the Consumer Credit Act, which must be enforced in the County Court). Provisions for the transfer of County Court judgments to the High Court for enforcement by the sheriff are governed by section 42 of the County Courts Act 1984 and by CPR Sch 2, CCR O.25, r. 13. Transfers may now take place through Sheriff's Lodgment Centres, and are subject to a fee.

There are certain cases where permission to issue writs of fi-fa or warrants of execution is necessary.[93] These include cases where more than six years have elapsed since the date of the judgment or order. In such cases, permission will not be granted unless the applicant (JC) satisfies the court that it is demonstrably just to extend the time for enforcement.[94] For the extension to be granted, it must be more than 'just': the court must be satisfied that it is 'demonstrably' just.[95]

The HCEOs or bailiffs need lawful access to the premises where the goods are held in order to levy execution. If the relevant premises are the dwelling house of the JD, they are not allowed to break open the outer door,[96] nor is it lawful for them to force their way in by other methods.[97] The outer door may be broken open if the premises are the JD's workshop or other building not being his dwelling house.[98]

---

[91] A paper containing the particulars of a writ. For both the fi-fa and the *praecipe* there exist standard forms to be filled in by the JC and stamped when the appropriate fee has been paid.
[92] RSC Ord 46 r 6.   [93] See RSC ord 46 and CCR ord 26 r 5.
[94] *Duer v Frazer* [2001] 1 All ER 249 (QBD).
[95] *Patel v Singh* [2002] EWCA Civ. 1938 (CA).
[96] *Semayne's Case* (1604) 5 Co 91; *Khazanchi v Faircharm Investments Ltd* [1998] 1 WLR 1603 (CA).
[97] *Vaughan v McKenzie* [1969] 1 QB 557 (Divisional Court); [1968] 1 All ER 1154, DC.
[98] *Hodder v Williams* [1895] 2 QB 663(CA).

The HCEOs or bailiffs may seize any of the JD's goods, including motor vehicles, money, promissory notes and securities, except goods that are necessary to the JD for use personally by him in his employment, business or vocation, and goods necessary for satisfying the basic domestic needs of the JD and his family.[99] The burden of showing that any goods are protected from seizure lies on the JD.[100] Where the goods are being held on third-party premises, whether the HCEOs or bailiffs can gain lawful access to the goods wholly depends on the circumstances of the case. The basic rule, however, is that a HCEO or County Court bailiff may break into a third party's premises if goods have been taken there to avoid lawful execution and request for entry has been refused.

At common law the general rule is that distress should not occur between sunset and sunrise or on a Sunday. However, some of the statutory regimes also lay down rules about when the distrainor may distrain. In accordance with the National Standards for Enforcement Agents produced by The Lord Chancellor's Department (now the DCA),[101] visits should ideally only be made between 6 am and 9 pm (or, for business premises, any time that the debtor is conducting business).

Unless the court orders otherwise, a writ of fi-fa or a warrant of execution must not be executed on a Sunday, Good Friday, or Christmas Day.[102] Otherwise the sheriff may distrain at any time. The National Standards for Enforcement Agent state that other religions and cultures should be upheld, and visits avoided on appropriate festivals and holidays.

Distress for indirect taxes must commence between 8 am and 8 pm on any day of the week, but it may continue outside those hours until the levy is completed. Persons holding themselves out as conducting any profession, trade or business during hours which are, wholly or partly, outside this period are subject to a levy during their trading hours. By contrast, there are no restrictions on the time during which a collector can distrain for income tax. However, a warrant authorizing a tax collector to break open premises can only be lawfully executed 'in the daytime'.

After the goods have been seized, the HCEOs or bailiffs usually enter into an agreement with someone responsible in the premises to take 'walking possession' of the goods. This means that the goods have been seized but can remain in the premises provided the responsible person promises not to remove or damage them without the HCEO's or bailiff's permission and to allow the HCEO or bailiff to re-enter the premises at any time to

[99] Supreme Court Act 1981, s 138(3A); County Courts Act 1984, s 89(1).
[100] *Toseland Building Supplies Ltd v Bishop (t/a Bishop Groundworks)* 28 Oct 1993, CA (unrep.)
[101] These are endorsed by a range of central and local government departments and the bailiffs' trade bodies, all of whose members are encouraged to comply with it.
[102] PD RSC 46 para 1.1.

complete the enforcement process.[103] Accordingly, it has long been considered that the HCEO or bailiff having walking possession of the goods may then break the lock or force his way in to gain access to the goods. However, in a recent Court of Appeal case,[104] it was held that unless the walking possession agreement or the circumstance of the case explicitly allowed forcible re-entry in the absence of the JD, such power should not be inferred.

The seized goods are released when the JD pays the judgment debt. If the JD persists in not paying, then the goods may be removed and sold at a public auction. If the JD is unable to pay or alleges that it is inexpedient to enforce any or part of the order, the JD may apply for a stay of execution.[105] The stay of execution, if granted, will usually be accompanied by an order that the JD pay the judgment debt by instalments. The court may also make a charging order on the JD's premises without the JC having to go through the Part 73 procedure.

VII. OBTAINING INFORMATION FROM JUDGMENT DEBTORS

The JC needs specific information about the JD, his assets, employer or bank in order to choose which method or methods of enforcement to use. This information can be obtained through the 'order to obtain information' (previously 'oral examination') procedure, which is now governed by simpler rules under CPR Part 71. Under this procedure, the JD is ordered to attend court to provide information about his means and any other information needed for enforcement of the judgment.[106]

Notice need not be given and the application may be dealt with by a court officer without a hearing.[107] The applicant has a right to the issue of the court order,[108] provided the application is in the correct form and contains the information required by CPR 71 PD 1. The order must be served by the JC personally (ie by himself or by someone acting on his behalf), except that in County Court proceedings only, it will be served by the court bailiff if the JC is an individual litigant in person. The court may also order service by an alternative method under CPR 6.8. The JC is entitled to fixed costs[109] and to an additional £15 if service was done personally[110] in order to compensate him, at least in part, for his time.

---

[103] *National Commercial Bank of Scotland v Arcam Demolition and Construction Ltd* [1966] 2 QB 593 (CA).

[104] *Khazanchi v Faircharm International McLeod v Butterwick* [1998] 1 WLR 1603 (CA), overruling on this point [1996] 1 WLR 995 (ChD).

[105] RSC 47.1; CCR 25.8.   [106] CPR 71.2.   [107] ibid.

[108] Previously, the court had a discretion to issue the order.   [109] CPR 45.6.

[110] CPR 45.5.

Within seven days of service of the order, the JD may ask for a sum sufficient to cover his travelling expenses to and from court and if such request is made, the JC must pay the sum requested.[111] An affidavit stating whether such a request has or has not been made and whether any sum has been paid must either be filed not less than two days before the hearing or be produced at the hearing.[112]

At the hearing, a set of standard questions will be put to the JD by a court officer. The JC may also ask questions, or may request the court officer to ask additional, written questions.[113] The questioning will be carried out by a court officer unless there are compelling reasons[114] or difficulties, which will require the greater authority of a judge. If this is so, then the JD will have to attend court. The JD will be questioned on oath and will have to answer such questions as the court may require.[115] In *Interpool Ltd v Galani*[116] it was held that the JD is also required to answer questions about any of his assets which are outside the jurisdiction.

A JD who fails to comply with the order is in contempt of court and the matter will be referred to a High Court judge or circuit judge, who may make a committal order against him.[117] Failure to comply with the order includes failure to answer questions on oath at the hearing but the most common type of failure to comply will be non-attendance at court. In the latter case, a committal order will only be made if the JC has complied with any request for travelling expenses and filed the required affidavit under CPR 71.4 and CPR 71.5. The judge will suspend the order provided the JD comes to court on a subsequent occasion. If the JD fails to do so again, then a warrant is issued for his arrest and he is taken to court for the examination. The judge may then either discharge the committal order or sentence the JD.

VIII. THE JUDGMENT DEBTOR'S AND THIRD PARTIES' REMEDIES

The remedies currently available to the judgment debtor in respect of unlawful enforcement action arise from various statutes and common law. JCs and enforcement agents may be held liable for trespass or for wrongful,

---

[111] CPR 71.4.   [112] CPR 71.5.
[113] PD 71 para 4.2.   [114] PD 71 para 2.2.
[115] CPR 71.2 (6)(c). The oral examination procedure is intended to be 'a cross-examination ... of the severest kind'—per James LJ in *Republic of Costa Rica v Strousberg* (1880) 16 Chapter D 8—the rationale being to prevent the JD defeating a judgment by dissipating or concealing assets.
[116] [1988] QB 738 (CA).
[117] PD 71 paras 7.2, 8.4 See also, Civil Procedure (Amendment No 4) Rules 2001 (25), Civil Procedure (Amendment No 5) Rules 2001 (31). The procedure for committal is to be found in CPR Sch 1, RSC Ord 52.

illegal or excessive seizure. If the distrainor was not entitled to seize the goods in the first place, the goods may be rescued. In such cases, the remedy of 'claim and delivery' (or 'replevin') may be available to the debtor, where the JD recovers the goods in return for (1) an undertaking to bring an action to determine the right to distrain and (2) tendering sufficient security for the debt and costs of the action. For other cases of unlawful seizure of goods, the remedy is damages. The remedies available are little used. This is possibly because the remedial structure is old and complex and JDs do not know their rights.[118]

If a third party makes a claim against any goods, money, or chattels that a distrainor has seized or intends to seize in execution of a debt, the sheriff's officers or bailiffs may apply to the court for relief by way of interpleader. The court may then make an order as to who has title to the goods. Interpleader relief is also available to any other person who is under liability in respect of a debt or money, goods or chattels and who is, or expects to be, sued by two or more persons making adverse claims to that debt or money, goods, or chattels.

The confrontational nature of enforcement means that grievances will be common and therefore a simple remedial structure is necessary. In the *White Paper*, Government plans to have irregular (including excessive) action[119] dealt with by the Complaints Board of the Security Industry Authority. However, illegal action,[120] including wrongful execution, will continue to be dealt with by the courts. Whereas there is currently a distinction between distraint (seizure of goods for non-payment of rent, rates, and taxes) and execution (the seizure and sale of goods to satisfy a judgment debt), the proposal would remove this distinction and the remedy would be simple damages up to the value of the goods plus any relevant special damages.

The Government also wishes to limit interpleader actions to claims of full ownership.[121] Therefore it proposes that 'if on application made within seven days after the date of execution of the warrant by the JD or any other person who owns a seized article the judge is satisfied that the article is exempt from distress, an order releasing the article from the distress shall be made.'[122]

---

[118] The Court Service publishes a guidance booklet: 'About Bailiffs' and Sheriffs' Officers' (Ex 345, available on the Court Service website), which gives a succinct overview of non-technical language of the various avenues of recourse.

[119] This will occur where the levy was carried out correctly but the distrainor subsequently does something unlawful.

[120] An illegal action will occur where it is wrongful from the outset, for example where the enforcement agent committed a wrongful act at the beginning of the levy which invalidated the subsequent proceedings.

[121] CPR Sch 1 RSC O 17 and Sch 2 CCR O 33.

[122] White Paper on Enforcement, 35, n 37.

Furthermore, the Government proposes abolishing the ancient and little-used remedy of replevin as it considers that the remedies for illegalities and irregularities will be sufficient and therefore should no longer be necessary to have a separate remedy for illegal seizure of goods.

IX. EFFICIENCY OF THE SYSTEM

A. *Inefficiency Due to Difficulties in Gathering Information*

It is widely acknowledged that the existing system of judgment enforcement is ineffective primarily because it is an outdated system that has not evolved in line with the demands of the modern world and modern commercial practice. It is for this reason that the present Government has undertaken a complete review of the system and recently issued a *White Paper*[123] with a view to reform.

Court service statistics show that, in relation to warrants of execution, which make up approximately 85 per cent of all enforcement action, about 35 per cent of warrants actually issued are paid.[124] This figure would rise to 75 per cent if 'unenforceable' warrants were excluded. Unenforceable means those that are not legally enforceable by reason of an incorrect address or for some other reason such as that the JD is bankrupt.

The high volume of warrants of execution in comparison to the other enforcement methods can perhaps be partly attributed to the century-old tradition of this method but it must also be said that it is indicative of the fact that JCs have little information about the JD on which they are able to take an informed decision. All that is required to issue a warrant of execution is the JD's name and address. In contrast, for example, an attachment of earnings order requires the JD's earnings, their expenditure and their employer's details. As the current system relies on the creditor obtaining information from the JD, it is not surprising that the JC opts for methods that require as little information as possible but prove not to be the most successful enforcement method. If, on the other hand, more information were readily available for the creditor, then he would be more likely to choose an effective method.

There are of course means of obtaining information about the JD, such as Part 71 orders. However, such a procedure takes time and is costly. Also,

---

[123] See para 3(c) above.
[124] Lord Chancellor's Department *Enforcement Review Report of the First Phase of the Enforcement Review* July 2000, 12. Moreover, the figures concerning the enforcement of 'default' judgments, which make up more than 90 per cent of the totality of claims issued and dealt with by the civil courts in England and Wales, are even lower: J Baldwin 'The Enforcement of Judgments in Undefended Claims in the Civil Courts in England and Wales' (2004) 23 CJQ 354.

disclosure orders in connection with freezing injunctions may elicit information, but they are expensive and suitable only in respect of larger cases.

It is for this reason that one of the recommendations put forward by the Lord Chancellor's Review has been that information about the JD be made available from other sources so as to reduce delay in enforcement is reduced (information coming from an independent source by its very nature being more reliable). In the *White Paper*, the Government plans to implement this recommendation through the creation of a Data Disclosure Order.

B. Inefficiency of the Current Fee Structure

The current fee system is governed by the principle that the JD should bear the costs if he delays payment of the debt. The problem is that the JC obtains debt recovery services from the public and private sector but does not pay for them fully. JCs therefore have no interest in what the service costs. On the other hand, the system is not favourable to the JC either. The more the JD has to pay in costs, the less the creditor recovers. Attachment of earnings would therefore in many cases be more beneficial to both JD and creditor but execution against goods is most often resorted to.

The Government proposes a major change to the existing fee structure by introducing an upfront fee payable by the JC before any enforcement action is taken. This represents a radical departure from the current principle that the JD should bear all the costs. At present, besides the court fee for issuing the enforcement measures, enforcement agents' fees are often calculated on a *per diem* or percentile basis and added to the overall debt.[125] The Government's economic analysis identified this up-front fee, in conjunction with better access to information, as a key element in the profitability and probability of enforcement. It is suggested that an upfront fee will encourage the JC to improve the quality of the information that he has to provide to the enforcement agent. The Government's preferred option is a negotiable fee within a bandwidth with a fixed floor and a ceiling for debts below a value threshold to be determined by regulation—the floor providing a minimum return for the enforcement agent and the ceiling protecting the JD, the fee being recoverable when enforcement is successful.

Currently, problems are caused if the JD offers to repay the debt directly to the JC after the warrant has been handed to the enforcement agent, as the agent may have undertaken work for which he may charge a legitimate fee. If, however, the JC does accept payment from the JD after issuing the

---

[125] The fees charged by Sheriffs are set out in the Sheriffs' Fees (Amendment) Order 1956 and other secondary legislation. For an overview of the present fees and charges system, see *Green Paper*, Annex C, available at http://www.dca.gov.uk/enforcement/enfrev01/repac.htm.

warrant, the amount of the up-front fee which he will already have paid to the enforcement agent, should be recoverable in addition to the judgment debt. The enforcement agent will retain the fee and the fee will be deducted from the amount owed by the JD to the JC.

CHAPTER 8

FRANCE

Marie-Laure Niboyet and Sabine Lacassagne[1]

Enforcement of judicial decisions in France is principally governed by the law of 9 July 1991[2] (L.) and its application decree of the 31 December 1992 (R.). [3] The scope of this law only concerns enforcement of movable properties and protective measures.[4] The 'saisie immobilière' is concerned with enforcement against immovable property and is governed by Articles 673–779 of the 1806 Napoleon Code of Civil Procedure. Some other enforcement procedures are codified in special codes. For these measures, the 1991 law represents what could be called the 'ordinary' law of enforcement.[5]

The 1991 law is the result of a far-reaching reform of enforcement law. Before this date, enforcement procedures were codified in the 1806 Napoleonic code of civil procedure and had never been changed with a global reform. This is the reason why it appears necessary to adapt enforcement procedures to the evolution of two centuries of judicial enforcement and the diversity of assets, the various forms of hiding assets, and the development of consumer credit. The reform pursued the aim of instituting adequate enforcement to the variety of assets and the different measures available to the creditors (levy under a lien, seizure of movable assets, seizure of cars or movables placed in a safe etc). Provisions have also been taken in order to facilitate the disclosure of the debtor's assets and to simplify the recovery of debts. The 1991 law increases the value of the *titre exécutoire* (warrant of execution) so that the creditor, in most cases, can obtain forced execution without any judicial intervention. The reform instituted a unique

---

[1] Centre de Droit Civil des Affaires et du Contentieux Economique, Université Paris X-Nanterre.

[2] JO 14 July 1991, 9228. The initial text was modified and completed by different laws enacted in December 1991 (Art 86), July 1992 (Art 18 and 83 *bis*), December 1992 (Art 41), Feb 1994 (Art 22-1) and July 1998 (Art 62 and 21-1).

[3] JO 5 Aug 1992, 10530. The text was modified by different decrees enacted in July 1993 (Art 29-2 and R. 145-3, 145-27 and 145-31 Code du travail), Dec 1996 and Apr 1997 (Art 19), Oct and Dec 1998.

[4] Judicial seizure and the taking of security by the court (*nantissement de fonds de commerce, hypothèques*) is also covered.

[5] The rules of the 1991 law are applicable until no special provision governs the question.

judge (JEX)[6] in charge of resolving execution difficulties during enforcement procedures.[7]

This report will briefly describe the principles of forced execution and in particular the place occupied by the execution agents, the different methods of forced execution, the enforcement procedure, and the research of information on the debtor's assets.

First of all, it is important to recall that, in the French enforcement law, the creditor has total control of all stages of the execution procedure, as it can only be carried out on his initiative. However, the creditor is not allowed to conduct the enforcement procedure. This remains the monopoly of specialized agents in forced execution.

I. THE ENFORCEMENT AGENTS

The power to exercise coercion against debtors or their assets used to be up to the creditor himself, who could proceed, on his own, and exercise private seizure of the debtor personally or of the debtor's assets. Nowadays, the exercise of coercion belongs mainly and mostly to the *huissiers de justice.* Forced execution is considered an extension of the state's *imperium* and its implementation is carried out by these public officers. The creditor is, for example, not allowed, except in very limited circumstances, to witness the different acts of enforcement (Article R.4).

A. The huissiers de justice

The *huissiers* are public officers in charge of different judicial performances. They may serve as official court attendants,[8] but most of them are in charge of delivering judicial and extra-judicial documents and are also in charge of enforcement proceedings.[9]

---

[6] The JEX is the president of the tribunal de grande instance (or the judge delegated by him). He shares the charge of judicial enforcement procedures with the president of the tribunal d'instance who is the only one competent in attachment of earnings (Art 145-5 code du travail); the president of the tribunal de commerce who can be competent in ordering protective measures in commercial litigation; and one of the judges of the tribunal de grande instance. These are the only members of the judiciary competent in *exequatur* procedures and sale of a minor's assets.

[7] The procedure before the JEX is oral and does not require representation by a lawyer.

[8] These bailiffs, called *huissiers audienciers*, are selected annually by the court from among the *huissiers* practising in the district. They are in charge of documentary delivery between lawyers. These functions require a lot of time so that the *huissiers audienciers* do not have any charge in enforcement procedures.

[9] They can also be appointed to undertake investigations. The *huissiers* may not give any opinion as to the factual or legal consequences to be drawn therefrom (in accordance with Art 249 of the new code of civil procedure). In procedure of interim payment, they are allowed to legally represent and to assist the defendants.

The *huissiers de justice* are governed by an order of 1945 and its application decree of 1956. They have authority within a defined territory:[10] the writs and procedures are done by the *huissiers* within the district of the *tribunal d'instance* corresponding to the debtor's residence. Within this district the *huissiers* are in competition with each other.

The *huissier* is the principal authority of the enforcement procedure. Any person who infringes the *huissier's* authority is liable criminally and under civil law.[11] As a public officer, he must give his assistance to the creditors within his territorial competence. However he can refuse this charge if the demand appears to be illicit or abusive.[12] The *huissier* also has an obligation to provide advice and information to both the debtor and the creditor.

The *huissier* is considered to be under the creditor's mandate. He can only proceed when the creditor gives him power to do so. His deliverance of the *titre exécutoire* (warrant of execution) to the *huissier* is proof of such empowerment. The commencement of the enforcement procedure, and the choice of the measure belong to the sole creditor,[13] as does the choice of the asset subject to execution. However, the creditor may be sanctioned if found to be abusing the system by way of initiating these execution procedures.

The public officer is responsible for the entire enforcement procedure. In case of difficulty, he must refer to the JEX or to the department of the public prosecutor to obtain authorizations and injunctions.[14] The *huissier* can never represent the parties before the JEX.

II. THE OTHER ENFORCEMENT AGENTS

A. *The auctioneer* (commissaire-priseur)

These public officers have a monopoly on the judicially ordered auction sale of movable personal property.[15] They take part in the enforcement procedure whenever the auction sale is ordered after an attachment of movable property.

---

[10] Arts 5–8 of the 1956 decree.

[11] Art 258, 258-1 of the penal code.

[12] For example, if the value of the costs for the execution measure exceeds the value of the initial demand (Art L.18-2).

[13] The creditor can choose to proceed or not, even if the value of his claim is very low. He can choose the type of measures to enforce and also the good that would be concerned by the enforcement procedure. Cf Art L.22-1 *'le créancier a le choix des mesures propres à assurer l'exécution ou la conservation de sa créance'*.

[14] Art L.10-1.

[15] Art 3 of the 1816 order, modified in June 1975.

B. *The court broker* (courtier en marchandise)

The tribunal de commerce can appoint the broker to sell on auction the wholesale goods that have been the subject of an attachment measure.[16]

C. *The court clerk* (greffier du tribunal d'instance)

The clerk of the *tribunal d'instance* is the only person allowed to proceed to an attachment of earnings of the debtor.[17]

D. *Notaries and solicitors*

Notaries and solicitors play both a residual role in enforcement procedure. They can register judicial securities and can also issue the order for attachment of immovable property.

III. THE DIFFERENT WAYS OF ENFORCEMENT

Forced execution against the person of the debtor is nowadays residual. Civil imprisonment, governed by Articles 749–62 of the penal code is not applicable any more in civil and in commercial matters since the law of 22 July 1867. Some infringements still punish the debtor in person for his debts,[18] but coercion is mostly exercised on the debtor's assets whenever specific performance is not the remedy sought.

A. *Execution on property*

In French law, the debtor's property is considered the common pledge of the creditors.[19] Forced execution consequently concerns all the debtor's assets. The execution measures have to be exercised on assets belonging to the debtor that are disposable. Execution on property takes the form of an attachment that freezes the assets in a way to protect them until a judicial

---

[16] Art 17 of the 1964 decree.

[17] Art R.145-10 to R. 145-30 of the code du travail.

[18] The most important of these infringements is the *délit d'abandon de famille* governed by Art 227-3 of the penal code whenever the debtor of an alimony allowance is reluctant to pay. Art 314-7 governs the infraction of insolvency's organization, Art 314-6 the misappropriation of seized properties. Art 197 of the 1985 law relative to insolvency procedures governs the infraction of bankruptcy.

[19] The price is distributed among them proportionately unless there are creditors with legitimate grounds for preference (Art 2093 code civil).

sale takes place. There are attachments of movable property[20] and attachments of immovable property.

1. Attachment of movable property

(a) Judicial sale
The judicial sale concerns movable property of the debtor. The creditor who holds a *titre exécutoire* obtains the attachment and the sale of the assets in order to be paid, whether it is in possession of the debtor or a third party. If the amount of the credit does not exceed EUR525, the measure is subsidiary. The creditor must first ask the debtor to give the name and address of his employer and/or the location of his bank account. If the debtor does not answer, it is then possible to obtain the authorization of judicial sale from the JEX. The debtor still has the use of the assets until the sale. There are certain non-attachable assets such as basic household equipment necessary to perform his or her profession or items vital for the care of a disabled or ill person.

(b) Attachment of a motor vehicle
There are two different ways of attaching a motor vehicle. The first one is the registration of the seizure of a vehicle in the office of the *'préfecture'* (R165 to R 69), and this renders impossible any transaction concerning the vehicle. The attachment is notified to the debtor within a period of eight days after the registration. The freezing effect of the measure lasts for two years but it can be renewed. The second one consists of the physical immobilization of the vehicle (Article L.58).[21] The *huissier* indicates his name and address on the vehicle. The attachment is notified to the debtor, who has one month to contest the measure or to pay the creditor. At the expiry, the creditor can obtain the judicial sale of the vehicle or its delivery.

(c) Attachment of earnings
Article L.145–1 of the *code du travail* provides the possibility for the creditor to seize directly in the hands of the employer the salary of his own debtor. Only a portion of the salary is liable to seizure. A second portion can be seized only by the sole alimony creditors. The last portion is not liable to seizure (an amount equal to the minimum wage). The JEX is not competent to order this measure. The president of the *Tribunal d'Instance* is the only judge that is competent in the same way as the JEX in other

---

[20] Judicial sale (*saisie-vente*), garnishment (*saisie-attribution*), attachment of transferable securities issued by stock companies (*saisie de valeurs mobilières*), attachment of a motor vehicle (*saisie de véhicule*).
[21] The *huissier* decides on the appropriate measure to effect immobilization; it must not damage the vehicle.

enforcement measures. The seizure is automatically preceded by an attempt of conciliation (the creditor addresses a petition to the judge, who calls on the debtor). If it is unsuccessful, the judge will order enforcement. The measure is notified to the employer and to the debtor within eight days. The employer must inform the tribunal of the employment details of the debtor within 15 days of the notification. The employer must then deduct from the employee's salary the maximum amount permitted under law in monthly fixed amounts until the full recovery of the debt. This amount is paid by the employer to the court clerk. The court clerk is responsible for distributing such amounts between the creditors.

(d) Garnishee orders
Garnishee orders allow the creditor who has a *titre exécutoire,* to prevent a third party against whom the debtor is judicially enforcing a debt from paying the debtor and to obtain from such third party (debtor of the debtor), and in priority to the debtor, satisfaction of the debt.[22] As soon as the garnishee order is notified to the third party, the preferential creditor becomes entitled to the third party debt up to the amount of the debt owed by the third party to the debtor. If insolvency proceedings have been instituted, the creditor still remains protected if the notification took place before the beginning of the procedure. Third parties must inform the *huissier* about the scope of their own debt to the debtor. The *huissier* notifies the debtor within the period of eight days. After a month, if the debtor has not contested the measure, the creditor is authorized to be paid.

Whenever the third party is a bank or similar institution, it must inform the *huissier* about the accounts opened in name of the debtor and their balance. A difficulty appears in such a situation. Article R.74 provides that the garnishee order has a freezing effect on all the bank accounts, even if the credit amount exceeds the sum owed by the garnishor. This can be very prejudicial for the economic activity of the debtor. In practice banks have re-interpreted this provision. Banks place the amount seized in a special bank account and leave the remaning sum to be freely disposable by the debtor, although the debtor is asked to provide other guarantees to protect them and other creditors. This requires the agreement of all parties and/or the intervention of the JEX.

2. Attachment of immovable property

This measure is enforced by the creditor who has a *titre exécutoire*. It can be ordered against a third party possessor of the property if the creditor is

---

[22] Arts L.42–L.49 and R.55–R.79.

the beneficiary of a mortgage or other privilege.(Articles 673 to 748 of the former civil procedure code).

B. Specific performance

Every obligation to do or not to do gives rise to an action for damages, in the event of non-performance on the part of the obligor (Article 1142 code civil). It is impossible to condemn the debtor to change his behaviour or to compel him to do something without undermining his integrity.[23] However, it remains unbearable for the judge to see his judicial authority flouted. French law provides for direct and indirect ways to obtain specific performance.[24]

The obligee has the right to demand destruction of whatever has been done in violation of an undertaking and may obtain authorization to destroy it himself at the expense of the obligor, without prejudice to payment of damages, in a property case. The obligee may also, in case of non-performance, be authorized to perform the obligation himself at the expense of the obligor. If the obligation is to refrain from doing something, the party who violates it is liable by the mere fact of such a violation.

1. Incentive measures

Indirect incentive measures are still the best way to enforce obligation to do or not to do something. Tribunals may order an *astreinte* (a pecuniary penalty) secondarily to the principal sum owed, to encourage the debtor to comply with a decision.[25] The *astreinte* is independent of damages. This penalty arises when the debtor does not comply with the payment order. The penalty usually grows in time as the debtor resists paying. An accrued *astreinte* that is not paid allows a *saisie conservatoire* (protective measure) on the debtor's personal property. All money deriving from the *astreinte* is for the benefit of the creditor.

In an *astreinte provisoire* the sum fixed is only provisional and cannot be enforced until the court has 'liquidated' it at the end of the period given to the debtor to perform. In an *astreinte définitive* the sum payable is not subject to revision.

The *astreinte* can be ordered by any judge in any matter. The JEX can order an *astreinte* to support its own decisions but also decisions of other judicial authorities if circumstances make it necessary.[26]

---

[23] *Nemo praecise cogi potest ad factum*: nobody can be compelled to act.
[24] Expulsion (Arts L.61–L.66 and R.194–R.209). Garnishment (Arts L.56–R.140 and R.154).
[25] Art L.33. [26] Art L.33-2.

The liquidation of the *astreinte* transforms the threat of a pecuniary penalty into a real debt in the event of a total or partial failure of execution or of a delay in execution. The liquidation must be requested by the creditor. The JEX is competent to liquidate the *astreinte*, except if the judge who ordered the *astreinte* is still competent, or asks to remain competent for the liquidation. Except where it is established that the failure to execute the judicial decision results from an accident or force majeure, the *astreinte* will be enforced. If the *astreinte* is provisional, the judge may increase or decrease the amount of the penalty depending on the debtor's conduct.

2. Attachment-Return

The measure consists of the return of movable property in the debtor's possession to the creditor (the creditor being the rightful owner or he who has a right of usage) (Article L.56). This enforcement measure is based on a document authorizing execution or on an injunction from the JEX and can be enforced against the debtor or a third party in possession. The creditor can be authorized to enforce a provisional measure in order to guarantee the efficiency of the return (R.155 and R.156). This prevents the asset from being disposed of.

IV. THE ENFORCEMENT PROCEDURE

A. Non-attachable property

Jurisdictional and executionary immunity prevent property from being attachable, as do reasons dictated by the law, or in some cases due to the debtor's own will (Article L.14).

Assets that are not attachable by operation of the law relate to basic household goods of the debtor and his family, equipment necessary for his profession, or vital for the care of a disabled or sick person. A portion of the salary or income, including unemployment benefits and social insurance, is also not attachable, as well as a bill of exchange, a check to order or drafts.

Some assets are not attachable due to the will of the debtor: family assets, dowries (before the reform of matrimonial regime that abolished dowries)[??], and assets mentioned in a 'not attachable clause' included in a gift.

B. Conditions of enforcement procedure

1. Material conditions

Execution measures cannot take place on Sundays or bank holidays, neither can they be performed before 6 am or after 9 pm, except with the special authorization of the JEX (Article L.28). Creditors cannot witness the operations, except with the special authorization from the JEX (Article R.4).

The debtor or the third party who is indirectly concerned with the attachment should preferably witness the enforcement procedure, even if it is not necessary.

Specialists who are to perform some enforcement operations (locksmiths etc) are also asked to attend.

If it is necessary to enter *manu militari* in private premises or to access private property, the creditor must have a *titre exécutoire* and must respect some other conditions.[27] In a judicial sale or in an attachment of immovable property, the *huissier* cannot force doors or windows in order to access the property. If the order is to expel a person from the property, he cannot oblige the person to leave the property by force. He must address the administrative authority.

The intervention of the administrative authorities is sometimes limited to the witnessing of the execution. A list specifies the people who can witness this if access to private property is required.[28]

If there is a public security risk or the protection of persons becomes necessary during the procedure, the *huissier* can request the assistance of public force (Article L.16). The *huissier* may ask the *Préfet* or any delegated authority for assistance. In order to do this he must show the *titre exécutoire*, the necessity of police intervention, and his inability to perform the necessary measures of his own accord. The demand can be refused because of higher public interests. The refusal must be motivated and will be transmitted to the department of the public prosecutor (*Procureur de la République*) who can ask for an explanation and try to prove the opportunity or necessity of a police intervention.[29] The department of the public prosecutor may exceed its own authority by reviewing the judicial decision. In case of refusal, even if the decision is motivated, the creditor can always ask for remedies against the State due to the loss incurred.[30]

---

[27] In case of expulsion, a delay must be respected to let the debtor quit the premises before a specific time. In case of judicial sale, a delay of eight days must be respected after the putting in default.

[28] This can be the mayor or his deputy, a civil servant designated by the mayor, a representative of the police force or the gendarmerie and in their absence, two persons who are not known by the creditor or by the *huissier*.

[29] A failure to answer within a two-month period is considered a refusal.

[30] The equality of citizen before public charges is the cause of action. When the State places public interests higher than the right of the creditor to obtain enforcement, the entire community must compensate for any loss. The *tribunal administratif* within the district of the *Préfet* is competent to resolve the action.

2. The legal conditions

(a) The titre exécutoire *(warrant of exécution)*

The *titre exécutoire* is the title delivered in the name of the State which gives the creditor power to obtain enforcement of the judicial decision. Forced execution is a measure that can only be requested by the creditor of a liquid debt, due and owing. The executory character of the title comes from the insertion of the *formule exécutoire* on a copy of the decision. Article L.3 provides an enumeration of executory titles.

(b) Judicial decisions and similar acts

Final decisions that are not subject to appeal and that are delivered to the debtor are considered enforceable. Judgments can also be enforced before the expiry of the period to file an appeal if the judge and the clerk make this clear on the act by means of their signature.

This type of interim execution requires notification to the debtor, although during the time in which the judgment can be appealed, there can be no execution on immovable assets. Interim execution may also be conditioned upon the giving of a guarantee, real or personal, sufficient to cover all restitutions or reparations. The debtor may avoid execution upon his property by depositing assets or money sufficient to cover the amount for which he has been found liable.

Reconciliation or settlement reports that have been approved by court (homologation),[31] as well as foreign judgments and arbitral awards that have been approved by a court (by an *exequatur* procedure) are assimilated to national judgments.

(c) Notarial acts can constitute a titre exécutoire

No order of priority in execution measures

In principle, the creditor is allowed to choose between the enforcement measures available. However, the 1991 law provides exceptions if enforcement is performed against a sole trader,[32] or if it concerns private premises,[33] or in case of attachment of immovable property.[34]

(d) Reports on enforcement procedures

The *huissier* must prepare a single report of the enforcement proceedings. The report contains the date, name of the creditor and that of the debtor,

---

[31] Art 131 and 1441-4 NCPC.
[32] Execution is performed on assets used for one's work and after on personal assets (Art L.22-1).
[33] Subsidiarity of judicial sale: Art L.51.
[34] Arts 2206, 2209, and 2210 of the code civil.

name, signature and address of the *huissier*, and references provided by the 1992 decree for each specific measure. The report must be delivered by the *huissier* or by ordinary or registered letter.

V. RESEARCH OF INFORMATION ABOUT THE DEBTOR'S ASSETS

Research of information comes up in French law against the principle of privacy, of bank secrecy and the prohibition on the existence of a centralized database on the debtor's assets.

However, it seems intolerable to the French legislator that it may not be possible to enforce judicial decisions due to a lack of information on the debtor's assets. The law of 1991 provides in its Article 41 (see Article R.54) for the power of the *huissier* to ask the department of the public prosecutor for assistance in order for the debtor's assets to be disclosed.

A. Assistance of department of the public prosecutor

Research of information is strictly controlled by law. The department of the public prosecutor is the only authority empowered to ask for information relating to the debtor.[35] The *huissier* does not have any direct access to information. He must ask the department of the public prosecutor for the information he needs. The department of the public prosecutor performs the research (Articles L.49–51).[36] The aim of the legislators in 1991 was mainly to channel the information into the hands of the judicial authority. The creditors must not have access to confidential information.

The system is not very successful. Part of the failure of this procedure results from the heavy workload of the department of the public prosecutor in criminal and civil procedures. The research of information takes time and the department of the public prosecutor lacks this. Most of the time, the information is obsolete when or if it is communicated to the *huissier*. This explains the development of private organizations (such as private detectives) with much-debated results.

When the department of the public prosecutor does research, it concerns itself only with the information listed in the 1991 law.

---

[35] This power cannotcannot even be delegated to police officers or *huissiers de justice*.

[36] He must prove the *titre exécutoire*, and attach a certificate of unsuccessful research. The *huissier* must have the assistance of the debtor himself. If the debtor does not answer, and if the *huissier* made hast, the public ministry can perform. The department of the public prosecutor has discretion to appreciate if the *huissier* made hast and can enjoin him to continue by himself.

1. Restrictive list of available information

The *huissier* can obtain from the department of the public prosecutor :

- the debtor's address
- the address of the debtor's employer
- the debtor's bank account details.[37]

This information is available from the central archives of the Banque de France or from the bank, post office, etc.[38] All entities under the supervision of the State (including concessions) are required to deliver such information. However, the police authorities are not subject to this requirement unless the information is in their hands (ie they are not required to acquire fresh information for the *huissier*).

2. Use of information

The required information can only be used for the enforcement of the judgment or other document with a *titre exécutoire* for which they were requested. They cannot be handed over to a third party. The use of information must be limited. If not, any person in possession of such information will be severely penalized.[39] Some academics greatly doubt the enforceability of the sanctions.[40] It seems highly improbable that Article L.41-1 could be applied, except in case of *flagrante delicto*.

If the research is unsuccessful, the department of the public prosecutor must inform the *huissier* who himself informs the creditor so that the latter can draw conclusions from such failure. After a three-month period without an answer from the Public Ministry, the research is considered unsuccessful. If the department of the public prosecutor has carried out adequate research there is no State responsibility. If the department of the public prosecutor has not carried out proper research, the State is responsible but can retain an action against the civil servant who committed the fault.[41]

B. *Other sources of information*

In matters of alimony, Article 7 of the 1973 law provides the right for the

---

[37] It is not possible to know if the account is in the black or in the red. This information is only available when the *huissier* performs a seizure on the bank account.
[38] The information concerns all the account in the same bank opened in the name of the debtor.
[39] Art 226-21 of the penal code. The *huissier* and creditor involve their civil and professional liabilities.
[40] R Perrot and P Thery *Procédures civiles d'exécution* (Dalloz 2000), spéc. n°336, 356.
[41] Art L.181-1 of the code de l'organization judiciaire.

creditor to obtain from public organizations the information necessary for enforcement.

In fiscal matters, as well as in matters of insolvency, Article 83 of the *Livre de procédure fiscale* and article 19 of the 1985 law contain a similar obligation.

When the enforcement procedure involves a third party, the 1991 law imposes on the third party the obligation to lend his support to the court (article 10 of the civil code, L.24 al. 1er).The third party's obligations are to guard or to assist in the deliverance of the attached assets, as well as to inform the creditor of his own obligations towards the debtor (Article L.44). Otherwise the third party is liable. If he does not cooperate, he could be sentenced to the amount of the debt or to incentive measures in order to obtain information.

VI. REMEDIES IN CASE OF UNJUSTIFIED OR IRREGULAR ENFORCEMENT PROCEEDINGS

The debtor does not have any remedy in order to contest the *titre exécutoire* at the enforcement proceedings stage.

In a situation where a settlement is transformed into a *titre exécutoire* by the judge, there may have been no real control on the legitimacy of the agreement or its respect for the rights of the parties(including due process).[42]

The absence of an appeal against the *titre exécutoire* poses particular problems in the context of the project to create a European *titre exécutoire*. In order to reach adequate harmonization between the law of the Member States it must be decided whether or not it is possible for the local jurisdiction to verify whether the *titre exécutoire* was granted following principles of due process.

The debtor can obtain the stay of execution or the withdrawal of the measure through different methods. The JEX is competent to rule on this claim as well as to decide if the *huissier*/creditor are responsible for damages for enforcing unjustified or irregular execution.

---

[42] The homologation is an *inaudita altera parte* procedure (Art 1441-4 of the NCPC)

CHAPTER 9

GERMANY

Burkhard Hess and Marcus Mack[1]

I. BASIC FEATURES OF THE GERMAN ENFORCEMENT SYSTEM

German enforcement law for civil claims is set out in Chapter 8 (ss 704–945) of the Code of Civil Procedure, *Zivilprozessordnung* (ZPO). Additional provisions relating to the execution in immovable property are to be found in the Code Regulating Sequestration and Public Sale (*Gesetz über die Zwangsversteigerung und Zwangsverwaltung*, ZVG). The organization of the courts and the status of the bailiffs and of the court officers is determined in the Act on the Organization of the Civil Courts, *Gerichtsverfassungsgesetz* (GVG) and in the Act on Court Officers, *Rechtspflegergesetz* (RPflG).

Enforceable instruments are mainly judgments which have become *res judicata* and provisionally enforceable judgments.[2] Section 794 ZPO contains an additional list of enforceable instruments such as court settlements (*Prozessvergleiche*), court cost orders (*Kostenfestsetzungsbeschlüsse*), enforceable default summons (*Vollstreckungsbescheide*), based on orders for payment (*Mahnbescheide*), decisions granting the *exequatur* on arbitral awards and enforceable instruments of public notaries (Notarielle Urkunden).

II. THE STRUCTURE OF THE ENFORCEMENT AGENCIES—THEIR TASKS IN RELATION TO ENFORCEMENT MEASURES

A. The 'decentralized' structure of the German enforcement system

German law distinguishes between the enforcement of monetary claims (ss 803–82a ZPO) and non-monetary claims (ss 883–98 ZPO). For monetary

---

[1] Professor and Wissenschaftliches Assistent, Karl-Ruprechts-University Heidelberg.

[2] For an introduction to the German approach to provisional enforceability, see KD Kerameus 'Enforcement in the International Context' 264 Receuil des Cours 181, 238 (1997 [in English]); B Hess in Wiezorek & Schütze *Commentary on the German Code of Civil Procedure* (3rd edn 1999), Preliminary remarks to s 707–720a [in German].

claims the German Code of Civil Procedure provides different procedures relating to the execution in movable property and to the garnishment of claims or other property rights. The enforcement imposed on the immovable property of the debtor is regulated in sections 864–71 ZPO and in the Code Regulating Sequestration and Public Sale (Zwangsversteigerungsgesetz, ZVG).

Different enforcement organs are responsible for the different means of enforcement. The main competence lies with the bailiffs (*Gerichtsvollzieher*) who are responsible for the attachment of movable property, the (limited) disclosure of the debtor's assets and the delivery of or recovery of goods and also for evictions. Garnishments are effected by court officers (*Rechtspfleger*) acting within the local courts *(Amtsgerichte)*. Court officers are also competent for the execution upon real estate of the debtor. These procedures are set out in the Code Regulating Sequestration and Execution by Public Sale   (*Zwangsversteigerungsgesetz*). If the creditor's claim is enforced by an execution lien in the debtor's land, the land register office (*Grundbuchamt*) will register a mortgage to enforce the claim.

Non-monetary claims (especially enforceable claims to refrain from a certain act) are normally enforced by the district courts themselves by imposing fines upon the debtor.

The German systems relies on the initiative of the judgment creditor and of his counsel: It is up to the creditor to gather the necessary information and to decide on the method of enforcement by applying directly to the competent organ. The competent organ then carries out the enforcement on its own responsibility according to the legal procedures. However, it is up to the creditor to control the procedure and to choose a different method if the selected enforcement measure should fail.

B. The Courts

As far as the courts are concerned, a double distinction has to be made. The first difference relates to the competencies of the court. The second relates to the persons who are responsible for the performance and the supervision of the enforcement proceedings. As German law does not provide a single, comprehensive enforcement court, the allocation of different enforcement matters to different types of personnel (bailiffs, court officers, enforcement judges) is a much more important feature than the organization of the enforcement courts themselves.

1. Competence

(a) Local courts acting as enforcement courts (Vollstreckungsgericht)
Several functions of the enforcement proceedings are allocated to the so-called 'enforcement court' (*Vollstreckungsgericht*), which is, according to

section 764(1) ZPO, the local court (*Amtsgericht*) where the property to be seized or attached is located. Normally, the enforcement court is organized as a division of the local court. Its competencies relate to the enforcement for monetary claims by means of:

- garnishment of monetary claims (for example bank accounts) or other property rights (s 828–63 ZPO);[3]
- execution against immovable property of the debtor by way of the registration of an enforcement mortgage (s 867 ZPO),[4] or by forced sale or forced administration of the real estate (ss 864–71 ZPO, s 1 ZVG);
- imposing a fine if the debtor refuses to disclose assets under oath (ss 899, 901 ZPO).
- Finally, while bailiffs are responsible for the execution relating to movable property, some of their activities (such as searching a home without the consent of the owner, section 758a ZPO) are subject to a prior authorization of the enforcement court. The intervention of the judge is required by the German constitution (Article 13(2) Basic Law).[5]

(b) Courts of first instance acting as enforcement organs.
In exceptional circumstances the responsibility for enforcement measures lies with the courts of first instance.[6] In these instances, these courts are also competent for the enforcement of judgments made by a court of a higher instance (Court of Appeal or the Supreme Federal Civil Court).

This is the case for the enforcement of injunctions relating to acts which must be performed personally by the debtor (eg the rendering of an account or giving a particular information). The first instance courts may impose disciplinary fines on the debtor who refuses to perform the act, section 888 ZPO. Reluctant debtors may also be sanctioned by a term of imprisonment.

A similar legal situation applies in the case of judgments requiring the debtor to refrain from a certain act. These judgments are enforced through contempt of court orders (s 890 ZPO).[7]

---

[3] Garnishment takes place, at least conceptually, in two steps, although these are generally contained in a single document. In the first step, the 'attachment decision' (Pfändungsbeschluß), the court orders that the garnishee not make payment to the debtor (Arrestatorium) and that the debtor not dispose of the claim against the garnishee (Inhibitorium). In the second step—the 'transfer decision' (Überweisungsbeschluß)—the court assigns this claim to the garnishor or judgment creditor. It is then up to the creditor to recover the sum from the garnishee.

[4] Strictly speaking, it is the land register office that is competent as such for the inscription of the mortgage.

[5] F Baur and R Stürner, Zwangsvollstreckungsrecht vol 1, 12. ed. 1995, §8 n° 8.12.

[6] According to s 23, 71 GVG first instance courts are the local courts [Amtsgerichte] (up to an amount of €5,000) and the district courts [Landgerichte]).

[7] Fines (which are to be paid to the Exchequer) are executed on the basis of the federal Justizbeitreibungordnung (JBeitrO). It only applies to payments ordered by federal courts. The relevant enforcement laws of all federal states however refer directly to the JBeitrO.

In exceptional instances, courts of any instance enforce their judgments themselves:

- if according to the judgment, the debtor is obliged to perform an act which can also be performed by a third person (*Vollstreckung vertretbarer Handlungen*), section 887 ZPO. In this situation, the judgment authorises the creditor to carry out the act himself or with the help of a third person and orders the debtor to advance the costs likely to be incurred in carrying out the act.[8]
- if the plaintiff obtains a judgment imposing an obligation on the defendant to make a declaration (*Willenserklärung,* for example to consent to contract), this declaration is presumed to have been given when the judgment becomes *res judicata*, section 894 ZPO.

2. Competent agents in the enforcement courts

Court officers (Rechtspfleger): Most of the functions conferred on the enforcement court are performed by court officers (*Rechtspfleger,* s 20 n° 17 RPflG). Their responsibilities include garnishment proceedings (s 20 n° 16 RPfG, s 828 et seq. ZPO) and enforcement measures relating to real estate (s 3 (1) (i) RPflG).[9]

Judges (Richter): The main competence of the judges in relation to enforcement matters relates to the control of the court officers' and the bailiffs' actions. Additionally, the intervention of the judge is also necessary if enforcement measures infringe upon certain constitutional rights of the debtor, for example, if the bailiff intends to search the house of the debtor without his consent (Article 13 German Constitution) or if the creditor applies for an arrest (detention) of the debtor (Article 104 German Constitution).

C. Bailiffs (Gerichtsvollzieher)

Bailiffs are responsible for the enforcement of tangible property (including negotiable instruments)[10] by way of seizure and public sale, as well as for the delivery or recovery of goods and for evictions. Bailiffs also perform the service of documents relating to other forms of seizure. In 1998, German

---

[8] Such obligations of the debtor are regularly enforced by garnishment or the seizure of his movables.

[9] Court Officers also perform a wide range of other tasks than enforcement matters. They run the land registry and other registries, and are responsible in as different areas as guardianship and succession, insolvency, legal aid and the like. Within a local court, though, the different functions are conferred to specialised court officers.

[10] See A Viertelhausen 'Vollstreckung in Wertpapiere' Deutsche Gerichtsvollzieherzeitschrift (DGVZ) 2000, 129.

legislation has conferred to the bailiffs the additional responsibility of obtaining the declaration of the debtor's assets (s 899 et seq ZPO).

Based on the structure of the German Procedural Code, the bailiff is in effect the most prominent enforcement organ: The eighth book of the ZPO (which deals with enforcement proceedings) largely refers to the bailiff (see especially s 750 et seq ZPO). However, the most important enforcement agents *in practice* are the court officers (*Rechtspfleger*), as they are competent for most of the other forms of seizure, especially garnishments. The value of attached claims is in fact several times higher than the value of the seized movable property.

III. THE PRESENCE AND DISTRIBUTION

A. Courts: judges and court officers

Judges and *Rechtspfleger* act within the court system and their presence on the territory is determined accordingly. Federal statistics do not show specific figures of 'enforcement courts'. As enforcement courts are normally organized as departments of the local courts, the number of local courts corresponds to the structure of enforcement courts. In 2000 federal statistics revealed 685 local courts in Germany.[11]

The size of the local court districts varies from State to State. While the Federal State of *Hamburg* provides seven local courts for a territory of 755 km2 with 1.7 million inhabitants (ie one court for roughly 250,000 citizens), the more rural Federal State of *Baden-Württemberg* provides 108 local courts for a territory of 35.751 km2 inhabited by 10.5 million persons (ie one court for roughly 100,000 citizens) in 2001. The federal statistics of the year 2000 counted 20,880 judges (16,606 in civil and criminal matter courts (*ordentliche Gerichtsbarkeit*) and labour courts) and 14,000 court officers (*Rechtspfleger*) in the whole country .[12]

B. Bailiffs

Normally, several bailiffs are appointed to the local courts. The size of the local courts differs according to the size of the municipality where the court is located. On average, six to eight bailiffs are attached to one enforcement court. Judgment creditors may apply directly to the general court office which will help them to identify the competent bailiff. The competence of

[11] BMJ (ed) Zahlen aus der Justiz (2002) 5 <http://www.bmj.bund.de/images/11315.pdf>.
[12] See Annex 1 to this chapter (provided by the web site of the Statistisches Bundesamt <http://www.destatis.de>)

the responsible bailiff is determined by reference to the domicile of the debtor or the location of the assets to be seized.

Section 16 (1) of the *Gerichtsvollzieherordnung* (Regulation on the Status of Bailiffs, GVO) provides:

If in a local court district there is employed more than one bailiff [. . .], the supervising judge assigns to each bailiff a territorially delimited district (bailiff district/*Gerichtsvollzieherbezirk*). When allocating the districts, the judge will consider the need for an even distribution of business and the possibility of an efficient arrangement of the bailiffs' official journeys. To every bailiff, he assigns one or [. . .] more [of the other] bailiffs as permanent substitute. With permission of the President of the District Court, the tasks can be assigned in a way other than by territory.

While in the 19th and early 20th centuries a competitive system was used,[13] nowadays in Germany commissioned *Gerichtsvollzieher*[14] normally have a monopoly on a definite area of territorial competence (*Bezirkssystem*). Accordingly, the earnings of a bailiff depend to some extent on the kind of district he is responsible for (rural, downtown, etc).[15] The territorial distribution excludes any competition.

The federal statistics of 2000 indicates 4,427 bailiffs (of which 879 were women) for Germany as a whole. However, there are considerable differences between the federal states. For example, in the City of Hamburg, with seven local court districts, the number of bailiffs has been increased from 91 to 98 due work-overload in 2000.[16] In 1999, there was one bailiff for every 18,733 citizens in Hamburg. The best bailiff–citizen ratio could be found in 1999 in the *Land* of *Berlin* (1:13.926), the least advantageous[17] in the *Land* of *Baden-Württemberg* (1:22,715), which increased it is ratio to 1 : 20,547 in 2000 with 511 *Gerichtsvollzieher* to 10.5 million citizens (2002: 537 bailiffs).[18]

IV. THE LEGAL STATUS OF ENFORCEMENT AGENCIES: PUBLIC AND PRIVATE

In Germany enforcement proceedings are considered to be an essential function of the State power which is exclusively exercised by State organs

---

[13] See W Kennett *Regulation of Enforcement Agents in Europe* vol 1 (2001) 41.
[14] The exception clause in s 16 (1) S. 4 GVO is hardly ever used.
[15] See above para 9.1.2.
[16] See the tables published annually in the DGVZ.
[17] Drucksache 15/630, Schleswigholsteinischer Landtag, 15. Wahlperiode. These numbers might also be attributable to the different economic circumstances in the different Länder and the resultant differences in the degree of forced execution.
[18] Landtag of Baden Württemberg, Drucksache 13/2184, p 3; <http://www3.Landtag-bw/WP13/Drucksachen/2000/13_2148_d.pdf>.

according to binding legal provisions.[19] Therefore, apart from the rare and limited exception of self-help (in cases of distress, section 226 German Civil Code), any kind of private (forced) enforcement is strictly forbidden (see below 10.3.). Bailiffs and court officers are civil servants, subject to the rule of law. The federation and the federal states must provide for effective enforcement institutions, because, according to the case law[20] of the German Constitutional Court, the constitutional guarantee of access to justice also includes efficient enforcement proceedings.[21]

However, the prohibition on empowering private 'enforcement agencies' to exercise force does not exclude private services for the recovery of debts (see below 10.3.).

V. THEIR TASKS IN RELATION TO THE DISCLOSURE OF THE DEBTOR'S ASSETS

In Germany it is the creditor's task to gather information on the debtor's location[22] and to find out the whereabouts of suitable assets out of which enforcement can be obtained. Normally, the enforcement authorities do not investigate the debtor's assets. German law does not allow enforcement agents special access to information. The current situation is very burdensome for the judgment creditors and their counsel. It is therefore sharply criticized in the legal literature.[23] In practice, some private investigators provide information about the location and the financial situation of the debtor.[24]

---

[19] From a systematic point of view some scholars (and a decision of the Federal Supreme Court (Bundesgerichtshof, BGH) 66 BGHZ 79, 80, overruled in 121 BGHZ 98, 121) consider enforcement proceedings to be a part of administrative law; eg J Blomeyer *Die Erinnerungsbefugnis Dritter in der Mobiliarvollstreckung* (1966) 28 ; R Bruns 'Die Vollstreckung in künftige Vermögensstücke des Schuldners', 171 AcP 358, 362. The predominant opinion of today considers enforcement proceedings as jurisdiction in a formal sense, see L Rosenberg, HF Gaul, and E Schilken *Zwangsvollstreckungsrecht* (11th edn 1997), §2 and passim, F Baur and R Stürner, 'Zwangsvollstreckungsrecht', vol. 1 (1995), §5 para 5.2.

[20] F Stein, M Jonas, and W Münzberg *ZPO—Kommentar zur Zivilprozessordnung* (22nd edn 2002) preliminary remarks to §704 ZPO, paras 43–4.

[21] This case law corresponds to the recent case law of the European Court of Human Rights (ECHR), 19 Mar1997, Hornsby v Greece, Recueil 1997, II para 33, 495, 510; 21 Apr 1998, Estima Jorge/Portugal, Recueil 1998 II para 727.

[22] Information about the debtor's current address is available to everybody on payment of a small fee. The main disadvantage lies in the fact that the information must be obtained at the local authorities. Creditors (as persons with a justifiable interest) are also entitled to obtain additional information, including the date of birth and the previous addresses of the debtors, s 21 Melderechtsrahmengesetz.

[23] In 1991, legislation adopted some minor changes allowing the bailiff to search the debtor's premises for additional information. See Hess in A Verbeke and M Caupain *La transparence patrimoniale* (Paris 1999), 47–50, 300–17.

[24] Commercial access to information is provided by the Schutzgemeinschaft für allgemeine

In the 1990s German enforcement law was changed in order to improve the judgment creditor's possibilities of finding out the whereabouts of the debtor's assets. If the bailiff when undertaking a seizure of property does not find sufficient assets for satisfaction of the creditor's debt, he can interrogate the debtor about any claims he holds against third parties. The information obtained is transferred to the judgment creditor.[25] The bailiff can also ask any person in the debtor's household about the debtor's employer and pass this information on to the creditor. Third parties are not, however, obliged to respond to his questions. The bailiff must inform them about their right to refuse to answer his questions.[26]

However, the position of the creditor is improved if the bailiff does not seize movable assets at the debtor's home.[27] If attempts at enforcement have been or are likely to be unsuccessful, the judgment creditor can request the bailiff to summon the debtor for a so-called 'debtor's declaration', sections 807, 899, et seq. ZPO.[28] The debtor is required to attend a hearing and to disclose his assets on solemn declaration. If the debtor contests his obligation, the enforcement court (court officer) will hear the case under section 900 (4) ZPO. On request of the creditor, the enforcement court (judge) may even order the imprisonment (of up to six months) of a debtor who refuses to give the solemn declaration (s 901 ZPO). After the hearing, the bailiff normally deposes the declaration (which is delivered on the basis of a standard form) at the enforcement register and sends a copy to the creditor, section 900 (5) ZPO. During a period of three years, a debtor can only be required to give an additional declaration if a creditor (in possession of a title) shows that there are reasons to believe that the debtor has a new source of income.[29] Registration lapses after three years, but the debtor can also get his name removed from the register if he satisfies the judgment debt in the interim (s 915(2) ZPO).

Kreditsicherung (SCHUFA), an organization of credit providers, which gives details of bad credit, unpaid cheques, applications for payment orders (Mahnbescheid), declarations of assets, and forced seizures in so far as they are known about. This information is only provided to members of the organization. Other commercial providers of information include Schimmelpfennig and Creditreform.

[25] Section 806a (1) ZPO.

[26] Section 806a (2) ZPO.

[27] As the intervention of the bailiff is a precondition for obtaining the asset's declaration, many creditors first apply for enforcement measures of the bailiffs.

[28] On demand of the debtor and with the consent of the creditor, the bailiff can take such a declaration directly after the unsuccessful attempt of seizure, s 900 (2) ZPO. Otherwise, he summons the debtor for the declaration which is delivered in a hearing at the bailiff's office, s 900 (3) ZPO.

[29] Otherwise, only creditors can request a copy of the first declaration from the enforcement court, see H Musielak and W Voit *Zivilprozessordnung- Kommentar* (3rd edn 2002) s 903 para 4

In practice, the main function of the debtor's declaration is not to disclose his assets but to provide an incentive for the debtor to pay voluntarily. The declaration of assets is registered in the 'debtor's register' which is maintained by the enforcement court and available to any creditor seeking information about the financial situation of the debtor (some local courts even offer electronic registers accessible via internet). The debtor's creditworthiness is thus a matter of public record.[30] Persons who figure in the 'debtors' list', immediately lose their creditworthiness and they have no real chance of getting any additional credit from a bank. They may even face serious difficulties in operating a bank account. These serious consequences normally provide an effective incentive to the debtor to comply voluntarily with the judgment.

VI. THE DEGREE OF SUPERVISION

A. Bailiffs

Bailiffs act outside the enforcement court, but under the supervision of the enforcement judge. They maintain an office under their own responsibility and at their own expense, section 46 et seq. *Gerichtsvollzieherordnung* (Regulation on the status of bailiffs, GVO). Sometimes bailiffs employ office clerks to cope with their workload.[31] They can form an office partnership[32] with other bailiffs, but they remain solely responsible for their duties in the respective districts. Bailiffs run their day-to-day business in enforcement matters independently (s 58 GVGA)[33] but they are subject to relatively strict control by the enforcement court. According to section 766 ZPO,[34] the judgment creditor and the debtor as well as any affected third person may challenge the legality of any action of the bailiff at the enforcement court.

---

[30] W Kennett *Regulation of Enforcement Agents in Europe* vol 1 (2001), 236.

[31] In practice, if the bailiff is married, both spouses run the office together.

[32] The office partnership, Bürogemeinschaft, means the sharing of an office for management purposes; it does not involve the sharing of professional activities.

[33] Details of the bailiff's procedure are regulated by administrative regulation, the Geschäftsanweisung für Gerichtsvollzieher (GVGA), which to a large extend simply explains the ZPO as in a commentary.

[34] Section 766 reads as follows: '(1) The court of execution rules on petitions, objections and complaints which affect the mode of enforcement or the procedure to be followed by the bailiff in carrying it out. . . . (2) The court of execution also has the authority to rule if a bailiff refuses to accept instructions to carry out an execution or to carry out an act of execution in compliance with the instructions, or if a complaint is made about the costs placed into account by the bailiff.'

In addition, the *Gerichtsvollzieherordnung* (ss 55–71) sets out in detail the books that need to be kept by the bailiff and the way that they should be handled. Quarterly inspections of each office are made by the supervisory judge or his appointed inspector (although the number of inspections can be increased or decreased in the light of experience).[35]

If the bailiff neglects his duties by negligence, the federal state employing the bailiff is liable for damages occurring to debtors or creditors under the terms of State responsibility (s 839 German Civil Code, Article 34 German Constitution). In case of gross negligence, the bailiff will be held personally liable to recourse by the State.[36]

B. Court officers

In terms of their personal status, court officers are civil servants. Therefore, they are fully subject to disciplinary control, including their working hours. However, section 9 RPflG grants them independence as to their judicial and administrative activities (*sachliche Unabhängigkeit*) similar to judicial independence. Therefore, court officers are basically independent in how they deal with the enforcement matters. Their decisions are only subject to the law. In difficult cases, however, especially matters involving the constitutionality of an relevant legal provision[37] or the application of foreign law, the court officer must refer the case to the judge. In summary, the supervision of the court officers does not correspond at all to the close supervision of bailiffs by the enforcement judge.

As a matter of principle, the *Rechtspfleger* is not subject to the supervision of the enforcement judge. In 1998, German legislation revised section 11 RPflG, the general remedy against the decisions of the *Rechtspfleger*. According to the new provision, decisions of the *Rechtspfleger* may be challenged by an appeal which must be lodged in the district court (*Landgericht*, s 72 GVG).

---

[35] According to §99 GVO, the inspector will check in particular:
- that new instructions have been entered properly in the Dienstregister and any advance payment has been properly entered in the accounts;
- that instructions are promptly carried out; that costs are properly calculated and entered in the accounts;
- that monies collected are properly and promptly given to the client (or other party to whom they are due) or paid into court;
- that different records tally;
- that the accounts are in order;
- that there are not too many enforcement proceedings that prove unsuccessful; and
- that the costs of enforcement are not disproportionately greater than the result to be achieved.

[36] BGH, Wertpapiermitteilungen (WM) 1999, 1842.

[37] Court officers cannot address directly the European Court of Justice under Art 234 EC Treaty—they must present the reference to the judge, see B Hess 108 ZZP 59 (1995).

C. Judges

According to Article 92 *Grundgesetz* (GG, German Constitution), judges are 'independent and only subject to the law'. Accordingly, section 26 (1) of the Law on Judges (*Deutsches Richtergesetz, DRiG*) provides that judges are subject to disciplinary supervision only to the extent that their independence is not infringed.[38] Disciplinary matters are decided by special 'Judicial Service Courts' on federal and state level (*Dienstgerichte des Bundes und der Länder*, s 61, 77 DRiG). Additionally, judicial review is exercised by the superior courts (below 7).

VII. LEGAL REMEDIES

A. Legal remedies available against unlawful enforcement

The German system of legal remedies in enforcement matters is particularly complicated and confusing.[39] Generally, the remedies can be divided into three groups. The first group (discussed at 7.1.1.) deals with irregularities during the enforcement procedure proper. The second group deals with objections and complaints derived from substantive law such as the action *to defend against execution* execution (s 767 ZPO: *Vollstreckungsabwehrklage/Vollstreckungsgegenklage*) and the third party complaint in opposition (s 771 ZPO: *Drittwiderspruchsklage*)[40] (7.1.2). The third group consists of remedies relating to the issuing of the enforceable copy, which is a prerequisite for the commencement of enforcement proceedings. These remedies are closely linked to the principle of formalization of the execution proceedings (7.1.3). The execution in immovable property also has its own rules with respect to remedies (7.1.4). Finally, the constitutional principle of proportionality allows for additional relief (7.1.5).

1. Remedies related to the enforcement procedure

(a) The Execution Complaint (Vollstreckungserinnerung, s 766 ZPO)

As far as the first group is concerned, the main remedy is the 'execution complaint' (s 766 ZPO: *Vollstreckungserinnerung*). It provides the basic remedy against procedural mistakes by the enforcement organs with regard to enforcement measures (including a bailiff's failure to act or refusal to

---

[38] Section 26 (2) reads: 'Notwithstanding paragraph 1, disciplinary supervision includes the right to hold before a judge any disorderly conduct as to his office and to admonish him to fulfil his duties in a proper and instantaneous way.'

[39] KD Karameus 'Enforcement in the international context' 264 RdC 197, 285 (1997).

[40] The third party complaint in opposition asserts that the third party claimant has a right in the object seized which prevents its alienation by the enforcement agents.

follow specific orders of the creditor). The judges of the enforcement courts are competent to decide on such complaints (s 766 (1) S. 1 ZPO, s 20 n° 17 S.2 RPflG) on application of the creditor, the debtor or a third party concerned (eg someone living with the debtor in the apartment searched by the bailiff).

As far as the conduct of the court officer is concerned, the situation is more complicated. This is due to the basic distinction between enforcement measures (*Maßnahmen*) and enforcement decisions (*Entscheidungen*), drawn by legal theory. Enforcement measures, normally of a rather administrative nature, are ordered in accordance with a motion of a party without the other side being heard (*ex parte* proceedings).[41] The attachment of a claim is a typical example of such an enforcement measure.

If the affected party is not heard before the enforcement measure is ordered, he or she may challenge the legality of the enforcement measure of a *Rechtspfleger* by a 'modified complaint' which is first reviewed by the *Rechtspfleger* of the execution court himself (*Abhilfeverfahren*).[42] A positive decision in regard to such a complaint constitutes an enforcement decision, which is subject to review by the district court (section 793 ZPO *sofortige Beschwerde*).[43] If the court officer does not amend the enforcement measure in accordance with the complaint, the file is transferred to the judge of the execution court for decision (see below; s 766 ZPO, s 20 n° 17 RPflG).

However, if the court officer deals with the case after hearing the affected person[44] and, therefore, makes an enforcement decision, this person can immediately apply to the district court (section 11 (1) RPflG, section 793 ZPO).

*(b) The Immediate Appeal (*Sofortige Beschwerde, s 793 ZPO*)*
Any decision of the enforcement court can be appealed under section 793 ZPO (*sofortige Beschwerde*), which relates to the competence of the District Court (section 567 (1) ZPO, section 72 GVG). A second appeal (*Rechtsbeschwerde*) which is limited to questions of law is open to the Federal Supreme Civil Court (s 572 (4), 574 (1) n° 2 ZPO, s 133 GVG).

---

[41] Including written statements.
[42] H Thomas and H Putzo (25th edn 2003) ZPO §766 °9, OLG Frankfurt OLGR 1999, 324.
[43] OLG Frankfurt OLGR 1999, 323.
[44] This includes those instances where the creditor's request is not granted. If the Rechtspfleger follows the request (for example for example to attach claims) only in part, creditor and debtor are entitled to different remedies decided upon (at first) by different courts. The creditor can file an appeal to the district court under s 793 ZPO against the enforcement decision not to attach all claims. The debtor can raise the execution complaint under s 766 ZPO against the enforcement measure to attach (some) claims, decided upon by the execution court. However, under s 793 ZPO the district court will also decide upon an appeal of the creditor against such a decision of the execution court.

However, leave for a second appeal is only granted if the case relates to question of general importance (s 574 (2) ZPO).

2. *Remedies relating to questions of substantial law*

(a) *The Action to Defend against Execution (*Vollstreckungsabwehrklage*) s 767 ZPO)*

This remedy allows the debtor to address objections based on substantive law against the claim determined by judgment.[45] The only objections admitted are those which arose after the end of the last hearing, section 767 (2) ZPO.[46] This action is sometimes used when the debtor paid after the judgment, thereby extinguishing the claim. If he can prove payment, the court will declare any enforcement to be unfounded ('inadmissible' or *unzulässig*).[47]

(b) *The third party complaint in opposition (s 771 ZPO:* Drittwiderspruchsklage*)*

This action is filed by a third party who asserts a right in relation to an object involved in the execution, where that action seeks to 'prevent alienation', ie a party whose property rights would be infringed by an assignment of the object from the debtor to the creditor.[48] Such a substantive right will normally be a right *in rem* (eg ownership of an object or of a claim). A simple claim for the transfer of ownership of the object (for example sales contract) does not suffice.[49] As to the effects of the successful complaint, see the relevant case study, infra at 12.1.

---

[45] 118 BGHZ 229, 234. To most of the other titles, s 767 applies mutatis mutandis.

[46] Section 767 (2) ZPO is based on the idea that final judgments are res judicata. In case of provisional enforceable titles, additional remedies to avoid execution are available (s 719 (1), 707 ZPO).

[47] 118 BGHZ 229, 234. The seizure of movable assets can already be stopped by payment of the sum to the bailiff, §754 ZPO, or by transferring the money via a bank to the creditors account and presenting documentary evidence of this (even an account statement) to the bailiff, s 775 No. 5 ZPO. In order to receive a ruling (with res judicata effect) on the extinction of the claim, the debtor must apply for such a declaratory ruling (Zwischenfeststellungsklage, s 256 ZPO), H Thomas and H Putzo ZPO s 767 para 3, F Stein, M Jonas, and W Münzberg *ZPO* s 767 para 5.

[48] Reichsgericht (Imperial Supreme Court) 116 RGZ 363, 366 (even though, literally, such 'transfer' would technically not be hindered, due to the option of acquiring ownership by good faith).

[49] This is obvious if the seller (debtor) is the owner of the object but it is also true if the seller is not. The main obligation of seller is to transfer to the buyer a special relationship towards the object (ownership). However, until the seller chooses to do so, the buyer does not receive the benefit of the relationship. See H Prütting and S Weth 'Die Drittwiderspruchsklage gemäß §771 ZPO' Juristische Schulung 1988, 505, 511; H Thomas and H Putzo, *ZPO* s 771 para 18. The situation is different in the case of loans, leases, etc.: The borrower only has a legal right derived from the lender; the lender has a better claim to possession of the object than borrower, who is obliged to give the object back once the lending agreement is termi-

3. *The 'Klauselverfahren' and the Principle of Formalization of Execution*

The issuing of the enforceable copy (*Klauselverfahren*) links the adjudication proceedings conducted by judges with the enforcement proceedings undertaken by paralegals (*Rechtspfleger, Gerichtsvollzieher*). Its function is derived from the organizational separation of courts and enforcement organs. The issuing of the enforceable copy as a proceeding apart from execution, subject to special remedies, is a necessary prerequisite to the 'principle of formalization' of enforcement proceedings. This principle states that the enforcement organs are prohibited from checking the legality of the title and that the creditor has a right to execution if he proves the formal prerequisites of execution,[50] consisting of an enforceable title directed against the debtor, an enforceable copy of this title, and service of the copy to the debtor.[51]

If relevant changes, such as succession of parties, transfer of disputed property or modification in a corporate scheme occur after the termination of the adjudication proceedings, the enforceable copy needs to be transferred to the successor or otherwise adapted (*Titelumschreibung*). As such 'copy proceedings' require scrutiny in law as well as in fact, they are entrusted to the *Rechtspfleger*. In the cases described above, or if the title grants only a conditional right to the creditor, the *Rechtspfleger* issues a 'qualified' enforceable copy (*Qualifizierte Vollstreckungsklausel*, s 726 et seq. ZPO, s 20 no. 12 RPflG).

Normally, however, it is the task of the court clerk (*Urkundsbeamter der Geschäftstelle*, s 724 (2) ZPO) to check the validity of the title. He does so (rather rapidly) on the basis of the court files, taking into account the formal requirements that ensure intrusion into the protected private sphere of the debtor is justified (ie signature of the judge, whether appeal has been filed (demanding for a declaration of provisional enforceability), whether the decision has an enforceable content, whether it is formulated clearly enough to be enforced).[52] He then makes a copy[53] of the title and marks it with the 'execution clause' (*Vollstreckungsklausel*) as enforceable copy, s 724 (1) ZPO.

---

nated. The lender could therefore successfully file under s 771, if the object was attached while in the borrower's possession. Conversely, like the claim of a buyer, the claim of a borrower to receive the object from the lender does not qualify for s 771, if the object was attached while still in the lender's possession after conclusion of the loan contract.

[50] F Baur and R Stürner Zwangsvollstreckungsrecht §6 para 6.53.

[51] Service can take place at the beginning of the execution by the bailiff.

[52] Of course, scrutiny by the court clerk with respect to conditions 3 and 4 of the section can only be superficial. In case of doubt, he will confer with the judge. In practice these conditions only come into play in the remedy proceedings.

[53] Section 733 ZPO provides for additional enforceable copies if needed.

The *Klauselverfahren* opens up two sets of remedies of its own, depending on whether a simple[54] or qualified[55] enforceable copy is in question.

4. *Additional remedies* are available concerning enforcement against immovable assets (s 96 et seq. ZVG, s 71 et seq. GBO (*Grundbuchordnung*, Act relating to the land registry).

5. *Protection against enforcement (*Vollstreckungsschutz, s 765a ZPO).

This remedy, which was included in the procedural laws in 1933, is sometimes called a 'procedural hardship clause'. Today it is used to implement the constitutional principles of proportionality and to protect the human rights of the debtor. Section 765a ZPO reads: 'Upon petition by the debtor, the enforcement court may cancel an act of execution in whole or in part, decline it or temporarily suspend it, after giving full consideration to the need to protect the interests of the creditor, if the act would impose a hardship due to very unusual circumstances and that hardship cannot be reconciled with public policy.' As the debtor's minimum subsistence is already protected by various other provisions, section 765a ZPO only applies in exceptional circumstances. One example concerns the eviction of tenants by landlords if there is an immediate risk of a suicide on the part of the debtor.[56]

---

[54] The creditor can file (within two weeks) a complaint to the court that decided on the merits of the case (Erinnerung, s 573 (1) ZPO)). Immediate appeal (s 567 (1), 573 (2) ZPO, sofortige Beschwerde) is directed to the district court or the regional court (Oberlandesgericht, s 72, 119 (2) no. 2 GVG); a further appeal (Rechtsbeschwerde, s 572 IV, 574 (1) No. 2 ZPO) to the Supreme Court (Bundesgerichtshof, s 133 GVG) is possible, if the case is of general importance. The basic remedy of the debtor is the Klauselerinnerung, s 732 ZPO. Competence is granted to the court, the clerk of which has granted the enforceable copy, s 732 (1) S.1. ZPO. See S Jungbauer, 'Die Zwangsvollstreckungsklausel- Rechtsmittel und Rechtsbehelfe nach der ZPO Reform', JurBüro 2002, 285

[55] Qualified copies will be denied if the creditor fails to prove by public documents the succession or the fulfilment of conditions of conditional claims (s 726 (1) ZPO). According to ss 730, 793, 567 (1), 573 (2) ZPO, s 11 I RPflG the creditor can then file an immediate appeal (and further appeal) against the decision of the Rechtspfleger (see 7.1.1.2.) However, the appeal will only have success if the creditor can proof succession or the fulfilment of the condition by way of public documents. Otherwise he has to sue for an enforceable copy under s 731 ZPO (Klage auf Erteilung der Vollstreckungsklausel). It is the court of first instance that decided on the merits and produced the title, which is also competent to decide on such an action, for which all possible proofs are admitted. Regarding the debtor, as in case of the simple copy, s 732 applies; see S Jungbauer, JurBüro 2002, 285, 289. Additionally, under s 768 ZPO, which regulates the less formal debtor's action against the granting of the enforceable copy (Klauselgegenklage), the debtor can claim that the substantial conditions set out for a qualified enforceable copy in s 726 (for examplefor example, succession) were not fulfilled.

[56] As Art 2 (2) of the German Constitution imposes a duty on all state organs to protect the life of human beings, the Constitutional Court suspended on several occasions the enforcement proceedings in order to protect the debtors' lives. For examples see BVerfG NJW 1998, 295, 296; NZM 2001, 951.

B. *The influence of constitutional standards and of Article 6 of the
European Convention on Human Rights*

From a comparative perspective, the German enforcement procedures are
characterized by the deepest involvement of constitutional standards in
Europe.[57] This development is due to the extensive implementation of
constitutional standards in the German legal system in general.
Additionally, a constitutional complaint is open to any person whose
constitutional rights are infringed by public authorities (which include, of
course, judgments and enforcement measures).[58] Constitutional standards
apply to the protection of property,[59] the inviolability of the home,[60]
personal freedom and human dignity as well as the protection of the family.
However, the case law of the Constitutional Court is mainly oriented
toward the protection of the debtor's rights. The case law of the European
Court of Human Rights[61] pertaining to enforcement has not affected
German procedural practice until now. Rather, this case law is oriented
towards the protection of the creditor's position.[62]

C. *Coordination with remedies against the titre exécutoire*

1. *Basic principles of provisional enforceability*

As stated above, section 704 (1) ZPO generally treats judgments as *res judicata* and provisionally enforceable judgments similarly with regard to
enforcement purposes. Section 708 et seq. ZPO deal with provisional

---

[57]   KD Kerameus 'Enforcement in the International Context' 264 RdC 197, 267 (1997).

[58]   In the legal literature this development is called the 'constitutionalization of procedural
law' F Stein, M Jonas, and W Münzberg ZPO Vor §704 ZPO para 43 ; R Zöller and MG
Vollkommer Commentary of the ZPO (23rd edn 2002) Einleitung (Introduction) para 100–3.

[59]   46 BVerfGE 325 (on the question of selling at 'fire-sale' prices in case of forced sale); 49
BVerfGE 228.

[60]   BVerfG NJW 1998, 295, 296; NZM 2001, 951 (both on the problem of possible suicide).

[61]   With the exception of cases dealing with enforcement issues in the context of Art 8 ECHR
and the Hague Convention on Cross Border Child Abductions, see B Hess
'Menschenrechtsschutz im europäischen Zivilprozessrecht' Juristenzeitung 2003.

[62]   European Court of Human Rights (ECHR), 19 Mar 1997, *Hornsby v Greece*, Recueil
1997, II para 33, 495; 11 Jan 2001, *Tanganelli v Italy* (not yet officially available)—both
applying Art 6 CPHR, see Fricero *Droit et Procédures* (2001), 170 ; P Yessiou-Faltsi 'Le droit
de l'exécution selon la Cour Européenne des Droits de l'Homme: Analyse et Prospective' in
UIHJ (Hrg.) *Le droit processuel et le droit d'exécution* (2002), 195 . Besides Art 6 CPHR, Art
8 CPHR (protection of family life; see, eg, ECHR, 20 Jan 2000, *Ignaccolo-Zenide c.
Roumanie*, 31679/96 (not yet officially available)), and Art 1 of the first supplementary protocol (protection of property) play an important role in enforcement matters, Cf ECHR, 28 Sept
1995, *Scollo/Italien*, Ser. A Nr 315-C.; 11 Jan 2001, *Lunari/Italy* (not yet officially available).
Art 5 CPHR applies also to committal orders, Cf W Rechberger and P Oberhammer
Exekutionsrecht (3rd edn 2002) para 5.

enforceability. As the *res judicata* effect requires the exhaustion (or waiver) of all methods of appeal, provisional enforceability is extended, as a rule, to all judgments.[63] Discrepancies based on the different courts rendering the judgment come into play only with respect to the question of whether the creditor has to post a security (see section 708 No. 10 ZPO), and whether the debtor can avoid provisional enforcement by posting a security (ss 709–11 ZPO).[64]

Section 712 ZPO enables the debtor to request that the court include in its judgment an order that he or she be allowed to avoid enforcement by posting a security. The request will be granted, if (provisional) enforcement has a negative impact on the debtor that cannot be mended by compensation, rendering the potential posting of a security by the creditor inefficient.

According to the prevailing view, the redemption of the claim through such enforcement is only provisional, as it always depends on the lack of success of the appeal. If the provisional title is set aside on appeal, the creditor must compensate the debtor for any damage, section 717 (2) ZPO (strict liability). The creditor may reduce that risk by restricting the enforcement to protective measures (*Sicherungsvollstreckung*, s 720a ZPO; for example attachment of movable property without realization through public auction).

2. Stay of provisional enforcement

On application of the debtor, the court of first instance may, under sections 719(1), 707 ZPO, stay provisional enforcement with or without security (to be posted by the debtor), or even order the creditor to post security before allowing execution to proceed. Such a stay is only granted, where an appeal *(Berufung)* with a good probability of success has been lodged.[65] In case of second appeal *(Revision)*, it is the *judex ad quem* (ie the *Bundesgerichtshof*, s 133 GVG) that decides upon the stay of enforcement, section 719 (2) ZPO.

D. The Impact of the implementation of the European Enforceable Order

To date, enforceable instruments of foreign jurisdictions (including those of EU Member States) need to be provided with a *Vollstreckungsklausel* in

---

[63] Judgments in matrimonial and parenthood matters are not provisionally enforceable, s 704 (2) ZPO.

[64] Cf K D Kerameus, 264 RdC 238, 248 (1997); B Wieczorek and B Hess *Commentary on s 704–20a ZPO* (3rd edn 1999).

[65] L Rosenberg, HF Gaul, and E Schilken *Zwangsvollstreckungsrecht* (11th edn 1997) §14 VII 221.

order to be enforceable in Germany. However, the *Klauselverfahren* (above 7.1.3) will most probably not comply with the European Enforceable Order for Uncontested Claims (EEO).[66]

Technical problems may arise in this respect with regard to remedies such as section 767 ZPO (*Vollstreckungsabwehrklage*, above 7.1.2.1). For remedy purposes, the EEO proposal refers to national law.[67] Section 14 and 9 of the German Act on the Implementation of International Covenants and European Regulations on Recognition and Enforcement of Foreign judgments (*Anerkennungs- und Vollstreckungsausführungsgesetz*; AVAG) declare, that the court providing the *Klausel* shall be competent for the *Vollstreckungsabwehrklage*. This head of jurisdiction has been challenged by legal literature.[68] Under the new Brussels Regulation, any formal recognition of a foreign judgment and similar 'secondary proceedings' are excluded. As a result, a German debtor must seek redress in the foreign court where the judgment was rendered.

VIII. PROVISIONAL MEASURES

Provisional measures are basically governed by two[69] different sets of rules:

Section 916 et seq. ZPO (*Arrest*), deal with the provisional attachment of assets (*dinglicher Arrest*, arrest *in rem*). In exceptional circumstances, an arrest operating *in personam* (*persönlicher Arrest*, section 918 ZPO) may be granted. Both remedies are designed to secure the future enforcement of a monetary judgment.

Temporary injunctions are dealt with in section 935 et seq. ZPO (*einstweilige Verfügungen*). They are aimed at protecting the creditor of a non-monetary claim.[70]

A two-step approach applies to provisional measures: First, the creditor must obtain a court order. Subsequently, the order is enforced by the competent authorities.

---

[66] P Yessiou-Faltsi 'Der Europäische Vollstreckungstitel und die Folgen für das Vollstreckungsrecht in Europa', lecture of 11 Apr 2003, Tübinger Tagung der Wissenschaftlichen Vereinigung für Internationales Verfahrensrecht, Part III 3.

[67] ibid Part IV 1.

[68] A Nelle *Anspruch, Titel und Vollstreckung im internationalen Rechtsverkehr* (2000).

[69] Provisional measures in family law matters are dealt with by a third set of rules, s 620 ZPO (einstweilige Anordnung).

[70] See P Schlosser 'Protective Measures in Various European Countries' in J Goldsmith (ed) *International Dispute Resolution* (1997) 186–97.

A. *Arrest*

An *Arrest* presupposes a liquidated sum of money or a claim which can be liquidated (s 916 ZPO). Further, there must be a danger of deterioration of the financial situation of the debtor. As a rule, an arrest normally operates in rem, allowing the attachment of the assets of the debtor. An arrest operating *in personam* (which is enforced by an imprisonment of the debtor) only takes place if other measures (including the attachment of assets) would be unlikely to succeed, section 919 ZPO. In practice, an arrest operating *in personam* is very seldom ordered.

Section 919 ZPO provides for the jurisdiction of both the local court where assets of the debtor are located (or where the debtor is present, in case of an arrest operating *in personam*), and of the court where the main proceedings are pending. It is at the discretion of the court whether the debtor will be heard before provisional measures are ordered. The debtor is entitled to oppose the *Arrest* (section 924 ZPO, *Widerspruch*) and he may avoid its enforcement by posting a security (section 923 ZPO).

B. *Einstweilige Verfügung*

Under section 935 ZPO, temporary injunctions may be ordered in regard to the object of litigation, if there is a risk that later enforcement of the rights of one party as to this object might be infringed by a change of the status quo (*Sicherungsverfügung*). Under section 938 ZPO, in addition to restraining orders, the court may make other mandatory orders, including, under exceptional circumstances, interim payments.[71] Finally, section 940 ZPO allows for temporary regulation of the legal relationship between the parties (*Regelungsverfügung*).

Section 936 ZPO applies the rules governing the *Arrest* to temporary injunctions, subject to exceptions in section 937 et seq. ZPO.

Under section 937 the competent court is the court in which the claim is pending. In urgent cases, section 942 ZPO additionally confers jurisdiction on the local court where the object in dispute is located. However, in such cases, the local court must also set a time frame during which the requesting party has to commence a procedure (at least) on the question of provisional measures in the court that is competent to decide on the merits of the claim.

C. *Enforcement of Provisional Measures*

Section 928 ZPO incorporates by reference the general provisions of enforcement proceedings contained in the eighth book of the ZPO. Several

---

[71] See Schlosser 'Judicial and Administrative Cooperation', RdC 284, 9, 159+165 (2000).

modifications are found in section 929 et seq. ZPO. An important modification relates to competence. The court granting the arrest order is also competent to attach the claims of the debtor against third parties. In practice, the decision of the court granting the *arrest* is often combined with a garnishment order. If access to other assets of the debtor is sought, the *arrest* is executed by the same officials (bailiffs) as in the case of enforcement of a monetary judgment. The arrest order must be served, on request of the creditor, by a bailiff to the debtor and assets of the debtor must be seized within one month after the service. According to section 930 ZPO, the enforcement of an arrest is restricted to protective measures. Thus, assets seized by the bailiff or by a garnishment order are merely frozen. Garnished debts are not transferred to the creditor. Only if the creditor pursues his claim in the main proceedings, and obtains a judgment against the debtor, may he continue the enforcement proceedings and execute the claim.

IX. ENFORCEMENT FEES AND COSTS

A. Court costs

The costs of enforcement proceedings are regulated in the *Gerichtskostengesetz* (GKG, Act on Courts' Costs), particularly in section 11 GKG and in an attached cost scale (n° 1640 et seq.). As a rule, court fees are related to the sum being claimed. However, in enforcement matters, fees are to a large extent determined independently from the amount in dispute. Nos 1640 et seq. of the scale to the GKG provide for fixed fees attributed to most *enforcement measures* (eg n° 1640: EUR10 for the attachment of a claim). These fees are relatively low. According to section 65 (V) GKG, the creditor has to advance these costs.

B. Bailiffs

In acting as civil servants, bailiffs are salaried (ss 10–11 GVO). The amount of the remuneration is fixed by the *Bundesbesoldungsgesetz*, and is dependent mainly on the period of the services performed and on the age of the bailiff. At the entry level, basic monthly salaries vary between €1,700–2273 (*Eingangsamt Besoldungsstufe 8*). Additional payments (eg for additional living expenses in specific areas) may be provided.

This basic salary is complimented by a fee element. Fees are regulated by the Act Regulating the Remuneration of Bailiffs (*Gerichtsvollzieher-kostengesetz*, GVKostG).[72] The bailiff can also claim expenses. Under

---

[72] All fees are payable by the debtor, or if recovery from the debtor is not possible, from the creditor.

section 13 GVKostG, fees are a 'full fee' which is calculated by reference to the amount collected by the bailiff and a fixed fee which relates to the individual activities of the bailiff. Fees are mainly intended to cover the costs of the bailiff's office.[73] The bailiff can also claim expenses. In practice, an additional source of income for bailiffs is the fees for the so-called travel expenses (*Wegegeld*) incurred for the personal service of documents.[74]

The charges levied on the basis of the GVKostG are payable to the federal state where the bailiff is employed. Only a proportion of them is kept by the bailiff. According to section 1 of the *Verordnung über die Vergütung von Vollstreckungsbeamten* (Regulation on the Remuneration of Bailiffs) the relevant proportion is 15 per cent. Section 9 contains the proviso that the amount payable to a bailiff as 15 per cent of the charges levied is capped at a certain annual amount (approx. €2,500). The bailiff can only retain 40 per cent of its normal entitlement to fee income above that amount.

According to section 4 GVKostG, the creditor has to pay an advance covering the probable costs of execution.[75]

C. The remuneration of court officers

This is comprehensively regulated by salary which is fixed by the *Bundesbesoldungsgesetz*. Any remuneration by the creditor is excluded.

D. Counsel fees

Attorneys' legal fees are fixed by the federal regulation on the fees of attorneys (*Bundesrechtsanwaltsgebührenordnung* (BRAGO)), particularly by section 57 et seq. Fees are based principally on the amount of the claim (*Gegenstandswert*). Enforcement proceedings attract part fees. According to section 57 BRAGO, the counsel is entitled to 30 per cent of a 'normal fee' based on the amount in dispute. However, if the value of the assets seized is lower, the lower value is applied. According to section 58 BRAGO each enforcement measure is a separate legal action for the purposes of enforcement.

E. Bearing of costs

German procedural law follows the general rule that the losing party has to

---

[73] Proposals for reforms of the current system are regularly met by harsh criticisms, see K Köhler 'Götterdämmerung des Gerichtsvollziehersystems?' DGVZ 2002, 19; also T Seip 'Die Zukunft des Gerichtsvollziehers' DGVZ 1999, 113, 114.

[74] This background explains the high amount of personal services rendered by bailiffs.

[75] This does not apply if the creditor has been awarded legal aid, s 4 (1) S.3 GVKostG.

bear the costs of the litigation, section 91 ZPO. This principle also applies in enforcement matters, section 788 ZPO. This rule, however, only refers to the 'necessary costs' of the proceedings. Two important points need to be mentioned in this respect:

(1) The creditor can only recover expenses for enforcement measures that could be considered necessary when he commenced the action. If the debtor seriously offers (full) payment, the costs of the creditor are not remunerated.

(2) The creditor may engage an attorney, if the debtor does not pay within a reasonable period after the judgment.[76] Only the fees set by the BRAGO are recoverable from the debtor, even though the creditor can agree to higher fees with his attorneys (eg on an hourly basis).

X. ENFORCEMENT PRACTICE

A. Statistics

In 2000, 4,426 bailiffs were in active service in Germany.[77] They received 8,859,470 applications (mostly for enforcement) and they received 3,084,072 requests to take a declaration of assets. Only in 869,926 cases was the declaration effected. The bailiffs distributed 2,984 million DM (approx. €1,500 million) to creditors (this number does not include payments made directly by debtors to creditors in order to avoid/stop further enforcement).

Up to 75 per cent of the seizures of movable assets ended without success,[78] leaving the creditor with only small hope to obtain disclosure of additional assets of the creditor by requesting the declaration of assets (ss 807, 899, et seq. ZPO). As a rule, this procedure is especially slow, because the creditor already had to wait about six months for any activity of the bailiff. Such delays have now become a reality in many federal States.[79]

B. Causes of Delay

Most commentators agree that the main cause of delays is the insufficient

---

[76] H Brox and W Walker n° 1676.

[77] Further information may be found at the table provided at DGVZ 2001, 143.

[78] B Winterstein and R Hippler 'Dienstleistungsunternehmen Gerichtsvollzieher' DGVZ 1999, 108.

[79] DPA, 8 Jan 2003, Cf F Däumichen 'Hat die Übertragung des Verfahrens zur Abgabe der eidesstattlichen Versicherung auf den Gerichtsvollzieher einen positiven Effekt erzielt?', DGVZ 2000, 183, 184.

number of bailiffs. While many bailiffs of course agree with that view,[80] some ministries of justice do not necessarily share it.[81] What is clear is that the current workload allows practically every bailiff to reach the maximum amount of fees he can earn (see above 9.1.2). This situation does not increase bailiff's willingness to start additional activities.[82]

Based on this fact, it can be stated that a structural reform of the German bailiff system seems to be necessary.

C. Private Debt Collection (Inkasso)

In Germany, the collection of debts by private persons/agencies does not fall under the definition of 'enforcement proceedings', since such collection entities act without any official authority. Their activities are strictly regulated by law. Attempts by private firms to 'enforce' payment by services as the so-called 'black shadow' (a man in a black suit with a black top hat who follows a debtor with a poster announcing that this person does not pay his or her debts) were immediately stopped by German courts.[83]

The main task of collecting agencies is to search for the address and the assets of debtors. Besides tracing the whereabouts of the debtor, their task is mostly the kind of work a solicitor normally does: writing urging letters to reluctant debtors. In practice, these services are often offered by lawyers, because the German *Rechtsberatungsgesetz* (RBerG) gives German lawyers an in principle monopoly on the giving of legal advice. Thus any activities of private debt collection agencies (*Inkassobüros*) are subject to gaining permission of the President of the local *Landgericht*, section 1 (1) n°5 RBerG, section 11 of the Verordnung (regulation) supplementing the RBerG (RBerV)).[84] Debt collection agencies are only allowed to give legal advice relating to the enforcement of a claim—but not regarding the existence of the claim.[85]

---

[80] F Däumichen DGVZ 2000, 184, B Winterstein and R Hippler DGVZ 1999, 109; Köhler 'Götterdämmerung des Gerichtsvollziehersystems', DGVZ 2002, 19, 20; Seip 'Die Zukunft des Gerichtsvollziehers' DGVZ 1999, 114.

[81] See the response of the Government of the Land of Schleswig-Holstein to an inquiry in this matter, Landtag SH, Drucksache 15/630, 15. WP (declaring the number of bailiffs sufficient); see also Press Release of the Ministry of Justice of Baden Württemberg of 14 May 2003 (declaring the need for additional 120 bailiffs).

[82] B Winterstein and R Hippler DGVZ 1999, 109, 112.

[83] Landgericht Leipzig, NJW 1995, 3190; S Edenfeld 'Der Schuldner am Pranger- Grenzen zivilrechtlicher Schuldenbeitreibung' JZ 1998, 645.

[84] The person requesting such a permission must be reliable and competent, §1 II RBerG. The RBerG does not apply, inter alia, to the collection of debts by consumer protection organizations acting within the scope of consumer protection, §3 No 8 RBerG.

[85] BGH WM 2000, 2423; G Rennen and G Caliebe *Rechtsberatungsgesetz* (2nd edn) Art 1 para 78.

Since permission is only granted for 'out of court recovery of debts' (*außergerichtliche Einziehung von Forderungen*, s 1 (1) n° 5 RBerG), it does not encompass the right to sue the debtor without the assistance of a lawyer, neither on behalf of the creditor, nor in their own name after the debt has been transferred.[86] The current situation may change in a near future. Pursuant to a recent reform of the *Rechtsberatungsgesetz*, consumer associations are now entitled to collect the claims of consumers in various areas of law, including securities actions, consumer fraud and in relation to standard terms.[87]

A vigorous debate has arisen as to whether the agencies are entitled to apply to the bailiff for the taking of a debtor's declaration once this responsibility has been shifted to the bailiffs.[88] As section 900 (3) ZPO gives the bailiff discretionary power, some (but not all) ministries of justice[89] took the view that this imbues the bailiff with (quasi-) judicial status. They concluded that the filing of such applications was therefore not within the scope of any possible permission. The courts are also divided on the subject.[90]

XI. REFORMING THE CURRENT SYSTEM

Due to the problems described, and in the light of important budgetary problems, the Government of the *Land* of Baden-Württemberg plans to propose a reform on the federal level introducing a system of bailiffs oper-

---

[86] In order to avoid evasive tactics, some courts (including the Federal Supreme Administrative Court, BVerwG NJW 1991, 58) and writers even took the point of view that the agency is not allowed any contact with the courts at all in such matters, not even when mediated by a lawyer; see Rennen and Caliebe, Rechtsberatungsgesetz 1 para 83 More recent decisions of the Federal Supreme Civil Court (BGH WM 1994, 453 ; WM 2000, 2423) and of the Federal Supreme Administrative Court (BVerwG NJW 1999, 440) have settled this question in favour of the agencies.

[87] Cf Hess and Michailidou 'Die kollektive Durchsetzung von Schadensersatzansprüchen im Kapitalmarktrecht' in Wertpapiermitteilungen (2003), 2318.

[88] H Ormanschick and O Rieke 'Aufträge zur Abnahme der eidesstattlichen Versicherung durch Inkassounternehmen', DGVZ 2000, 181; 'Viertelshausen, Tätigkeitsgrenzen der Inkassounternehmen in der Zwangsvollstreckung' DGVZ 2000, 181, Caliebe, NJW 2000, 1623.

[89] See H Ormanschick and O Rieke `Aufträge zur Abnahme der eidesstattlichen Versicherung durch Inkassounternehmen' DGVZ 2000, 181 at 182.

[90] For opinions against this, see LG Frankfurt Rechtspfleger (2000), 558 ; LG Wuppertal DGVZ (2000), 39. For opinions in favour, see LG Bremen MDR (2001) 351 ; AG Zerbst MDR (2000) 1338. This matter has been left open by LG Köln MDR 2002, 1215 (deciding that the agency is not allowed to demand that the debtor is taken into custody). The question was also left open by a panel of the Constitutional Court when not accepting a constitutional complaint of an agency based on the constitutional freedom to choose and to exercise a profession (Art 12 GG), even though the panel raised doubts as to the judicial nature of the proceeding before the bailiff (NJW (2002) 285).

ating on a private basis (comparable to that in France). The proposal is still being discussed and evaluated by a working group of the Ministry of Justice of Baden-Württemberg.[91]

A similar proposal was made by a reform commission of the largest bailiff's association. The proposal also included demands for additional responsibilities, notably with respect to the attachment of claims and the enforcement of claims under public law.[92]

Annex 1

Lawyers in Numbers [1]

Function:	1998 All	Women	2000 All	Women
Judges	20,969	5,511	20,880	5,780
Federal	493	64	495	70
State	20,476	5,447	20,385	5,710
Kind of Court[2]				
Civil and Criminal Courts[3]	15,548	4,142	15,464	4,368
Labour Courts	1,163	346	1,142	355
Administrative Courts	2,375	544	2,361	558
Tax Courts	635	95	641	103
Social Courts	1,220	374	1,228	388
Rechtspfleger (Court Officers)	14,102	7,452	14,036	7,638
Public Prosecutors	4,998	1,412	5,044	1,559
Amtsanwälte[4]	965	304	965	339
Solicitors[5]	88,861	22,403	101,503	27,159
Anwaltsnotare[6]	8,930	736	8,864	765
Notary Publics	1,663	306	1,665	308

[1] Reference Date: 31 Dec; Counsels/notary publics: 1 Jan of the following year
[2] Not included: Constitutional Courts and Disciplinary Courts
[3] Including Federal Court of Patents
[4] *Rechtspfleger* acting as Public Prosecutors
[5] Not included: *Anwaltsnotare*
[6] Solicitors acting as Notary Publics

Statistisches Bundesamt Deutschland 2002
Translation by the Authors

[91] Press Release of the Ministry of Justice of 14 May 2003; Cf the parliamentary enquiry of 25 June 2003, Landtag of Baden Württemberg, Drucksache 13/2184, p 3; <http://www3.Landtag-bw/WP13/Drucksachen/2000/13_2148_d.pdf>.
[92] See the evaluation by Schilken, DGVZ (2003) 65.

CHAPTER 10

THE NETHERLANDS

Ton Jongbloed[1]

I. INTRODUCTION

Dutch enforcement law is mostly codified in Books 2 and 3, title 4 of the *Wetboek van Burgerlijke Rechtsvordering* (Code of Civil Procedure) which came into force in 1838, hereinafter referred to as *Rechtsvordering* or *Rv.*[2] Just as in German law, civil procedure and enforcement are jointly governed in one Act.

When Napoleon was defeated at Waterloo in 1813, the Netherlands became 'independent' again and the question rose as to what legislation was going to apply. But the Code of Civil Procedure was introduced after only 25 years, as late as 1838.[3] Though the Constitution 1814 said in section 100: 'There shall be a code of civil law, corporal punishment, commerce and the composition of the judiciary', French law was to remain in force as long as there were no national codes yet.

The ensuing delay was due to the fact that Belgium, which was in favour of an amended version of the French code, had become part of the Kingdom of the Netherlands by that time. Finally, many years later,[4] Parliament adopted codes which were pretty close to their French predecessors. These codes were to be enacted 'at the stroke of midnight between 31 January and 1 February 1831', but now it was the Belgium secession that threw a spanner

---

[1] Professor of the Law of Enforcement and Seizure, Molengraaff Institute for Private Law, University of Utrecht, Utrecht University, The Netherlands. Deputy Justice Court of Appeal Leeuwarden, The Netherlands.

[2] Rv is mostly used in combination with an Art; eg Art 430 Rv.

[3] The title-page of the official edition says: 'Wetboek van Burgerlijke Regtsvordering, ter Algemeene Lands Drukkerij 1838 (Code of Civil procedure, printed by the Algemeene Lands Drukkerij). It is a volume of some 200 pages. The code counted 899 ss and ended with title VII of the Third book called About the state of apparent insolvency. The code was put before Parliament in October 1827 and was to become law on 1831, were it not for the fact that Belgium broke away from the Netherlands resulting in the actual implementation as late as 1838.

[4] See S van Brakel 'De geschiedenis van de totstandkoming van het Burgerlijk Wetboek van 1820 tot 1838' Gedenkboek Burgerlijk Wetboek 1838–1938, P Scholten E M Meijers. and WEJ Tjeenk Willink Zwolle (eds) (1938), 307–26. In the same Gedenkboek, see J van Kan 'Het BW en de Code Civil', 243–76 and RP Cleveringa Jzn 'De ontwerpen–1816 en–1820', 277–305.

in the works.[5] It was the draft Code of Civil law in particular that needed adapting and some 'Dutch' arrangements,[6] which had been eliminated due to Belgium pressure, were now re-introduced. Incidentally, from the beginning, the law of procedure was strongly influenced by its French counterpart as it would have been well-nigh impossible to deduce one national system from the very different regional systems for the conduct of civil procedure. The delay resulted in a revision, which was not too radical, and was announced in several acts in Staatsblad 1837, nn 24–6, 28–42, and 44–50, after which by Decree of 10 April 1838, Staatsblad 12, the Code, including amendments, was enacted on 1 October 1838.[7]

In 1992 a major part of a New Civil Code came into force and that meant a major change of this part of *Rechtsvordering*. Most articles had never been changed in those 150 years, but the Dutch legislator thought this was a good opportunity to 'update' these rules. On 1 January 2002 Book 1 *Rechtsvordering* was changed to speed up civil procedure. The average procedure lasted for almost 23 months and now the intention is that most procedures will only last for approximately eight months and the average will be one year.[8] Apart from the provisional enforcement, Book 3 deals with 'special proceedings', such as procedures regarding the law of traffic, the law of succession, family law (among other things divorce) and provisions on the recognition of foreign judgments and their endorsement as being enforceable (*exequatur* procedure, article 985 ff.).[9] Book 4 *Rechtsvordering* is the Dutch law regarding arbitration and it is the consequence of the New York Arbitration Convention of 1958.

II. ENFORCEMENT

A. Introduction

The purpose of enforcement in The Netherlands is generally to recover sums of money, but it may also be to have some other kind of duty performed (duty to do something or refrain from doing something).

---

[5] The Decree of 5 Jan 1834, no 1 adjourned its introduction for an indefinite period of time.
[6] eg the system of complete joint family assets and liabilities, which became the main rule again.
[7] See R van Boneval Faure *Het Nederlandsche Burgerlijk Procesrecht*, Part 1 (3rd re edn E J Brill Leiden 1893) 15–17 and also *Mr W van Rossem's verklaring van het Nederlandse Wetboek van Burgerlijke rechtsvordering* by R P Cleveringa, part 1 (4th edn), W E J Tjeenk Willink Zwolle 1972, Inleidende aantekeningen, xxi–xli.
[8] M de Tombe-Grootenhuis 'Relationships between Parties, Lawyers and Judges in Civil Contentious Proceedings' in M Elizondo Gasperín *Relaciones entre las Partes, los Jueces y los Abogados*, Instituto Nacional de Estudios Superiores en Derecho Penal, AC División Editorial, (Mexico 2003), 389–413.
[9] There is a special law regarding the enforceability of decisions given by judges in other EU Member States, making the enforceability more or less automatic.

In practice, a creditor needs to have an enforceable document (a court judgment or a deed) if he wishes to apply for enforcement.

The recovery of sums of money will take one of the following forms:

Attachment of goods:[10] goods belonging to the debtor will be placed under the control of the courts and sold (public sale or auction) so that the creditor can be paid back from the proceeds. The bailiff will seize the goods after giving the debtor a two-day period to pay his debts according to the judicial decision. If the debtor is not able to pay or is refusing to pay, the bailiff will sell the goods. The debtor is obliged to let the bailiff enter his house, because article 444 Rv gives the bailiff the opportunity to go to any place as it is necessary to fulfil his duty. If the debtor is unwilling to let the bailiff go into his house, the bailiff can enter with the assistance of a locksmith and in the company of the mayor or (this is the usual situation) a high-ranking police officer. The police officer has to ensure that the bailiff is doing his job according to the law.

Attachment of bank assets:[11] the debtor's account is blocked (seizure of assets) and the credit balance is seized. The bailiff will send a note and a copy of the garnishment order to the bank that he is seizing the debtor's account. From the moment the bank receives this note the debtor can not withdraw any money: the account is 'frozen', although the money the debtor receives is not seized in advance. In practice this means that the bailiff sometimes will seize the bank account a couple of days later for the second time. In future it is expected that bailiffs can seize bank accounts from their office by sending a note by e-mail.

Assignment of earnings:[12] part of the debtor's wages or salary can be seized and the creditor will be paid from it. The bailiff has to go to the employer and give him a copy of the garnishment order. From that moment the employer has to pay a portion of the debtor's monthly or weekly wages or salary to the bailiff. Only a portion can be seized because the legislator has realized that a debtor has to pay his housing, has to eat, and so on. In practice the debtor will keep (if (s)he is married or living together and the spouse has no income) monthly approximately €1,040.[13] Has the debtor a monthly salary of €1,500, probably €460 can be seized. At the end of May bailiffs are very busy, because that month most employers will pay the holiday allowance. That means that a creditor can receive more money, probably €1900 that month.

---

[10] Art 439 ff and 711.   [11] Art 475 and 718.
[12] ibid.
[13] If he or she is older than 65 years of age: EUR 1.097,84. If he or she is a single according to age and income between €179,79 (not yet 21 years old), €520,30 (21 years old and monthly income less than €578,11), €728,42 (21 years old and monthly income more than €809,35) and €778,37 (65 years old).

Execution against real property,[14] whereby the debtor is evicted[15] from property, which is confiscated and sold (at auction) to pay the creditors. A bailiff can also seize real property. In such a case he does not has to leave his office, because he just has to send a note to the land registry office that he is seizing the real property. The cadastral registration will be marked with the seizure and in practice none will buy the property any more. If the debtor pays his debts in time a notary public can sell the real property in a Dutch auction.[16]

It should also be mentioned that there are certain categories of the debtor's assets and claims that cannot be attached (clothing, food, certain items of furniture, a portion of his or her salary) so that debtors and their family can still enjoy a reasonable standard of living.[17]

If someone fears that his debtor will take advantage of the drawn-out procedures and the various redress facilities to escape his creditors before judgment is actually given, eg by organizing his own insolvency or transferring his assets, it is in the creditor's interests to apply to the court for interim measures.

The court may order interim or precautionary measures against the debtor's assets. The purpose of all these measures is to anticipate the final judgment on the merits for a certain period so as to ensure that it will be possible to enforce it. But several situations have to be distinguished.

1. Precautionary measures

They have been defined by the Court of Justice of the European Communities as measures designed to safeguard rights the recognition of which is applied for in other proceedings in the court hearing the case on the merits and to preserve the status quo in both fact and law. In practice, such measures will enable the creditor to cover himself against the risk of not being paid by using two techniques: either the debtor is prevented from disposing of his assets or charges are registered on them so that if he does dispose of them they can be recovered from subsequent acquirers.

Examples of precautionary measures include:

- Preventive attachment of movable property or sums of money belonging to the debtor;
- Court receivership of contested property that must be preserved in its present condition until judgment has been given;

---

[14] Art 502 and 725.   [15] Art 555.
[16] Compare MJW van Ingen and A W Jongbloed, Onderhandse executie; 'Executoriale verkoop uit de hand' ex Art 3:251 lid 1 BW en met name Art 3:268 lid 2 BW, Kluwer Deventer 1998.
[17] See also <http://europa.eu.int/comm/justice_home/ejn/enforce_judgment/enforce_judgment_gen_en.htm>.

- Attachment by way of mortgage on real property, business assets and valuable securities. There are rules as to publicity.

(a) Conditions for ordering precautionary measures

When the creditor files his application, the court may ask the creditor to provide evidence that his claim has a chance of succeeding and that there is a risk the creditor will not be able to recover the debt from the debtor.

The court's Order will specify the assets covered by the measure, up to a certain amount in proportion to the creditor's claim. There are lists of goods and assets that cannot be attached (clothing, food, certain items of furniture, a portion of wages or salaries) to ensure that the debtor and his family can still enjoy a decent standard of living. The debtor can challenge the measure and apply for the attachment to be lifted. If, after the case has been heard on the merits, the creditor has obtained an enforceable final judgment, he can have the precautionary attachment converted into an execution order.

2. Interim Measures

In other urgent situations, purely precautionary measures will not always be enough. The court may therefore order certain interim measures having similar effects to the expected judgment on the merits. The final judgment may confirm or revoke these interim measures.

Like precautionary measures, interim measures are taken before judgment is given on the merits, which distinguishes them from provisional execution.

3. Provisional Execution

The creditor has had judgment given for him but there is still the possibility of an appeal or challenge. The creditor wishes to have the judgment enforced immediately as he is afraid that the debtor might appeal simply in order to delay the proceedings. In many such cases the court will order provisional execution of the judgment. Certain requirements may be imposed, depending on the merits of the case (urgency, security given by the creditor, principle of adversarial proceedings, claim not open to challenge although the judgment can still be appealed against, etc.). For instance, the urgency requirement is more and more often interpreted in quite broad terms.[18]

[18] See <http://europa.eu.int/comm/justice_home/ejn/interim_measures/interim_measures_gen_en.htm>.

B. *Rules for enforcement*

In Book 2 and 3 title 4 *Rechtsvordering* rules are given for the enforcement of the instruments stipulated in Article 430 Rv. These include not only the decisions of civil courts and arbitral tribunals but also decisions on monetary claims of criminal courts, administrative authorities, social insurance institutions, as well as enforceable notarial instruments.

As mentioned, civil procedure and enforcement are jointly governed in one Act. This means that the general provisions of *Rechtsvordering* governing parties, proceedings and oral hearings, evidence, judicial orders and directions and appeals apply also in enforcement law. For example, for a seize order as mentioned in Article 700 Rv the rules regarding applications (Art 261 ff. Rv) are applicable.

Enforcement law is governed almost exclusively by *Rechtsvordering*; in addition a few provisions of enforcement law are found in secondary legislation, but these are not relevant for this article since they are nearly all more technical in nature.[19]

Rechtsvordering governs different areas of enforcement law. In Book 2 *Rechtsvordering* (Art 430 ff.) rules are given for the enforcement of judgments and the other instruments stipulated in Article 430 Rv. In Book 3 title 4 (Art 700 ff. Rv) rules regarding the provisional enforcement are to be found. In Article 585 ff. Rv rules regarding the imprisonment for debt and in Article 611a ff. Rv rules concerning the 'dwangsom' (*astreinte*) are given.[20]

1. *Rules for enforcement by attachment*

Both books—2 and 3 title 4 Rv—start with 'General Provisions' (Arts 430–8b and 700–10a). Most other articles (Art 439 ff and 711 ff) are regarding 'The Enforcement of Money Debts', but in Articles 491–500 and 730–7 special rules regarding the enforcement of obligations to give an object can be found. These rules were introduced in 1992. Until that moment only money claims could be directly enforced.

Every part of the rules regarding the enforcement of and seizure for money debts contains rules especially for movable property (439 ff and 711 ff.), shares (474a ff and 714 ff), immovable property (502 ff and 725 ff),

---

[19] Special rules regarding the seizure and enforcement of, for example, patents and copyright can be found in special laws regarding those subjects in a general way.

[20] Rv does not contain a definition of astreinte. Astreinte was defined by legal scholars as an additional order to the debtor to pay his creditor a sum of money, without any connection to the damage the creditor suffered or will suffer, in case of non-performance or overdue performance of the principal obligation, in order to put the debtor under pressure so that he will fulfil the main obligation as established by the judge. Astreinte is most frequently calculated per day that the performance of the judicial decision is delayed or per individual violation of the judicial decision. See below IV.

ships (562a ff and 728 ff), airplanes (584a ff and 729 ff). Garnishment orders are to be found in Articles 475 ff and 718 ff. Special rules regarding (provisional) martial arrest are inserted in Article 768 ff: when the judge gives a decree for divorce, at the same moment (if necessary) a ruling for the splitting up of the spouses goods is given. Rules making it possible to seize a property in The Netherlands belonging to someone living outside The Netherlands are to be found in Article 765 ff.

In every enforcement case the bailiff has to act: only a bailiff can attach goods, it cannot be done by for example a notary public. Sometimes the bailiff has to enter the debtor's premises (to attach movable goods, aircraft, and ships) and the goods should be specified (eg a television set, brand name Philips, type 2004X; four wooden chairs, a round table diameter one and a half meter, etc), but otherwise he can attach the good in his office (eg immovable goods) by sending a notice to the Official register of immovable goods with a copy to the debtor. The bailiff has to warn the debtor that attachment is imminent: the debtor has to pay his debt within two days and otherwise the bailiff will attach the goods. If there is fear of embezzling the goods the bailiff may attach them immediately (eg when the bailiff arrives and the neighbours tell him the debtor already has taken away half of his belongings and that the removal firm will arrive the next morning to remove the furniture).

A debtor can not prevent the bailiff from entering his premises: the judge can give special consent although the Constitution (Art 12) says that none can enter without the resident's approval because the law—Rechtsvordering—has made an exception for such cases.

Finally the debtor will sell all the attached goods. The money he receives will be paid to the creditor after deducting the bailiff's costs.[21] When there are more creditors the bailiff has to divide the money proportionately to the claim of each creditor.

Enforcement measures by attachment occur frequently in The Netherlands, either independently or following protective measures by attachment. Yet in many cases enforcement by attachment is not effective: often, once this stage has been reached there is no further redress against the debtor (if the debtor had been capable of paying, he would have paid much sooner).

---

[21] The costs differ. For seizure of movable property the bailiff usually can charge an amount of €92,61(but if it is necessary that a third person—eg a police-officer—opens doors to let the bailiff go into a house €124,35) and for seizure of immovable property and airplanes an amount of €127,22. If the bailiffs seizes movable property to hand the property to the creditor he can charge €85,10 and after the judgment as he hands over the property once more €213,74. For garnishing wages the normal charge is €105,03. These amounts can be found in an special decree regarding the tariffs bailiffs may charge (Besluit tarieven ambtshandelingen gerechtsdeurwaarders) and change every year according to a decision given by the department of justice.

Information concerning the debtor can be obtained electronically by a bailiff (not by other persons) from official (parish) registers. There are official arrangements made to ensure that bailiffs always can obtain confirmation of the correct information about a party's name, address or place of residence.[22] Such information is also readily available through commercially provided databases and other information sources. But a bailiff could rely upon the protection of the law in going to a particular address, even although it was the wrong address for the debtor, if that was the address provided in the court action. Dutch bailiffs have no access to registers connected with the social security system or the tax authorities. Neither is there an official register of places of employment.

2. Other enforcement measures than attachment

There are other enforcement measures than attachment. The main enforcement measure other than attachment is enforcement by the creditor himself pursuant to judicial authorization, This is a type of specific performance. Enforcement with the assistance of the police—for instance the eviction of squatters with the help of the riot police—also forms a direct and specific way of enforcement. The same applies to enforcement by delivery as provided in Article 491 ff and to the specific performance of Articles 3:300–1 Civil Code. The latter introduced in 1992 an interesting novum in the renewed Civil Code: when the debtor refuses to perform a legal act to which he is committed, the court may order that the effect of its judgment is identical to the effect of a legally drawn-up deed from the debtor, or the court may appoint a compulsory representative to perform the act on behalf of the debtor. In the case the defendant is under an obligation to draw up a deed together with the claimant, the court may determine that its judgment shall take the place of the deed or a part of the deed. By recording the Court's decision in the public registers it is also possible to effect delivery of registered goods (especially immovable property and larger aircraft and ships).[23]

C. Effectiveness

Van Koppen and Malsch write that in most cases the defendant will 'win', because in most cases the defendant has nothing to pay, will not pay, or the debt is irrecoverable. [24]

---

[22] Otherwise they could not serve the writ of summons correctly.

[23] See H.J. Snijders `Netherlands Civil Procedure' in *Access to civil procedure abroad* (CH Beck Verlag München e.a.) 272.

[24] PJ van Koppen and M Malsch 'De waarde van civiele vonnissen' in PJ van Koppen (ed) *Het recht van binnen; psychologie van het recht* (Kluwer Deventer 2002) 889–96.

Their findings are set out in the following table:

		Action by Claimant			
	None	Seizure	Negotiations	Seizure and negotiations	Per-centage
No payment (326)	45	25	26	21	35
Partial payment (205)		8	32	35	49 22
Total payment (399)	47	44	39	30	43
Total Percentage	100	100	100	100	100
Total Cases (930)	473	149	214	94	

(left axis label: Action by defendant)

They also found out after studying 4,131 cases, that in 48 per cent there was a default judgment.[25] But in the 52 per cent of the cases where the defendant came into court and made a defence, only in 25 per cent the action was granted en in 27 per cent the action was denied. The result of the 48 per cent default cases and the 25 per cent cases that the action was granted, led to 26 per cent no payment at all, 16 per cent partly paid and 32 per cent fully paid. That means that adding 27 per cent (action denied) plus 26 per cent (defendant paid nothing), in 53 per cent of the cases the defendant 'won' and that in only 32 per cent the plaintiff got what he wanted: all the money.

III. FUNDAMENTALS AND RECENT REFORMS

When *Rechtsvordering* entered into force in 1838 it superseded French *Code de Procédure Civile*, framed under the supervision of Napoleon Bonaparte, which had remained in force after 1813 when The Netherlands became once more independent. This is one of the reasons why Dutch execution law resembles its French counterpArticle Another reason is that when in the 19th century new institutions were introduced the Dutch had to look south, because there was not yet a German *Zivilprozeßordnung*. So for instance the function of the *Gerechtsdeurwaarder* (court bailiff) is

---

[25] PJ van Koppen (ed) *Het recht van binnen; psychologie van het recht* 894.

similar to that of the French *huissier de justice* and not the German *Gerichtsvollzieher*. But since 1838 there have been many legal developments and less Dutch are reading and/or speaking French. Now English is the *lingua franca*, but the English court system—and their enforcement system as well—differs a lot from the Dutch. This is the reason why in Dutch enforcement practice references to foreign cases or foreign literature are rare.

The basic structure of Dutch enforcement law has not changed since *Rechtsvordering* entered into force in 1838, but this Act was amended for numerous times, especially in 1991,[26] 1992,[27] 1993/4,[28] 1995,[29] and 2002[30] when numerous aspects were reformed.

Now a special commission is drafting a report answering the question: must Dutch civil procedure be changed drastically to speed procedures even more, to increase efficiency in court proceedings and to make use of modern information technology.[31] Increased efficiency in court proceedings can be achieved especially by using information technology for dealing with matters which arise en masse in the same form.

To date no such technical innovations in the court process have been introduced. The legislator introduced in 1991 a form that could be filled in by the creditor so he would not need a writ of summons. In 2002 this form was abolished: most people thought it was too difficult to fill in such a form and the courts had to carry out a lot of redundant activities.[32]

For the moment the legislator only has planned to change the rules regarding the procedure and not the rules regarding seizure and enforcement. But it will be necessary. We only have to think of garnishing a bank account. Now the bailiff has to go the office of the bank, but it could be done by e-mail.

The majority of civil judicially enforceable instruments derive from default payment orders. In Germany and Austria the *Mahnverfahren* (*ex*

[26] The possibility to seize social security benefits was introduced on 1 Apr 1991 (wet–law—van 13 december 1991, Stb—Dutch Statutebook—605).
[27] Introduction of the New Civil Code (wet van 3 juli 1989, Stb 289, and wet van 2 april 1991, Stb. 199).
[28] New divorce proceedings (wet van 1 juli 1992, Stb 373 en wet van 23 december 1992, Stb 1993, 15).
[29] Less rules concerning family law proceedings (wet van 7 juli 1994, Stb 570): 130 Arts were abolished and only 20 new articles were introduced.
[30] Speeding up civil procedure (wet van 6 december 2001, Stb 580, 581 and 584; wet van 13 december 2001, Stb. 622 and wet van 14 december 2001, Stb 623).
[31] WDH Asser, HA Groen, and JBV Vranken *Een nieuwe balans; Interimrapport Fundamentele herbezinning Nederlands burgerlijk procesrecht* (Boom Juridische uitgevers Den Haag 2003). See also ML Hendrikse and AW Jongbloed (eds) *De toekomst van het Nederlands burgerlijk procesrecht* (Kluwer Deventer 2004).
[32] eg someone buys a lounge suit, but three months later it went to pieces. Who has sold it: a shop. But was it a limited or a natural person? Sometimes it is not easy to find out who was the seller.

parte orders for payment) exists, but the Dutch legislator is not very fond of this type of proceeding, not only because approximately 15–20 per cent of the orders can not be executed because of an incorrect name or address, but also because in 2002 just one civil procedure remained and creditors are satisfied with the current Dutch system.

IV. ASTREINTE

Astreinte is not available in every EU Member State, but is highly successful in the Netherlands. It was defined by legal scholars as an additional order to the debtor to pay his creditor a sum of money, without any connection to the damage the creditor suffered or will suffer, in case of no-performance or overdue performance of the principal obligation, in order to put the debtor under pressure so that he will fulfil the main obligation as established by the judge. *Astreinte* is most frequently calculated per day that the performance of the judicial decision is delayed or per individual violation of the judicial decision.

Astreinte was introduced in Dutch law in 1933,[33] but now a uniform Benelux[34] statute concerning the coercive civil fine (in French: *astreinte*; in Dutch: 'dwangsom') applies in The Netherlands since January 1, 1978. Articles 611a to 611h *Rechtvordering* are the transformation into Dutch law of the uniform Benelux statute on *astreinte*.[35] The uniform statute contains a statutory system which is currently in force in Belgium, the Netherlands and Luxembourg. The unity of interpretation of the rules concerning *astreinte* in the three countries is guaranteed by the Benelux Court. The members of that Court are Justices of the Supreme Courts of the three countries constituting the Benelux.

Astreinte is considered to be an indirect means of enforcing a judgment. Since imprisonment for debt de facto[36] has been abolished in The Netherlands, *astreinte* is the central indirect way of enforcing a judgment. It is indirect because it does not directly grant the creditor what he is entitled to. It is a means of enforcing a judgment, just like a seizure resulting in a forced public sale of (part of) the assets of the debtor, because the intention

[33] Astreinte was introduced by the law of 29 Dec 1932, Stb 1932, 676; effective 1 Apr 1933, Arts 611a and 611b DCCP.
[34] Belgium, The Netherlands and Luxembourg.
[35] The articles in the Dutch Code of Civil Procedure governing astreinte were introduced by Statute of 27 Mar 1977 containing ratification of the Benelux Treaty concerning the uniform statute on astreinte, and of the Enclosure (uniform statute on astreinte), signed at 's-Gravenhage on 26 Nov 1973.
[36] Every year there are only a few imprisonments for debt mostly on behalf of the Dutch Department of Finance (Tax-division) or on behalf of ex-spouses in cases regarding alimentation.

of *astreinte* is to encourage the debtor to perform his obligation, as established by a court order.

Astreinte is frequently used in The Netherlands. The institution as such is widely accepted by legal scholars, although it is obvious that coercive civil fines should only be imposed with great caution and care, given the possibility of their considerable financial impact. The possible threat for one's financial position is precisely why coercive civil fines should be considered to be due only in cases where the defendant undoubtedly infringed upon the main court order. Reasonable doubt should always be to the advantage of the debtor when coercive civil fines are concerned.

The range of court orders to which an *astreinte* can be attached is remarkably broad. Any court decision ordering a person, a company or even a governmental body to do, give or refrain from doing something, could be enforced by means of an *astreinte*. Coercive civil fines have been attached to orders to stop infringements on intellectual property, to restore a piece of land on which a building has been built without a permit to its original condition, to respect the rights of both parents to see the couple's children after a divorce, to coerce a person to refrain from harassing an ex-lover etc.

Astreinte is considered by most legal scholars to be a useful instrument to enhance the efficiency of judicial decisions. The system of the uniform Benelux statute grants plaintiffs an instrument to obtain specific performance of court decisions, often in cases where there are no other means available to obtain specific performance. At the same time, the uniform statute contains several guarantees protecting the defendant. The judge is never obliged to follow the point of view of the plaintiff. It is the judge who determines at his discretion the amount of *astreinte* and the conditions under which it becomes due. The suggestions of the plaintiff in that respect are not binding on the judge. If it would appear after the court order has been pronounced that the main obligation is impossible to perform, the defendant can request the judge who imposed *astreinte* to moderate (lower or abolish) *astreinte*. Another guarantee for the defendant is that once *astreinte* is due, the collection of the amounts due needs to be initiated within six months at most, in order to avoid a situation where a passive attitude on the part of the plaintiff results in astronomical amounts becoming due.

Any judge (including arbitrators) can impose an *astreinte*, as long as he is requested to do so by one of the parties.[37] No judge in the Dutch legal system can impose an *astreinte* if he is not requested to do so. On the other hand, a judge is always free to refuse to impose an *astreinte*. There are no

---

[37] Art 611i Rv Pursuant to that provision, arbitrators may impose an astreinte, according to the same set of rules as any other judge (ie Arts 611a–611h DCCP).

specific requirements for a judge to be able to refuse to impose an *astreinte*.

Since enhancing the authority of judicial decisions is one of the aims of *astreinte*, it is clear that coercive civil fines which would be so low that the debtor might prefer to pay the fine instead of performing the obligation imposed upon him by the judge should be avoided. Thus, the judge is authorized to impose a higher coercive civil fine than the amount requested by the plaintiff. As long as an *astreinte* is requested by the plaintiff, even without specifying a particular amount of money, the judge is free to grant or refuse it. If the judge decides to impose an *astreinte*, he can determine the amount and the conditions under which it becomes due at his discretion. If the plaintiff requests the judge to impose an *astreinte* which will be due by the defendant per day while a particular obligation is not performed, the judge is not obliged to impose an *astreinte* due on a daily basis. The judge could also rephrase the obligation and impose an *astreinte* per violation of the order, or even an *astreinte* determined for a single amount, to be incurred by the debtor in case of one or more violations of the order. This could be useful in cases where infringing upon the main court order more than once is not possible, or where there would not be much of a difference between one, two or more violations. If the judge decides to impose an *astreinte* per unit of time, he is free to choose whatever unit of time he wishes. The unit of time is in most cases one day, but it could also be one hour, one working day, one week, one month, etc.

If the judge does not indicate a maximum amount, then there is no limit as to the amounts which can become due pursuant to violations of the court order. The absence of any automatic limitation of *astreinte* could result in stubborn debtors having to pay very substantial amounts of money, particularly when *astreinte* becomes due per unit of time. The law does, however, contain a rule protecting the debtor in this respect. The creditor can only initiate enforcement proceedings on the basis of coercive civil fines incurred by the debtor within a period of six months preceding the beginning of the enforcement proceedings. The main reason for this rule (contained in Art 611g Rv) is precisely to avoid a creditor's passive attitude resulting in large amounts becoming due.

The judge is always free to determine a maximum amount above which no coercive civil fines can become due (Art 611b Rv). Obviously, this maximum should be sufficiently high in order to avoid that the debtor would prefer to pay *astreinte* instead of performing his obligation. There is no maximum as to the number of times a judgment imposing an *astreinte* can be obtained, as long as the plaintiff does not request the judge to decide on a matter on which a court of law has already taken a decision.

V. ENFORCEMENT AGENTS

As mentioned before it is not necessary to have a court order for a warrant of execution. Enforcement is possible on the ground of the instruments stipulated in Article 430 Rv: these include not only the decisions of civil courts and arbitral tribunals but also decisions on monetary claims of criminal courts, administrative authorities, social insurance institutions as well as enforceable notarial instruments.

This means that it is not necessary to obtain a special writ of enforcement,[38] that court clerks do not have a special function in the enforcement proceedings and that there is no special enforcement officer (*Rechtspfleger*).

Three different people deal with execution in the Netherlands, but the most important person to enforce court rulings is the (court) bailiff (*gerechtsdeurwaarder*).

The notary (public)[39] is only involved if the execution regards the sale of immovable property.

State-employed enforcement agents are only responsible for the collection of public taxes and dues. However, sometimes some of this work is now offered, by tender, to the third group: the (court) bailiff. In fact this person has a monopoly on the formal service of documents and the enforcement of private law claims.

At the moment there are about 325 bailiffs and 225 deputy bailiffs[40] in The Netherlands. From the middle of the 1980s most Dutch bailiffs' practices developed successfully and turnover increased steadily. Before there was a small staff and the average bailiff practised only with the traditional administrative tasks such as serving processes, serving judgments, carrying out preventive attachments or attachments of goods, simple evictions and supervising public auctions.

Within the Dutch legal system the bailiff nowadays has a central position. Civil services are the foundation. But unlike many of his foreign colleagues the *Dutch* bailiff is allowed to also undertake non-administrative practices. It is that combination that gives the Dutch bailiff an added value compared with the recovery agencies.

On 15 July 2001 a new Act on Bailiffs came into force. The Act introduces more market orientation within the profession. The new Act is a result of a Government operation called 'Market forces, deregulation and legislative quality operation'.

---

[38] The only exception is imprisonment for debt (Art 434 Rv).

[39] This is a private person, but is entrusted with public duties.

[40] Sometimes they are called junior bailiffs. As there a lot of things to do, the 325 bailiffs need some help. Both the bailiff and the junior bailiff can act in the same matters, the difference is that a bailiff is appointed by the Queen and has his own office.

A committee examined the feasibility and usefulness of promoting the operation of free market forces for bailiffs. The rules relating to the exclusive competence, policy on location of practices, fees, codes of conduct and professional codes, training and title protection were examined.

This new Act introduced a more market-orientated thinking within the profession. This is achieved in several ways:

* Relaxing the requirements on beginning a practice.
* More freedom in price agreements with clients.
* Increasing the supervision of the profession.

The Royal Society of Bailiffs (*Koninklijke Vereniging van Gerechtsdeurwaarders*) was converted into a professional organization of public law: the Royal Professional Organization of Bailiffs (*Koninklijke Beroepsorganizatie van Gerechtsdeurwaarders*). It is compulsory for every Bailiff to be a member of this organization.

The organization is able to adopt further regulations governing the profession.

The bailiff has to fulfil his duties in accordance with law and the principles of professional ethics. The bailiff has an independent position in the Dutch legal system. Consequently it is inappropriate for the Government to lay down one-sided standards of conduct for the practising of the profession. At the same time introducing greater competition, which is one of the aims of the new Act, means it is important that activities of the bailiffs are regulated.

The Act provides for a more stringent supervision: bailiffs are governed by statutory disciplinary rules, codes of conduct and professional codes.

A. Organization of bailiffs

According to the new Act there is a central board, the national council of bailiffs and the General assembly of bailiffs.

The *board* is entrusted with the general management of the organization, the promotion of proper professional conduct and their professional skills, for example in the form of bylaws codes, the administration etc. A bureau assists the board.

The Board consists of an odd number of at least seven members. Both the chairman and the vice-chairman are bailiffs. Both the bailiffs and the junior bailiffs should be represented equally within the board. They are chosen for a period of three years and can be re-elected once more.

The chairman of the board also is entrusted with the chair of the general meeting.

The *Council of members* consists of 30 members and 30 substitute members. Each area of the High Court, there are five in the Netherlands, chooses six members and six substitute members.

Each member is a junior bailiff or a bailiff. They are chosen for three years and can be re-elected for three years once again.

The council

- formulates the general policy of the organization and confers, if necessary, with the board. The council has the right to request information from the board and to instruct the board to investigate matters that could be relevant to the formulation of the organization's policy;
- adopts bylaws after conferring with the board about these bylaws; and
- appoints the board and supervises the board and may suspend or discharge members if they have lost confidence in them.

The council advises the annual general meeting on the report of activities of the board in the financial accounting and the draft budget.

The *General Assembly* of bailiffs advises the Council about the professional codes. They approve the report of the Board, the accounting reports and the voting of the budget.

The *KBvG* may charge its members annual dues to cover the costs. The general meeting, at the proposal of the board, determines the size of the dues.

B. Appointment as a bailiff

The new Act sets out the way to become a bailiff. A bailiff may be appointed at the location where he wishes to set up his practice if he or she:

- is a Dutch national;
- has attended professional training;
- has been a candidate (junior) bailiff for two years;
- has received positive feedback on his business plan from a committee of experts;
- has a good conduct certificate; and
- has a certificate of the Chamber of Bailiffs (the professional disciplinary body)[41] from which it can be ascertained whether any disciplinary measures have been taken against him or her.

Technically a bailiff is appointed by the Queen. The professional training is at university level and in the near future it will result in a university degree. A person who wants to become a bailiff will then, in addition to the university degree, have to undergo training.

A business plan shall be drawn up which at least shows:

---

[41] This chamber consists of five members: three judges and two bailiffs. It acts as a judicial institution.

- that the applicant has adequate financial means to keep up a practice that corresponds with the requirements of the office; and
- that there are reasonable grounds to expect that the practice will break even in three years' time.

A Committee of Experts to be appointed by the Minister of Justice issues a recommendation with regard to the business plan. In connection with the scrutiny of the business plan, the Committee is authorized to make enquiries with the KBvG and the Financial Supervision Office. The recommendation shall be added to the business plan as an annex.

The procedure is as follows: the candidate bailiff who wishes to qualify for appointment as bailiff shall file an application with the Minister of Justice, stating the place in which he intends establishing himself as bailiff. With this application he shall submit documentary evidence showing that he fulfils the requirements I just mentioned, including the business plan.

In the application he shall also state the office(s) where he has worked as an assigned candidate bailiff.

The Minister of Justice sends a copy of the application plus annexes to the board of the KBvG, with the request that wants to be informed within three months of any facts or circumstances known to the KBvG that it believes could result in refusal of the application (for instance, disciplinary measures undertaken against the candidate).

Article 7 of the Law on Bailiffs sets out the circumstances in which as application can be refused:

only if one or several of the criteria set out has not been fulfilled or if, given the applicant's antecedents, there is solid reason to assume that the candidate bailiff will commit an act or omission contrary to the provisions laid down by or pursuant to the law or that the image or discharge of the office of bailiff will be otherwise affected or obstructed. An order to refuse appointment shall be given by the Minister.

Within four months of receipt a decision shall be taken on the application. Within two months of the date of appointment as a bailiff the new bailiff takes the oath or affirmation before the President of the district court in whose district his place of practice is located. The bailiff has to keep office in the place of practice.

C. Complaints against enforcement procedures

This can be achieved in two ways:

1. Legal remedies against the enforcement

The debtor, creditor and third parties can, according to the provisions of

Rechtsvorderings file complaints against the enforcement in the court. There is a special summary proceedings before the president of the District Court (Art 438a Rv).

If the executing party abuses his right of execution (for example execution of a clearly ill-founded judgment declared to be executable by anticipation) the court may order the execution to be halted. If the bailiff finds any difficulties with the enforcement or has a dispute with his principal he can also turn to the president of the District Court for advice in a special summary proceedings.

2. Disciplinary rules

The bailiff or the deputy bailiff can be disciplined for infringements of their duties and for not acting in accordance with the dignity and respect of their profession.

The Chamber of Bailiffs examines the disciplinary cases in the first instance. This chamber is a five-person panel, which consists of three persons who are appointed by the Minister of Justice and two members who are appointed also by the Minister of Justice but at the intercession of the national organization of bailiffs. These two members are bailiffs. The other three members are members of the judiciary.

The members are appointed for a period of four years. After this period they can be reappointed once for a new period of four years. The members can not , at the same time, be a member of the board of the national organization. The Minister of Justice appoints the President of the Chamber, who is a judge. He or she can try to settle the matters or refuse a complaint if he thinks the complaint is inadmissible or unfounded.

The sessions of the Chamber and Higher Court are open to the public.

The parties have the right to appeal against its decisions to the Higher Disciplinary Court. The Court of Appeal in Amsterdam acts as this higher disciplinary court. Appeal is possible within 30 days of the award being served upon them. The chamber of civil matters deals with the appeal.

Both the chamber and the higher disciplinary court enjoy wide powers to:

- suspend the bailiff for a period of 12 months awaiting the judgment;
- reprimand the bailiff;
- reprimand him with notice that a next violation will result in a penalty, suspend or dismissal;
- impose a penalty of approximately €5000;
- suspend him for a of maximum one year;
- disqualification

Under the new law there are also rules about records and accounting:

- The bailiff keeps records both with regard to his work and with regard to his business assets. These records shall at all times show his rights and obligations. He also keeps records with regard to his personal assets, including the assets of any community property in which he is married.[??] Every year the bailiff shall draw up a balance sheet both with regard to his business assets and his personal assets as well as a statement of income and expenditure with regard to his business.
- The records regarding his work as such shall relate to the official acts as well as the other activities carried out by the bailiff. The records relating to the official acts shall include a register and a repertory.
- The register contains, ordered by date, the copies of the records of service drawn up or signed by the bailiff, affidavits, deeds and statements.

A new feature in the law was also the keeping of *special accounts* in the name of the bailiff with a credit stating his capacity, which shall be earmarked solely for moneys of which he takes receipt for third parties in connection with his work. Any moneys entrusted to the bailiff in connection with his work for third parties shall be paid into that account.

These accounts were meant to protect the money the bailiff receives on behalf of his clients. No garnishee order can be enforced against the credit institution on the share of a rightful claimant in this special account.

By ministerial order regulations are laid down with regard to the manner of computation and payment of the interest on the moneys paid into the special account above €500.

One of the most important changes is the grounding of the *Financial Supervision Office*.

This Bureau supervises the financial organization of the bailiffs' offices. Once a year an accountant has to audit the accounts. The auditor's report must be sent to the Bureau within six months of the end of each financial year. With regard to the firm's annual accounts the report at least has to have the character of an assessment. The Bureau may require the bailiff to grant access to his business and personal records and related documents, balance sheets, statements of income and expenditure, the register and the repertory. The Bureau may require the bailiff to provide copies of these documents. If in its surveillance the Bureau becomes aware of facts or circumstances that in its opinion constitute a reason to take disciplinary action, it will notify its findings, if necessary (in case of irregularities or breaches of the relevant regulatory legislation) in the form of a complaint, to the chairman of the Chamber of Bailiffs. One could say that the Bureau works like a kind of public prosecutor.

CHAPTER 11

SPAIN

Juan Pablo Correa Delcasso[1]

I. ENFORCEMENT PRACTICE IN SPANISH LAW

Enforcement of judicial decisions is governed by Articles 538 et seq. of the *Ley de Enjuiciamento Civil* (LEC), which provides for a unified regime for the satisfaction of all sorts of claims, both judicial and extrajudicial.[2]

As will be outlined, enforcement in Spain remains an activity wholly reserved for the courts, which must 'pass judgment and enforce that which has been decided', as prescribed by Article 117 of the Spanish Constitution.

The different judicial enforcement bodies will be analysed together with a study of their powers. After this, the different procedural stages that must be followed by all judgment creditors (or a creditor who has been rendered a favourable arbitral award) will be tackled, followed by a conclusion on the efficiency of the system.

A. The judicial enforcement bodies

The judicial enforcement bodies are as follows:

(i) The sole district court judge (Juzgado de Primera Instancia), who is competent on the substantial matter, is responsible for both the 'passing of judgment and enforcement of that which has been decided'. The judge is not therefore determined in accordance with the location of the assets.

The functions that are exercised by such judge as ascribed to him by the LEC (apart from the general management of the procedure) are as follows:

- to ascertain his territorial competence to take on the execution of such arbitral or judicial decision (Art 546 LEC);
- to refuse or to grant the enforcement requested by the creditor by a judicial order (*auto*), this being appellable before the *Audiencia Provincial* (Article 553);

---

[1] Doctor of Law, Advocate and Professor, University of Barcelona.
[2] In the previous LEC of 1881, the enforcement of judgments was considered different from the enforcement of extrajudicial claims. Although this is no longer the case, the previous legislation has left numerous impressions in the new law.

- to identify the beneficiaries of a judgment in favour of consumer organizations (Art 519 and 221 LEC);
- to recognize and to enforce judgments and foreign enforcement orders, in accordance with international treaties (Art 523 LEC);
- divide the jointly held assets of spouses when the debt is due by only one of them, and the other spouse requests it (article 541 LEC);
- determine exactly (Art 553 LEC):
    the persons against whom enforcement will be directed;
    the amount being enforced;
    the measures that will need to be carried out to find the assets;
    the enforcement measures that will need to be carried out, as for example, the attachment of assets of the debtor that will be executed immediately, even before the notification of the judicial decision of the enforcement judge (Art 553.2 LEC); and
    the content of the notification to the debtor, if an extrajudicial decision is to be enforced;
- to join various enforcement actions between the same parties at the creditor's request, if the judge in charge of enforcing the oldest judgment believes this to be more favourable to the debtor (Art 555 LEC);
- to hear any appeal by the debtor to the enforcement in the cases stated by the law (Art 556 and 563 LEC);
- to order the stay or the termination of the enforcement in the cases specified in the law (such as if a bankruptcy proceeding is commenced or a criminal action is sought: Arts 565–70 LEC);
- to order the debtor to list his assets (Art 589 LEC);
- to order the gathering of information from financial institutions, public or private registries, individuals or moral persons among others (Art 590 LEC);
- to determine the order by which seizures will be effected following the scale at Article 592 LEC, if there is no agreement between the creditor and the debtor (Art 592 LEC), as well as determining the total salary to be seized following the criteria established by Articles 607 and 608 LEC;
- to resolve the case where a third party alleges that an asset of his has been unduly seized (*terceria de dominio*) or that he possesses a preferential credit (*terceria de major derecho*);
- to order the seizure of assets that have already been seized by a third party for the residual amount of the execution, or to order the seizure of the residual amount of the execution once the assets have been executed (Arts 610 and 611);
- to order a preliminary inscription of a seizure of an immovable good on the land registry (Art 629 LEC);
- to order the judicial administration of a business or a business group (Arts 630–3 LEC);

- to order the direct transfer of assets that have been seized to the creditor, this concerning cash seized from current bank accounts, as well as the sale of all his assets following the judge's order, such sale being undertaken in a manner agreed by the parties, or by a private institution (under judicial supervision), or by the court itself (Art 636 LEC);
- to designate an expert to evaluate the seized assets where necessary (Arts 637–9 LEC);
- to order the administration of the seized assets by the creditor, if the revenues they produce may satisfy the debt (Arts 676–80 LEC);
- to impose fines on the debtor, if he has not complied with a judicial order to hand over a good or to take an action (Arts 701, 709, and 710 LEC);
- to order the return of fungible goods, or this failing, their equivalent in cash (Art 702 LEC);
- to evict the occupants of a property that is to be handed over to the creditor and who do not possess the title to occupy such property (Art 704 LEC);
- to designate an expert to evaluate the cost of specific performance, when it is to be performed by a third party (Art 706); and
- to fix, at the creditor's request, the damages and interest if these have not been fixed by the judgment (Arts 712–20 LEC).

(ii) The court clerk of the district court (secretario judicial).

He will exercise the following functions:

- he will exercise public faith and assist court in the exercise of its functions;
- he directs the court's personnel;
- he is responsible for the archives and the safekeeping and deposit of documents, as well as for the assets deposited at certain institutions (Art 473 of *Ley Organica del Poder Judicial* or LOPJ).

In practice, the functions of the court clerk in the enforcement of judgments are essentially related to the control of the communications that are rendered to the court from third party debtors, public and private institutions, as well as the payment to the creditor of any amounts received during the enforcement proceedings.

(iii) The Agente Judicial

This agent is in charge of effecting attachments and vacating the occupants of property, with or without title, by order of the judge (Art 487 LOPJ).

In practice, the execution of attachments on movable property will be carried out by listing and describing in as much detail as possible the various assets that are attached (article 624 LEC).

(iv) the court official (Official de Justicia), who acts by delegation from the court clerk (Art 487 LOPJ), particularly when the seizure of movables is carried out.

*(v) the lawyer (*abogado*) and the* procurador intervene in all cases where the amount of the execution exceeds €900 (Art 539 LEC):

• the lawyer will exercise his functions as counsel as are granted to him in the great majority of European countries;
• the *procurador*, legal representative before the court (article 23 LEC), will receive all the communications addressed to him by the court and will intervene during the execution to carry out the judge's orders to third party debtors or to different private institutions (Art 167 LEC).

(vi) Major cities such as Barcelona have a **Common communication services** *(Servicio Comun de Actos de Notificacion*, Art 163 LEC), charged with carrying out the notification of judicial orders to the parties.

II. THE ENFORCEMENT PROCEDURE

As previously mentioned, forced enforcement of judgments is governed by Article 538 et seq. of the LEC. These sections provide for a unified treatment of the enforcement of judicial and extra-judicial decisions.

In summary, the different steps to be followed by any creditor in possession of a *titre executoire* are the following:

A. Presentation of an enforcement notice (Art 549 LEC)

After the expiry of the period established by Article 548 LEC for the debtor to comply voluntarily with the judge's decision (20 days from the date of his or her notification), the creditor (through an advocate and *procurador* if the sum of the order exceeds €900)[3] must present an enforcement order

---

[3] In effect, Art 539 LEC states that 'the creditor and debtor shall be directed by an abogado and represented by a procurador, except for the execution of decisions issued in procedures in which the intervention of such professionals is not compulsory. For the execution in procesos monitorios (a simplified type of procedure, for smaller amounts of money) in which there has been no confrontation, the intervention of an abogado and a procurador is required when the amount for which the execution is demanded Euro 900. In actions of the execution procedure for which this Statute expressly provides a pronouncement about the litigation costs, the parties shall satisfy their respective costs in accordance with Art 241 of this Statute, without prejudice to their right of due reimbursement after the Court's decision. The litigation costs not included in the previous paragraph shall be at the expense of the executed party with no need for a specific judicial decision; until the settlement however, the executing party shall satisfy the expenses and costs corresponding to the actions realized upon request by the executed party or other persons, which will be paid by whoever demanded such action'.

to the court that heard the case at first instance or '*Juzgado de Primera instancia* (Art 545 LEC); this must specify:

(i)   the *titre exécutoire* on which the claimant is relying on in order to request enforcement (a *titre exécutoire* is considered to be, among other things, a final judgment or an arbitral award);

(ii)   the method of enforcement sought, together with the amount claimed plus interest and costs, which must not exceed 30 per cent of the principal (the enforcement costs can amount to 30–40 per cent of the costs of the trial as such, although it is often less, including lawyers' costs and the costs relating to each enforcement measure taken);

(iii) a list of the assets that can be seized, together with a statement as to whether the debtor considers them sufficient to cover the debt;

(iv)   should the creditor have indicated that he does not know of sufficient of the debtor's assets to cover the debt, he may ask the court to investigate the financial institutions, public entities and public registers as well as the individual and legal persons the creditor indicates, so that these may state the assets of the debtor. The court will not carry out such investigations if the creditor could obtain the information himself or through his representative; and

(v)   the debtor's identity together with the identity of any other person who may be liable for the debt.

A *titre exécutoire* does not have to be final, and there are important new provisions for provisional enforcement.

This order may eventually be accompanied by documents indicated by Article 550 LEC (the powers of the *procurador*, extrajudicial enforcement claims, and other supporting documents).

B. Service of the enforcement order

If the request meets the conditions laid down by law, the court gives an enforcement order that is not subject to appeal. In the interim this may be objected to restrictively in writing:

(i)   the debtor may allege *pluspetición*, or excess, when the court has, for example, granted more than that which was fixed in the enforcement claim. A very simple procedure will therefore be carried out to determine the exact sum, but this will not suspend the enforcement process (Art 558 LEC);

(ii)   the debtor may oppose the order on the grounds of form or procedure (lack of representation, capacity to act and so forth). In certain cases, the court may accordingly suspend the enforcement proceedings (Art 559 LEC); and

(iii) the debtor may oppose enforcement on substantive grounds. The judge may agree to a hearing in which both the debtor and the creditor will be heard if the parties have requested it. The substantive grounds include payment of the debt or taking of the action required by the judgment, limitation of the enforcement action which occurs within five years of the judgment (these two grounds would not normally suspend execution), or out of court settlement. Opposition to enforcement based on these grounds will not suspend enforcement. Whatever the judge decides in this case may be appealed.

The debtor may wish to oppose not the enforcement itself, but a particular act of enforcement. He may do this on two grounds. First, because the rules regulating the enforcement procedure have been infringed (for example if the court has infringed a particular procedure). Secondly, because the court has not acted in accordance with the judgment (in this event it is the injured party—whether the debtor or the creditor—who can appeal).

Finally, if after the trial new facts or acts come to light that cannot be used to oppose enforcement through the above-mentioned causes of opposition to enforcement, but are legally relevant in relation to the enforcement, the debtor may allege such facts or acts in court (Art 564 LEC).

In every case, the parties to the enforcement procedure will, throughout the process, have the possibility of denying the commission of the legal infraction in question (Art 562 LEC). A judgment will not be suspended provisionally, even though the judgment has been appealed. However, if the debtor proves that the enforcement of the appealed decision would produce damages difficult to restore, he may ask the court to suspend the enforcement if he deposits an amount sufficient to cover any damages resulting from the delay in the execution (Art 567 LEC).

The order which grants the enforcement must state (Art 550 LEC):

(i)   the name of the persons to be served with the enforcement order;
(ii)   the amount sought;
(iii) the measures of location and investigation that have been approved;
(iv)   the means which will be employed by the court to seize the debtor's goods; and
(v)   the debtor's previous summons if the matter relates to an extrajudicial claim.

C. Enforcement

Once the order has been delivered, the court puts the 'judicial machinery' into action and orders the appropriate type of enforcement (warrant sale, power to seize, etc).

The law on the enforced recovery of sums of money (*ejecución dineraria*), governed by some 133 articles, and the enforcement of obligations to do or refrain from doing something (*ejecución por obligaciones de hacer y no hacer*) established by Articles 705–11 LEC, are placed under two distinct headings. The law sets out the following requirements:

First, the seizure of goods must always be proportionate, in the sense that one must never reclaim a value greater than the amount stipulated in the order, unless there are no less valuable goods in the debtor's property (Art 584 LEC);

Secondly, the enforcement procedures may always be averted or annulled through payment of the amount required by the order (Art 585 LEC);

Thirdly, sums of money that have been deposited by the debtor are delivered to the creditor, unless an opposition to the enforcement order has been lodged (article 586 LEC).

Fourthly, the *Agentes Judiciales* effect seizures. They have police authority to do this.

Fifthly, the seizure has full effect from the moment that the assets are on the list drawn up to the point of its enactment, independently of the measures which may be taken *a posteriori* to ensure its full effectiveness or subsequent publication (such as an entry in the land register (Art 587 LEC)). If there is a question of the seizure of other assets which need not be indicated at the time the plan is drawn up, as soon as it is practicable (whether such a seizure is, for example, on a bank account) the seizure will produce full effect from the moment that the court grants it by means of a specific decision, which is immediately communicated to the relevant person or organization.

Sixthly, the court will rely on the creditor to provide any information on the debtor's assets. He may access all sorts of public registers (land registry, companies registry, car registry, movable goods registry, missing debtors registry (for debtors whose domicile is unknown) as well as private registers accessible to creditors only (such as the ASNEF), although he would normally delegate a search to a private agent. Should the creditor not be able to provide such information, the debtor will be required by the court (on the debtor's request or of the court's own initiative) to provide a list of sufficient assets to cover the debt. The court may penalise non-compliance with such an order with fines or even imprisonment (of between six months and a year). The court's power to order fines or imprisonment for such non-compliance is being exercised with increasing frequency. Even with this powerful judicial tool, the creditor will often prefer to obtain a report on the debtor's assets by a detective (some €600) in order to contrast it with any information the debtor may provide on cross-examination.

The creditor (and he may only do this once he has a *titre exécutoire*) may also ask the court to require financial entities (banks), public registers and public entities generally (tax authorities, social security authorities) to which he does not have access, as well as individuals and moral persons (such as employers) the creditor may indicate, to provide the court with a list of the assets belonging to the debtor of which they have a record. The creditor must specify the reasons why such entity or person has such information. The court will not require any information from any entity or person if the creditor could obtain such information himself or through his representative (*procurador*). All such persons and entities are obliged to cooperate to the fullest extent (and the court may impose periodic fines for non-cooperation ranging from €180 to €6000) save if human rights will be infringed in such cooperation. It is notable that special regional fiscal authorities (*oficinas de averiguacion patrimonial*) have been created in order to assist the court in the retrieval of tax information relating to the debtor. This is particularly efficient. The social security authorities are also very cooperative with the judge in providing him with information on the debtor's salary, pensions or other income received.

It must be noted that there exists no difference in the access to information on the debtor's assets if the judgment is foreign or if it is Spanish. The foreign judgment will normally be subject to an *exequatur* procedure, and once the *titre executoire* has been recognized, it will be the locally competent judge who will be in charge of the information gathering process.

Like most legal systems in the European Union, Spanish law envisages the difficulties resulting from the disposal of goods that have been seized. In the absence of a specific agreement between the creditor and debtor, the court will order the seizure of assets that are easiest to sell and whose sale is least onerous for the debtor (the court will never delegate such task to a private figure such as the French *huissier de justice*). If the application of such criteria is difficult or impossible, then the judge will seize assets in the following order: the court will seize sums of money placed in a bank; next, shares, titles and the like which may be sold on a secondary market (on the stock exchange, in particular); jewellery and works of art; revenues of a certain value; movable property; immovable property; wages; pensions; and finally, titles and loans which may mature in the long term (article 592 LEC). A business may also be seized if the court decides it is appropriate.

The seizure of salaries, pensions or other monetary revenues is done by court order (on the creditor's request) to the appropriate entity or person, and such person will be obliged to transfer the amount indicated to an account.

The seizure of a bank account is fairly simple, and rapid when the debtor's bank account details are known. If they are not known, it may still be very efficient where the tax authorities have their information systems directly linked up with the bank's. The time necessary to seize a bank account will usually therefore be between 24 hours and one week.

The creditor's lawyer drafts a petition for seizure and this is presented to the court by the *procurador*. The debtor is notified and will usually file any opposition in writing. The court will order (through the medium of the *procurador*) the financial institution to retain a certain amount within the debtor's bank account, and the debtor may freely dispose of anything other than that amount. The bank (or any third party debtor) must communicate to the judge the amount it owes to the debtor (a false statement being subject to criminal sanctions). The bank shall first of all transfer any amount seized to the court's bank account (although the bank must respect any general rules on unseizable amounts), and the court shall then transfer such amount to the creditor. Should the creditor not know where the debtor has a bank account, the court will have notice of the debtor's bank account either through the tax authorities or by the debtor's own declaration. Should the account not have sufficient funds to cover the debt, the judge may order that any further amounts to be deposited shall become the subject of seizure. The seizure shall cease only after the creditor has had his debt completely satisfied and when the judge orders it. The effect of any movements the creditor has effected on his account prior to the seizure shall be determined by the judge.

The cost will vary, although it is recoverable by the creditor on execution. If €10,000 is to be recovered, the cost of the procurador will typically run to €300, the cost of the lawyer to €1,620 (although this is variable), and as from 1 April 2003 there is a court fee to pay, which will vary in accordance with the amount claimed.

Should the seizure of a bank account be ordered through an EU judgment, the law applicable to such seizure shall be the law of the place of seizure. The seizure of immovable property is done by a provisional inscription in the public land registry.

Some assets cannot be seized by law. Such is the case of household goods, or the debtor's clothes and the debtor's books and instruments that are necessary for him to exercise his profession. Income equivalent to the minimum wage is also unseizable, whether received by wage, pension or other form payment. For amounts above the minimum wage, there is a sliding scale on the amounts that can be seized (ie up to double the minimum wage only 30 per cent of such amount can be seized, up to triple the amount of the minimum wage only 50 per cent of such amount can be seized etc.). Such a sliding scale does not apply if the payment of alimony is being enforced.

Once the goods have been seized, the law prescribes measures by which the seizure is guaranteed, which include:

- their deposit in the 'Deposits and Consignments Account' where cash is concerned, and which is a de facto current account held by each court with Banesto Bank. When a case concerns sums of money deposited in a bank account or proceeds from a salary, the court will order the financial entity or payer of salaries or any other income to retain such sums and, in the case of collection of wages, to transfer them to the court's account (Art 621 LEC).

- a precise identification of the object in the instructions at the time of the seizure, where movable property is concerned; the instructions must also appoint an agent—a function which may be discharged by the debtor himself, by a public authority or another third party (Arts 624 and 626 LEC).
- the recording of the seizure in the Property Register in the case of immovable property or other goods eligible for entry in the aforementioned Register, which will be made the same day as the facsimile transmission of the court's order (Art 629 LEC).

Once the goods have been seized, the law governs their sale. In this area, the new *Ley de Enjuiciamiento Civil* introduced important legislative innovations; it intended to do away with sale by court auction, given the inefficiency of that process. Since then, in order to obtain the highest possible sale price,[4] sale by auction is made subordinate to other methods put into effect by the parties and above all to sale by a specialist establishment. In this way the value of the good that has been seized will typically be established by an expert selected by the court (in the absence of an agreement between the parties) as established by Articles 637–9 LEC. There are three methods by which to effect the sale of the seized good:

- by the accord of the parties through an agreement of sale which must be approved by the court (Art 640 LEC);
- sale by a specialist establishment, under the control of the court, as prescribed by Art 641 LEC; and
- sale by auction, as a final remedy (Art 636 LEC), which is regulated by Articles 643–54 for movable property, 655–76 for immovable property (681–700 in the case of mortgaged estates).

If the creditor requests it, or if the debtor requests it and the creditor

---

[4] As the legal commentary emphasizes: 'Not few are the changes, and mainly the legal certainty and security, introduced by this Statute in the procedimiento de apremio or phase of realization, once the evaluation of the assets affected to the execution has been done, depending on their different nature. In addition to filling numerous legal gaps, a single auction is established, with provisions aimed to achieve a more satisfactory result for the executing debtor, according to market rules as far as possible, trying moreover to reduce the economic cost. Irrespective of the improvements introduced in auctions' regulation, the statute paves the way for means of alternative forced alienation that in some circumstances will speed up the realization and improve their efficiency. Thus, the realization agreements between the creditor and the debtor are regulated, as well as the possibility for the judge to rule the assets alienation by a specialized person or entity out the judicial auction, upon request by the executing party or with its consent.'

consents, the court may agree the sale of the assets by a specialist person or entity in the sale of such type of assets. If the parties have not agreed otherwise, the specialist cannot sell the asset for less than 50 per cent of the value given to such asset by the valuer (70 per cent of the value if it is an immovable asset). The specialist will deposit the proceeds from the sale (less fees and disbursements) in a designated bank account. The specialist has six months in which to sell the asset(s), after which his mandate will be revoked. He may be granted a further six months to sell the asset(s) if he was not able to sell them due to circumstances beyond his control.

In all of these modes of disposition—which each merit their own analysis—it is important to note:

- the fact that the legislator has concerned himself for the first time with the communications that need to be made to the tenants or occupants of the building in order that they produce for the court those documents which legitimate their rights;
- the phasing out of the previous system of sale by auction, which allowed the auction of goods at derisory prices (Arts 669–71); and
- the possibility for the contractor to ask the court to put him in possession of the building and to evict any tenants who might be living there.

The law is also concerned with the regulation of a number of other areas, for instance, that the administration of a good in lieu of payment if the creditor requests it (that is, in order to manage the income or benefit that it might produce, which will contribute towards the reduction of the total amount of the judgment): Articles 676–80 LEC.

The intervention of third parties who have a preferential credit (*tercería de mejor derecho*). Should an asset belonging to a third party be seized, such seizure and its ulterior sale shall be valid. However, a third party has a particular action to protect his right to the property (and to prevent its sale) if he uses it before the sale of such asset (*tercería de dominio*). If after the sale of an asset, it is established that it belonged to a third party, the third party will only have an action for damages against the debtor (Art 594 LEC).

Provisional enforcement must be requested by the claimant, and will be carried out even on a judgment from the district court, except in order to effect the nullity of titles relating to industrial property or to effect the inscription of title to property on public registers (or in certain cases relating to family law). The rules relating to the acquisition of information on the debtor's assets are the same as those that apply to a final judgment. It will only be carried out after the expiry of the 20-day period for voluntary fulfilment of the judgment. The claimant does not have to make a deposit at court for the amount being executed as was the case previously. The defendant cannot oppose provisional enforcement of money claims, but may oppose the particular method of enforcement used (such opposition being directed to the enforcing judge with no appeal possible on his decision) if it is to cause damages that are impossible to restore or to compensate if the judgment was overturned. He may also avoid provisional enforcement of a money claim if he deposits the amount to which he is liable (debt, interest and costs) with the court. In the case of monetary claims, should the judgment be overturned once provisional enforcement has begun or been finalized, the execution will cease, the original creditor will return any amounts received, together with any costs resulting from enforcement that the debtor has been obliged to satisfy, and the creditor will be liable for the debtor's damages and interest on such amount. Should the judgment be overturned only partially, the creditor will return only the proportional amount due, plus interest on such amount from the day it was perceived.

Provisional enforcement of EU judgments that are not yet final is also possible. If the requirements specified in Regulation 44/2001 are complied with, and the law of the place judgment permits it, the Spanish judge is obliged to follow through with the requested provisional enforcement. In the case of non-EU provisional judgments, the general rule is that they will not have the benefit of provisional enforcement (if they are final, enforcement will depend on international treaty).

Provisional enforcement and protective measures are two radically opposed concepts in Spanish law. Provisional enforcement will only be granted once the period for voluntary compliance with a judgment has expired, whereas provisional measures take effect only until the judgment is final or has been the subject of a provisional enforcement order. A foreign judgment that is not final may benefit from protective measures even though it is not entitled to provisional execution.

Protective measures are those measures ordered by the court that is to take charge of the proceedings at the claimant's request, under his responsibility, to insure the enforcement of a future judgment that may be favourable to the claimant. The judge may order any protective measure he sees fit in order to insure enforcement. There is no appeal to his decision to grant or refuse a protective measure.

In order for the judge to order a protective measure, the creditor must appear to the judge to have a right to such credit, the measure must avoid the frustration of a future judgment, the creditor must provide security for costs and they must be ordered while proceedings are in progress or just before they commence if it is very urgent.

The debtor will be allowed to oppose the measure, unless the creditor persuades the judge of the urgency required, in which case the debtor will not be heard prior to the measure being taken (although he will be able to oppose such measure once it is taken).

Protective measures may be requested by a creditor who is in pursuit of a claim abroad as long as he can prove that he is a claimant to such action and as long as the Spanish courts do not have exclusive jurisdiction. The worldwide Mareva Injunction does not exist in Spain.

Concerning the enforcement of orders to do, or refrain from doing, something, the law introduces the following innovations:

The possibility of imposing penalties on the condemned party if he or she does not comply with the obligation within the time period determined by the court (Art 699 LEC), which may amount to 20 per cent of the value of the good in the case of monthly penalties, and 50 per cent of the value in the case of a single penalties (Art 711 LEC).

The eventual seizure of goods which the court might order to ensure compliance with the obligation (a seizure which might be substituted by a guarantee) if it extends beyond a certain period of time (Art 700 LEC).

The separate mechanisms which are used to enforce the law in each case, distinguishing those instances where it is a question of enforcing fulfilment of an obligation to deliver movable property, fungible goods or, on the other hand, to bring about a decision to do or refrain from doing something (Arts 701–10 LEC).

Finally, the law sets out in Articles 712–720 LEC the damages and interest which must be settled during the enforcement procedure (either requested during the declaratory phase of the proceedings or because a non-pecuniary judgment could not be rendered); it also lays down the payment of revenue earned by the debtor and the monitoring by the court of the process of administration.

III. CONCLUSION : THE EFFICIENCY OF THE ENFORCEMENT SYSTEM

To conclude, one may affirm that the new code of civil procedure (LEC 1/2000, of 7 January) has greatly improved enforcement procedure by the introduction of new institutions such as the forced declaration of assets to be done by the debtor, the sale through specialist institutions, or the obligation of cooperation for public bodies and third party debtors in general in order to locate the debtor's assets.

Nevertheless, despite these efforts, the Spanish enforcement system is still slow and inefficient given that the courts, already often overworked, are in charge of the majority of the enforcement procedure. In this regard, we consider it necessary that the *procuradores* (who already provide a great service in reducing the courts' workload, especially in the transmission of judicial orders to third party and public and private institutions), assume more and more responsibilities in this field, approaching those of the French *huissier de justice*.

Without doubt, a greater intervention of a professional such as the *procurador* in the enforcement procedure, together with a reform of the role of the judiciary as required continuously by the great majority of authors, will contribute very considerably to increase the efficiency of the Spanish enforcement system, which has always been considered as one of the areas needing reform in our legal system.

CHAPTER 12

SWEDEN

Torbjörn Andersson and Hugo Fridén

A Note on 'Inkasso'

Before starting with the topics mentioned in the questionnaire we will draw your attention to, so to speak, a pre-state to execution by the enforcement authority. Sweden's system is generally based on smaller or larger debt-collection agencies. These are often called inkasso-agencies and their work with collection of debts is regulated in the Code of *Inkasso* from 1974. According to this law the concept of *inkasso* covers all activities in order to make the debtor pay his debt, expect giving information about basic things like day of maturity and that the debt will be transferred to inkasso.

I. THE STRUCTURE OF ENFORCEMENT AGENCIES

A. *Their nature (public/private etc) and location within the Member State*

In Sweden the nature of the agency is public. There is nothing like the private bailiffs which exist in France, the Netherlands or the UK. The Swedish Enforcement Authority /Enforcement Agency (*Kronofogdemyndigheten*), together with the National Tax Board (*Riksskatteverket*), forms what may be called the state branch of execution. The National Tax Board possesses chief authority and is a governmental, central agency of administration. (Swedish Ordinance 1988:784 on instructions for the branch of execution.)

Under the Swedish Code of Execution (*Utsökningsbalken*) the enforcement authority is a state authority set up to enforce court judgments and decisions containing direct obligations to pay or other direct obligations. The Enforcement Authority must also enforce decisions on payment or other direct obligations, where organs other than courts, for example an administrative agency, take such decisions. But the Code of Execution requires that enforcement orders, other than court judgments and decisions, be directly enforceable under statutory law. Apart from court judgments, decisions and, where this is specifically provided for, administrative decisions, arbitration awards obliging a party to pay or to perform in some

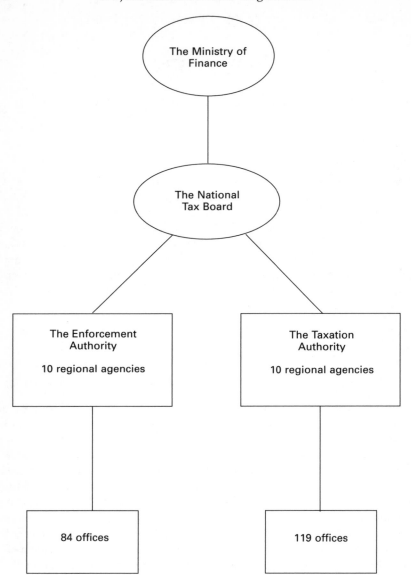

other way, are also executable (*titres exécutoires*) and thus require the assistance of the Enforcement Authority on application. That means that the Enforcement Authority is a public body which is independent from the courts.

B. *Organization of Enforcement Agencies, including education and status of personnel*

Since 1997 the Enforcement Authority has been divided into 10 regional agencies. These regional agencies are in turn split up into 84 offices. Each regional agency has a board and an executive director. Generally, the regional organization contains seven units, which deal with administration, summary proceedings, reconstruction of bad debts, field activities, special collection recovery and supervision of bankruptcies, respectively.

At present there is an ongoing enquiry and debate as to whether the Enforcement Authority should be organized in a way that separates it, and its regional branches, from the Tax Board. The tasks that currently are attributed to the Enforcement Authority are expected to remain. What is looked into, though, is whether the Authority should keep its role as claimant in public cases. A proposed alternative would be to confer the role of claimant to the tax authorities, as representatives of the state. As recently as 30 October 2003 the Swedish Parliament reconstructed some of this organization and from 1 January 2004 all the regional tax authorities, with their 119 tax offices, together with the National Tax Board, will form one body named The Tax Department (skatteverket). However, the future structure of the branch of execution is still being investigated and discussed.

The staff of the Enforcement Authority consists of lawyers (primarily occupied with execution/enforcement), executive civil servants and administrative and educational staff. Of course, the lawyers have law degrees, but also generally experience from court and from courses given internally at the Enforcement Agency on specific executive matters.

The executive staff are educated internally, although their education to some extent has been connected to law studies at university level. The internal courses provided by the Enforcement Agency for the benefit of all executive personnel are rather solid, theoretically as well as practically. In each specific case the Swedish Tax Board confers competence to the 'Crown Inspector' (*Kronoinspektören*, cf 'public bailiff') to carry out executive tasks like seizure and eviction. Generally the administrative staff is educated, but is also offered internal courses. Those responsible for recruitment and education have a university background.

C. Efficiency (based on time, cost, incentives for agents)

Statistics are a source of constant discussion and misunderstanding. Therefore, the following text is merely an attempt to catch a glimpse of the efficiency of Swedish execution in practice. It is based on a follow-up of the Enforcement Authority by the Tax Board (published on 28 February 2003). As far as possible the data concern the period 1992–2002 and Sweden as a whole; they encompass all the 10 regional enforcement agencies (public bailiffs) in Sweden. The subject matters dealt with are divided into 'A-matters' (mainly concerning public claims) and 'E-matters' (mainly private claims). To a large extent the statistics correspond to these categories.

The number of new debtors subject to applications for execution decreased over the period. In 1992, 460,000 new debtors were made the subject of enforcement measures, while in 2002 the number was 210,000, a reduction of more than 50 per cent. Almost 80 per cent of the total number of debtors over the period are private individuals. Legal persons make up circa 15 per cent.

The number of matters which are still in the system is somewhere between 550,000 and 650,000, and the number has been more or less constant throughout the period. According to the Tax Board, the Enforcement Agency copes with less matters today in comparison. It is also held that the flow of matters has slowed down.

During the relevant period, the number of 'A-matters' varied a lot, but that is probably due to the introduction of new types of 'A-matters'as well as variations in routines for categorising as 'A-matters'. The backlog of 'A-matters' tends to grow irrespective of the number of applications. During 2002, some 2,202,000 new 'A-matters'were received and some 6,654,000 remained in the system.

Another conclusion made by the Tax Board is that the percentage of enforced 'A-matters' is well in line with the economic cycles of society at large.

The flow of 'E-matters' (private claims primarily) has decreased, just like the flow of 'A-matters'. Meanwhile the back log has grown over the ten-year period, but not for the last six years. At least part of this increase may be explained by reference to the recent introduction of a possibility for claimants to renew their applications. After the expiry of the one-year limit for dealing with a matter of enforcement, a claimant may apply for renewal and presumably obtain continued enforcement, which accordingly adds to the back log of matters. The number of applications for renewal has been 150,000 annually for the last three years. During 2002 360,000 'E-matters' were received and 416,000 remained by the end of the year.

The applicant can apply for a complete or a limited inquiry of the debtor's assets. Where the former is applied for the Enforcement Authority must 'to the extent necessary considering the substance of the application, the situation of the debtor and other circumstances, investigate into the debtor's situation in respect of employment and wages and whether he possesses property fit to distraint'.[1] In cases where the applicant has applied for a limited inquiry, the Enforcement Authority merely looks into the prospect of attachment of the debtor's earnings. Among the 'E-matters' received, some 80 per cent requested a limited inquiry of the debtor's assets. This is an increase in comparison to 1992, when the number was only 65 per cent.

During the last five-year period the percentage of enforced 'A-matters' has been between 40 per cent and 50 per cent. The corresponding number of 'E-matters' is between 25 per cent and 30 per cent. The efficiency of enforcement, with respect to costs and calculated on the basis of actually concluded A- and 'E-matters', seems to be developing positively. The Tax Board, though, holds that the flow of matters is faster than the flow of debtors.

As to the timeframe for the processing of inquiries, in respect of the two categories of matters, 'E-matters' are dealt with more swiftly. Around 75–80 per cent of them are handled in less than three months. In respect of 'A-matters' the corresponding amount is 50–65 per cent. This difference may be explained with reference to the formal time limit for dealing with 'E-matters', a limit which does not exist for 'A-matters'. An application for execution of a private claim must only be dealt with for one year, unless the claimant applies for renewal. A public claim will be handled with no time limit, that is, for as long as the debtor does not pay or until the debt itself is time barred under substantive law.

D. Fees charged for the provision of these services

The costs, attached to a case before the Enforcement Authority, are covered by fees for recovery of debts. There are four fees: basic fee, preparation fee, sales fee and special fee. The basic fee varies depending upon whether the applicant applies for a complete (€100) or a limited inquiry (€50). It may be added that the fees for recovery are determined by the actual process and that the cost for the work of the Enforcement Authority is related to the expected outcome for the applicant.

E. Supervision by courts, regulatory bodies and other organizations

Execution is regulated by law, by the Code of Execution and the Ordinance on Execution, both of which were enacted in the beginning of the 1980s.

[1] Code of Execution Chap 4 s 9c.

There is no such thing as 'private execution' of claims in Sweden, although of course a debtor may avoid enforcement by paying his debts privately. Prior to the actual enforcement by the Enforcement Authority, there is no judicial control of the activities by the Authority. The coercive measures are decided by the Authority alone and although such decisions may be appealed to a court, the measures of coercion remain executed until the judgment of the court; that is, unless the court upon application issues an order for interim relief. The actual decision to carry out enforcement in a particular case may be subject to appeal to a court. The appeal as such, though, does not bring about a stay of the enforcement.

Under Swedish constitutional law domestic agencies and authorities are independent. This means that the government, the parliament etc, must not interfere with the way, for example, the Enforcement Authority deals with or decides a specific matter. State supervision is thus limited to statutory regulation and to court control.

F. Remedies, including stays of execution

The system laid down by the Code of Execution presupposes independent enforcement agencies. For simplification of the procedure, there is a possibility for self-regulation, whereby the Enforcement Agency, on its own initiative, or after complaint, corrects its decisions.[2] For instance, the Enforcement Agency may cancel a decision to seize, relieving the debtor of having to go to court.

As submitted above, practically every decision made by the Execution Authority may be subject to court procedure after appeal.[3] An appeal by the applicant or by the debtor has to be taken within three weeks from the day the decision of seizure was served to the debtor and it is supposed to be lodged with the Enforcement Authority in question.[4] However, an appeal by a third party is not subject to time limits. The court in question is the District Court and in such cases its decision may be subject to appeal to the Court of Appeal and, after a review dispensation, the Supreme Court.

How burdensome the recourse to remedies is, is hard to say in general. A common impression based on limited personal experience is that it is fairly easy to have recourse since the Enforcement Authority nowadays can make a self-correction.[5] However, in some cases this can only be done during a limited time after the seizure has been made. It is the author's opinion that in most cases this burden is reasonable.

---

[2] ibid ss 33–5.
[3] ibid Chap 18 s 7 para 2 and Chap 18 s 8.
[4] ibid Chap 18 s 7 para 2 and Chap 18 s 8.
[5] ibid Chap 4 s 33–5.

As submitted before, an application for enforcement must be founded upon a *titre exécutoire*. The most important among the *titres exécutoire* recognized under the Code of Execution are judgments and other decisions by courts. Such *titres* may be enforced immediately, thus before the time limit for appeal has lapsed. The effects of the possibility to prompt enforcement [??] are mitigated by the fact that generally enforcement may not be completed before the time limit has lapsed and the judgment etc stands. For example, seizure may be made in respect of a debt founded upon a judgment by a District Court, notwithstanding that the time limit for appeal against the judgment is still running. But the Enforcement Authority must not sell the property subject to seizure and monetary assets received must not be handed over to the applicant before the time limit has lapsed.[6] And this is the case whether or not the judgment has been appealed.

In order to stop a commenced enforcement, the debtor or occasionally some third party must appeal against the *titre exécutoire* and concurrently apply to the court for interim relief in respect of the enforcement.

The order of things is systematically similar, where an enforcement decision by the Enforcement Authority is appealed against before the District Court. The enforcement is not stayed because of the appeal, but in addition the complainant has to apply for interim relief before the District Court.

G. *The impact of national constitutional law*

In Sweden there is generally a direct and clear connection between the Instrument of Government (*Regeringsformen*) and exercise of public powers. Under Swedish constitutional law parliament possesses the power to legislate and the government is equipped with the competence to pass ordinances, either after being empowered by parliament or by way of implementing legislation. The latter kind of ordinances may not add to the statutes enacted by parliament. At a lower level of regulatory hierarchy, you find authorization from the government to state agencies to issue regulations.

Within the law of execution, the Tax Board has been entrusted the role of chief administrative authority.[7] In this capacity the Board is subject to a general obligation to issue regulations upon authorization in statutory law.[8] A clear example of this is the delegation of competence to issue regulations concerning attachment of earnings. Here parliament has provided that the government, or the administrative entity indicated by the government, may annually lay down standard amounts for establishing how much the debtor

---

[6] ibid Chap 3, s 4.
[7] Swedish Ordinance 1988: 784 on instructions for the branch of execution.
[8] SFS 1988:784 Chap 2 s 2

should be entitled to keep covering his and his family's expenses. The government has, by way of delegation, provided that the Tax Board may issue regulations on further details concerning this standard amount; this competence is annually made use of by the Tax Board. In the same ordinance by which the Tax Board is appointed chief administrative authority it is also laid down that the Board has the general task to promote law-abidance, consistency and uniformity in the application of law of execution. In order to fulfil that aim, the Board has been provided with competence to issue recommendations; this power is used quite frequently.

Constitutional influence upon the organs of execution may also work by way of a number of requirements laid down in the Instrument of Government; more or less directly these provisions regulate the exercise of public powers. Among these is the requirement that public powers must only be exercised under the law (the principle of legality). Another example would be the right to (judicial) review of regulations, which in short provides that courts and other public bodies are obliged to set aside norms which conflict with the Constitution or norms enacted in breach of the Constitution. The order of execution mentioned above has a clear connection to the principle of proportionality, constitutionally conditioning public interference with individual rights.

II. THE EUROPEAN DIMENSION

A. The impact of European human rights instruments (ECHR and the European Charter).

The ECHR is incorporated into Swedish legislation and granted a status somewhere between an Act of Parliament and constitutional law.

As submitted above, almost all decisions during the different phases of an enforcement case may be subject to judicial determination. So it seems like the Swedish system of enforcement suffers from no fundamental problems in respect of Article 6 ECHR. Still, there are a few questions, which may be interesting to elaborate on further. For instance, the Enforcement Authority has been generously provided with competence to use coercive measures. Generally, the use of such measures does not require a prior judicial determination, but merely an opportunity to appeal afterwards. Furthermore, the Enforcement Authority is under an obligation to use the assets found, primarily, to recover tax debts owed to the State. This has had the effect, on occasion, that a creditor having found assets and briefed the Enforcement Authority about it, has been left with reduced recovery, since the tax debts have absorbed the assets.

The fact that the Enforcement Authority is obliged to recover debts to the state may raise questions in respect of the impartiality and objectivity of the Authority as well as of the enforcement system as such. The difference between public and private claims in respect of the former, but not the latter, being enforced without time limit, adds to this. Consequently, it is not surprising that a separation between the Tax Board and the Enforcement Agency is currently being seriously considered.

(a) Cooperation of enforcement agencies at European level, including the role of private debt collectors and professional bodies

The following is a very brief and in no way complete sketch. But our ambition is to present at least something of an overall picture. For this reason it is sufficient to distinguish between the enforcement of Swedish claims abroad and foreign claims subject to enforcement in Sweden. Furthermore, you may make a distinction between private and public claims.

When enforcing Swedish private claims abroad, the Enforcement Agency plays a modest role. Where the Enforcement Agency, in a matter concerning a private claim, concludes that enforcement cannot be undertaken in Sweden, the matter is returned to the claimant. Then it is up to the claimant to apply for execution abroad. Thus, the enforcement procedure at the Enforcement Agency ceases when no executable assets belonging to the debtor can be found in the country.

The procedure for enforcement of Swedish claims abroad may be better described by the representatives of the relevant foreign jurisdictions, but at least in Europe the procedure is more or less the same as the one described in the following.

Often when private claims based on foreign titles of execution are enforced in Sweden, a Swedish court must carry out a formal decision containing a consideration of the enforceability of the title. The court competent to make such decisions is the Court of Appeal in Stockholm. In order to trigger an enforceability consideration there must be an applicable Convention, incorporated by Swedish legislation, in force between Sweden and the other State involved.

An affirmative decision on the title's enforceability constitutes a title of execution under Swedish law. Where there this no Convention and/or no statutory support for recognizing foreign titles, the claimant is left to commence legal proceedings before a Swedish court in order to receive a *titre exécutoire* if that is at all possible.

Enforcement in Sweden of foreign public claims and, as its corollary, of Swedish public claims abroad, always requires Conventions as a basis. In this category one may find Conventions on taxation, on legal assistance and also EC directives on enforcement. From the Swedish act on mutual assistance in tax matters it is clear how the procedure is generally framed. The concept of assistance is legally defined to encompass more than the concept of enforcement, since the former includes exchange of information and serving of documents. Where the Enforcement Agency requests enforcement of tax debts in another Nordic country, or vice versa, the agency in Stockholm has to apply for, or receive an application for, enforcement.

Assume that the enforcement agency in Gothenburg wants to enforce a claim for tax debts in Denmark. The Gothenburg agency then asks the Stockholm agency to apply for enforcement to the competent Danish authority. Accordingly, when an enforcement authority situated in Copenhagen wishes to enforce claims for Danish tax debts from a Swede living in Malmö, it applies for assistance to the enforcement agency in Stockholm.

In cases concerning Swedish public claims against individuals with assets situated outside the Nordic countries, the Swedish Enforcement Agency contacts the Tax Board, which is competent to receive applications for the enforcement of claims for tax debts outside the Nordic countries. Also non-Nordic authorities requesting enforcement of foreign tax may make applications to the Tax Board.

The competent authorities, that is, the Tax Board and the enforcement agency in Stockholm, make an appreciation as to whether the legal requirements are met and send the applications to the relevant authority in Sweden or abroad. One of the conditions which have to be met is that the tax debt must be encompassed by the Convention in question and that no measures will be taken which are in breach of Swedish law, administrative practice, public policy or public interests.

B. The European enforcement order and its implications for the system of remedies against execution

1. The European enforcement order

The proposed European enforcement order has as its purpose to make the cross-border enforcement of judgments speedier and more efficient. Under the Brussels I Regulation declarations of enforceability made by a competent court or authority in the country where enforcement is sought are provided for.[9] This opens up the possibility of having a foreign judgment enforced without any review in substance by the courts in the state of enforcement.[10] Nonetheless, the declaration procedure of the Brussels I Regulation does require at least a formal declarative decision by a court in the state of enforcement, and such a decision may be appealed against.[11] Thus, although the declaration procedure makes recognition and enforcement over EU borders more efficient and speedier in comparison to gener-

---

[9] Regulation 44/2001 Art 38.
[10] Art 41 compared with Arts 53, 34, and 35.
[11] Regulation 44/2001, Art 43.

ally applicable *exequatur* procedures, ie requiring a test of whether the foreign judgments meet domestic public policy criteria, it presupposes the participation of courts of the state where enforcement is sought. The objective of the proposed European enforcement order is the abolition of *exequatur* procedures in respect of uncontested claims. This means that a judgment delivered in one Member State should be enforced in another, without any checks of the judgment being undertaken by courts of the State where enforcement is sought.

It must be said that this is a big step to take. The Commission and the Council in their draft proposals refer to the principle of mutual recognition and the Commission submits that the mutual trust needs to be strengthened by providing for some common minimum procedural standards. This is also thought essential in order to strictly observe the requirements for a fair trial in keeping with Article 6 of the ECHR. This system of mutual trust and recognition of judgments will be applicable as to uncontested judgments in an area covering 25 European States, of which most just recently belonged to the legal and bureaucratic ideals of Eastern Europe and the Soviet Union. In view of the fact that Sweden has managed to have the Swedish Enforcement Service regarded as a court, in the meaning of the Brussels I Regulation and the future Regulation on the European Enforcement Order, and that from a Swedish perspective it is even doubtful whether one can trust the Service's reliability in applying the regulations, the trust in decisions by fellow European courts cannot be expected to be robust, in general. The latest alterations made by the Presidency in the proposal presented on 30 June 2004, seem to lean towards the principle of mutual recognition, reducing the scope of the minimum standards which are tools for harmonization. This may make political consensus easier to attain, perhaps, but obviously it further weakens the possibilities for creating an environment of mutual trust. Allowing domestic law to rule summary proceedings, of course, means recognizing the enforcement of foreign judgments, the standards of which you cannot exercise any control over in the absence of minimal rules laid down at EC level.

This being said, in the following we will consider the impact of the proposal, in its present shape, on the Swedish law of execution.

Under Swedish law the creditor must present the original document of the title of execution, unless the Enforcement Agency considers that a verified copy will do.[12] This deviates slightly from Article 7(3) in the European order, where it is submitted that the number of authenticated copies of the certificate shall correspond to the number of authenticated copies of the judgment supplied to the creditor. The possibly varying national requirements on execution titles having to be presented in original documents, lead

---

[12] Code of Execution Chap 2 s 3 para 3.

to the bigger issue of parallel execution. Are there any measures to protect the debtor from being subject to enforcement in a number of States simultaneously, which would amount to unjust execution? In what way can the enforcement service of one State obtain information as to how far a parallel and simultaneous enforcement procedure in another state has progressed, in case the various enforcement proceedings have as their subject only one claim manifest in several authentic copies? The cooperation referred to in Article 26a does not seem to cover information exchange between enforcement services in respect of a particular case.

Something which was discussed during the preparation of the European enforcement order (see the explanatory memorandum concerning Article 5), is whether the judgment must have acquired the authority of a final decision. In the latest draft by the Presidency, Article 5a does not require that the decision enforced be final. As is clear from the report above, the general rule in Sweden is that the termination of the time limit for appeal does not have to be awaited before enforcement is sought. And this applies without there being a need for the creditor to apply for interim enforcement; such orders are regulated separately. The decision of a summary proceeding, that is a so-called Order for Payment, is fully enforced by way of seizure, possibly sale and payment to the creditor, even though the time limit for appeal against the decision has not passed. Generally, this is only exempted where the property seized is real estate or of considerable value. In such situations, the enforcement service either waits for the expiry of the time limit for appeal or obtains the consent of the debtor, before the executive sale of the property is carried out.[13] As a requirement of finality is laid down in Article 5a of the Regulation, a creditor seeking enforcement outside the Swedish borders will be at a disadvantage in comparison to creditors seeking enforcement in Sweden. Furthermore, creditors with claims based upon foreign decisions would not, contrary to creditors with claims based upon Swedish decisions, seek enforcement before the expiry of the time limit. In order to avoid discrimination of foreign creditors and claims this may call for a change of Swedish law, which will in fact lead to a slow down of the enforcement procedure in Sweden. On the other hand, the Regulation, even if it would include a requirement of finality, will simplify enforcement abroad in comparison to the present system where *exequatur* proceedings are necessary.

The rules on service of documents, as laid down in the proposed regulation, have as their sole, yet important, purpose to make it acceptable to have foreign summary judgments enforced without *exequatur*, thereby simplifying the cross-border enforcement of uncontested claims. Obviously, enforcement of uncontested claims puts the rights of the defence at risk.

---

[13] ibid Chap 3 s 11 and Chap 8 s 4 paras 1–3.

Generally in this kind of procedure, the actual service of the document instituting the proceedings is the only real contact between the court (or enforcement service) and the debtor. In order to guarantee the attainment of a basic level of legal certainty, the regulation contains minimum standards for uncontested claims procedures. These minimum standards may be said to be met by Swedish law in its existing shape. Still, as to one of the earlier drafts of Article 15 one may doubt in respect of the requirement of service in sufficient time to arrange for defence. The earlier draft required that at least 14 calendar days pass, as from the day of service, allowing the debtor to object to the claim in the summary proceedings. Under Swedish law it is clear that the time limit for objection must not be set for a longer period than 14 days, unless extraordinary circumstances are at hand.[14] However, in practice the time is generally set at 10 days.

As to methods of service, most of the methods allowed under Swedish law meet the minimum standards laid down in the regulation. Still, there may be deviations. Under Swedish law it is generally considered that service is lawfully undertaken, where, in case personal service on the debtor has failed, the document is placed in the debtor's mail box or nailed to the door of the debtor's personal domicile.[15] The latter method of service is probably not reconcilable with Articles 11–12. Another method for service which is possible under Swedish law, but which seems contrary to the proposed regulation, would be personal service at the debtor's domicile on the landlord of the house.[16]

In the context of the service of documents and the protection of the interests of the defendant, we observe that the Parliament proposed a reinforcement of the defendant's position by suggesting a requirement that an application for a European enforcement order be served on the debtor.[17] This new article was apparently struck down without comment in the proposal delivered by the presidency on 30 June 2004. It is difficult to say whether the idea of requiring service on the debtor of an application for a European enforcement order is abolished. If not, it would seem appropriate to make the minimum standards applicable also in respect of such applications.

[14] Act on Summary Proceedings s 25.
[15] Cf ibid s 29 and Act on Service of Documents s 15.
[16] Cf Act on service of documents s 12 first para.
[17] See Art 6a in COM (2003) 341 final, 11 June 2003.

PART III

HARMONIZATION AND MUTUAL RECOGNITION IN EUROPEAN CIVIL PROCEDURE

CHAPTER 13

HARMONIZATION AND MUTUAL RECOGNITION: HOW TO HANDLE MUTUAL DISTRUST[1]

Torbjörn Andersson

I. EUROPEAN APPROXIMATION OF PROCEDURAL LAW

It is a well-known fact that it is difficult to attain EC approximation in the field of procedural law. There are ideological reasons for this. Courts and the organization of courts are part of the State organization, State identity, and State constitution, and foreign influences in this field represent, or may represent, a threat to the State identity. Some would perhaps say that, at least in some legal orders, procedural law might be regarded as the highest expression of legal culture.

There are also practical reasons for the difficulty in achieving harmonization in the field of procedural law. Procedural law has, traditionally, been domestically rooted and there has been a lesser need for foreign influence and impulse for change.[2] But the times they are a-changing: with increased cooperation at a legislative level within the European Union, it has become apparent that Member States can benefit from closer cooperation in the field of procedural law.

Procedural approximation would probably contribute to an increased cross-border mobility for persons as well as having an impact on the other fundamental freedoms of the Community, particularly in respect to increased cross-border trade. That is the combination of objectives stated as driving efforts for cooperation in this field of procedural development. At the end of the twentieth century, such considerations prompted Member States to agree on closer cooperation on matters of procedural law. One

---

[1] This chapter is based on proceedings from the final meeting for this project held at the British Institute of International and Comparative Law in London on 23 Apr 2004 and entitled Enforcement Agency Practice in Europe: Cooperation or Harmonization?

[2] From a Swedish perspective, one might observe that in the field of private law, there is a significant legal discourse and close cooperation between the Nordic countries on very detailed technical issues and you may see references to German scholars on private law questions but that is not the case within the field of procedural law, at least not to the same extent.

effect of this was the transfer of an 'area of freedom, security and justice' in the third pillar into the first pillar of the union, thereby including the willingness to cooperate on matters of international private and procedural law as part of procedure.

II. HARMONIZATION AND RECOGNITION

If you look into integration, you might say that in this field there are two ways forward. The first is harmonization, by which you would establish a set of common procedural rules either in a specific area or more broadly across an increased number of procedural practices. Approximation of this sort was the objective of the Storme Report. An alternative way would be recognition. Member States recognize judgments from other Member States, even though those judgments stem from unfamiliar procedural systems based upon alien procedural values or ideologies. Recognition must be the least preferable option from an 'integrational' perspective as it would make a difference for undertakings and individuals where proceedings are commenced. Still, at least parties may be certain that a court judgment obtained will be recognized in other Member States.

Consequently, harmonization is the most agreeable solution from a European perspective. Ideally undertakings and individuals would be keen to engage in cross-border activity where only one set of procedural rules were to apply, irrespective of where you lodged your court proceedings. Therefore, harmonization must be considered the option most likely to promote European integration.

But there are some disadvantages to harmonization. This may be disputed, but I would say that it is inevitable that harmonized legislation leads to a deterioration of quality in respect of purely domestic law. If one has to make 15 states, or even 25 states, agree on the same set of principles to achieve a compromise, it is inevitable that the quality of the rules will deteriorate.

A second disadvantage would be that if you harmonize rules and restrict them to cross-border situations you will have trouble distinguishing those types of situations from purely domestic situations, resulting in an awkward application of procedural rules designed to promote certainty. Establishing two sets of rules for cross-border and domestic situations is likely to cause delay in the proceedings and might also create confusion and damage the certainty of the procedure.

An additional disadvantage from a European perspective is the likelihood of encountering significant political difficulties when instituting common procedural rules. Member States will have to scrutinize and probably surrender some of their ideological values and cultural identity, if they are to agree on harmonized rules. Drafting, coordinating and implementing harmonized rules will be a protracted process. This is likely to upset the usual functioning and organization of the court and will inevitably create problems that are difficult to foresee and remedy.

Now, if you favour the principle of recognition, some of the disadvantages of harmonization will be overcome yet to the detriment of a more concentrated form of European integration. The principle of recognition will not affect purely domestic situations as it would be relatively simple to restrict recognition to cross-border situations. In addition important obstacles to cross-border activities would be removed without the need to reconcile all the Member States to a common set of procedural rules and ideological values. The internal systems peculiar to each Member State will remain intact, only slowly adjusting to a common European standard due to minimum requirements built into EC law based upon the principle of recognition.

III. (THE PRINCIPLE OF) MUTUAL TRUST

The big problem, in this author's view, with the principle of mutual recognition or the idea of recognition is that it requires mutual trust. The advantage of common procedural rules is that every Member State has or would have an opportunity to contribute to the drafting process. Even if a Member State has to forfeit some ideological values and has had to alter the structure of domestic legislation on some point, it must accept the new rules, or at least be familiar with them.

A principle of recognition of foreign judgments, by comparison, requires, in its extreme, that a domestic legal system allows for enforcement of judgments based on procedural rules and ideological values over which the Member State has no influence and very little knowledge. Today, Member State control over European Union judgments is exercised by way of the executor procedure provided for in the Brussels I Regulation, and it is possible for a court in the state where enforcement is sought to refuse enforcement with reference, for instance, to domestic public policy.

As of today, the cross-border enforcement of judgments may be said to have as its basis the principle of mutual recognition but not the objective of eventually creating procedural rules and the chosen way towards 'free movement of judgments' is mitigated with respect to the *exequatur* procedure provided for. Apparently, this is somewhat of a drawback for European integration. First, it does not achieve the higher level of integration, ie common procedural rules. Secondly, it makes cross-border enforcement of judgments a slow process in comparison to domestic enforcement of judgments, providing a disincentive for cross-border trade and movement of persons, goods, services and so forth. Domestic trade will have an advantage.

IV. THE EUROPEAN ENFORCEMENT OF ORDER AND SERVICE OF DOCUMENTS

The legislative work for the now-adopted regulation on the European Enforcement Order for uncontested claims must be seen in the context of the discussion above. The Commission, at the initial stage, assessed that the declaration of enforceability, provided for under the Brussels I Regulation, does not remove all obstacles for the unhindered movement of judgments within the Union, and leaves intermediate measures that are still too restrictive. It was considered a contradiction in terms that the enforcement of judgments concerning claims that have not been challenged by the debtor, should be delayed due to an *exequatur* procedure in the state of enforcement.

Abolishing the *exequatur* procedure was considered vital, because rapid recovery of outstanding debts is an absolute necessity for business and a constant concern for the economic sectors whose interest lies in the proper operation of the internal market. Therefore the proposal, which is now adopted, contained a provision under which a claimant may obtain a European enforcement order by a court in the state of origin and that the order may suffice to enforcement in another Member State without an *exequatur* procedure. That is well known.

Now, as will be clear from what has been said about the abolishment of the *exequatur* procedure for judgments concerning uncontested claims, that would also mean giving up Member State control over the judgments they are to enforce. In order to mitigate this drawback for Member State control, and the potential threat that poses for domestic procedural values, it is claimed that mutual trust between the Member State systems must be strengthened and this must be done by way of some common minimum standards.

Thus, minimum standards are proposed with regard to the service of documents, the time of service, which enables the preparation of a defence, and the communication of appropriate information about the debtor. These minimum standards would aim to create mutual trust and provide for legal certainty of the debtor. Since judgments based upon uncontested claims are often default judgments, mutual trust and legal certainty require that a debtor has had a fair opportunity to make an objection before the court. In the proposal now adopted, the minimum standards must be met for the claimant to obtain a European enforcement order.

As to the minimum standards in respect of service of documents, the proposed regulation originally required that documents had been served on the debtor personally, by post or electronically where the claimant had obtained a receipt. Only when reasonable efforts to serve the debtor personally had been unsuccessful, substitute service could be permitted. This would include personal service at a debtor's domicile on adults domiciled in the same household, service on a company where the debtor is self-employed or deposit of documents in the debtor's mail box where the debtor is self-employed.

These minimum standards may have caused difficulties in some Member States. For instance, Swedish rules on service of documents would not have met these minimum requirements. The minimum standards of service on documents were altered, eventually, by the Council. First, the hierarchy between the methods of service was abolished and it was deemed possible to serve the debtor by post where his address is in the state of origin.

The Council also introduced a requirement that the laws in the state of origin must provide that a debtor, subject to any of the methods of service in the regulation, may apply for a full review where he has not been served in time to prepare a proper defence. This was thought to mitigate the possibility of service by mail. In respect of this proposal, the Commission hopes that compliance with these minimum standards concerning service of documents justifies the abolition of the control of the rights of the defence in the Member State where judgment is to be enforced. The Commission agrees with the Council that the proposal strikes a fair balance between simplification of cross-border enforcement and the adequate protection of debtor's rights.

It is interesting to observe that the ratio of minimum standards, for methods of service of documents, has been subject to a slight shift in the reasoning of both the Commission and Council. Originally the emphasis was placed on mutual trust between Member States, now it seems to be placed on legal certainty and the rights of the debtor. Those two are inter-related of course, but the arguments differ. In addition, the requirements contained in the minimum standards have grown more relaxed. In my opinion, Swedish law on service of documents now meets the requirements prescribed by the Council. Furthermore, this relaxation has been mitigated with reference to national rules providing for full review where the minimum standards fall short of adequate protection of the debtor. This illustrates a shift towards effective enforcement and a move away from the rights of the defendant.

V. MUTUAL DISTRUST

Mutual trust cannot be created on demand. Mutual trust and legal certainty are, as I have said above, inter-related. The courts and other officials of the state of enforcement are likely to trust foreign judgments if they know or have reason to believe that the rules governing the procedure leading to that judgment affords, inter alia, adequate protection of the uncontesting debtor.

And the yard-stick for the domestic officials of the state administering enforcement, as concerns adequate protection, will of course be the domestic conception of what adequate protection means.

This issue of distrust can be divided into three sections. First, there is the problem of information. Mutual recognition needs a minimum standard to be set in order to inform judges, officials and the public of the basic core of foreign rules and foreign procedures. The credibility of foreign procedural rules rests in the fact that they contain familiar minimum standards which will have been applied at domestic level in the foreign state. If the minimum standards are relaxed then part of their value is lost as they will yield less information about the foreign procedural system. In this context, it is interesting that reference to foreign procedural rules, as on full review, as in the adopted regulation, does not cure the information problem completely because the state of enforcement will not know whether or not the foreign procedure affords adequate protection. For example, to my knowledge nothing is said about time limits in the adopted regulation.

An additional element to the problem of distrust is the deviations between procedural systems in the levels of protection of the debtor yet this is a difference that would be overcome by a minimum standards requirement or some alternative form of harmonizing rules. It is very interesting to see in this context what alterations may be necessary at a domestic level. Member States may have to alter their rules if they fail to comply with the minimum standards yet commentators should be alert to the fact that this process may engender a situation where Member States apply a more 'relaxed' approach to the minimum standards shared throughout the Community in an effort to safeguard existing values. This of course could raise feelings of mistrust between Member States when pursuing a common system of procedural regulation.

A third section of the problem of distrust is, of course, suspicion. Even if you have a minimum standard in some respects, there may be suspicions in the particular State of enforcement that the actual practice in the State of origin deviates from those minimum standards. I would say that a requirement for minimum standards or full harmonization may create mutual trust in the communication of information and actual deviations at legislative level. But a suspicion that a practice other than that contained within the minimum standards is being used cannot be overcome by minimum standards.

In order to have an optimal effect on the problem of information and actual deviations and to promote the rights of defence, minimum standards should not allow for too many variations and should not rely too heavily on domestic law. By enabling foreign judgments for uncontested claims to be easily enforced in other Member States there is a risk that officials involved in enforcement will contest or try to obstruct its operation. This is of particular importance following the enlargement of the European Community in May this year which increases the likelihood of judgments on uncontested claims decided within a value system and procedural framework quite unfamiliar to the State of enforcement.

It has long been my belief that approximation of procedural rules should be undertaken carefully and preferably indirectly by harmonizing only substantive rules and letting the procedural rules emerge much later. As to this particular area, I have an opinion to the contrary. In order to overcome mutual distrust it will be necessary to set some clear minimum standards or preferably harmonized procedural rules on service of documents, default judgments and summary proceedings. That is in fact the next step. I doubt that the new regulation which has been adopted, although a significant step forward, will have the desired effect and create mutual trust. But that may be the opinion of a pessimistic Swede and a natural or born sceptic.

CHAPTER 14

CAN THERE BE A EUROPEAN BAILIFF?

Ton Jongbloed

I. INTRODUCTION

In all the countries I examined for a Dutch research project,[1] there is legislation outlining the tasks and powers of court bailiffs. In some countries, that legislation can be traced to decrees issued by the French King Philips Le Bel from November 1302 and June 1309, but in countries where this is not the case, a large degree of agreement seems to exist.

It is important that this legislation has been recently modified in some countries or that another form of the profession of Court bailiff has been chosen: in 2001, in the Netherlands; in 2002, in Latvia; and in 2003, in Hungary and Portugal.

Further, it must be noted that borders, which disappeared a long time ago enabling free movement of persons, goods, services and capital, are no longer an obstacle because calculating debtors, for example, establish themselves right across the border. It also has to be considered that in this 'Europe without borders' in which the centre of gravity in political decision-making moves from national parliaments to 'Brussels', it is less evident that court bailiffs work for their national governments.

Moreover, now that there is freedom of choice and nobody is obliged to use the services of a certain court bailiff, there is an incentive to offer higher quality. It will also lead to cooperation between court bailiffs in the Member States. Not only can it lead to cost savings, but tasks within those cooperation bonds can also be divided in an adequate manner, both at the country level and at the level of several countries.

---

[1] Belgium, Denmark, Finland, France, Germany, Greece, Hungary, Latvia, The Netherlands, Portugal, Scotland, and Sweden. The report will be published by Kluwer, Deventer, The Netherlands.

II. MAIN TASKS

An important question is which tasks must belong to the court bailiff.[2] A 'wide' and 'narrow' conception can be used.

In the narrow conception the court bailiff has been particularly charged with performing acts concerning seizures: it concerns seizures themselves (either execution by sale of debtor's chattels or seizure for security) and that which is directly linked with it such as judicial eviction, executory sale, doing the notifications preceding the seizure, supervision at voluntary public sales, etc.

The wider conception includes the tasks of the narrow model, but the Court bailiff is also considered as an usher to whom judicial communications are notified and then passed on to parties or interested parties. In the latter case it is also his responsibility to perform the trial introduction and other notifications, belonging to the first process or the instruction of lawsuits, as well as performing judicial summons, disclosures, protest etc. Given the national reports previously examined, it can be argued, the wide conception is more prevalent, thus the court bailiff is exclusively competent in the field of seizures.[3] In all the countries I examined, the court bailiff already has an important task in the seizure area, so it can be assumed that sufficient knowledge and experience exists in that area. But, moreover, the court bailiff can also have the task or receive the task to do judicial notifications. The latter task does not have to be attributed exclusively to the court bailiff but it can be considered that within the framework of judicial security it is suitable that certain notifications take place. We can think of a denunciation of the lease by the landlord. It would be unfortunate when, due to a mistake by the mail office,[4] somebody would not be informed of his rights and obligations, because in such a case we cannot speak of an 'honest process' as exhibited in article 6 ECHR. Further, in countries such as Finland and Greece, where the court bailiff does not notify summons, it appears that in many cases (approximately 60 per cent and 30 per cent respectively) the enforcement of a legal judgment is not effective because the debtor either no longer has property or the address of the person concerned cannot be retrieved. It seems that if the court bailiff brings out a notice of summons this leads to a higher execution turnover. It can be considered that a court bailiff will also take care of the possibilities of execution and recourse when bringing out the notice. Thus, procedures whereby recourse

[2] I realize that I am influenced for an important part by the existing practice in the Netherlands which I know very well.

[3] This including the actual execution by means of an auction (of movables) and if any imprisonment for debts.

[4] This often happens in practice, because postmen do not have the same training as court bailiffs and do not have the responsibility of a court bailiff.

is not expected to be possible will not be held and this discharges the court of such useless procedures.

III. SUBSIDIARY ACTIVITIES

A begging question is that of subsidiary activities. Whereas in some countries, eg Belgium, subsidiary activities are either prohibited or strongly restricted, this is not the case in most of the other countries 'as long as this does not damage the good and independent achievement of the court bailiff's office, or does not obstruct its esteem'. If a court bailiff does not receive a monthly honorarium by the government, but has to acquire his income, it goes without saying that subsidiary activities within limits can be accepted. The court bailiff can be assumed to be an expert in the legal area in general and is considered as a specialist in a number of areas. Is it possible that someone is forbidden to apply his knowledge and experience for the benefit of others as long as his main position is not compromised?

If we assume that a court bailiff does not obtain a monthly financial honouring by the government, but rather earns his own income, then it must be guaranteed that this court bailiff has sufficient venture skills to carry out his trade and will not suffer financially or commercially in a short period. For this reason a regulation must be achieved concerning a venture plan with regard to the (intended) establishment of a Court bailiff. It goes without saying that the appointing agency is informed by a commission of experts.

Furthermore, a regulation concerning the office of court bailiff and the tariffs belonging to it must be achieved. Given that the price level strongly diverges in several countries this is something for the long term. Eventually one could consider what a reasonable income is for a court bailiff considering his training and his experience, but also with regard to the fact that a court bailiff must be incorruptible and should withstand the seduction of fraudulent activities. There should be a standard income on the basis of which the tariffs can be determined. Such a standard income must be such that a court bailiff has the choice to not perform subsidiary activities.

In this view, it is also appropriate that the court bailiff has the possibility of free establishment: he establishes himself in a place of his own personal preference, but obviously takes into account the number of bailiffs who are already established in a certain area. To prevent financial obstructions arising from settling in scarcely populated areas, one can think of a regulation where financial support is offered when a bailiff wishes to settle in such an area. Of course the situation must be avoided where court bailiffs establish themselves only in urban surroundings.[5]

---

[5] Also a mixed system can be considered—such as in Hungary—with independent court

If one opts for the possibility of free establishment this means that no language demands (like in Belgium) have to be made. A court bailiff who wants to earn his living must be able to communicate with his 'customers'. If proper communication can not be established by one bailiff, another bailiff with a better command of the language will inevitably replace this poor communicator.

IV. (IN)EFFECTIVE ENFORCEMENT

From this research, it becomes clear that in some countries, in a lot of cases, legal judgments cannot be successfully implemented. In this context especially, Finland and Greece can be singled out where approximately 60 per cent and 30 per cent respectively of the legal judgments prove to be ineffective. Beside the fact that the court bailiff in these countries does not bring out the writ of summons and can not consider if recourse will be possible, it appears that this percentage is also influenced (negatively) because in countries such as Greece and Slovenia cases are assigned to a specific court bailiff who cannot transfer the matter concerned to another court bailiff. It seems clear that sickness and holidays can lead to the delay or even failure of the enforcement in a number of these cases. It is therefore recommended that a court bailiff be able to transfer the matter to a colleague. It could even be considered to establish court bailiffs' offices consisting of at least two court bailiffs and one candidate court bailiff to guarantee continuity for enforcement as well as with regard to sickness and malfunction.

V. COURT BAILIFFS AS EMPLOYERS?

A point of discussion will be whether court bailiffs can be employed by other court bailiffs. On the one hand the situation must be avoided where some court bailiffs obtain such an influence on the activities of the whole occupational group by employing others that they can be certain of their votes at general member meetings. On the other hand not every court bailiff is as enterprising and not every court bailiff wants to accept the financial dangers linked to conducting a business. Subsequently the question arises, what is wrong if a court bailiff who performs activities at a high level, is prepared to carry out these activities at a fixed amount per month thus excluding financial risks? In a similar vein, can non-court bailiffs financially take part in a bailiff's office? As long as the court bailiff or the court bailiffs

bailiffs and court bailiffs linked to district courts. The government could employ court bailiffs in thinly populated areas and guarantee them a minimum income.

jointly have a majority it seems that that possibility must exist. If it is a larger office with multiple staff and someone, not a court bailiff, acts as manager and knows exactly how to run the office, then it should not be excluded that this person is bound to the office by making him a co-proprietor.

VI. NATIONALITY REQUIREMENTS AND LIABILITY REGULATION

What is absolutely out of the question is a nationality requirement. Any citizen from the EU, who also has the knowledge and skills required outside the birth country or the country of which one holds the nationality,[6] should be eligible for appointment as court bailiff. Portugal and Hungary are appropriate examples of this.[7] In all cases rules must be established concerning the number of substitute court bailiffs (or candidate court bailiffs) per office,[8] the duration for which they have been added[9] to the office as well as concerning the training and continuing education of court bailiffs and their executive staff. A regulation could also be designed concerning the maximum size of offices, thus maintaining sufficient competition. Further rules have to be established concerning the right of nondisclosure, professional secrecy, the oath of secrecy in procedures, the administrative obligations, the ministry duty and the privacy of those with whom a court bailiff has official involvement.

Because the court bailiff receives his position from the government—which wants to ban injustice—there will be a special regulation on the liability and consequently the insurance of bailiffs. A continuation of this is disciplinary jurisdiction.

VII. AGE, GENDER, AND APPOINTMENT

What should not be a point of discussion is the minimum, and maximum, age. For the maximum age, taking into consideration an appointment for

---

[6] If in the future there is no longer a Belgian, Danish, German, Finnish, French, etc. nationality, but a European one, the problem has also been solved.

[7] Comp Art 254 s 4 Hungarian Enforcement law.

[8] If a maximum is set this means that when it is reached or exceeded there are enough indications that there are sufficient possibilities for the establishment of still another independent court bailiff in that area.

[9] There need not be 'lifelong' additions, nor the court bailiff nor the candidate can take advantage of that. court bailiffs will hesitate to employ someone, being afraid if the quantity of work reduces the person concerned will stay in office. Candidates are advised to contact several offices to have a wide experience. A 'lifelong' addition will mean they will not change office quickly.

life, one can look for a link with the general pensionable age. A minimum age is not necessary if a certain training is assumed. Before obtaining this knowledge and experience, a candidate will already be in their twenties. From the national reports, it appears that it is not considered as a problem. Likewise the flow to the profession of court bailiff should not be stopped unnecessarily by requiring that someone is under a certain age when the appointment takes place. Court bailiffs must have a lot of experience: they must be good lawyers, but also have social skills. Thus, it must be possible that if somebody with a lot of experience decides to become a court bailiff at an older age they are not prevented from doing so. Nor is it a point of discussion either that a court bailiff must have a certificate of good character delivered by the government.

It should be clear that women are under-represented among court bailiffs. Only Denmark, Greece and Sweden have a substantial number of female Ccurt bailiffs. It has also been commonly confessed that there are differences in approach by women than by men. Now that half of the population are women, one should strive to increase the number of female court bailiffs. Formerly, court bailiffs had to command respect by their force and appearance; this is no longer the case. Court bailiffs need to have a thorough judicial knowledge from which comes the respect they need to take measures and give advice. Furthermore, it is has been suggested that women are less aggressive and that would imply that disputes could possibly be settled amicably, at an earlier stage.

An appointment must take place by either the government or the minister of justice emphasizing the special position of the court bailiff as a civil servant. It is preferable that, preceding the appointment, a recommendation has to be obtained by the president of the Court because it is recognition that a court bailiff fulfils an important legal position. Previously, because of the strong link between court and the bailiff, a court bailiff would frequently serve at the meeting, however, this is no longer necessary. The court bailiff has been trained in such a way as to confer the burden of those duties onto someone else.

Further, it is also unnecessary for a candidate to have worked for a certain period at a court bailiff's office in the capacity of a trainee bailiff. However, there can be a difference of opinion concerning the requirement of a legal training for a trainee Court bailiff. In many countries, it is a condition that the trainee court bailiff be a qualified lawyer. Currently that is not an unjustified requirement: a court bailiff must first of all be a good lawyer, paying attention to the nature of his activities and those with whom he officially deals. Furthermore, a court bailiff must have certain skills if he wants to fulfil his occupation successfully. It is necessary to provide guidance to subordinates. This guidance must be with respect to the financial aspects of running an office as well as the aptitude to acquire skills essential to an independently-established court bailiff. This requires a certain minimum training. One can wonder if this has to be an academic training. Courses at universities pretend to be of a scientific nature, but it is not expected that a court bailiff, for a good execution of his occupation, will publish articles in journals or books. As yet (the first 10 years) a higher professional training in the social-judicial area would be more reasonable as a minimum condition: that opens the possibility to come to a uniform training requirement from the present range of training. At the moment it cannot be expected that, for example, in Germany a course at the university level will be thought necessary in a few years' time.

Moreover, if an occupational profile of the court bailiff exists, then it is possible to formulate so-called final exams for a course and a tailor-made training could be initiated. A similar practice exists in France; the tailor-made training only focuses on that which is necessary for the competent execution of one's professional duties. [10] That level should correspond with an LL.B. Those who wish to study another specialist field after some time can undertake different training and possibly find another occupation with the previously obtained diploma.

Subsequently (in approximately 10 years) the LL M additional training must be started (the nature of the activities also implies this). When this step is taken, one can say that the training of court bailiffs does not substantially differ from that for lawyers, notaries and other professionals, and the theory and practice will correspond with each other. At the moment, it can be put that although training is not yet compulsory at that level, the court bailiffs already work at a high standard.

It is remarkable that in only a few countries after the Declaration in Bologna in 1999, whereby the ministers of Education decided to introduce the Bachelor-Master-structure to achieve a higher exchange of students inside Europe for tertiary education, the education for Court bailiffs is organized differently. One wonders if a Swedish *kronofogde* must have completed university legal training in Sweden or in Denmark, Finland, Iceland or Norway and whether there should not be a more general exchange of professional competences, because having finished such study in a country other than Sweden is no real objection.

---

[10] To give an example: the knowledge in the field of enforcement and seizure law will have to be thorough. Knowledge of state and government law, as well as penal law, can be less thorough. In these cases a restriction to the main branches and subjects relevant to the Court bailiffs can be introduced.

VIII. ADDITIONAL POINTS OF INTEREST

Whether someone is suitable for appointment to Court bailiff could be assessed by means of the following points:[11]

A. Personality

- family circumstances and details;
- attitude and presence;
- behaviour and morality;
- physical and psychic resistance;
- sociability and social motivation;
- intelligence;
- critical sense;
- sense for analysis and synthesis;
- openness and maturity of mind;
- circumspection, moderation, composure;
- intelligence level and degree of training (studies completed, postgraduate training, training, possible editions, etc.
- intellectual and social points of interest (among others feeling with the general social and economic context in which the candidate will fulfil his office);
- ability to communicate, and
- oral and written expression.

B. Professional framework

- sense for completion;
- sense for responsibility;
- integrity, independence, impartiality;
- decision-making;
- sound judgment and tactfulness;
- capacity to get to the bottom of a problem;
- commitment;
- punctuality, ability to meet deadlines;
- sense for order and method;
- consideration and meticulousness;
- sense for initiative;
- working pace and perseverance;
- collegiality;

[11] One and other comes from a circular letter dated 15 May 1996 of the Belgian minister of Justice then in office.

- contact with superiors, staff, colleagues from the court, litigants;
- if the candidate is a replacing judge: thoroughly motivated advice concerning the quality and quantity of the performances, and
- if the candidate is a judicial trainee, the advice has to confirm at least the training reports, otherwise contradictions have to be motivated.

C. Discipline

- remarks made by the leading person(s) regarding the performances and
- disciplinary sanctions (also half official remarks) and judgments, to be circumscribed and assessed in view of the job aimed at.

IX. MEMBERSHIP OF PROFESSIONAL ORGANIZATION

Membership of a professional organization designed to regulate the office of court bailiff might be thought preferable. In that manner the interests of the occupational group can be optimally looked after. This would ensure that justice is performed in accordance with democratic principles: everyone has a voting right, can have his voice heard and thus exert influence. This prevents 'Scottish situations': in Scotland, some large offices have ended their membership of the Society, thus reducing its impact as a interlocutor. Tasks can be attributed to such a representative organization of court bailiffs regarding, among them being continuing education and disciplining. It is not suitable that such an organization has a direct impact on the way of examination.[12]

It is interesting to know that in Sweden, one of the tasks of the court bailiff is to provide information to prevent people from having financial problems. If someone has financial problems, the court bailiff is the first one to be informed. In a number of cases these problems can still be solved relatively easily. The court bailiff can, on the basis of his practical experience, give advice so that the expense pattern can be regulated.

---

[12] Indirectly, this will be the case because such an organization will advise concerning the knowledge necessary for a good fulfilment of the occupation. A direct impact would be that if there is a threat of less Court bailiffs, the level of the exam would be lowered, whereas there is a threat of a surplus, the opposite will be the case. Thus, it prevents high fees from dissuading candidates.

PART IV

HARMONIZING PROVISIONAL AND PROTECTIVE MEASURES IN THE EUROPEAN JUDICIAL AREA

CHAPTER 15

MINIMUM PROCEDURAL STANDARDS FOR ENFORCEMENT OF PROVISIONAL AND PROTECTIVE MEASURES AT EUROPEAN LEVEL[1]

Burkhard Hess

I. DIFFERENT TYPES OF PROVISIONAL RELIEF

The Member States of the European Union[2] provide for provisional and protective measures to secure creditors' claims in cases of urgency.[3] There is a consensus in legal theory and praxis that provisional measures are aimed at protecting the future enforcement of a judgment. These measures are seen as instruments to prevent the evasion of legal responsibilities of a debtor and to avoid a situation where the debtor would be unable to pay the judgment.[4] Provisional remedies, characterized by speed and efficiency, are normally ordered in instances of urgency, to maintain the status quo or to safeguard certain rights, so that the parties may proceed to argue their claims on the merits.[5] The fundamental structure of provisional remedies is similar in all jurisdictions. A creditor seeking provisional relief must

---

[1] The following presentation is an abbreviated extract from the Study JAI A3/02/2002 on making more efficient the enforcement of judicial decisions within the European Union: transparency of a debtor's assets, provisional enforcement and protective measures, attachment of bank accounts which elaborated the author for the European Commission in 2003.

[2] All references to the Member States of the European Union only include the Member States of 30 Apr 2004.

[3] There is a trend in some Member States to interpret the urgency factor loosely.

[4] On the political underpinnings see W Kennett *Enforcement* 151, distinguishing different approaches in the common law and continental law jurisdictions. These differences are, however, rather limited: German law, for example, adopts the same rationales as the English system.

[5] According to the European Court of Justice, the purpose of provisional measures is to safeguard rights which the court dealing with the merits of a case is, in any event, requested to recognize while preserving the status quo both in fact and in law, see ECJ, 26 Mar 1992, case C-261/90, *Reichert II*, ECJ Reports 1992 I 2149.

establish the existence of the claim (*fumus boni juris*) and prove that an infringement of that claim is imminent (*pericula in mora*).[6] If the court is satisfied that these conditions are met, it will (often at its discretion) grant an interim order to preserve the status quo of the parties (especially freezing (specific) assets of the defendant), provide for the interim satisfaction of the claim, or order any other anticipatory enforcement of the judgment.[7] Provisional measures are limited in a twofold way: they do not become *res judicata* and their legal effects are strictly limited up to the effects of the relief sought in the main proceedings.

During the last 25 years, national courts[8] (and to some degree national legislators)[9] have developed various types of provisional measures, and thereby improved the position of creditors. At the same time, the impact of cross-border provisional relief (which also includes cooperation between the courts of different Member States) has been enhanced considerably.[10] Within the European Union, cooperation between different courts, within the context of cross-border actions is supported by articles 31 and 32 of the Brussels Regulation. Provisional and protective remedies have been the subject of considerable review and examination in legal literature.[11] Comparative research shows different types of provisional remedies can be classified according to their legal effects. The following types of provisional remedies can be distinguished:

- those aimed at reserving a future enforcement (preliminary attachments or freezing orders);
- provisional measures designed to regulate the status quo of the parties; and
- measures that protect future specific performance (especially interim payments).[12]

---

[6] On these similarities cf Commission's Communication of 27 Nov 1998, COM(1997) 609 final, n° 23–4.

[7] See Art 10.1.2. of the Draft Recommendation on the Approximation of Judiciary Laws in Europe presented by M Storme and G Tarzia (1984).

[8] The most prominent evolution took place in England, see below at n where provisional relief is available when the High Court in London, under Lord Denning MR, granted a Mareva Injunction for the first time, a decision in the case of *Nippon Yusen Kaisha v Kara Georgis* [1975] 1 WLR 1093. A similar decision was afterwards made in another case, the case of *Mareva Companiera SA v International Bulk Carriers Ltd* [1975] 2 Lloyd's Rep. 509, on the evolution of the English law see Cuniberti, *Les mesures provisioires* (2000) nn 67.

[9] Especially the French legislation of 1991 introduced the 'juge de référé' with a large empowerment for provisional and protective measures, see above.

[10] This improvement of cross-border provisional relief is largely influenced by the European instruments which provide for the recognition of provisional remedies, Cf P Schlosser, *RdC* 284 (2000) 190.

[11] Recent literature G Cuniberti *Les mesures conservatoires* (Paris 2000); T Ingenhoven *Grenzüberschreitender Rechtsschutz durch englische Gerichte* (2001).

[12] F Baur *Studien zum einstweiligen Rechtsschutz* (1967) 23–34; R Stürner *Generalbericht*

A. Preliminary attachments and freezing orders

All Member States provide for provisional remedies aimed at securing the future enforcement of monetary claims.[13] Two types of provisional measures exist. In Austria, Belgium, Denmark, Finland, France, Germany, Greece, Italy, Luxembourg, Portugal, Spain, Scotland, and Sweden, creditors can apply for an order attaching the defendant's assets. Nevertheless, differences concerning the operation of the seizure do exist, such that it operates in a general way in certain of these Member States,[14] while in others it will affect specific assets.[15] Either the court orders a specific seizure (for example of a bank account) or grants general permission to the creditor to seize whatever assets of the defendant may be detected. As a rule, the seizure operates *in rem*. Accordingly, the account or targeted asset is directly frozen and any operation of the account/asset is deemed to be invalid against the creditor.[16]

However, in England and Ireland, provisional and protective measures do not operate *in rem* but *in personam*.[17] In these jurisdictions, the defendant may be ordered to do or to refrain from doing something, for example from dealing with or disposing of money deposited in a bank. Yet, the operation of the account remains legally possible.[18] If the defendant (or any third party) does not comply with the court order, they will be indirectly sanctioned by the court which may impose penalties for contempt. Some continental jurisdictions also combine *in rem* and *in personam* remedies. In France, provisional measures under articles 808 and 812 NCPC operate *in rem*, but are often combined with an *astreinte* (penalty).[19] Scottish law provides for provisional remedies which operate *in rem* (arrestment) and

---

in M Storme (ed) *Procedural Laws in Europe* (2003) 161 ff. This classification was also used by M Storme and G Tarzia *Rapprochement* 105 ff; Art 10.1.2., 203, it is also found in the Commission Communication of 27 Nov 1997, COM(1997) 609 final, n° 23.

[13] See the answers to the questions 1.2.1–1.2.3 of the questionnaire on provisional measures. The classification is not used in Italy, where provisional and anticipatory measures are distinguished, Italian Report on Provisional Measures, 1.1.

[14] In France, by operation of law (Art 47 of the law of July 1991), the seizure has a blocking effect with respect to all accounts kept by the bank (in any of its branches) for the debtor.

[15] Cf the answers in the National Reports to question 2.5.3. Some Member States (eg Belgium, Luxemburg) empower the creditor to seize the accounts of the debtor with the help of the plaintiff, while other entrust the enforcement courts. Note also Scotland, where the competence of the court clark has been challenged due to Art 6 ECHR. Since 2002, only a judge can grant the arrestment: Scottish Report on Provisional Measures, 2.5.2.

[16] eg ss 135, 136 German Civil Code, German Report on Provisional Measures, 2.5.3. The same situation exists in Scotland, Scottish Report on Provisional Measures, 2.5.3. and 2.5.3.2.

[17] English Report on Provisional and Protective Measures, 2.5, A Briggs [2003] *LMCLQ* 418, 425.

[18] The addressee of the injunction may therefore continue to contract with third parties and the validity of these transactions depends on the bad faith of the third party.

[19] French Report on Provisional Measures, 5.3.3.3.

for others operating *in personam* (interim inderdict). Both are used for the blocking off assets; *in personam* relief entails extraterritorial effects.[20]

B. Provisional protection of non-pecuniary claims

All Member States provide provisional remedies designed to regulate the status quo of the parties or to safeguard future performance.[21] In practice, injunctions enjoining a person from doing a certain act are of utmost importance. As a rule, they include an *astreinte* (penalty) which is recognized in the other Member States under article 49 of the Reg. 44/01.[22] These injunctions are closely related to the substantive rights that they protect. Accordingly, considerable differences exist between the Member States. In many jurisdictions, the courts have significant discretion concerning the means used to protect affected parties. In some Member States, the ordinary courts are also entrusted with the enforcement of their orders, while in other Member States provisional protection may also be obtained from enforcement organs.[23] Due to the significant differences between the national systems, it does not seem advisable to propose any Community action for harmonization of these injunctions.[24]

C. Interim payments

The third type of provisional measures are interim payments. Interim payments are similar to provisional remedies in non-pecuniary matters. They are designed to regulate the status quo of the parties or to order interim performance. In many Member States, courts are empowered, on the presentation of sufficient evidence refuting the creditor's alleged claim, to order interim payments from the debtor. This kind of provisional protection is of particular importance in France and the Benelux Countries, where *juges de référé* are specifically empowered to order these kinds of

[20] G Maher and B Rodger 'Provisional and Protective Remedies, The British Experience of the Brussels' Convention' (1999) 48 ICLQ 302, 330; Scottish Report on Provisional Measures, 2.5.3.2.

[21] Cf the answers to questions 1.2.2. and 3 of the Questionnaire on Provisional and Protective Measures.

[22] As an alternative to Art 49, the courts of another Member State may order a penalty (in favour of a foreign judgment which is recognized under Art 32 of the Reg 44/01) if the debtor does not comply with the foreign judgment, German Supreme Civil Court, Wertpapiermitteilungen 2000, 635, 637.

[23] The differences between the Italian and the German systems are explained in BGH, Wertpapiermitteilungen 2000, 635 (*Italian Leather/WECO*). ECJ Case C-80/00, *Italian Leather/WECO*, did not address the issue. On this case law cf the comments of B Hess IPRax 2005.

[24] R Stürner 'Einstweiliger Rechtsschutz: Generalbericht' in M Storme (ed) *Procedural Laws in Europe* (Maklu Antwerp 2003) 143, 175.

payments.[25] As a result, these Member States adopted a two-tier system of provisional measures: on the one hand provisional attachments (*saisie conservatoire*), on the other hand provisional injunctions (référé).[26] Interim payments are available in Austria,[27] Belgium,[28] France,[29] Greece,[30] Luxembourg,[31] the Netherlands,[32] Sweden,[33] and England.[34] In Germany, the introduction of a similar remedy is currently discussed.[35] However, considerable variations exist between the national systems, especially with regard to the conditions and scope of application. While in some Member States interim payments are regarded as a general remedy that requires only proof of the (mere) existence of the secured claim,[36] other Member States require proof of a particular need by the creditor (urgency).[37] In France, interim payments are based on both the existence of the claim or of the creditor's specific need for protection.[38] However, creditors in Denmark, Finland, Germany,[39] Ireland[40], Italy[41], Scotland,[42] and Spain[43] generally do

---

[25] See generally van Compernolle 'Introduction générale', in J van Compernolle and G Tarzia *Les mesures provisoires en droit belge, français et italien—Étude de droit comparé* (1998), 5.

[26] It should be noted that référé proceedings mainly relate to non-pecunary claims, enjoining persons from doing an act.

[27] Sections 381, no 2, 382 *Exekutionsordnung* Austrian Report on Provisional Measures, 1.2.3.

[28] *Référé–provision.* However, none of the provision of the Belgium Code Judiciaire empowers explicitly the president of the instance court to order interim payments. The present situation is largely influenced by French developments see J van Compernolle in J van Compernolle and G Tarzia (eds) *Les mesures provisoires* 14–15.

[29] Art 809 (2) NCPC, French Report on Provisional Measures, 1.2.3.

[30] Art 728 CCP, Greek Report on Provisional Measures, 4.1–4.2. This provisional remedy is, however, limited to certain categories of pecuniary claims, especially maintenance claims, tortious liability (especially interim payments for medical expenses,) and workers compensation.

[31] Ordonnance de référé–provision, Art 933 (2) cpc of Greek Report on Provisional Measures 1.2.3.

[32] Dutch Report on Provisional Measures, 1.2.3. and 4, the proceedings vary in the 19 district courts, much depends on local custom.

[33] Chapter 15, s 4 CJPr (providing for summary proceedings), Swedish Report on Provisional and Protective Measures, Preliminary Remarks, D.

[34] Order for payment, CPR 25 r. 1(k), English Report on Provisional Measures, 4.1–4.9.

[35] Bundestagsdrucksache 14/8784: Vorläufige Zahlungsanordnung.

[36] Belgium, France, Luxembourg, and The Netherlands. Cf also ECJ, Case-80/00 *Italian Leather/WECO* para 39.

[37] Especially Austria, Greece.

[38] Cf Arts 809 (1) and 809 (2) NCPC, French Report on Provisional Measures, 1.1.

[39] With the exception of maintenance claims, see ss 935, 940 ZPO.

[40] n Ireland, no provisional measures for the enforcement of claims for payment exist in Irish law. In actions where the claimant seeks only to recover a debt or liquidated demand in money payable by the defendant, the summary summons procedure is used, Irish Report, Part D, 2.1.

[41] Comparable protection can be obtained by the summary proceedings for uncontested debts, Italian Report on Provisional Measures, 1.2.3.

[42] Scottish Report on Provisional Measures, 1.2.3.

[43] Spanish Report on Provisional and Protective Measures, 1.2.3.

not grant this type of interim relief. Nonetheless, alternate accelerated proceedings may be applied to offer similar protection.[44] In addition, the well-performing judicial systems in some of these jurisdictions (where a judgment of a first instance court is obtained in an average of six months)[45] do not require any additional provisional protection.

In many Member States, provisional remedies are considered an efficient alternative to costly and time-consuming main proceedings. Therefore, interim payments are largely replacing main proceedings. This is acceptable if the debtor is given a fair chance to contest the claim by way of an oral hearing.[46]

II. THE PROCEDURE FOR OBTAINING PROVISIONAL OR PROTECTIVE MEASURES

A. Pre-conditions for obtaining provisional measures

In all Member States, the creditor must, when applying for provisional and protective measures, assert the existence of a claim on the merits and a danger that the enforcement of the claim may be frustrated. Nonetheless, all national systems lower the standard of proof somewhat in relation to the claim on the merits.[47] In Belgium, the applicant must only provide sufficient evidence to establish that the claim exists, in Denmark, Portugal and Spain a *prima facie* standard applies, while in England the claimant must present a 'good arguable case'.[48] In Austria and Germany, the courts may order an '*arrest*' even if the applicant fails to establish the existence of a claim, although in this case the creditor must provide a security as a condition of the provisional measure.

The second condition is urgency, which is interpreted in different ways. Most of the jurisdictions require that the applicant shows there is a risk (whether imminent or not) that an eventual judgment will remain unsatisfied.[49] In most of the Member States, especially in Austria, Denmark, Finland, Germany, Greece, Italy, the Netherlands and Portugal the creditor

[44] In Germany, a maintenance creditor may apply for a preliminary injunction if the payment of the debt is urgently needed. In Italy, Arts 186 *bis* cpc and 186 quater provide for summary proceedings which replace largely proceedings on the merits, R Stürner in M Storme (ed) *Procedural Law* 173, Italian Report on Provisional Measures, 1.1. (in fine).
[45] This is the case in Germany and in Belgium, see R Stürner in M Storme (ed), *Procedural Laws* 142, 174.
[46] In France, about 11 per cent of all cases dealt by the tribunaux de grande instance are decided as référé; about 35 per cent of these judgments are not followed by ordinary proceedings, French Report on Provisional and Protective Measures, 5.1. In the Netherlands, in 95 per cent of all *kort geding* proceedings, no procedure on the merits will follow, Dutch Report on Provisional and Protective Measures, 3.8.
[47] See the answers in the national reports on question 2.4.4.
[48] The practical differences of these divergent formulations do not seem to be great.
[49] See the answers in the national reports on question 2.3.2.

is not allowed to rely on showing the need for protection based on the existence of competing creditors and the risk of the debtor becoming insolvent. In France and Belgium and Luxembourg, urgency is not always a pre-requisite for provisional relief. In these jurisdictions, provisional measures are granted in a 'two-tier' system. Creditors can seek an arrest of the defendants' assets (*saisie conservatoire*) or directly address the president of the competent (or local) court for protective relief in *référé*—proceedings.[50] In these processes, urgency is not a pre-requisite for provisional relief, as long as the claim on the merits appears to be well-founded.[51] In addition, in many Member States urgency is loosely interpreted, because, the claim on the merits does not have to be due, so even future and conditional claims may be secured.[52]

B. The examination of the court

Provisional measures are granted in an accelerated, often informal procedure. There are differences in the Member States relating to the requirement for an adversarial hearing. Although in Austria, France (Article 67 Act of 1991), Luxemburg and the Netherlands provisional measures are regularly granted *ex parte*, other Member States require the debtor to be heard (especially Spain). Nevertheless, in these Member States provisional measures are also granted *ex parte* if the creditor asserts particular urgency or the danger of frustration.[53] If provisional measures are granted *ex parte*, the debtor must be immediately informed about enforcement measures and has a right to oppose to the measures in a contested hearing.[54]

C. The need for a security

In most of the Member States there is an obligation on the applicant to compensate the defendant for any loss or damage if the provisional measure should be set aside in the main proceedings.[55] On the Continent, the courts often require a security from the creditor which is usually provided in the

[50] Art 808 (2) NCPC; the French model has been adopted by the other jurisdictions under consideration, French report, Dutch report, Belgium report, Luxemburg report.
[51] However, it should be noted that in these Member States *référé*—proceedings (for interim payments of a debt) to some extent replace summary procedures, W Kennett *Enforcement* 171.
[52] Austria, s 378 (2) EO; Germany, s 916 (2) ZPO; Belgium, Art 1415 (2) Code Judiciaire ; Luxembourg and England, *Zucker v Tyndall Holdings plc* [1992] 1 WLR 1127; Scotland: *Gillanders v Gillanders* (1966) SC 54.
[53] See the answers in the national reports to question 2.4.3.1.
[54] In Spain the debtor is customarily heard, in accordance with Art 733 LEC. If provisional measures are granted *ex parte*, the debtor must oppose the order within 20 days. Scotland: *Gillanders v Gillanders* (1966) SC 54.
[55] Cf the answers of the national reports on provisional measures to questions 2.6 and 3.6.

form of a bank guarantee. In some jurisdictions, the court has discretion when ordering the security;[56] much depends on the creditor's prospects of success in the main proceedings or on the latter's financial ability to provide a security.[57]

In England and Ireland, the applicant is required to give an undertaking as to damages.[58] This undertaking is made to the court, not to the other party.[59] Under such an undertaking the applicant will compensate the affected party for any losses they would suffer by reason of the injunction being granted if the applicant's case ultimately fails at trial. The undertaking is called on at the end of the trial if the substantive action fails; the defendant does not have to commence fresh proceedings for damages to cover his or her loss. In addition, the applicant is also required to indemnify the reasonable costs of any non-party complying with the order and to compensate any loss caused by the order.[60] If a court is satisfied that an undertaking would be without value, it can either require that some form of security be given to support the undertaking (usually in the form of a bond) or it can refuse the application for an injunction.

III. 'ENFORCING' PROVISIONAL MEASURES

As a matter of principle, provisional measures are immediately enforceable.[61] However, there exist considerable differences in the details of the order (especially as to whether specific assets must be identified or whether the order may be drafted in a general form).[62] These differences relate to the way in which provisional measures are enforced. Most of the legal systems refer to the general rules on the enforcement of judgments for the enforcement of provisional measures. However, when provisional measures are enforced, these rules are only applied insofar as they provide for the freezing of the debtor's assets. Satisfaction of the claim is effected unless the creditor obtains a judgment on the merits.

---

[56] This is the case in Germany, where according to s 921 ZPO, the court may order an arrest even if the existence of the claim has not been sufficiently established.

[57] See the answers of the national reports on provisional measures to question 2.6.3.

[58] Cf the English and Irish Reports on Provisional Measures, 3.6. In Scotland, the creditor must not give a security, Scottish Report on Provisional Measures, 2.6.1.

[59] In the case of a freezing order which is granted *ex parte*, the applicant must notify the defendant forthwith of the order and serve on the defendant a copy of the affidavit used in support of the application, together with the claim form and the order, English Report on Provisional Measures, 3.6.2.

[60] N Andrews in M Storme (ed) *Procedural Laws in Europe* (Maklu Antwerp 2003) 267, 292. A similar obligation does not exist on the Continent.

[61] French Report on Provisional and Protective Measures, 2.7.2.

[62] Cf P Schlosser *RdC* 284 (2000), 167–8.

There are considerable differences to the position of a debtor in this situation. While in Germany and Portugal, the creditor is entitled to a lien, according to him or her priority even over competing creditors,[63] the position in English law is quite different: the debtor is entitled only to a security, a freezing injunction does not create any rights *in rem* and leaves issues of priority among creditors unaffected.[64] In order to provide for efficient protection of the secured claim, some Member States have modified the competencies of enforcement organs. Under German law, the garnishment of a bank account is not ordered by the judicial officer (*Rechtspfleger*) of the enforcement court, but by the court ordering the provisional measure (*Arrestgericht*).[65] Similar modifications are found in other Member States.[66]

By contrast, in England there exists a clear separation between the asset-freezing measures (which are derived from recent case law) and the enforcement mechanisms relating to judgments. While provisional measures are mainly enforced by injunctions against the debtor and the third debtor from disposing of their assets (injunction *in personam*), and sanctioned by contempt orders, the garnishment of bank accounts in enforcement proceedings operates *in rem*.[67]

The national systems also diverge in regard to the enforcement structures. Some legal systems require, as a pre-requisite to the making of asset-freezing orders, that the applicants specify the assets targeted for seizure,[68] while others do not consider this necessary and grant wide-ranging orders for seizure. This is the case in France, where the creditor may obtain and enforce an order freezing the balance of all the accounts the debtor may have in the bank, even if the bank operates on a nation-wide business.[69] The same situation is encountered in the Netherlands, where no identification of the targeted account is required.[70] In most Member States, the ambit of a provisional measure is not limited to specific assets and, therefore, all assets of the debtor can be targeted. His legal position is protected by the immunities (relating to salaries etc.) which are provided by the general laws

---

[63] Sections 930, 804 ZPO, German Report on Provisional and Protective Measures, 2.5.3.1.; Art 622 no 2 Codigo Civil, Portuguese Report on Provisional and Protective Measures, 2.5.3.4.

[64] English Report on Provisional and Protective Measures, 2.5.3.4.

[65] German Report on Provisional and Protective Measures, 2.4.1.2.

[66] eg the large discretionary power of a Greek court. See the Greek Report on Provisional and Protective Measures, 2.5.2.

[67] W Kennett *Enforcement* 164; S Goldstein *Commercial Litigation—Pre-emptive Remedies* A2-013; A Briggs [2003] Lloyds' MCLQ 418, 425.

[68] Especially Austria and Germany, National Reports on Provisional Measures, 2.5.3.1.

[69] P Schlosser *RdC* 284 (2000) 168.

[70] National Report Netherlands on Garnishment, 2.2.2.: as a rule, the three largest banks are regularly the subject of applications by creditors seeking to enforce provisonal measures. A similar situation exists in Scotland, Scottish Report on Garnishment, 2.2.1.1.

on enforcement. The same considerations apply to the position of third debtors and other third parties: they are protected by the procedural safeguards, which are found in the general laws of enforcement.

If provisional relief is granted before the main proceedings are commenced, the applicant is obliged to initiate these proceedings within a definite period. There are some variations in the national systems, as some Member States provide for a specific period of time set in legislation,[71] whereas in other Member States, the court fixes the period according to the circumstances.[72] In some Member States, the debtor may apply for the revocation of the provisional measure if the creditor fails to comply with the formal conditions regulating the granting of that measure.[73] As a rule, the provisional measure will be set aside if the debtor should succeed in the main proceedings or is able to prove a change of the circumstances. If the provisional measure is set aside, the creditor must compensate the debtor's loss. As a result, it can be said that there are considerable differences in the details of the relationship between provisional measures and substantive proceedings in the Member States. Nevertheless, a common denominator can be found in the fact that the court hearing the substantive matter always has competence in relation to the supervision of the provisional measures which had been granted in ancillary proceedings.[74]

V. THE CROSS-BORDER CONTEXT

A. *Jurisdictional issues*

All Member States grant competence to order provisional measures to the courts deciding the main proceedings.[75] In the European context, the competence of the court deciding the main proceedings is determined by Articles 2–24 of Reg. 44/01. This competence may also be exercised before the main proceedings are initiated. According to the procedural laws of most of the Member States, the applicant must then initiate the main

[71] eg Denmark: 40 days, Greece and Italy: 30 days. [72] eg Austria, Finland.
[73] eg Germany.
[74] Recently, the Swiss Federal Tribunal, referring to this principle, held that the *exequatur* decision for a foreign provisional measure becomes void if that measure should be set aside by the competent court for the main proceedings, BGE 129 III 626 (*Motorola*), judgment of 30 July 2003.
[75] Cf the answers to question 6.1. in the national reports on provisional and protective measures. In France and the Low Countries, the competence for ordering *référé*-measures lies with the president of the court which decides the main proceeding.

proceedings within a period of time fixed by the court (often two weeks or one month). If the proceedings are not initiated within this time, the provisional measure will automatically become ineffective or will—following an application of the defendant—be set aside by the court.[76]

In addition to the competence of the court deciding on the merits of the case, all Member States—with the exception of Spain[77]—confer additional jurisdiction on the court where enforcement takes place[78] (ie the place where the defendant's assets are located or the court at the defendant's domicile).[79] This competence is derived from practical necessity. Often the evidence, assets or the occurrences forming the basis of the case are located where the enforcement of the provisional measure is sought.[80] The allocation of competences between the court hearing the main proceedings and the court at the place of enforcement has a long tradition in the Member States. However, it presumes preliminary and main proceedings can be coordinated and, therefore, that there will be close cooperation between the courts involved.[81]

The domestic heads of competence are also applied if provisional measures are sought in the European cross-border context. Accordingly, a creditor may apply for the seizure (or freezing) of local assets even when the main proceedings are pending abroad. The European instruments on civil procedure do not directly address these jurisdictional issues. As the national reports show, all Member States provide for support of main proceedings in other Member States and considerable case law has been reported.[82] As a result, it can be stated that collaboration between the courts of different Member States in provisional and main proceedings has become a reality in the European Judicial Area.

---

[76] This is the legal position in Germany, s 926 ZPO.

[77] In Spain, the courts of justice are responsible for the enforcement of their judgments. However, the Spanish legal system also provides for some support of the competent court by local enforcement agents where the enforcement takes place, Spanish Report on Provisional Measures, 6.1. and 6.2.

[78] In England, Ireland, and Scotland the competence of the domestic courts to support main proceedings abroad was explicitly stated when the Brussels Convention was ratified. The Civil Jurisdiction and Judgments Act 1982 (CJJA '82), s 25(1), conferred on the High Court in England power to grant interim relief in the absence of substantive proceedings, provided proceedings have been or will be commenced in another State. With effect from 1 April 1997, the power to grant interim relief was extended to any proceedings in any State, regardless of whether it is a Brussels or Lugano contracting State or whether the proceedings fall within the scope of the Conventions (Civil Jurisdiction and Judgments Act 1982 (Interim Relief) Order 1997 (SI 1997/302)), Cf English Report on Provisional Measures, 6.1.1.3. The legal situation in Ireland is similar, see Sec. 13 (1) of the Jurisdiction of Courts and Enforcement Act of 1998, Irish Report on Provisional Measures, 6.1.

[79] This criteria corresponds to Art 39 (2) of Reg 44/01.

[80] W Kennett *Enforcement* 134.

[81] ibid 155; Schlosser, *RdC* 284 (2000), 174–82.

[82] Cf the answers to question 6.2.2. in the Dutch, English, French, German, Greek, Irish, Italian, Scottish, and Swedish Reports on Provisional Measures.

Nevertheless, in practice, the coordination of provisional and main proceedings at the European level has proved to be difficult. A key reason is that Article 31 of the Reg. 44/01 does not address the jurisdictional issues but simply refers to the domestic rules of the Member States. These rules often include exorbitant heads of jurisdiction.[83] Additionally, in some Member States creditors may even seek extraterritorial protective measures. This is especially the case in England and Ireland where the worldwide *Mareva* injunction (now: freezing order, C.P.R. 25) is aimed at freezing all assets of a debtor wherever they are located.[84] Accordingly, creditors who have conducted main proceedings in other European countries, have often applied to the English High Court for a freezing order/Mareva injunction with the aim of blocking the defendant's assets abroad.[85] In *Crédit Suisse Fides v Cuoghi*, the Court of Appeal explicitly rejected the argument that jurisdiction to grant asset-freezing measures (as ancillary measures) should be restricted to the courts where the assets are located.[86] This position is shared by Ireland, but it is not found in the other Member States.[87]

In the decisions *van Uden* and *Mietz,* the ECJ imposed far-reaching jurisdictional limits on provisional measures at the European level.[88] According to the Court: 'the granting of provisional or protective measures on the basis of article 24 of the Convention of 27 September is conditional on, inter alia, the existence of a real connecting link between the subject-matter of the measure sought and the territorial jurisdiction of the Contracting State the court before which those measures are sought'.[89] According to this decision any ancillary protective measure aimed at supporting main proceedings in another Member State presumes the existence of assets within the jurisdiction of the court which determines the matter.[90]

---

[83] Example: in France, the juge de référé may base his competence on the exorbitant competences of Arts 14 and 15 Code Civil; in the *van Uden* case, the competence of the president of the Dutch first instant court in kort geding proceedings was derived from (former) Art 126 (3) bv, Cf B Hess and G Vollkommer IPRax (1999) 220, 222.

[84] English Report on Provisional Measures, 6.2.5; C Heinze *Internationaler einstweiliger Rechtschutz,* Recht der internationalen Wirtschaft 2003, 923, 924. Scottish law does not permit a cross-border freezing of assets abroad, Scottish Report on Provisional Measures, 6.2.5., *Steward v The Royal Bank of Scotland* (1994) SLT (ShCt) 27.

[85] *Republic of Haiti v Duvalier* [1990] 1 QB 202 [1989] 1 All ER 456; *Credit Suisse Fides Trust SA v Cuoghi* [1998] QB 818; *Refco Inc v Eastern Trading Co* [1999] 1 Lloyds Rep 159.

[86] *Credit Suisse Fides Trust SA v Cuoghi* [1998] QB 818.

[87] P Schlosser RdC 284 (2000) 181; Cf the answers of the national reports to question 6.2.5. of the questionnaire on provisional and protective measures.

[88] ECJ Case C-391/95 *Van Uden* [1998] ECR I-7091; Case C-99/96 *Mietz* [1999] ECR I-3637.

[89] ECJ Case C-391/95 *Van Uden* [1998] ECR I-7091, 7122, para 48.

[90] According to the ECJ, Art 24 presumes that '. . . the measure sought relates to specific assets of the defendant located or to be located within the confines of the territorial jurisdiction of the court to which application is made', ECJ Case C-391/95, *van Uden* [1998] ECR I 7091, 71.

However, this limitation does not rule out the possibility that the ancillary measure might be enforced in another Member State, if there are additional assets which can be seized. Yet, the principal effects of ancillary protective measures which are given on the basis of domestic competences, remain strictly territorial.[91]

The ECJ largely relied on the traditional approach[92] according to which the parties are protected mainly by provisional measures which must be sought from the court determining the merits of the case. The effects of ancillary measures remain limited to the assets located in the district of the assisting court. As a consequence, within the scope of Article 24 of the Reg. 44/01, a worldwide freezing order can only be sought when the English court is competent for the decision on the merits or when (considerable) assets are located within England.[93] Under Article 31 of the Reg. 44/01, a far-reaching freezing order as given in the *Duvalier*[94] and the *Cuoghi*[95] cases seems to be excluded.[96] However, in the legal literature, the interpretation of the 'territorial connection criteria' remains largely disputed.[97] Recent case law shows that English Courts are still granting ancillary protection with extraterritorial effect even if the main proceedings are pending abroad.[98] Foreign litigants are using the 'magic curial arm' (Schlosser) of the English judiciary in order to overcome the short-comings of foreign civil procedures.[99]

---

[91] A Stadler *Erlaß und Freizügigkeit einstweiliger Maßnahmen im Anwendungsbereich des EuGVÜ*, JZ 1999, 1089, 1093; Schulz *Einstweilige Maßnahmen nach dem Brüsseler Gerichtsstands- und Vollstreckungsübereinkommen in der Rechtssprechung des Gerichtshofs der Europäischen Gemeinschaften*, ZEuP 2001, 805, 815 ss H Gaudemet-Tallon, *Compétence et Exécution*, no 311 s.

[92] As described above.

[93] However, the question remains open as to whether ancillary provisional measures can be sought from a court which is competent according to Arts 2–25 of the Reg. 44/01, Cf B Hess and G Vollkommer, IPRax 1999, 220, 222; T Rauscher and S Leible *Commentary* on Art 31 Brussels' Regulation (2003), no 20; Swiss Federal Tribunal, 30 July 2003, BGE 129 III 626 (*Motorola*); contrary opinion Wolf *Europäisches Wirtschafts- und Steuerrecht* 2000, 11, 16–17.

[94] *Republic of Haiti v Duvalier* [1990] 1 QB 202, [1989] 1 All ER 456; *Credit Suisse Fides Trust SA v Cuoghi* [1998] QB 818; *Refco Inc v Eastern Trading Co* [1999] 1 Lloyds Rep 159.

[95] *Credit Suisse Fides Trust SA v Cuoghi* [1998] QB 818.

[96] The same opinion is expressed by A Stadler *JZ* 1999, 1089, 1093. For a different opinion see P Schlosser *RdC* 284 (2000) 188, who stresses that the rulings of the ECJ in *van Uden* and *Mietz* should be limited to interim payments.

[97] Cf the answers of the national reports to question 6.3.5.

[98] *Motorola Credit Corp v Uzan* [2003] CP Rep 56, paras 61.

[99] P Schlosser `Coordinated Transnational Interaction in Civil Litigation and Arbitration' (1990) 12 Mid L Rev 150, 152; McLachlan `International Litigation and the Reworking of the Conflict of Laws' (2004) 120 LQ Rev 581, 590–3.

B. *The recognition of provisional measures*

Under the traditional doctrine, the recognition of a foreign judgment presumes its finality. Therefore, interim measures for protection could not be recognized and enforced abroad. Article 25 of the Brussels Convention (now article 32 of the Reg. 44/01) adopted an innovative approach and allowed the recognition of provisionally enforceable judgments and provisional measures.[100] However, the ECJ restricted the application of Article 25 of the Brussels Convention in the famous case *Denilauler v Couchez Frères*[101] and excluded the recognition of protective orders under the Convention which had been obtained ex parte. The main arguments for the exclusion of these orders (which were set out in the concluding passages of the judgment of AG *Mayras*) were the drastic effects of those measures, the protection of the defendant (who did not know that proceedings had been instituted against him abroad) and the effect on third parties resulting from the blocking of an account in respect of counter-action cannot immediately be taken.[102] Therefore, in order to protect those persons, the ECJ concluded that affected parties should be afforded an opportunity to object to such a measure in a forum which is geographically close, is based on a legal system which is familiar to the affected parties and which does not pose any linguistic barriers.[103]

Since *Denilauler*, ex parte decisions have not been recognized and enforced in the European Judicial Area.[104] This restrictive position undermines the efficient protection of creditors, because the cross-border 'surprise effect' of provisional measures is not available. As an alternative, creditors must apply directly at the place of enforcement for ancillary protective orders[105] or relinquish any surprise effect and apply for a contested hearing when seeking provisional relief. Now that 25 years have passed since *Denilauler*, the decision should be reappraised.[106] Today, allowing the cross-border recognition of *ex parte* orders securing the enforcement of pecuniary claims would be a clear step towards the principle of mutual trust in the judicial systems of other Member states. However,

---

[100] P Schlosser *RdC* 284 (2000) 190.
[101] ECJ, Case 125/79, *Denilauler/Couchet Frères* [1980] ECR 1553. This case is discussed by W Kennett *Enforcement* 146.
[102] ECJ, Case 125/79 *Denilauler/Couchet Frères* [1980] ECR 1553.
[103] The main arguments are summarized by W Kennett *Enforcement* 147.
[104] See the answers to question 6.4. in the national reports on provisional and protective measures.
[105] Recourse to several jurisdictions entails additional costs and (often) delay. In addition, the debtor might be alerted when the creditor seeks to obtain provisional measures in several jurisdictions and might be able to transfer his assets out of the reach of the creditor.
[106] For a concurring opinion see W Kennett *Enforcement* 148; Swedish Report on Garnishments, preliminary remarks in fine; Scottish Report on Provisional Measures, 7.2.1. and 7.2.2.1.

there are considerable differences in the national legal systems in regard to the conditions for obtaining, and the legal effects of, provisional measures. Therefore, in the absence of prior harmonization of minimum standards that provide efficient protection of the affected persons, the application of the principle of mutual recognition of provisional measures seems to be excluded. Nevertheless, as most of the Member states provide for measures designated to secure the (future) enforcement of a claim in the case of urgency, Community action in this field seems to be advisable. This action should reinforce and restructure the existing cooperation between national courts granting provisional relief in support of main proceedings in other Member States.

Finally, it should be noted that the different structure of provisional measures (operating in personam/in rem; affecting specific assets or all assets of the debtor) has not been an obstacle for their recognition and enforcement within the European Judicial Area. Accordingly, the English 'freezing order' (formerly Mareva injunction) has been recognized in France,[107] Germany[108] and in Switzerland[109] (although these Member States do not provide for comparable provisional relief). This example shows that, in practice, 'mutual trust' (or the willingness to accept a different but functional similar solutions of a foreign jurisdiction) has become a reality in case law of the different European courts.

VI. POLICY RECOMMENDATIONS

A. Clarifications of Article 31 of the Brussels Regulation

There is a general consensus amongst the Member States (also reflected in the answers of the national reporters to question 7.1) that Article 31 of the Regulation 44/01 should be clarified. The decision of the Working Party on the revision of the Brussels and Lugano Conventions, not to change these provisions, was unfortunate.[110] Despite the clarifications of the European Court of Justice in *van Uden* and *Mietz*, many uncertainties still exist in regard to the limitations of the judicial competences for (ancillary) provisional measures.

---

[107] CA Paris, 5 Oct 2000, Gaz Pal 2002 no 204 (M-L Niboyet); Cour de Cassation, judgment of June 30, 2004 (aff *Stolzenberg*).
[108] OLG Karlsruhe, ZZP Int 1996, 91, 93 ; OLG Frankfurt, OLG Report 1998, 213, 214 ; OLG Frankfurt, OLG Report 1999, 74, 75.
[109] BGE 129 III 626, *Motorola*, judgment of 30 July 2003.
[110] The same opinion is expressed by Stadler, JZ 1999, 1089, 1099; W Kennett *Enforcement* 140; H Gaudemet-Tallon *Compétence et reconnaisance* no 312.

First, it would be useful to address the question of whether interim payments are 'provisional measures' in the sense of Article 31 Reg. 44/01. Despite the case law of the ECJ,[111] there are compelling reasons to exclude interim payments from Article 31.[112] The main reason is that the function of these remedies is not only to protect the creditor efficiently for the future realization of the judgment (in the main proceedings), but to replace the lengthy and time consuming main proceedings themselves.[113] In many Member States, these remedies are not considered to be 'provisional measures', but a form of summary proceedings. Therefore, interim payments should be linked to other summary proceedings.[114] This proposal does not lead to an exclusion of those remedies from the Regulation 44/01. Hence, interim payments can be obtained from a court which is competent according to Article 2–24 of Regulation 44/01. They are therefore recognized under Articles 32 et seq. of the Regulation.[115] If the jurisdictional limits of the Regulation are respected, it would even be conceivable to remove the additional requirement (as stated in *Van Uden*) that the repayment of the sum must be guaranteed by a security.

Secondly, it seems advisable to clarify and improve. Article 31 of Reg. 44/01. A second paragraph should contain the following definition of provisional measures:[116]

---

[111] Case C-99/96 *Mietz* [1999] ECR I-3637.

[112] It should be added that the safeguards which the European Court of Justice established in the *Mietz* case, largely hinder the free movement of such measures within the European Union. For example: the European Court requires that the creditor must provide securitiy before obtaining an interim payment. However, according to Art 46 of the Regulation, the party against whom enforcement is sought may seek a stay of the proceedings or the provision of a security when the decision which is being enforced is appealed or opposed in its state of origin. Therefore, according to the structure of the Regulation, the provisional enforceable judgment may be recognized without any prior security of a creditor. Thus, the position of the ECJ relating to provisional measures is more restricted than the position of the Regulation itself, Cf A Stadler *JZ* (1999) 1089, 1099.

[113] In 1991 the Luxembourg Court of Appeal held that a *référé*-provision' (interim payment) could not be considered as a provisional measure in the sum of Art 24 Brussels' Convention, Judgment of 26 Nov 1991, no 12898, Luxembourg Report on Provisional Measures, response no 6.

[114] Cf the Green Paper on a European order for payment procedure and on measues to simplify and speed up small claims litigation, 18–19, COM/2002/0746/final.

[115] This proposal corresponds to the exclusion of interim payments in no 22 of the International Law Association's Principles on Protective Measures in International Litigation (Helsinki, Principles of 1996), which reads as follows: 'The procedure in domestic law under which a court may order an interim payment (ie an outright payment to the claimant which may be subsequently revised on final judgment) is not a provisional and protective measures in the context of international litigation', ILA Reports 1996, 185–96; W Kennett *Enforcement* 373–5.

[116] It is advisable to rely on Art 1 of the ILA Principles on provisional and protective measures, which reads as follows: Provisional and protective measures perform two principal purposes in civil and commercial litigation: (a) to maintain the status quo pending determina-

For the purposes of the first paragraph, provisional, including protective measures are measures to maintain the status quo pending determination of the issues at trial; or measures to secure assets out of which an ultimate judgment may be satisfied.[117]

In addition, the jurisdiction of a court to grant provisional and protective measures should be clarified: this jurisdiction should be in line with the case law of the ECJ and provide that the principal responsibility lies with the court that is competent according to the Regulation to determine the main proceedings in the case under Article 2-25 [and that, additionally, ancillary protective measures may be obtained from a court in whose jurisdiction assets of the debtor are located or the protective measure is enforced.[118] Therefore, the definition under Article 31 of the Brussels I Regulation should continue to apply to any provisional measure (with the exception of an interim payment) which is sought in order to block the defendant's assets or to preserve the status quo pending a final decision on the merits. Thus, it is recommended to clarify the actual legal provision of the Brussels I Regulation on provisional measures.

B. A European Protective Order for Cross-Border Garnishment

1. Outline

It seems advisable to set up a Community instrument on a European Protective Order for the Cross-border Garnishment of Bank Accounts. This instrument should supplement the legal protection of creditors provided for by the Brussels Regulation. This instrument should be part of a larger Community measure dealing with enforcement matters.

The European protective order should be based on the principle of mutual trust in the judicial systems of the Member States;[119] it should provide for comprehensive responsibility of the court exercising jurisdiction over the substance of the matter. This court should be empowered to grant provisional and protective measures which are automatically enforced in all

---

tion of the issues at trial; or (b) to secure assets out of which an ultimate judgment may be satisfied'. According to this definition, a paradigm case under category (b) are measures to freeze the assets of a defendant held in the form of sums on deposit in a bank account with a third-party bank (no 2 of the Helsinki Principles).

[117] It seems to be advisable to include in the Preamble of Reg 44/01 the indication that interim payments are subject to the legal regime of the Regulation (but not on Art 31) and that provisional measures securing proofs fall within the scope of Art 31, see above at n . This proposal also closely follows the wording of the ILA principles, below n 789.

[118] A similar opinion is expressed by N Andrews in M Storme (ed) *Procedural Laws in Europe* (2003) 263, 270.

[119] Cf no 36 of the final Conclusion of the Finish Presidency at the Tampere Council, 14–15 Dec 1999; ECJ, Case C-116/02, *Gasser/Misat*, para 72; Case C-159/02; *Turner/Grovit*, para 24.

other Member States (on the basis of a form).[120] Under exceptional circumstances (urgency) these measures may be ordered ex parte.[121] They would always be ordered on the condition that the applicant gives a security which covers any eventual loss or damage suffered by the defendant if the action should fail on the merits. The legal effects of the cross-border garnishment would be the blocking of (specific) bank accounts of the debtor in other Member States.[122] The European Protective Order should be served on the debtor and the debtor should be obliged to disclose the whereabouts of his assets on the basis of the European Assets Declaration.[123] The bank where the account of the debtor is held shall also be obliged to provide information on the status of the account on the basis of a claim form (European Third Debtors' Assets Declaration).[124] These cross-border proceedings would be supported by the competent organ/court of the Member State where the account is located. These courts or organs may order ancillary protective measures which are strictly confined to the assets located in that Member State. In addition, these organs may adjudicate upon any objection of the debtor or the third party debtor against the seizure which may be based on the enforcement laws of the Member State addressed. Hence, close cooperation between the courts involved would be needed. Any ancillary measure would have to be immediately communicated to the court hearing the main proceedings.[125] This cooperation may be supported by the European Judicial Network.

2. *Guiding principles*

Cooperation between the courts of the Member States should be based on the following principles:

The main responsibility for ordering provisional and protective measures should fall on the court which is to determine the merits of the case. This

---

[120] Same opinion Andrews in Storme (ed) *Procedural Laws in Europe* 267, 272.

[121] These circumstances must be established by the claimant; the claimant must ensure that the defendant is promptly informed of the order, cf ILA Helsinki principle no 7. This proposal corresponds (at least from its effects) to the proposal of R Perrot and G de Leval at the seminar held in Lisbon (1999) on the 'inversion of the proceedings' (*L'inversion du contentieux*), cf initial Caupain and G de Leval (eds) *L'efficacité de la justice civile en Europe*, 200–4 and 433–5.

[122] The legal effect of the order should be determined by the procedural laws of the Member State where the account is located, Cf above C, text at n. 733–6.

[123] See Study JAI A3/02/2002.

[124] The third debtor's declaration should be given on a standard form.

[125] Recently, the Swiss Supreme Federal Court held that the *exequatur*-decision under Arts 25 Lugano Convention would automatically become void if a provisional measure should be set aside by the court addressing the main proceedings, BGE 129 III 626 (judgment of 30 July 2003). According to this case law, there exists a clear 'priority' of the court addressing the main proceedings.

responsibility does not depend on the commencement of main proceedings.[126] However, any provisional measure which is granted prior to the commencement of main proceedings should be conditional upon those proceedings being instituted.

Therefore, the court deciding on the merits may order the freezing (blocking) of the debtor's assets in several Member States. This order should regularly be obtained after the debtor is heard; only in cases of urgency would it be possible to make an order ex parte.[127] The order would be automatically recognized and enforced in the other Member States, according to the principles of the European garnishment order.[128] Accordingly, the competent court may itself freeze bank accounts which are located in other Member States. The legal effects of that order, however, would be determined by the enforcement law of the Member State where the account is located.

The grant of such relief should be discretionary. It should be available on (a) a showing of a case on the merits to a standard of proof which is less than that required for the merits under the applicable law; and (b) showing that the potential injury to the plaintiff outweighs the potential injury to the defendant[129]

Provisional measures should be issued as an interim order on the basis of a claim form which informs the third party debtor about the effects of the seizure and which requires the third party debtor to provide any information on the account seized. This information shall be given on the form of the European Third Debtor Assets Declaration.[130] In addition, the court may order that the debtor gives a European Assets Declaration on the whereabouts of his or her assets.[131]

As a rule, the defendant should be heard before the order is issued. If the order is (for reasons of urgency) obtained *ex parte*, the defendant should be heard within a reasonable time and should be granted the opportunity to object to the order[132]

---

[126] However, if a party applies for protective orders to a specific court which is competent under Arts 2–24 of the Reg 44/01, the application to that court should be considered as a choice of the court for the main proceedings.

[127] A similar proposal is found in Art 10.3.1. of the M Storme and G Tarzia Draft, Storme (ed) *Approximation of Judiciary Law* 204.

[128] See below C.

[129] This precondition corresponds to no 4 of the ILA Helsinki Principles on Provisional and Protective Measures and to Art 10.2. of the M Storme and G Tarzia Draft, Storme (ed) *Approximation of Judiciary Law* 204.

[130] Cf above C.

[131] The court may directly request the competent organ at the domicile/seat of the debtor to take the assets declaration, Cf above B.

[132] Cf Art 10.3.1 (2nd phrase) of the M Storme and G Tarzia Draft, Storme (ed) *Approximation of Judiciary Law* 204.

The court should have authority to require a security from the claimant or to impose other conditions to ensure the compensation of any loss or damage suffered by the defendant or third parties which may result from the granting of the order.

If the provisional measure is obtained before the main proceedings are commenced, the court granting the measure should make orders to the effect that the main proceedings be commenced within a short period of time. Otherwise, the provisional measure will be set aside *ex officio*.

In addition, the location of a bank account in a Member State would be a sufficient basis for granting additional provisional measures in respect of these assets. As a rule, the assets should be blocked in order to secure any future enforcement of the secured claim. These measures should be issued on the basis of a standard form, informing the third party debtor of their legal effects (which are determined by the procedural law of the Member State where the account is located). The third party debtor would be obliged to give all necessary information on the status of the bank account to the applicant.

If ancillary measures are sought before the commencement of the main proceedings, the court should impose a condition that the main action must be filed within a reasonable period of time. Otherwise, the provisional measures would be set aside. Any ancillary measures shall be subject to a security given by the applicant.

The court with jurisdiction in the main proceedings and the competent court for the ancillary provisional measures should cooperate closely: the court of the ancillary proceedings shall (with the support of the European judicial network) inform (on its own motion) the court of the main proceedings about the protective measure.[133] The court of the main proceedings shall exercise a supervisory function and shall be empowered to suspend or to amend the ancillary order.[134]

The court (or enforcement organs) at the place of enforcement shall be competent to decide on any objection to the seizure which may be derived from the *lex loci executionis* (the enforcement laws of that Member State which includes any release of parts of the sum seized) which might be based on immunities of the debtor or on a priority of concurrent creditors or of the bank.

---

[133] This corresponds to the cooperation in insolvency proceedings, see Art 31 of Reg 1346/00/EC. Cf also P Schlosser, *RdC* 284 (2000) 396–7 on 'joint transborder case management'.

[134] See also Swiss Federal Court, 30/7/2003, BGE 129 III 626, at 5.2.3. According to Art 20 (2) of Regulation Brussels II a, ancillary provisional measures 'cease to apply when the court of the Member State having jurisdiction as to the substance of the matter has taken the measures it considers appropriate' Reg EC 2201/2003 of 27 Nov 2003, OJ L 338/1 of 23 Dec 2003.

The proposed instrument would allow the close cooperation between civil courts and enforcement organs in the European Judicial Area, which is based on mutual trust in the well functioning of national jurisdictions. Furthermore, it would considerably improve the provision of creditors who would not only get a provisional protection of their claims within the European Union, but would also be able to trace the debtor's assets with the help of enforcement organs and third party debtors. As a result, the three-different strands of the present study: transparency, garnishment and provisional and protective measures, are simultaneously applied for an improvement of the judicial protection of the citizens within the European Judicial Area. Accordingly, it seems advisable to complement the Reg. 44/01 by a Regulation on European Enforcement.

CHAPTER 16

ENGLISH PRIVATE INTERNATIONAL LAW ASPECTS OF PROVISIONAL AND PROTECTIVE MEASURES

Andrew Dickinson[1]

Despite the nomenclature ('provisional or protective', 'interim', 'interlocutory') orders made before the trial of an action can have a decisive impact on litigation. Thus it is well recognized that the Court's decision to grant an interim injunction to preserve or restore the parties' positions, based on a preliminary assessment of the merits of the claim, can compel the defendant to settle on a favourable basis. Similarly, a decision refusing an interim order can steal momentum from the claimant's case. Little wonder, therefore, that satellite disputes commonly arise about the scope of the court's jurisdiction to grant provisional measures and its exercise. This phenomenon has not been limited to the domestic context, as appears below.

Provisional or protective orders made by the English courts may have cross-border connections in various ways. Thus:

1. An order made in substantive proceedings before the English Court may purport to affect the conduct of the defendant or non-parties in other jurisdictions without any steps being taken to enforce the order in those jurisdictions.
2. An English court may make an order in substantive proceedings of which it is seised with a view to that order being enforced in another jurisdiction.
3. An English court may make an order in support of substantive proceedings in another jurisdiction.
4. An English court may be called upon to enforce an order of a provisional or protective nature made by a court in another jurisdiction.

This chapter outlines the law and practice of the English courts in these four scenarios. Before doing so, it may be helpful briefly to explain the types of interim orders commonly made by English courts.

---

[1] Solicitor Advocate (Higher Courts—Civil). Consultant, Clifford Chance LLP. Visiting Fellow in Private International Law, British Institute of International and Comparative Law.

The procedures for obtaining interim orders are contained in Part 25 of the Civil Procedure Rules 1998. Rule 25.1(1) lists 20 types of interim orders which an English court may grant in civil proceedings. Although Rule 25.1(1) is neither exhaustive[2] nor conclusive as to the existence of jurisdiction to make any particular order,[3] the list provides a useful starting point and is reproduced in Annex A at the end of this chapter.

Foremost among these interim orders, in terms both of its attractiveness to claimants and the debate surrounding it is the 'freezing injunction', a form of relief still commonly referred to as a *Mareva* injunction.[4] The following features of a freezing injunction are noted:

(a) As its name suggests it is an *in personam* order made against a party to the action, usually the defendant against whom a cause of action has been asserted.[5]
(b) The order typically restrains the party in question from (i) removing his assets (whether in his own name or not) from England and Wales up to the value of the claim, or (ii) otherwise disposing of or dealing with his assets up to the same value, subject to very limited exceptions.
(c) The second limb of the order may be limited to assets in England and Wales (especially if those assets exceed the value of the claim) or may extend to assets outside the jurisdiction ('worldwide freezing injunction').[6]
(d) Exceptionally a party may be ordered to transfer the assets from one foreign jurisdiction to another, or not to transfer assets from one foreign jurisdiction to another, or to order the return to England of assets from abroad.[7]
(e) A freezing order is a purely personal remedy confers no proprietary interest, or priority, upon the party in whose favour it is granted.[8]

---

[2] CPR, r. 25.1(3): 'The fact that a particular kind of interim remedy is not listed in paragraph (1) does not affect any power that the court may have to grant that remedy.'

[3] In many cases the jurisdiction is statutory or derives from the inherent jurisdiction of the court: see note in Civil Procedure, para 25.1.1. The CPR cannot, of themselves, extend the jurisdiction of the English courts or create new remedies: see Civil Procedure Act 1997, s 1 and Sch 1.

[4] See *Mareva Compania Naviera SA v International Bulk Carriers SA* [1975] 2 Lloyd's Rep. 509 (CA).

[5] The injunction is not available if no cause of action has yet arisen: *Veracruz Transportation v VC Shipping Co Inc* [1992] 1 Lloyd's Rep 353 (CA). In limited circumstances, related persons may be joined as co-defendants in order that the injunction may bind them: see, eg, *C Inc. v L* [2002] 2 Lloyd's Rep 459 (Aikens J).

[6] See *Babanaft International Co. v Bassatne* [1990] Ch 13 (CA); *Republic of Haiti v Duvalier* [1990] 1 QB 202 (CA).

[7] *Derby & Co. Ltd v Weldon (No 6)* [1990] 1 WLR 1139 (CA).

[8] *Cretanor Maritime Co. v Irish Marine Management Ltd* [1978] 1 WLR 966 (CA); *The Angel Bell* [1981] QB 65 (Goff J); *A-G v Times Newspapers* [1992] 1 AC 191, at 215 (Lord Ackner) (HL).

(f) A party against whom the order is directed who knowingly disobeys the order is in (civil) contempt of court and may be fined or imprisoned. A non-party who assists in the disposal of assets having been notified of the order may also be in (criminal) contempt of court.

(g) Freezing injunctions (including worldwide freezing injunctions) are commonly granted after as well as before judgment to assist the enforcement process.[9]

(h) To obtain a freezing injunction the applicant must show that he has (at least) a good arguable claim on the merits, that the defendant has assets (within or outside the jurisdiction) and that there is a well-founded fear of those assets being dissipated or otherwise dealt with so as to defeat the ends of justice unless the order is made.[10] The order is discretionary and may be refused to an applicant who has failed to give full and frank disclosure on a without notice application, or who has misled the court.

The following paragraphs consider primarily the cross-border aspects of this important remedy using the framework described above. Although many of the points made below are of general application, the focus is upon the relationship with other European Union jurisdictions that are parties to the 1968 EC Convention on jurisdiction and the enforcement of judgments in civil and commercial matters (the 'Brussels Convention') and are now bound by Council Regulation No. 44/2001 on jurisdiction and the recognition and enforcement of judgments in civil and commercial matters (the 'EU Jurisdiction Regulation').[11]

I. INTERIM ORDERS IN ENGLISH SUBSTANTIVE PROCEEDINGS WITH (APPARENT) EXTRA-TERRITORIAL EFFECT

The most important example of this phenomenon is the worldwide freezing injunction, described above.[12] Although the order is made *in personam*

---

[9] *Babanaft* (see n 6 above). CPR, r 25.2(1)(b). See further para 8(c) below.

[10] *Ninemia Corp v Trave GmbH* [1983] 1 WLR 1412 (CA).

[11] Of the EU Member States, Denmark alone is a party to the Brussels Convention but not bound by the EU Jurisdiction Regulation. With effect from 1 May 2004, the 10 new Member States which have not yet acceded to the Convention are bound by the Regulation. For present purposes, differences in language between the Convention and the Regulation are immaterial. References below to the 'Lugano Convention' are to the 1988 EC/EFTA Convention on jurisdiction and the enforcement of judgments in civil and commercial matters, which extends to Iceland, Norway and Switzerland.

[12] See para 5(c). Note also that a search (formerly *Anton Piller*) order may be made in relation to premises outside England: *Cook Industries v Galliher* [1979] Ch 439; *Altertext Inc v Advanced Data Communications* [1985] 1 WLR 457 (Scott J).

against a party subject to (or to be subjected to[13]) the jurisdiction of the English courts, it clearly has extra-territorial effects and, as appears above, in exceptional cases may operate not only negatively (by prohibiting the defendant from dealing with his assets abroad) but positively (by requiring the defendant to move assets between jurisdictions).[14]

The following points arise from this description:

(a) The breadth of the order (and its extra-territorial character) should be taken into account by the court as a factor militating against the exercise of its discretion to make the order.[15]

(b) The fact that the English court has jurisdiction with respect to the substantive proceedings means that no additional conditions or restrictions are placed on the grant of relief by the Brussels Convention or the EU Jurisdiction Regulation, at least prior to judgment.[16] The jurisdiction to grant the freezing injunction is parasitic upon the court's jurisdiction to entertain the substantive proceedings.[17]

(c) After judgment, however, there is at least a question mark whether an English court retains the power to grant a worldwide freezing order which extends to assets in another Member State.[18]

Article 22.5 of the EU Jurisdiction Regulation provides that 'in proceedings concerned with the enforcement of judgments, the courts of the Member State in which the judgment has been or is to be enforced' shall have exclusive jurisdiction.

Admittedly, the predecessor to Article 22.5, Article 16.5 of the Brussels Convention (in identical terms), was held by the English Court of Appeal in *Babanaft v Bassatne* **not** to apply to a post-judgment *Mareva* injunction[19]

---

[13] An order for an interim remedy may be made at any time including before proceedings are started: CPR, r. 25.2(a). Unless the court otherwise, either the applicant must undertake to the court to issue a claim form immediately or the court will give directions for the commencement of the claim: CPR PD25 (interim injunctions), para 4.4.

[14] See para 5(d) above.

[15] *Rosseel NV v Oriental and Commercial Shipping (UK) Ltd* [1990] 1 WLR 1387 (CA); *Derby v Weldon (No 6)* (see n 7 above).

[16] *Van Uden Maritime BV v Firma Deco-Line* (Case C-391/95) [1998] ECR I-7091, para 22 (ECJ). Compare the position where the English court does not have substantive jurisdiction (discussed at s 3 below).

[17] Although perhaps of theoretical import only given the requirement to commence proceedings immediately (see n 13 above), query the position if a worldwide freezing injunction is granted on the basis of an undertaking to commence proceedings but the process is interrupted by the commencement of proceedings involving the same parties and the same cause of action before another Member State, so depriving the English court of its potential substantive jurisdiction under EU Jurisdiction Regulation, Art 27 (Brussels Convention, Art 21).

[18] Briggs and Rees *Civil Jurisdiction and Judgments* (3rd edn 2003) para 6.03, n 20.

[19] [1990] Ch 13, at 35 (Kerr LJ) 46 (Neill LJ).

and, subsequently, by European Court of Justice in *Reichert (No. 2)* not to apply to a pre-judgment action whose purpose was to facilitate enforcement.[20]

Moreover, practically speaking, it may cause injustice to claimants if the fact of a judgment in their favour required them immediately to take steps in several Member States[21] to maintain the protection to which they had previously been entitled.

However, the Court of Justice has not been averse to looking at the substance rather than the form of proceedings in applying the Brussels Convention[22] and the European Court's description in *Reichert (No. 2)* of the scope of Article 16.5[23] would seem apt to describe the effect of a post-judgment freezing order. In the recent case of *Turner v Grovit*,[24] the Court of Justice characterized an anti-suit injunction as interfering with the jurisdiction of a foreign (Spanish) court notwithstanding that it was an *in personam* order directed at the foreign claimants.[25]

Ultimately, however, although the point may not be as clear cut as the English court seemed to think it in *Babanaft*, the reasoning of the Court of Justice in *Webb v Webb*[26] (a judgment concerning Article 16.1 of the Brussels Convention) in maintaining a clear, and formal, distinction between rights *in rem* and rights *in personam* does support the conclusion that a post-judgment freezing injunction falls outside the scope of Article 22.5/Article 16.5.[27] In conclusion, the balance of authority is finely weighted, and, until an opportunity arises for further judicial consideration of the issue, all that one can say is that it is not as clear cut as the Court of Appeal in *Babanaft* appeared to think.

The English courts have long recognized the need to protect third parties in respect of the extra-territorial impact of a worldwide freezing injunction.[28] They have formulated two general propositions. First, the limit of

---

[20] *Reichert v Dresdner Bank (No 2)* (Case C-261/90) [1992] ECR I-2149 para 28 (ECJ).

[21] See Art 47.1 of the EU Jurisdiction Regulation.

[22] See, eg, *The Tatry* (Case C-406/92) [1994] ECR I-5439 paras 46–8.

[23] That an action falls within Art 16.5 only if it is intended to obtain a decision in proceedings relating to recourse to force, *constraint* or distraint on movable or immovable property *in order to ensure the effective implementation of judgments and authentic instrument (ibid)* [Emphasis added].

[24] Case C-159/02 [2004] 3 WLR 1193; see Dickenson [2004] LMCLQ 273.

[25] ibid paras 27–8.   [26] Case 294/92 [1994] ECR I-1717.

[27] The scales may tilt in the other direction when the Court of Justice comes to consider the reference by the House of Lords in *Turner v Grovit* as to the compatibility of anti-suit injunctions with the Brussels Convention. The main objection to such injunctions is that, although directed at a litigating party, they are in substance directed to a foreign court (see para 34 of the Advocate-General's opinion). The Court of Justice's decision is awaited with interest. See further paras. 23–4 below for a similar debate in connection with the availability of relief in support of proceedings in another Member/Contracting State.

[28] See *Babanaft* (n 6 above); *Derby & Co Ltd v Weldon (Nos. 3 and 4)* [1990] Ch 65 (CA); *Bank of China v NBM LLC* [2002] 1 WLR 844 (CA).

the court's territorial jurisdiction and the principle of comity require that the effectiveness of freezing orders operating upon third parties holding assets abroad should normally only derive from their recognition and enforcement by the local courts. Secondly, third parties amenable to the English jurisdiction should be given all reasonable protection.[29]

In recognition of these considerations, a worldwide freezing injunction should normally contain the provisos set out in Annex B at the end of this paper. These provisos were recently approved by the Court of Appeal[30] and are designed to provide sufficient protection to third parties both within and outside the jurisdiction. In particular:

(i) Persons outside England and Wales (other than the respondent or his officer or agent appointed by power of attorney) are not affected or concerned by the order unless:
  • they are subject to the jurisdiction of the English court, have been given written notice of the order at a residence or place of business in England and Wales and are able to prevent acts or omissions abroad which constitute or assist a breach of the terms of the order; or
  • the order has been declared enforceable in their own country, and then only to the extent that it has been declared enforceable.

(ii) In respect of assets located outside England and Wales, any third party may comply with what he reasonably believes to be his obligations under the laws of the country in which those assets are situated or the proper law of a contract with the respondent or with an order of the courts of that country or state.[31]

II. INTERIM ORDERS IN ENGLISH SUBSTANTIVE PROCEEDINGS—ENFORCEMENT ABROAD

Subject to the following observations, a worldwide freezing injunction granted by the English courts is a 'judgment' within the meaning of Article 32 of the EU Jurisdiction Regulation and may be enforced in other Member States in accordance with the provisions of the Regulation.[32]

---

[29] *Bank of China v NBM LLC* (n 26 above), at 851 (Tuckey LJ).

[30] *Bank of China v NBM LLC* (n 26 above).

[31] Provided that reasonable notice of any application by the third party for such an order is given to the applicant's solicitors.

[32] As is well known, the definition of 'judgment' in Art 32 is broad. For examples of the enforcement of freezing injunctions in other Member States, see the cases cited by Professor Dr Burkhard Hess *Study No JAI/A3/2002/02 on making more efficient the enforcement of judicial decisions within the European Union*, 18 Feb 2004, nn 793–5 <http://www.europa.eu.int/comm/justice_home/doc_centre/civil/studies/doc/enforcement_judicial_decisions_180204_en.pdf>. The nature of the relief means that it is unlikely to be enforceable outside the EU or the Contracting States to the Lugano Convention.

For obvious reasons, freezing injunctions are generally granted initially without notice to the respondent. A freezing injunction granted on this basis was not enforceable under the Brussels Convention; only an injunction made following a hearing of which the respondent had been given sufficient notice would suffice.[33]

Under the EU Jurisdiction Regulation, however, it seems that an order granted without notice *might* be enforceable if the defendant failed to institute proceedings to challenge the order when it was possible for him to do so.[34]

The normal procedure before the English Courts is that an order made without notice will give a return date for a further hearing at which the respondent can be present and will make clear the respondent's right in the meantime to apply to the court to vary or discharge the order.[35] A freezing injunction given without notice will normally be expressed to apply only 'until the return date or further order of the court'.[36] The time between the initial hearing and the return date will generally be only one or two weeks.

Further, the applicant may be required to give a formal undertaking not to seek to enforce the order outside England and Wales without the formal permission of the court.[37]

In the premises, the scope for enforcing a worldwide freezing injunction granted without notice is likely to be limited.

To the extent that a freezing injunction is enforceable, the fact that it has been given in the course of substantive proceedings will mean that the scope for reviewing the jurisdiction of the English court to make the order will be very limited.[38]

A further issue arises as to the methods of enforcement of freezing injunctions in other Member States, which (with the exception of Ireland) are understood not to have any direct equivalent. In this regard, two decisions of the Court of Justice appear relevant. First, *Hoffman v Krieg*[39] in which the Court stated that a foreign judgment which is to be recognized under the Brussels Convention 'must in principle have the same effects in the State in which enforcement is sought as it does in the State in which the judgment was given'. Secondly, *Kongress Agentur Hagen GmbH v Zeehaghe BV*[40] in which the court emphasised that the Brussels Convention was not intended to harmonize the Contracting States' rules of procedure.

---

[33] *Denilauler v SNC Couchet Freres* (Case 125/79) [1980] ECR 1553, para 13 (ECJ).

[34] EU Jurisdiction Regulation, Art 34.2. Cf Briggs and Rees (n 18 above) para 7.14.

[35] CPR PD25 (interim injunctions) para 5.1(3) and Specimen Injunction paras 2 and 3.

[36] ibid. Specimen Injunction, para 5.

[37] ibid Sch (B), para (10).

[38] *Mietz v Intership Yachting Sneek BV* (Case C-99/96) [1999] ECR I-2277, paras. 50–1 (ECJ).

[39] Case 145/86 [1988] ECR 645.

[40] Case C-365/88 [1990] ECR I-1845.

Against this background, the correct approach would appear to be for the enforcing court to characterize the order by reference to its effects under the law of the country of origin,[41] but then to apply its own procedural devices for enforcing the order.[42]

III. ENGLISH INTERIM ORDERS IN SUPPORT OF FOREIGN PROCEEDINGS

The English High Court has power to grant interim relief in support of proceedings in a foreign court even if (a) the court is not located in a Member State or otherwise in a Contracting State to the Lugano Convention, and (b) the subject matter of the proceedings is not within the scope of the EU Jurisdiction Regulation or the Brussels or Lugano Conventions.[43]

For this purpose, 'interim relief' means any kind of interim relief which the Court has power to grant in substantive proceedings before it, other than (a) a warrant for the arrest of property, or (b) provision for obtaining evidence.[44]

On an application for interim relief in support of substantive proceedings before a foreign court, the High Court may refuse to grant that relief if, in its opinion, the fact that it otherwise has no jurisdiction makes it inexpedient for the court to grant it.[45] This provision has led the English courts to adopt a two-stage approach. First, to consider whether the relief would have been granted in substantive proceedings before the English court. Secondly, to consider the issue of expediency.[46]

As to the second of these stages, the Court of Appeal has recently identified five particular considerations which the Court should bear in mind when considering it would be inexpedient to grant a worldwide freezing injunction:[47]

(a) Whether the making of the order will interfere with the management of the case in the primary court, for example if it is inconsistent or overlaps with an order made by that court.

---

[41] So that it would be inappropriate, eg, to attribute any proprietary effect to an English freezing injunction or to treat it as analogous to a local order having such effect.

[42] Briggs and Rees (n 18 above) para 6.17. An issue of this kind was raised in *Italian Leather SpA v WECO Polstermöbel* (Case C-80/00) [2002] ECR I-4995, but not answered.

[43] Civil Jurisdiction and Judgments Act 1982, s 25 ('CJJA 1982'), as extended by the Civil Jurisdiction and Judgments Act 1982 (Interim Relief) Order 1997 (SI 1997/302).

[44] CJJA 1982, s 25(7).   [45] ibid s 25(2).

[46] See *Motorola Credit Corpn v Uzan* [2004] 1 WLR 113 (CA). See also *Republic of Haiti v Duvalier* [1990] 1 QB 202 (CA); *Credit Suisse Fides Trust SA v Cuoghi* [1998] QB 818 (CA); *Refco Inc. v Eastern Trading Co* [1990] 1 Lloyd's Rep. 159 (CA).

[47] *Motorola* (n 44 above) para 115. In *Motorola*, the substantive proceedings were taking place in New York.

(b) Whether it is the policy of the primary jurisdiction not itself to make worldwide freezing/disclosure orders.

(c) Whether there is a danger that the orders will give rise to disharmony or confusion and/or the risk of conflicting, inconsistent or overlapping orders in other jurisdictions, in particular the courts of the state where the respondent resides or where the assets affected are located.

(d) Whether there is likely to be a potential conflict as to jurisdiction rendering it inappropriate and inexpedient to make a worldwide order.

(e) Whether in a case where jurisdiction is resisted and disobedience is to be expected, the court will be making an order which it cannot enforce.[48]

(f) In cases falling within the material scope of the EU Jurisdiction Regulation or the Brussels or Lugano Conventions where relief is sought in support of proceedings in another Member or Contracting State, the court must also consider whether the order is a 'provisional or protective measure' within the meaning of Article 31 of the EU Jurisdiction Regulation or Article 24 of the Conventions, as the case may be.

(g) The reference in Article 24 the Brussels Convention to 'provisional, including protective, measures' has been held to refer to measures which are intended to preserve a factual or legal situation so as to safeguard rights the recognition of which is otherwise sought from the court having jurisdiction of the substance of the case.[49]

(h) That statement, of itself, is plainly capable of encompassing a worldwide freezing injunction.[50] The European Court of Justice has, however, placed further limits on the power of Member State courts to grant provisional or protective measures. In particular, the granting of provisional or protective measures on the basis of Article 24 of the Brussels Convention was held in *Van Uden* to be conditional upon the existence of a real connecting link between the subject-matter of the measures sought and the territorial jurisdiction of the court before which those measures are sought.[51] The Court had also held previously in *Denilauler*, and repeated in *Van Uden*, that the courts of the place where assets subject to the measures are located are best able to assess the circumstances which may lead to the grant of those measures.[52]

---

[48] eg if neither the defendant nor any assets are known to be located within the jurisdiction. Cf *Republic of Haiti v Duvalier.*

[49] *Reichert (No 2)* (n 20 above), para 34; *Van Uden* (n 16 above) para 37.

[50] The provisional character of which is secured by an undertaking in damages by the applicant and, if appropriate, the provision of security.

[51] *Van Uden* (n 16 above) para 40.

[52] *Denilauler* (n 31 above) para 15; *Van Uden* (n 16 above) para 38.

(i) Worldwide freezing orders granted in support of proceedings before Contracting States to the Brussels or Lugano Convention have been upheld by the Court of Appeal on more than one occasion.[53] But no English case since *Van Uden*[54] has directly addressed the point whether the reasoning in that case deprives the English courts of the power to grant worldwide freezing injunctions in support of proceedings in other Member or Contracting States. The answer would appear to depend on whether one should look at the form or effect of the freezing injunction, a debate encountered above.[55] At presence, the balance of authority and argument looks to be evenly weighed and the continued use of the worldwide freezing injunction in this context may be open to question.[56]

(j) Even within the framework of the EU Jurisdiction Regulation and the Brussels and Lugano Conventions, a court is left to apply its own rules of jurisdiction and conditions for the grant of relief. Formerly, the question whether personal jurisdiction existed to make an interim order against a person outside England and Wales in support of foreign proceedings vexed the English courts on more than one occasion.[57] Now, however, permission may be sought to serve such a respondent outside the jurisdiction with the application notice.[58]

IV. ENFORCEMENT BY ENGLISH COURT OF FOREIGN INTERIM ORDER

This scenario can be dealt with more briefly:

(a) Outside the regime of the EU Jurisdiction Regulation and the Brussels and Lugano Conventions, the ability of the English courts to enforce interim orders (at least of an *in personam* nature) is severely restricted, if not altogether suffocated, by the requirement that a foreign judgment to be enforceable at common law be (i) for a fixed or ascertainable sum of money, and (ii) final and conclusive.

---

[53] *Republic of Haiti v Duvalier* (French courts); *Credit Suisse Fides v Cuoghi* (Swiss courts) (both n 44 above).

[54] At least to the writer's knowledge.

[55] On the question whether post-judgment worldwide freezing injunctions can be reconciled with the scheme of the EU Jurisdiction Regulation and the Conventions: see para 8(c).

[56] See Collins and others (ed), Dicey and Morris, *The Conflict of Laws* (13th edn 2000) para 8-027; Briggs and Rees n 18 above para 6.09.

[57] See *Mercedes Benz AG v Leiduck* [1996] 1 AC 274 (PC).

[58] CPR, r 6.20(4). The applicant must show that England and Wales is the proper place to bring the claim (CPR, r 6.21(2A)). Often the application for permission to serve the application notice will be made at the same time as the (without notice) application for the order and the two documents served together (see CPR, r 6.30).

(b) Within the Regulation/Convention regime, there are broadly two scenarios.

   (i) First, if the court whose order the English court is asked to enforce has before it the substantive dispute to which the interim order relates. In this scenario, the grounds for objecting to enforcement of the order are those set out in Arts. 34 and 35 of the Regulation or Arts. 27 and 28 of the Conventions and those alone.

   ii) Secondly, if the court whose order the English court is asked to enforce has no substantive jurisdiction[59] over the matters in dispute between the parties. In this scenario, the English court must examine whether the measure ordered was or was not a 'provisional or protective measure' within the meaning of Article 31 of the Regulation or Article 24 of the Conventions.[60] This proposition, which comes close to an investigation of the jurisdiction of the court of origin,[61] is designed to protect the integrity of the jurisdictional rules of the Regulation/the Conventions from being undermined.

(c) If the foreign interim order is enforceable under the Regulation or the Conventions, the English court should approach the matter in the manner described above, ie to characterize the order by reference to its effects under the law of the country of origin, but then to apply its own procedural devices for enforcing the order.[62]

ANNEX A

Civil Procedure Rules 1998, Rule 25.1(1)

The court may grant the following interim remedies—

(a) an interim injunction (GL);
(b) an interim declaration;
(c) an order—
   (i) for the detention, custody or preservation of relevant property;
   (ii) for the inspection of relevant property;
   (iii) for the taking of a sample of relevant property;
   (iv) for the carrying out of an experiment on or with relevant property;

---

[59] Or does not appear from its decision to be exercising such jurisdiction: *Mietz v Intership Yachting Sneek BV* (Case C-99/96) [1999] ECR I-2277, paras 53–5.

[60] *Mietz* (above), para 54. See paras 21–3 above.

[61] Barred by Art 35 of the EU Jurisdiction Regulation and Art 28 of the Conventions.

[62] See para 16.

    (v)   for the sale of relevant property which is of a perishable nature or which for any other good reason it is desirable to sell quickly; and

    (vi)   for the payment of income from relevant property until a claim is decided;

(d) an order authorising a person to enter any land or building in the possession of a party to the proceedings for the purposes of carrying out an order under sub-paragraph (c);

(e) an order under section 4 of the Torts (Interference with Goods) Act 1977(1) to deliver up goods;

(f)   an order (referred to as a 'freezing injunction' (GL)) –

    (i)   restraining a party from removing from the jurisdiction assets located there; or

    (ii)   restraining a party from dealing with any assets whether located within the jurisdiction or not;

(g) an order directing a party to provide information about the location of relevant property or assets or to provide information about relevant property or assets which are or may be the subject of an application for a freezing injunction (GL);

(h) an order (referred to as a 'search order') under section 7 of the Civil Procedure Act 1997(2) (order requiring a party to admit another party to premises for the purpose of preserving evidence etc.);

(i)   an order under section 33 of the Supreme Court Act 1981(3) or section 52 of the County Courts Act 1984(4) (order for disclosure of documents or inspection of property before a claim has been made);

(j)   an order under section 34 of the Supreme Court Act 1981(5) or section 53 of the County Courts Act 1984(6) (order in certain proceedings for disclosure of documents or inspection of property against a non-party);

(k) an order (referred to as an order for interim payment) under rule 25.6 for payment by a defendant on account of any damages, debt or other sum (except costs) which the court may hold the defendant liable to pay;

(l)   an order for a specified fund to be paid into court or otherwise secured, where there is a dispute over a party's right to the fund;

(m) an order permitting a party seeking to recover personal property to pay money into court pending the outcome of the proceedings and directing that, if he does so, the property shall be given up to him;

(n) an order directing a party to prepare and file accounts relating to the dispute;

(o) an order directing any account to be taken or inquiry to be made by the court.

ANNEX B

Extract from Specimen Worldwide Freezing Injunction—Provisos (CPR PD 25 (Interim Injunctions))

19. Persons outside England and Wales

(1) Except as provided in paragraph (2) below, the terms of this order do not affect or concern anyone outside the jurisdiction of this court.

(2) The terms of this order will affect the following persons in a country or state outside the jurisdiction of this court –

    (a) the Respondent or his officer or agent appointed by power of attorney;

    (b) any person who –

        (i)   is subject to the jurisdiction of this court;

        (ii) has been given written notice of this order at his residence or place of business within the jurisdiction of this court; and

        (iii) is able to prevent acts or omissions outside the jurisdiction of this court which constitute or assist in a breach of the terms of this order; and

    (c) any other person, only to the extent that this order is declared enforceable by or is enforced by a court in that country or state.

20. Assets located outside England and Wales

Nothing in this order shall, in respect of assets located outside England and Wales, prevent any third party from complying with—

(1) what it reasonably believes to be its obligations, contractual or otherwise, under the laws and obligations of the country or state in which those assets are situated or under the proper law of any contract between itself and the Respondent; and

(2) any orders of the courts of that country or state, provided that reasonable notice of any application for such an order is given to the Applicant's solicitors.

PART V

THE IMPACT OF THE EUROPEAN CONVENTION ON HUMAN RIGHTS AND FUNDAMENTAL LIBERTIES ON ENFORCEMENT PRACTICES WITHIN CERTAIN EUROPEAN JURISDICTIONS

CHAPTER 17

THE IMPACT OF THE EUROPEAN CONVENTION ON HUMAN RIGHTS AND FUNDAMENTAL LIBERTIES ON ENFORCEMENT PRACTICES[1]

George E Kodek[2]

I. INTRODUCTION

In the more than 40 years since its adoption, the ECHR has significantly influenced civil procedure in all European countries. While the right to be heard, generally expressed in the maxim *audiatur et altera pars*,[3] and general notions of procedural fairness, were by no means new to European States, the Convention has directed attention to many aspects hitherto neglected and has brought about significant improvements and refinements. This influence, however, has in large measure been restricted to the procedure until a judgment is rendered, whereas the possible implications of the Convention for enforcement proceedings have received comparatively little attention. Contrary to the considerable amount of literature dealing with domestic constitutional guarantees and enforcement law, relatively little has been written on the influence of the ECHR in this respect. Only in recent years have decisions concerning the enforcement of civil judgments become more frequent at the European Court of Human Rights.

---

[1] This chapter is based in part on proceedings from the final meeting for this project held at the British Institute of International and Comparative Law in London on 23 Apr 2004 and entitled *Enforcement Agency Practice in Europe: Cooperation or Harmonization?*

[2] LLM, Judge of the Vienna Court of Appeals.

[3] This maxim is, surprisingly, not of Roman origin. Rather, it was formulated in the Middle Ages (see A Wacke '*Audiatur et altera pars*' *Zum rechtlichen Gehör im römischen Zivil- und Strafprozess, Festschrift Waldstein* (1993) 369 [372]; see also CJ Claassen, *Dictionary of Legal Words and Phrases I* (1975) 155 ff). This does not imply, however, that this principle in substance was unknown to the Romans. (see A Wacke, FS Waldstein 369). In continental *ius commune* the principle was in part derived from a maxim of canon law dealing with the protection of possession ('contra inauditam partem nihil definiri potest' CJC X 2, 12, 1 *de causa posessionis*). See O Bülow *Gemeines deutsches Zivilprozessrecht* (2003) 157.

This paper will examine the influence of the ECHR in this respect on an abstract level, without any real reference to the background of any particular legal system. In light of the author's legal education and professional background, however, there is a propensity to place emphasis on civil law countries and particular German speaking countries, ie countries whose language and legal system I am most familiar.

Analysing the influence of the ECHR on enforcement proceedings is difficult in several respects. First, the wording of the Convention itself is not very specific. Thus, as a main source of the law we have to rely on decisions of the Court of Human Rights. Unfortunately, the decisions of the Court often lack the precision of reasoning we are used to, or at least expect from domestic courts. Therefore, the factual and domestic legal background of many decisions is not always entirely clear. What is more important, perhaps, is that the Court decides on a case-by-case basis, with the main emphasis clearly being placed on an attempt to do justice in individual cases.[4] The process of providing orientation for future cases and systematic development of the law seems to be of secondary importance to the Court. An attempt to deduce general principles from the decisions of the Court thus faces considerable difficulty. In many respects the case law of the Court seems to resemble the parts of a giant jigsaw puzzle which have to be assembled in order to get a full picture of the law of human rights. While certainly not endeavouring to assemble the entire puzzle, this paper attempts to explore how some parts of the case law may fit together. The requirements of the Convention in the area of enforcement law outlined in this article not only provide a guideline for present day enforcement practice, but may also serve as the framework for future reform in this field.

---

[4] Matscher, a former Judge of the European Court of Human Rights, has pointed out that the Court's case law is largely casuisitic and only occasionally contains statements capable of general application. See Matscher `Methods of Interpretation of the Convention' in R Macdonald, F Matscher, and H Petzold *The European System for the Protection of Human Rights* 63. This is due in part to deliberate self–restraint of the Court. It is often emphasized that the Court should not develop general theories, but should confine its attention, as far as possible, to the issues raised by the concrete case before it' (see, eg, *De Becker* judgment of 27 Mar 1962, Series A no 4, 26; *Golder* judgment of 21 Feb 1975, Series A no 18, § 39; *JB v Switzerland*, no 31827/96, ECHR 2001-III; *Weh v Austria*, 8 Apr 2004, § 49. See Matscher in R Macdonald, F Matscher, and H Petzold *The European System for the Protection of Human Rights* 64 n 4. For additional examples see J Callewaert 'The Judgments of the Court: Background and Content' in R Macdonald, F Matscher, and H Petzold *The European System for the Protection of Human Rights* 728 n 105.

II. SUBSTANTIVE GUARANTEES (A) FROM THE PERSPECTIVE OF THE JUDGMENT
CREDITOR

A. The protection of property (Article 1 of Protocol No 1)

Arguably the most important substantive guarantee the Convention
provides for a creditor is Article 1 of Protocol No. 1, which guarantees the
'peaceful enjoyment' of one's 'possessions'.[5] This provision contains the
only protection of a purely economic right in the framework of the
Convention.[6] While possessions in the sense of Article 1 of Protocol No. 1
are in the first place all those rights which are called property rights in the
national systems, the Convention guarantee is not limited to the technical
notion of property in national law. Rather, the term 'possession' or *'biens'*
in this provision has an autonomous meaning. Therefore, the Commission
has held from the very beginning that all rights which are well-founded in
national law can basically benefit from the guarantee of Article 1. They may
be claims, immaterial rights or even rights granted under public law.[7] Today
it is well established that a claim can constitute a 'possession' within the
meaning of Article 1 of Protocol No. 1 if it is sufficiently established to be
enforceable.[8]

While the State cannot be hold responsible for a debtor's lack of means,[9]
failure to provide adequate means to enforce a 'claim' may constitute a
violation of Article 1 of Protocol No. 1. It has to be pointed out, however,
that the protection granted by Article 1 of Protocol No. 1 is not absolute.
Member States clearly enjoy a wide *margin of appreciation* as to the ways
and means of enforcement of civil judgments[10] and as to ascertaining

---

[5] Art 1 para 1 of Protocol No 1 provides: 'Every natural or legal person is entitled to the
peaceful enjoyment of his possessions. No one shall be deprived of his possessions except in
the public interest and subject to the conditions provided for by law and by the general principles of international law.'

[6] It is worth noting that this provision is contained not in the original Convention, but in
an additional Protocol. The reason for this is that the parties originally failed to agree on a
protection of property in the Convention system. See J Frowein 'The Protection of Property'
in R Macdonald, F Matscher, and H Petzold *The European System for the Protection of
Human Rights* 515.

[7] J Frowein in R Macdonald, F Matscher, and H Petzold, *The European System for the
Protection of Human Rights* 517.

[8] *Stran Greek Refineries and Stratis Andreadis v Greece*, judgment of 9 Dec 1994, Series
A no 301-B, § 59; *Burdov v Russia*, judgment of 18 Apr 2002; *Immobiliare Saffi v Italy*, judgment of 28 July 1999 (eviction proceedings).

[9] See, eg, *Gasus Dosier- und Fördertechnik GmbH v The Netherlands*, judgment of 23 Feb
1995, A306-B, § 65 *in fine*.

[10] See also *Emsenhuber v Austria*, decision of 11 Sept 2003, no 54536/00, where the Court
found that a decision refusing a building permit did not necessarily have to be enforced by tear-
ing down the building built without a permit, but that another way to give effect to the decision would be by way of pecuniary compensation to the neighbour for the unlawfully erected
building.

whether the consequences of enforcement are justified in the general interest for the purpose of achieving the object of the law in question. Particularly in spheres such as housing, which lays a central role in the welfare and economic policies of modern societies, the Court will respect the legislature's judgment as to what is in the general interest unless that judgment is manifestly without reasonable foundation.[11] Thus, a temporary stay of enforcement proceedings for social reasons, for example in eviction proceedings, will generally be compatible with the Convention.[12]

A violation of a creditor's substantive rights as protected by the Convention, therefore, will only be found in extreme cases which amount to a *de facto* denial of enforcement. This may also be true if a retroactive statute were enacted which, in effect, completely bars enforcement of a court decision.[13] Similarly, a *gross violation of procedural fairness* which results in an arbitrary denial of an application for enforcement measures may amount to a violation of a creditor's substantive rights.[14] Apart from such extreme cases, however, Article 1 of Protocol No 1 offers little guidance as to the rights a creditor should enjoy in order to be able to enforce a judgment debt. In most cases, therefore, the focus of the examination of the influence of the Convention on enforcement proceedings will have to be directed at the applicability of the more specific procedural guarantees set forth in Article 6.[15]

B. *The right to respect for private and family life (Article 8)*

Occasionally a failure to enforce a judgment may also deserve scrutiny in light of Article 8 ECHR.[16] Thus, in 2004 in *Cvijetic v Croatia* the Court

[11] *Immobiliare Saffi v Italy*, judgment of 28 July 1999, § 49; *Palumbo v Italy*, judgment of 30 Nov 2000, § 26.

[12] A different result is reached, of course, if the duration of the stay in effect renders the right enforcement of which is sought nugatory. For repeated stays of execution by legislative measures, see *Immobiliare Saffi v Italy*, judgment of 28 July 1999; *Palumbo v Italy*, judgment of 30 Nov 2000.

[13] Most recently this issue was raised in a number of applications against Greece. See, eg, *Vasilopoulou v Greece*, judgment of 21 Mar 2002. The Court notes, however, that Member States here enjoy a wide margin of appreciation. This aspect of the Court's case law, however, is beyond the scope of this article since it deals with an outright denial of enforcement under national law rather than with the influence of the Convention on enforcement proceedings as such.

[14] It is well established in the Court's case law that a violation of Art 6 can in addition also constitute a violation of a substantive right. See, eg, the cases concerning the enforcement of custody rights and rights of access discussed below at 2.1 b).

[15] See below at 3.

[16] Art 8 ECHR provides:
(1): Everyone has the right to respect for his private and family life, his home and his correspondence.
(2) There shall be no interference by public authority with the exercise of that right except such as is in accordance with the law and is necessary in a democratic society in the interests of

held that a States' failure to enforce an eviction judgment may constitute a violation of Article 8. This, however, apparently is only true if someone seeks to regain his private dwelling place. Clearly Article 8 is not available to the owner of an apartment who seeks eviction of a tenant for failure to pay his rent without any intent of using the apartment himself.[17]

Another area where Article 8 is of possible relevance for enforcement proceedings is the enforcement of decisions on custody and rights of access. It is well established that the enforcement of these decisions falls under art 8 ECHR.[18] Thus, in this case Articles 8 and 6 overlap to a certain extent.[19] While the essential object of Article 8 is to protect the individual against arbitrary action by the public authorities, there are also positive obligations inherent in an effective 'respect' for family life.[20] The Court has repeatedly held that Article 8 includes a right for parents to have measures taken that will permit them to be reunited with their children and an obligation on the national authorities to take such action.[21] While due to the special nature of these cases, any obligation to apply coercion in this area is limited, the Court stresses that national authorities have to take all the necessary steps to facilitate execution as could reasonably demanded in the special circumstances of the case.[22] Necessary measures may include the advice of social

national security, public safety or the economic well-being of the country, for the prevention of disorder or crime, for the protection of health and morals, or for the protection of the rights and freedoms of others.

[17] That the Court is reluctant to stretch the protection under Art 8 too far is also apparent from *Kyrtatos v Greece*, judgment of 22 May 2003, where the Court found that extensive construction works in an environmentally protected swamp did not violate rights of neighbours under Art 8.

[18] *Margareta and Roger Andersson v Sweden*, judgment of 25 Feb 1992, series A no 226-A, *Nuutinen v Finland*, judgment of 27 June 2000, Reports 2000-VIII 1994, *Ignaccolo Zenide v Romania*, judgment of 25 Jan 2000, Reports 2000-I; *Sophia Gudrun Hansen v Turkey*, judgment of 23 Sept 2003 (_15,000 non-pecuniary damages awarded!), *Sylvester v Austria*, judgment of 24 Apr 2003.

[19] It has to be remembered, though, that these provisions serve to protect different interests. While Art 6 affords a procedural safeguard, Art 8 serves the wider purpose of ensuring proper respect for, *inter alia*, family life. In light of the different interests protected by these provisions it is justified to examine the same set of facts under both Arts. See, eg, *McMichael v United Kingdom*, judgment of 24 Feb 1995, series A no 307-B, 57, § 91. However, occasionally the Court focuses only on Art 8 in such cases, considering it not necessary to examine the facts of the case also under Art 6. See *Sylvester v Austria*, judgment of 24 Apr 2003, § 76.

[20] *Keegan v Ireland*, judgment of 26 May 1994, Series A no 290, § 49.

[21] *Eriksson v Sweden*, judgment of 2 June 1989, Series A no 156, 26–7, § 71; *Margareta and Roger Andersson v Sweden*, judgment of 25 Feb 1992, Series A no 226-A,p. 30, § 91; *Olsson v Sweden* (no 2), judgment of 27 Nov 1992, Series A no 250, 35–6, § 90; *Hokkanen v Finland*, judgment of 23 Sept 1994, Series A no 299-A, 20, § 55; *Nuutinen v Finland*, judgment of 27 June 2000, Reports 2000-VIII, 83, § 127; *Ignaccolo-Zenide v Romania*, judgment of 25 Jan 2000, Reports 2000-I, 265, § 94; *Sylvester v Austria*, judgment of 24 Apr 2003, § 58; *Sophia Gudrun Hansen v Turkey*, judgment of 23 Sept 2003, § 97.

[22] *Hokkanen v Finland*, judgment of 23 Sept 1994, Series A no 299-A, 22, § 58; *Ignaccolo-Zenide v Romania*, judgment of 25 Jan 2000, Reports 2000-I, 265, § 96; *Sophia Gudrun Hansen v Turkey*, judgment of 23 Sept 2003, § 99.

services, assistance of psychologists or child psychiatrists.[23] Furthermore, public authorities have to attempt to locate the child, at least to some extent, *ex officio*.[24]This position is likely to be in conflict with the traditional view, held in many countries, that it is for the creditor to take the initiative and point out to the authorities the location where enforcement measures are to take place.

C. From the perspective of the judgment debtor

1. The protection of property (Article 1 of Protocol No 1)

Article 1 of Protocol No 1 does not forbid enforcement proceedings *per se*.[25]A seizure of assets belonging to the debtor in the course of enforcement proceedings does not constitute an 'expropriation' in the sense of this provision. Moreover, such a measure clearly is in the public interest and 'provided for by law'. Several decisions of the Commission point out that Article 1 of Protocol No. 1 is primarily aimed at providing protection against arbitrary expropriation, but not against lawful enforcement of a court decision. In at least two decisions the Commission, in dismissing the complaint as manifestly ill-founded, indicated that there was no suggestion that the proceedings had not been fair and that the sale had not yielded an amount reasonable under the circumstances.[26] While this suggests that rights under this provision may be violated if the debtor's property is sold at an unreasonably low price, there is arguably no general '*proportionality*' requirement under the Convention. In this context it has to be remembered that a debtor—as long as he is solvent (otherwise he can, and in most countries has to, file for the opening of bankruptcy proceedings)—can always avoid enforcement proceedings by voluntarily complying with the judgment. Some national courts, however, assume that there is a prohibition under (domestic) constitutional law against sales at an unfairly low price.[27]

Some decisions of the Court even suggest that the seizure of goods belonging not to the debtor, but to a *third party*, may be permissible under certain circumstances.[28] In dealing with fiscal rights of preference under

[23] See the *Ignaccolo Zenide, Sophia Gudrun Hansen* judgments cited below.

[24] *Ignaccolo-Zenide v Romania*, judgment of 25 Jan 2000, Reports 2000-I, § 111; *Sylvester v Austria*, judgment of 24 Apr 2003, § 71.

[25] It is well recognized in other contexts that the fundamental rights have certain 'implicit limitations'. What these are cannot be determined by a general formula; it follows rather from the assessment of the individual case. See for examplefor example the *Golder* judgment of 21 Feb 1975, Series A no 18.

[26] Decision of 10 Dec 1979 and *X. v Germany*, decision of 14 Mar 1980, application no 8469/79.

[27] See German Constitutional Court BVerfGE 46, 325 (332) = NJW 1978, 368.

[28] See, particularly, *Gasus Dosier- und Fördertechnik GmbH v The Netherlands*, judgment of 23 Feb 1995 (concerning seizure of a concrete mixer in which the applicant had a fiduciary ownership).

Dutch law, the Court noted that the power of recovery against goods which are in fact in a debtor's possession, although nominally owned by a third party, was not an uncommon device to strengthen a creditor's position in enforcement proceedings; it could not be held incompatible per se with the requirements of Article 1 of Protocol No. 1.[29] Thus, the right of landlords levying distress for rent to seize any third party goods found on the rented premises under English law seems to be in accordance with the Convention. The same holds true for the traditional civil law rule that a landlord enjoys a lien *ex lege* on all goods found on the premises occupied by the tenant ('*invecta et illata*').

2. The right to respect for private and family life (Article 8)

A search of a debtor's residence and subsequent seizure of goods in the course of enforcement proceedings per se probably does not constitute a violation of art 8 ECHR. Even if this is seen as an interference, it will generally be justified as being 'in accordance with the law' and aimed at 'the protection of the rights and freedoms of others.'[30] While there is no general warrant requirement under Article 8, recent case law suggests that a warrant may be required if the statute authorizing the search and seizure lacks the necessary specificity.[31] Moreover, the absence of a warrant may be factor considered by a court when assessing the overall circumstances of a search or seizure.[32] Also, in many countries there may be a warrant requirement under domestic constitutional law.[33]

---

[29] *Gasus Dosier- und Fördertechnik GmbH v The Netherlands*, judgment of 23 Feb 1995, §66.

[30] See Commission decision 10 Dec 1979, no 7952/77, which held that entry into an applicant's home was justified under Art 8 para 2 ECHR if he does not want to pay his debts.

[31] *Crémieux v France* judgment of 25 Feb 1993, A256-B, §40, and *Funke v France*, judgment of 25 Feb 1993, A256-A §57: 'Above all, in the absence of any requirement of a judicial warrant the restrictions and conditions provided for in law . . .appear too lax and full of loopholes for the interferences with the applicant's rights to have been strictly proportionate to the legitimate aim pursued.' It should be pointed out, however, that these decisions did not concern civil enforcement proceedings, but a search by customs officials in a criminal proceeding. For another decision concerning a search by customs officials, see *Miailhe v France*, judgment of 26 Sept 1996, Reports 1996-IV.

[32] See also *Chapell v UK* , judgment of 30 Mar 1989, series A no 152-A (concerning an Anton Piller order, no violation found).

[33] See German Constitutional Court BVerfGE 51, 97 = NJW 1979, 1539: While the German Code of Civil Procedure (s 761 ZPO) requires a court authorization only for night-time entries of a home, the Constitutional Court has held that in light of the constitutional protection of homes this provision ought to be extended *per analogiam* to all entries of a home. The situation is less clear under Austrian law. Section 26 of the Enforcement Act (*Exekutionsordnung*) authorizes the bailiff to enter and search the debtor's residence. While constitutional law contains what would appear to be an unqualified warrant requirement for all searches, arguably historically the purpose of this provision was only to provide a protection against searches in the context of a criminal proceeding which were seen as particularly intrusive.

It should be noted that while the rights provided for by the Convention also generally apply to legal persons, only *individuals* are protected by Article 8. Thus, according to a decision of the *ECJ* concerning the search of business premises of *Hoechst AG*, Art 8 ECHR does not include *companies*.[34]

3. Compulsion and personal liberty

Enforcement law, particularly in connection with the enforcement of judgments enjoining a debtor to perform, or refrain from certain activity, often provides for sanctions in case the debtor fails to comply with the judgment. This is perfectly in line with the substantive guarantees of the Convention. In fact, Article 5 paragraph 2 ECHR expressly permits *detention* for non-compliance with a lawful court order or in order to secure the fulfilment of an obligation prescribed by law.[35]

Also in other contexts enforcement proceedings involve elements of compulsion. Thus, a debtor is often required to provide information as to his financial situation and the whereabouts of his assets. While such compulsion does not violate the Convention,[36] the subsequent use of such information in a criminal proceeding may be 'unfair' under Article 6 ECHR.[37]

III. PROCEDURAL GUARANTEES

A. Applicability of Article 6 ECHR

1. Introduction

While the substantive guarantees of the ECHR and Protocol No 1 generally

Some contemporary commentators believe that the warrant requirement also applies to seizures in the context of civil enforcement proceedings. See, eg, W Jelinek et al 'Verfassungsrechtliche Aspekte der Zwangsvollstreckung in Österreich', in Beys (ed), *Grundrechtsverletzungen bei der Zwangsvollstreckung* (1996) 3 Dike International 301 (357). While some authorities take the position that a court order authorizing enforcement of a civil judgment contained an implicit warrant to enter a debtor's home, this is questionable under today's law, because—unlike in the 19th century (see R von Canstein *Lehrbuch des österreichischen Civilprocessrechts* (2nd edn 783 n 5)—under today's enforcement practice the court decision authorizing execution does not have to contain the address where the seizure is to take place in order to provide greater flexibility for the bailiff.

[34] NJW 1989, 3080.
[35] For the procedural guarantees to be observed in such cases see below at 3.2 (k).
[36] The situation is different, of course, when someone is compelled to provide information in connection with a (pending or contemplated) criminal proceeding. See, eg, *Funke v France*, judgment of 25 Feb 1993, A256-A, § 42–4.
[37] See *Kansal v UK*, judgment 27 Apr 2004; German Constitutional Court BVerfGE 56, 37 = NJW 1981, 1431.

pose few problems in the context of enforcement proceedings since they are not very specific (they provide for numerous exceptions and States always have a certain margin of appreciation) the scope of applicability of the procedural guarantees of Article 6 to enforcement proceedings is more difficult to determine. Article 6 paragraph 1, first sentence ECHR provides: 'In the determination of his civil rights and obligations or of any criminal charge against him, everyone is entitled to a fair and public hearing within a reasonable time by an independent and impartial tribunal established by law.' As indicated in the introduction to this paper, the significance of this provision for enforcement proceedings has so far received little attention. National courts apparently have some difficulty in determining the possible impact of Article 6 on enforcement proceedings, sometimes resorting to apodictic, yet inconsistent if not outright contradictory views.[38] Yet the possible implications of a full applicability of Article 6 to enforcement proceedings are quite far-reaching: If this provision were fully applicable to enforcement proceedings, this would extend not just the reasonable time requirement and some very general notions of fairness to enforcement proceedings, but all specific guarantees provided by Article 6, such as the requirement of a public hearing and of a public tendering of the decision, would also apply to enforcement proceedings. This would place many continental procedural systems in considerable difficulty. Suffice it to point out that in some countries at least certain enforcement measures, particularly seizures, may take place without prior court authorization. Even in countries which require judicial authorization, the decision is usually made in an ex parte proceeding in which defendant is not heard. Furthermore, in most countries the decision on such applications is rendered without a hearing taking place; most countries resort to a mostly, if not exclusively, written procedure.

There may also be some less obvious consequences: In *Morel v France*, a decision concerning a French bankruptcy proceeding, the Court expressed reservations against a judge opening a bankruptcy proceeding if he had been previously involved in a reorganization proceeding.[39] Does this mean that, assuming Article 6 fully applies to enforcement proceedings, the judge authorizing enforcement proceedings must not be the same judge who rendered the judgment enforcement now sought? The answer is probably no. As the Commission has repeatedly stated: 'It does not jeopardize the impartiality of a judge if he has previously dealt with other cases brought

---

[38] A good example of the difficulties national courts have in dealing with this question is provided by the Austrian Supreme Court. In a 1998 decision it stated that there can be no doubt that Art 6 ECHR does not apply to enforcement proceedings (3 Ob 243/98a). A few years earlier, the same court stated that it had 'always' applied Art 6 to enforcement proceedings (3 Ob 42/95 = SZ 68/83).

[39] *Morel v France*, judgment of 16 May 2000, No 34130/96.

against the same person.'[40] The decision in *Morel*, which applied principles originally developed in the field of criminal procedure[41] to bankruptcy proceedings should probably be limited to the specific facts of the case. While in the case of a reorganization proceeding and a subsequent bankruptcy proceeding concerns about involvement of the judge in the reorganization proceeding may seem understandable (although, in the author's opinion, a little far-fetched), this certainly does not apply to an order authorizing enforcement proceedings. In light of both the routine character of such decisions, and of the fact that such decisions are rendered in a highly formalized proceeding leaving little room for judicial discretion, it appears extremely unlikely that participation of the judge sitting at the title stage in subsequent enforcement proceedings is considered a violation of Article 6.

Another problem which full applicability of Article 6 to enforcement proceedings would bring is the principle of 'equality of arms.' This principle, which the Court derives from the general fairness requirement of Article 6, can be defined as the requirement to be able to comment on all the evidence adduced or observations filed with a view to influencing the court's decision. It is worth noting here that in many European countries applications for the authorization of enforcement proceedings are dealt with ex parte.

In one of the few decisions squarely addressing the issue, the Commission has held:[42] 'As a general rule, enforcement proceedings following a civil court judgment do not come within the scope of art 6–1 ECHR. They do not themselves determine a dispute relating to civil rights, but presuppose a prior determination of these rights by an independent court. However, in the context of enforcement proceedings questions might have to be determined which involve a decision on civil rights of the parties, such as partition of property.' While the complaint was dismissed as manifestly ill-founded, the Commission noted: 'Insofar as the execution proceedings in the present case may be considered to constitute the determination of civil rights, the Commission has accordingly examined this complaint in light of art 6–1 of the Convention.' In the following sections an attempt will be made to explore what decisions have to be regarded as determinations of civil rights and obligations in an enforcement proceeding, and thus require that the guarantees provided for by Article 6 be complied with.

---

[40] Commission decision No 11831/85, DR 54, 144; decision *Krone v Austria*, 21 May 1997, No 28977/95.

[41] It is well established that under Art 6 the investigating judge (*juge d' instruction*) may not be the judge deciding on guilt or innocence of a defendant. See, eg, *DeCubber v Switzerland*, judgment of 26 Oct 1984.

[42] Commission decision of 21 May 1997, No 28977/95 *Krone v Austria*. See also CD 42, 145 and DR 48, 225 (application to question witnesses in a public hearing).

2. Development of the case law

The European Court of Human Rights reads Article 6 broadly and interprets it as a guarantee of a 'right to a court',[43] of which the right of access to a court is but one aspect.[44] While the wording of Article 6 seems not to cover enforcement proceedings, in a number of cases the Court applied the reasonable time requirement to enforcement proceedings. In the opinion of the Court, the right to a court guaranteed by Article 6 'would be illusory if a State's domestic legal system allowed a final, binding judicial decision to remain inoperative to the detriment of one pArticle It would be inconceivable that Article 6 ECHR should describe in detail procedural guarantees afforded to litigants—proceedings that are fair, public and expeditious—without protecting the implementation of judicial decisions; to construe Article 6 as being concerned exclusively with access to a court and the conduct of proceedings would be likely to lead to situations incompatible with the principle of the rule of law which the Contracting States undertook to respect when they ratified the Convention. . . . Execution of a judgment given by any court must therefore be regarded as an integral part of 'trial' for the purposes of Article 6.'[45] While sometimes the Court used the term 'enforcement' in a non-technical sense and subjected the implementation of the decision of an administrative court reversing the decision of an administrative authority to the reasonable time requirement,[46] several decisions of the Court actually deal with the duration of enforcement proceedings in the technical sense of the word.[47]

---

[43] *Golder v United Kingdom*, judgment of 21 Feb 1975, Series A No 18.

[44] The concept of 'access to court' refers to the right to have a legal claim determined by a court with full jurisdiction on the matter. See P van Dijk in R Macdonald, F Matscher, and H Petzold *The European System for the Protection of Human Rights* 345.

[45] See, eg, *Hornsby v Greece* judgment of 25 Feb 1997, Reports 1997-II, 510–11, § 40; *Immobiliare Saffi v Italy*, judgment of 28 July 1999, § 63, ECHR 1999-V; *Antonakopoulos et al v Greece* (1994); *Vasilopoulou v Greece* (2002); *Dimitrios Georgiades v Greece*, judgment of 28 Mar 2000; *Burdov v Russia*, judgment of 18 Apr 2002, § 34; *Rybakykh v Russia*, judgment of 24 July 2003, § 55.

[46] *Hornsby v Greece*, judgment of 25 Feb 1997. The case concerned an administrative decision on an application for a license to operate a foreign language school. The case is also significant in that it is one of the few cases that were decided both by the European Court of Human Rights and by the European Court of Justice (*Commission of the European Communities v the Hellenic Republic*, judgment of 15 Mar 1988, no 147/86). A more recent example is *Krombach v France* (judgment of the European Court of Human Rights of 13 Feb 2001; *Krombach v Bamberski*, judgment of the ECJ of 28 Mar 2000).

[47] *Martins Moreira v Portugal* (1988, defendant was bankrupt when proceedings were over); *Di Pede v Italy, Zappia v Italy* (1996: enforcement proceedings concerning a judgment debt of 5 million ITL from 1969 to 1993); *Comingersoll SA v Portugal*, judgment of 6 Apr 2000 (enforcement proceedings on bills of exchange 'which by their very nature need to be dealt with expeditiously' lasting 12 years); *Palumbo v Italy*, judgment of 30 Nov 2002 (eviction proceedings); *Cvijetic v Croatia*, judgment of 26 Feb 2004 (eviction proceedings lasting from 1994 to 2002. The delay was in part due to demonstrations of war veterans preventing eviction).

In what probably has to be regarded as a significant, if largely unobserved development, the Court recently held that *res judicata* is also protected under Article 6.[48] It would be an infringement of the rights guaranteed by Article 6 to allow a final decision to be set aside on the application of the public prosecutor, a procedural device traditionally found in many Eastern European countries. In the opinion of the Court, one of the fundamental aspects of the rule of law is the principle of legal certainty, which requires, among other things, that where the courts have finally determined an issue, their ruling should not be called into question.[49] Legal certainty presupposes respect of the principle of *res judicata*, that is the principle of finality of judgments. The Court also stated that departures from that principle are justified only when made necessary by circumstances of a substantial and compelling character.[50]

3. Analysis

When analysing the applicability of Article 6 to enforcement proceedings, a number of important principles of that article have to be remembered which, although well-established, frequently tend to be overlooked in the discussion of the matter: First, Article 6 applies only to decisions about *civil* rights and obligations, ie *substantive* rights and obligations, not to decisions on purely *procedural* questions. Secondly, from the fact that the French text of Article 6 speaks of '*contestation*' it has been inferred that for Article 6 to be applicable the settlement of a *dispute* concerning a right or obligation must be at issue.[51] Thus, Article 6 paragraph 1 requires not only that the matter concern civil rights or obligations, but that there be a dispute (contestation) concerning the particular rights or obligations. The dispute must be genuine and of a serious nature. The claimed judicial proceedings must lead to a 'determination' of civil rights or obligations.[52] Thirdly,

---

[48] *Rybakykh v Russia*, judgment of 24 July 2003; see also *Brumarescu v Romania*, judgment of 28 Oct 1999, Reports 1999-VII.

[49] *Rybakykh v Russia*, judgment of 24 July 2003, § 51; *Brumarescu v Romania*, judgment of 28 Oct 1999, Reports 1999-VII, §61.

[50] *Rybakykh v Russia*, judgment of 24 July 2003, §52.

[51] This concept of 'dispute', however, should not be construed too technically and should be given a substantive rather than a formal meaning: a difference of opinion between the parties concerned is sufficient, provided that it is 'genuine and of a serious nature'. This interpretation was enunciated for the first time in the *Le Compte, Van Leuven and De Meyere* judgment of 23 June 1981, Series A no 43, 20. See P van Dijk in R Macdonald, F Matscher, and H Petzold *The European System for the Protection of Human Rights* 354.

[52] However, the 'determination' need not form the main point or even the purpose of the proceedings. It is sufficient that the outcome of the claimed judicial proceedings may also be 'decisive for' or may 'affect' the determination or the exercise of the right, or the determination or fulfilment of the obligation. That right or obligation does not have to constitute the direct object of the procedure; moreover, the determination need not necessarily concern the

Article 6 only applies to *final* determinations as opposed to preliminary decisions.

While enforcement proceedings have to be seen as a part of the original proceedings for purposes of the reasonable time requirement,[53]they normally do not entail a decision about a 'civil right',[54] nor do they ordinarily decide a 'dispute' (contestation). This is true from the viewpoint of both parties: As for the debtor, the institution of enforcement proceedings ordinarily requires that a determination of the obligation of debtor has already occurred in a prior proceeding. Furthermore, in light of remedies available to the debtor, be it an appeal or the institution of a separate lawsuit challenging the enforcement proceedings, the decision on an application for authorization of enforcement proceedings (which in continental Europe is often granted ex parte) clearly does not constitute a final determination for purposes of Article 6. But the same is true from the creditor's point of view: The creditor generally has a choice of several enforcement methods; a decision on any one application for authorization of particular enforcement measures does not affect the existence of his claim.[55]

Yet the Court has found that enforcement proceedings constitute an *'integral part'* of the trial. While this phrase may be helpful in justifying the extension of the reasonable time requirement to enforcement proceedings (which apparently is the primary reason why the Court adopted it), it offers little guidance as to whether and to what extent the other guarantees provided for by Article 6 also apply to enforcement proceedings. Since enforcement proceedings normally do not fulfil the requirements for the applicability of Article 6 outlined above (a fact which can hardly be assumed to have escaped the Court), the term 'integral part of the trial' probably should not be understood as implying a full application of all guarantees provided by Article 6 to enforcement proceedings. The best explanation seems to be that for purposes of Article 6 the proceedings at the title stage and enforcement proceedings have to be examined together for some purposes without all guarantees of Article 6 necessarily also applying to the latter. Thus, apart from the reasonable time requirement (the application of which to enforcement proceedings is well established)

---

existence of a right or obligation, but may also relate to its scope or modalities (*Le Compte, Van Leuven and De Meyere* judgment of 23 June 1981, Series A no 43, 22; *Bentham* judgment of 23 Oct 1985, Series A no 97, 15 et al). See P van Dijk in R Macdonald, F Matscher, and H Petzold *The European System for the Protection of Human Rights* 354.

[53] See 3.1 (b) and 3.2. (f).

[54] For a discussion of possible exceptions, see 3.1 d).

[55] The result may be different if the only feasible way of enforcement is denied. This result, however, does not require us to assume that all guarantees of Art 6 apply to enforcement proceedings. Rather, it can also be explained by subjecting enforcement proceedings only to a general fairness test as suggested in the text below.

enforcement proceedings are probably only subject to a general fairness test, i.e. whether *basic notions of fairness* have been complied with.[56] For a proceeding to be *fair* under Article 6 ECHR, sufficient legal ways of enforcement have to be available (with States probably—as in the context of the 'right to a court' in general—enjoying a certain margin of appreciation here), but the only procedural requirements the Convention imposes on enforcement proceedings is that they are decided within a reasonable time and that they conform to general notions of fairness whereas the other more detailed guarantees of Article 6 do not apply to enforcement proceedings as such.[57] Thus, the Commission probably stated the law correctly when observing that 'as a general rule, enforcement proceedings following a civil court judgment do not come within the scope of Article 6.'[58] In some instances, however, a determination of civil rights and obligations does occur in enforcement proceedings. These instances will be examined in the next section of this paper.

4. Full application of the guarantees of Article 6 ECHR

If a determination of civil rights occurs only at the enforcement stage, the requirements of Article 6 ECHR have to be met in this respect. For purposes of the Convention, it is immaterial whether the proceeding leading to a decision is categorized as being part of the 'title stage' of the proceedings or part of enforcement proceedings under national law.[59] A good example for a determination of civil rights only at what is considered to be the enforcement stage under national law is Portuguese law according to which in an action for damages the final determination of '*quantum*' can be reserved for

[56] It is well established that the 'right to a court', of which the right of access is one aspect, is not absolute; it is subject to limitations permitted by implication and calls for regulation by the State, which enjoys a certain margin of appreciation in this regard (*Annoni di Gussola v France*, judgment 17 Oct 2000 §48; *Edificaciones March Gallego SA v Spain*, judgment 19 Feb 1998, Reports 1998-I, 290 §34; *García Manibardo v Spain*, judgment 15 Feb 2000, §36, ECHR 2000-II).

[57] This construction of Art 6 is similar to the Court's decisions on legal aid: while the Court consistently has held that an application for legal aid falls outside the scope of Art 6 (see, eg, *Ivanova v Finland*, judgment of 28 May 2002, No 53054/99), it has also pointed out that availability of legal aid for indigent defendants may be important in assessing the fairness of a proceeding (see *Airey v Ireland*, judgment of 9 Oct 1979, series A No 32) and that the decision on an application for legal aid may not be arbitrary.

[58] Commission decision of 21 May 1997, No 28977/95 *Krone v Austria*.

[59] It is well established that the nature of the right or obligation under domestic law is not decisive: what matters is whether according to general objective principles, in which context the legal systems of the other contracting States must also be taken into consideration, the character of a 'civil right' or 'civil obligation' can be assigned to the right or obligation at issue, taking into account in particular the capacity of the person claiming the right and the conditions in which he exercises or wishes to exercise it. See *König* judgment of 28 June 1978, Series A No 27, 30; *H v Belgium* judgment of 30 Nov 1987, Series A No 127, 33–4.

the enforcement proceedings.[60] In a number of decisions dealing with this aspect of Portuguese law, the Court has held that if the national law of a State makes provision for proceedings consisting of two stages—one when the court rules on the existence of an obligation to pay and another when it fixes the amount owed—it is reasonable to consider that, for purposes of Article 6 paragraph 1, a civil right is not 'determined' until the amount has been decided.[61] The determination of a right entails deciding not only on the existence of that right, but also on its scope or the manner in which it may be exercised.[62]

Another example are severance (partition) proceedings. In some countries the decision as to how a jointly owned property be partitioned is rendered only at the enforcement stage.[63] In these cases it is quite clear that the decision involves a 'determination of a civil right' even if it is rendered at a stage of the proceedings categorized as 'enforcement proceedings' under national law.[64]

Another area where Article 6 may be of importance on the enforcement stage is eviction proceedings. In *Immobiliare Saffi v Italy*,[65] the Court held that as the tenant did not contest termination, the only outstanding point concerned the date of repossession. For so long as that date was put back owing to the tenant's refusal to leave voluntarily, which entailed a *de facto* extension to the lease and a subsequent restriction on the applicant's right of property, there continued to be a dispute for the purposes of Article 6.

While this probably only was intended to justify the application of the time requirement of Article 6 ECHR, a determination of a 'civil right' may occur in eviction proceedings if the court can stay or defer enforcement and, thus, in effect extend the lease.[66]

The *imposition of sanctions* for failure to comply with a court order also raises questions as to whether Article 6 applies to such proceedings. While the kind of action(s) defendant is required to perform or abstain from has

---

[60] Section 661 para 2 Portuguese Code of Civil Procedure. See *Guincho v Portugal*, judgment of 10 July 1984, Series A No 81; *Silva Pontes v Portugal*, judgment of 22 Feb 1994; see also *Martin Moreira v Portugal*, judgment of 26 Oct 1988, Series A no 143, §44. In this case the Court found a violation because already the first stage of proceedings took too long.

[61] *Silva Pontes v Portugal*, judgment of 22 Feb 1994, §30.

[62] ibid, citing *Pudas v Sweden*, judgment of 27 Oct 1987, Series A no 125-A, §31. In *Silva Pontes*, the Court also expressly stated that the dispute (contestation) over the applicant's right to damages would only have been resolved by the final decision in the enforcement proceedings (ibid §33).

[63] See *W v Austria*, No 10757/84, DR 56, 36 (not decided because W lacked standing).

[64] See Commission decision of 21 May 1997, No 28977/95 *Krone v Austria*.

[65] *Immobiliare Saffi v Italy*, judgment of 28 July 1999.

[66] In *Immobiliare Saffi* the delay of the enforcement proceedings was in part (although not exclusively) due to a repeated extension of stays of eviction proceedings by legislative measures, not by court orders.

been determined at the title stage of the proceedings, the question whether defendant actually failed to comply with the decision was not.

One final example may illustrate some of the difficulties the issue of whether or not a determination of a civil right occurs in enforcement proceedings may pose in a civil law system: In some countries the court, by *ex parte* order, levies an attachment on defendant's wages and simultaneously orders the employer to pay the wages to the judgment creditor. It has been suggested that this was already a determination of civil rights and, therefore, the order to the employer should be issued separately only after the attachment order was served upon defendant and he had an opportunity to be heard.[67] Regardless of the possible merits of this view under national law, reliance on Article 6 of the Convention in this context seems misplaced. As pointed out above, the guarantees of this provision do not apply to all decisions having some influence on the civil rights of a person, but require that there is a genuine dispute. In the context of enforcement proceedings, since the possibility of attachment proceedings is a standard way of enforcement authorized by statute, it is hard to envisage in what respect there could be a genuine 'dispute' (contestation) triggering the guarantees of Article 6. Moreover, the Convention does not necessarily require that the defendant is heard ex ante; even if—*arguendo*—we assume that Article 6 applies to this situation at all, the requirements of the Convention could be satisfied if there are remedies ex post enabling the debtor to challenge the attachment.

B. Selected problems

1. Quality of judgment to be enforced

For the purposes of the Convention, there is no (general) requirement that the decision for which enforcement is sought be final. Indeed, in many countries finality of a decision is not traditionally a condition for enforcement.[68] That this position is in line with the Convention was graphically illustrated by a recent decision of the Court finding no violation of the Convention in a case where the opening of bankruptcy proceedings was based on a non-final assessment of taxes which was contested in pending court proceedings.[69]

---

[67] See T Hoeren, NJW (1991) 410; contrary W Kahlke, NJW (1991) 2688, according to whom the right to be heard is not so important in a highly formalized proceeding and the right to be heard *ex post* (*Erinnerung*, §766 ZPO) is sufficient to satisfy the requirements of German constitutional law.

[68] It may be worth noting here that when interpreting the Convention, the Court often takes into account the law of the Contracting States.

[69] *Västberga Taxi Aktiebolag and Vulic v Sweden*, judgment of 23 July 2002, No 36985/97: The Court emphasized, however, that because of the far-reaching consequences of the decision, there was a duty to decide on the tax proceedings quickly.

An interesting case in this context is *Annoni di Gussola et al v France*.[70] There the Court found a violation of Article 6 ECHR in a case where a cassation was (temporarily) struck off the list pursuant to French procedural law upon application of a creditor for the defendant's failure to comply with lower courts' judgments on the theory that the precarious financial situation of the debtor should have created a rebuttable presumption of the existence of 'manifestly unreasonable consequences' militating against striking the cassation. While the French system of temporarily striking cassations had the effect of a stay of cassation proceedings until the lower courts' judgments are fulfilled, the Court in *Annoni di Gussola* only addressed the applicant's difficulty to obtain a review of the lower courts' decisions in the court of cassation. What the Court found objectionable was that the cassation proceedings were stayed until the judgment was fulfilled, thus in effect depriving an indigent debtor of access to the court of cassation. Nothing in the decision, however, suggests that enforcement proceedings were only permissible after all available remedies have been exhausted.

Indeed, this position is also reflected in a Recommendation of the Council of Europe: Principle C 10 of the *Recommendation of the Council of Europe* No R (81) 7 On Measures Facilitating Access to Justice, provides:

So that the right of appeal should not be exercised improperly or in order to delay proceedings, particular attention should be given to the possibility of *provisional execution*[71] of court decisions which might lead to an appeal and to the rate of interest on the judgment sum pending execution. (Emphasis added.)

It should be noted, however, that in some countries *domestic constitutional law* may require that a judgment is final or that some balancing of interests takes place before a non-final judgment is enforced.[72]

2. Ex parte *Application*

In countries which require judicial authorization for enforcement measures, the application for instituting enforcement proceedings is often granted ex parte. Since the institution of enforcement proceedings as such does not

---

[70] *Annoni di Gussola et al v France*, judgment of 14 Nov 2000.

[71] Emphasis added.

[72] See, eg, Austrian Constitutional Court VfSlg 12.863. In this decision the Constitutional Court found the statutory provisions authorizing preliminary enforcement of awards to employees in labour law cases unconstitutional. Likewise the unconditional enforcement of non-final tax assessments was held to be unconstitutional on the ground that the burden of the consequences of a possibly wrong decision must not be placed on one party (VfSlg 11.196). On the other hand, the immediate enforceability of decisions as to the costs of enforcement proceedings without requirement of finality or even (prior) service upon defendant was held to be unobjectionable under the Austrian Constitution (Austrian Constitutional Court VfSlg 15.105 [1998]).

involve a (final) determination of civil rights and obligations, this seems to be in accordance with Article 6. Also, it has to be pointed out that the debtor was already heard in the previous proceeding from which the judgment sought to be enforced emanated. Thus, the opportunity for a debtor to raise his arguments *ex post* by appeal or by separate action is unobjectionable.[73] Of course, domestic law may go beyond the minimum requirements of Article 6 and provide for a right of debtor to be heard before execution proceedings are authorized.[74]

3. Requirement of court decision before enforcement?

Generally enforcement proceedings do not entail a decision on civil rights or obligations. This is certainly true from the perspective of the debtor. If all relevant aspects have been determined at the title stage of the proceedings, no additional judicial protection is necessary. Also, enforcement proceedings ordinarily do not entail a decision as to the judgment creditor's rights. While the enforcement of a judgment is protected, at least to some extent, under Article 6, this, applies only to enforcement per se (the right of access to the court would be meaningless if there were no way of enforcing the judgment), but not to any particular enforcement measure as such.

4. Remedies

Since the institution of enforcement proceedings does not ordinarily involve a determination of civil rights, it is unobjectionable under the Convention if an order authorizing or denying enforcement proceedings can be challenged by way of an ex parte appeal as provided for in some countries.[75] Thus, recently, the Austrian Supreme Court has held that appeals in enforcement matters are not covered by Article 6 ECHR and therefore there is no right of the creditor to file an answer to an appeal filed by debtor against a court decision ordering certain enforcement measures to be taken.

Often, however, civil law enforcement proceedings can be challenged by way of *collateral attack* by instituting separate lawsuits. Such proceedings

---

[73] This is also true, for example, under domestic constitutional law of Germany. See German Constitutional Court BVerfGE 9, 98, 102; 51, 97, 111; 57, 346, 358.

[74] This is primarily the case where surprise is not an issue. Thus, for example, under Austrian law a defendant may be heard before enforcement of a judgment ordering specific performance or providing for other injunctive relief.

[75] See also *Pérez de Rada Cavanilles v Spain*, judgment 28 Oct 1998, reports 1998-VIII. Here the Court found a violation of Art 6 because an appeal *(reposición)* of the creditor against a decision setting aside the title (settlement) had to be received by court within three days. It should be noted, however, that this decision did not concern the authorization (or denial) of enforcement proceedings per se, but the remedies against a decision setting aside the title which was the basis for the enforcement proceeding.

opposing enforcement proceedings on *substantive* grounds concern civil rights in the sense of Article 6. Therefore Article 6 applies to these kind of proceedings.

5. Collateral attack of the judgment

While this is beyond the scope of this article, it should be noted that the extension of the guarantees under Article 6 to the enforcement of a judgment may also affect collateral attacks on the judgment sought to be enforced by the creditor. Under civil law, enforcement proceedings can not only be challenged by an appeal or similar remedy against the order authorizing execution, but also by instituting a separate lawsuit challenging either the enforcement order or the underlying judgment.[76] If such a challenge is based on substantive grounds,[77] it would seem that Article 6 applies. Thus, the Commission[78] has held Article 6 to apply to an action for discontinuation of the enforcement proceedings (Impugnationsklage) in which it was argued that the applicant, as a consequence of several measures of corporate restructuring, was not bound by the injunction issued. On the other hand, purely *procedural* challenges to enforcement proceedings do not trigger the guarantees of Article 6.

Whereas in previous decisions the Commission has consistently held that Article 6 does not apply to collateral post-judgment remedies such as applications for re-opening proceedings etc,[79] recent case law considering *res judicata* to be protected by the Convention[80] may require to afford the guarantees under Article 6 ECHR to the judgment creditor if such a remedy is brought by the debtor (but not *vice versa*)![81] This result was already—albeit somewhat intuitively—reached by the Court in an earlier case where it afforded the creditor the protection of Article 6 in a proceeding in which the debtor sought to have the settlement, which was the basis for the execution, set aside.[82]

---

[76] Possible examples of such separate lawsuits include defendant's assertion that payment had already been made, that a change of circumstances has occurred which justifies a reappraisal of a maintenance award or a third party's claim of ownership.

[77] As in other contexts, the term 'substantive grounds' does not necessarily correlate to what national law qualifies as 'substantive', but has to be interpreted separately.

[78] Commission decision of 21 May 1997, *Krone v Austria*, No 28977/95.

[79] See the European Commission decisions of 5 Apr 1974, no 5495/72, CD 45, 57; 8 May 1978, no 7761/77, DR 14, 173; and 7 Dec 1982, no 9578/81, DR 31, 217.

[80] *Rybakykh v Russia*, judgment of 24 July 2003, §§51, 52.

[81] Since in *Rybakykh v Russia*, judgment 24 July 2003, §59, the Court already found an infringement of the applicant's right to a court by the very use of the supervisory-review procedure, it considered it unnecessary to consider whether the procedural guarantees of Art 6 of the Convention were available in those proceedings.

[82] *Pérez de Rada Cavanilles v Spain*, judgment 28 Oct 1998, reports 1998-VIII.

In *Stran Greek Refineries*,[83] the Court has held that the outcome of proceedings brought in the ordinary courts to have an *arbitration award* set aside is decisive for civil rights and so within the scope of Article 6 paragraph 1. This decision, however, did not arise in the context of *exequatur* or enforcement proceedings *per se*, but on the occasion of a challenge of an arbitral award brought by the debtor. This decision, therefore, does not imply that before authorizing execution of a judgment, a court has always to comply with the requirements of Article 6. Apart from involving a challenge of an arbitral award (which may well be treated differently from decisions emanating from ordinary courts), *Stran Greek Refineries* only addressed the guarantees to be provided *if* the debtor challenged an award. Thus, even if this decision would apply to challenges of judgments of ordinary courts (which in my opinion is by no means clear since the Convention does not grant a right to appeal), it would only require that a proceeding in line with Article 6 is available to the debtor; the mere abstract possibility that a debtor might wish to challenge an award, however, does not bring about the need to provide an occasion to do so before enforcement of a judgment is authorized. If, however, the procedural system of a State allows a debtor to bring such a challenge, the *creditor's* right to defend the judgment is protected under Article 6.

6. Reasonable time requirement

It is already well established that the reasonable time requirement of Article 6 also includes enforcement proceedings. Most of the cases decided by the Court concerned eviction proceedings,[84] but in some cases the Court had occasion to deal with the enforcement of monetary judgments.[85]

Under the Court's case law Article 6 paragraph 1 imposes on the States the duty to organize their judicial system in such a way that their courts can meet each of its requirements, including the obligation to hear cases within a reasonable time.[86] In a number of decisions, the Court has applied this principle to enforcement proceedings.[87] While the Court has noted that a

---

[83] *Stran Greek Refineries and Stratis Andreadis v Greece*, judgment of 9 Dec 1994, Series A, No 301-B.

[84] See, eg, *Palumbo v Italy*, judgment of 30 Nov 2002 (eviction proceedings); *Cvijetic v Croatia*, judgment of 26 Feb 2004 (eviction proceedings lasting from 1994 to 2002, enforcement proceedings delayed, inter alia, by demonstrations of war veterans).

[85] *Zappia v Italy*, judgment of 29 Aug 1996, Reports 1996-IV, 1410–11, §§16–20 (enforcement proceedings concerning a judgment debt of 5 million ITL lasting from 1969 to 1993); *Di Pede v Italy*, judgment of 26 Sept 1996, Reports 1996-IV, 1383—4, §§20–4; *Comingersoll SA v Portugal*, judgment of 6 Apr 2000 (enforcement proceedings on bills of exchange lasting 12 years).

[86] See, eg, *Kyrtatos v Greece*, judgment of 22 May 2003, §42.

[87] *Cvijetic v Croatia*, judgment of 26 Feb 2004, §41.

delay in the execution of a judgment may be justified in particular circumstances, the delay may not be such as to impair the essence of the right protected under Article 6 paragraph 1.[88] The time of enforcement proceedings has to be added to the title stage of the proceedings. The relevant time period starts from the application to institute enforcement proceedings.[89] The cases decided by the Court involved extreme delays of several years which in effect made the judicial protection provided in the title stage of the proceedings meaningless.[90] Hence the decisions provide little guidance as to the exact requirements of the Convention in this respect. The criteria for the 'reasonableness' of the duration of proceedings probably are the same as for the 'title stage' of the proceedings. Thus, the urgency of the case, its complexity and the conduct of the applicant and the conduct of the authorities have to be taken into account.[91] In one decision the Court suggested that enforcement of a claim based on bills of exchange by their very nature need to be 'dealt with expeditiously'.[92] On the other hand, if the duration of enforcement proceedings is due to the debtor's lack of means, this is not attributable to the State.[93]

While the Court recognizes that in exceptional cases States may intervene in proceedings for the enforcement of a judicial decision, for example by availing themselves of their margin of appreciation to control the use of property, the consequence of such intervention should not be that execution is prevented, invalidated or unduly delayed or, still less, that the substance of the decision is undermined, Thus, the Court criticized Italian law which repeatedly extended stays of execution in eviction proceedings.[94] On the other hand, a relatively short stay of eviction proceedings for social reasons normally would be unobjectionable.[95] However, the result would probably have to be different if the creditor seeks eviction of a flat he urgently needs for his own use.

---

[88] *Immobiliare Saffi v Italy*, judgment of 28 July 1999, §74, ECHR 1999-V; *Burdov v Russia*, judgment of 18 Apr 2002, §35.

[89] See, eg, *Martins Moreira v Portugal*, judgment of 7 Oct 1988, §44.

[90] In *Martins Moreira v Portugal*, judgment of 7 Oct 1988, defendant was bankrupt when the enforcement proceedings were over. Already the first stage of proceedings had lasted more than eight years. In *Immobiliare Saffi v Italy*, judgment of 28 July 1999, a creditor, in spite of pursuing his claim vigorously for more than 11 years, could obtain possession of his apartment only after defendant had died.

[91] See, eg, *Moreira v Portugal*, judgment of 7 Oct 1988, §§47

[92] *Comingersoll SA v Portugal*, judgment of 6 Apr 2000.

[93] This was expressed by the Court in several decisions as to Art 1 protocol No 1 (see, eg, *Gasus Dosier- und Fördertechnik GmbH v The Netherlands*, judgment of 23 Feb 1995, A306-B, §65 *in fine*), but equally applies to the reasonable time requirement.

[94] See, eg, *Immobiliare Safi v Italy*, judgment of 28 July 1999; *Palumbo v Italy*, judgment of 30 Nov 2000.

[95] The Court recognizes that States have a wide margin of appreciation in this respect. See 2.1(a).

7. *Extra-judicial enforcement proceedings*

There is no case directly addressing the issue whether and to what extent extra judicial enforcement proceedings are compatible with the Convention. In *Annoni di Gussola et al v France*[96] the Court expressed reservations against a 'privatization' of justice. However, this decision did not deal with enforcement proceedings[97] but with the striking of a cassation, on motion of the defendant in cassation, on the ground that the judgment of the lower court was not complied with. What aroused the Court's criticism was that a measure in the public interest such as the temporary striking of a cassation, was conditioned upon a motion by the applicant's opponent. This decision, therefore, is clearly limited to the facts of the case before the Court and provides little guidance for the permissibility, under the Convention, of extra-judicial enforcement proceedings.

Since Article 6 only applies to final determinations of dispute, thus requiring the existence of an actual dispute, no prior judicial authorization is necessary for enforcement proceedings. Thus it seems that extra judicial enforcement proceedings are in line with Article 6 as long as the right of access to a court under art 6 ECHR is not violated. This is also true for enforcement proceedings entrusted to private professionals like the *huissier* in Latin countries and the Scottish *sheriff's officer*. If, however, a debtor contests his obligation (and there has not already been a judicial decision in a prior proceeding), there has to be court proceeding available to decide on the parties' 'civil rights and obligations'.

It is likely, however, that the Court will view the activity of private individuals acting without prior court authorization with more scrutiny in light of Article 8 compared to searches and seizures performed in the exercise of a valid court order[98] Furthermore, often *domestic constitutional law* will place limits to the exercise of what are essentially governmental functions by private individuals.[99] Indeed it can well be argued, from a domestic civil law point of view, that the enforcement of court decisions belongs to the core of State functions and cannot be left to private individuals.[100]

---

[96] *Annoni di Gussola v France*, judgment of 14 Nov 2000.

[97] Although the case also involved a private sale of car in the course of 'enforcing' a debt, this issue was not reached by the court.

[98] For criticism of extra judicial seizure by customs officers in connection with a criminal proceeding see *Crémieux v France*, judgment of 25 Feb 1993, A256-B, §40, and *Funke v France*, judgment of 25 Feb 1993, A256–A § 57. For another decision concerning a search by customs officials, see *Miailhe v France*, judgment of 26 Sept 1996, Reports 1996-IV. See also 2.2(b).

[99] See, eg, Austrian Constitutional Court VfSlg 14.473 concerning the constitutional limits, under Austrian law, of the privatization of air traffic control and entrusting it to a limited liability company (Austro-Control').

[100] This consideration will only prevent a full privatization of enforcement proceedings in many countries. It does not affect, however, the organization of enforcement organs and their remuneration as long as there is sufficient control over them by public authorities.

8. Police assistance and other Assistance from the State

In a number of decisions the Court has made it clear that national authorities have to provide the means necessary for execution of a judgment. Such measures also include police assistance if the debtor seeks to resist enforcement.[101] This position was adopted in a long line of cases against Italy[102] and affirmed recently in a decision against Croatia.[103] The decision concerned a spectacular case where eviction proceedings were hindered by war veterans. In this decision, the Court also pointed out that where health problems of the debtor may result in a postponement of eviction, the creditor has to have access to an official physician to verify defendant's assertion of ill health.

Special problems are posed by child abduction cases and, generally, in case of enforcement of custody rights and rights of access. In several decisions the Court has held that the national authorities have to take all the necessary steps to facilitate execution.[104] Necessary measures may include the advice of social services, assistance of psychologists or child psychiatrists.[105]Also, while under national law it may be the responsibility of the creditor to indicate to the authorities where enforcement should take place, in these cases the public authorities have to attempt to locate the child, at least to some extent, ex officio.[106]

9. Procedural rights of debtor in enforcement proceedings

The procedural rights of a debtor in enforcement proceedings have so far received surprisingly little attention. While it seems well established that the full guarantees of Article 6 apply if a debtor challenges the enforcement of a judgment on substantive grounds by way of initiating a separate independent lawsuit,[107] the extent to which Article 6 applies to the actual enforcement proceeding itself is unclear. One of the few cases that dealt

---

[101] See, eg, *Immobiliare Saffi v Italy*, judgment of 28 July 1999 (eviction proceedings lasting 11 years until death of defendant); *Palumbo v Italy*, judgment of 30 Nov 2000. In these decisions, the Court also criticized that there was no judicial review available as to the prefect's refusal to grant police assistance (ibid §45).

[102] See, eg, *Immobiliare Saffi v Italy*, judgment of 28 July 1999; *Palumbo v Italy*, judgment of 30 Nov 2000.

[103] *Cvijetic v Croatia*, judgment of 26 Feb 2004 (eviction proceedings lasting from 1994 to 2002).

[104] See, eg, *Ignaccolo Zenide v Romania*, judgment of 25 Jan 2000, Reports 2000-I; *Sophia Gudrun Hansen v Turkey*, judgment of 23 Sept 2003 (_15,000 non-pecuniary damages awarded); *Sylvester v Austria*, judgment of 3 Apr 2003.

[105] See the *Ignaccolo Zenide* and *Sophia Gudrun Hansen* judgments cited above.

[106] Here the procedural guarantees provided by Art 6 and the substantive guarantees under Art 8 overlap to a certain extent. See also 2.1(b).

[107] See 3.2 (e).

with other aspects of Article 6 than the reasonable time requirement in enforcement proceedings is *Walston (No 1) v Norway*.[108]There, the Court found a violation of Art 6 ECHR, because the Norwegian court failed to forward a copy of the creditor's 'observation' to defendants in an enforcement proceeding.[109] However, the thrust of the applicant's argument before the domestic courts was placed on challenging the judge's ability to decide the case on grounds of his former employment with the creditor, and thus a purely procedural issue. While the Court held that the fact that the applicant may have been unable to comment on some documents objections to the judge did not constitute a violation of the Convention, the application was successful insofar as the applicant could not comment on a written observation of the creditor. It is not entirely clear from the decision, however, whether (and to what extent) at this stage of the proceedings substantive 'civil' rights were at stake. The implications of this decision on enforcement proceedings as such thus remains somewhat doubtful. In light of the ex parte character of the application for authorization of enforcement proceedings in many countries and the importance of surprise in some cases it may be worth noting that nothing in the decision suggests that a debtor may have a right of access to the court file or to obtain a copy of the court file under the Convention already at the very beginning of the proceeding. Rather, *Walston* apparently dealt with the final decision on whether or not the applicant's real estate should be sold in enforcement proceedings.

10. Forced sale

While public auction brings about a change in ownership and therefore arguably involves a decision about civil rights, Article 6 applies only if there is an actual *dispute* (*contestation*). Thus, if the conditions for a forced sale are stated sufficiently clearly in the law, from a perspective of the Convention there is normally no need for a judicial decision. Also, two decisions of the Commission concerning bankruptcy proceedings suggest that the *distribution of proceeds of a forced sale* does not entail a decision about civil rights[110].

11. Fines and imprisonment

In many countries the court can impose *sanctions* for failure to comply with

---

[108] *Walston (No 1) v Norway*, judgment of 13 May 2003. See also *Vermeulen v Belgium*, judgment of 22 Jan 1996, No 58/1994/505/587, concerning comments by the public prosecutor in bankruptcy proceedings.
[109] The creditor had applied for a compulsory sale of the applicant's property.
[110] Commission decisions DR 6, 107 and DR 24, 198.

a judgment, which is of particular importance in all cases where injunctive relief is granted. While the kind of action(s) defendant is required to perform or abstain from normally has been determined at the title stage of the proceedings, the question whether the defendant actually failed to comply with the decision, was not. Thus it might seem that Article 6 applies to the determination of this aspect.

However, the traditional view is that fines imposed in order to secure compliance with a civil court decision do not constitute 'criminal' sanctions under art 6 ECHR.[111]Detention for 'non-compliance with the lawful order of a court or in order to secure the fulfilment of an obligation prescribed by law' (Art 5 para 1 b ECHR) is distinct from 'lawful detention after conviction by a competent court' (Art 5 para 1 a ECHR). Thus, the guarantees provided by Article 6 for criminal proceedings do not apply to the imposition of sanctions for failure to comply with a court order. In at least one decision, the Commission has held that detention ordered by an enforcement court for non-compliance with an injunction issued in unfair competition proceedings after the unsuccessful imposition of fines falls to be considered under Article 5(1)(b) ECHR.[112] It should be pointed out, however, that according to the case law of the Court,[113] for a sanction to qualify as 'criminal' in the sense of Article 6 three elements need to be taken into account: Whether the sanction belongs to criminal law under domestic law, the nature of the offence and the severity of sanction risked. Thus, while the classification of the sanction under national law and the nature of the offence do not pose any difficulty, in light of the severity of the sanctions available in many countries, the continuing validity of the decisions denying the 'criminal' nature of sanctions in this context seems questionable.

Even if one adheres to the traditional view that the special guarantees provided for 'criminal' proceedings do not apply to sanctions imposed for failure to comply with a court decision, the guarantees of Article 6 may apply under the 'civil limb' of this provision. While not expressly addressing the question, the decisions of the Commission discussed above seem to suggest that the imposition of sanctions in order to compel a debtor to comply with a judgment does not qualify as a determination of civil rights and obligations in the sense of Article 6, but apparently should be regarded a measure belonging to public law instead. Thus, the guarantees of the Convention would only come into play if the court imposes imprisonment (in which case Article 5 paragraph 1 b applies), whereas the imposition of

---

[111] See Commission decision of 21 May 1997, *Krone Verlag v Austria*, No 28977/95. For a discussion of contempt of court proceedings, *The Times* judgment of 26 Apr 1979, Series A no. 30, §47.
[112] Commission No 12827/87, unpublished.
[113] See, eg, *Schmautzer v Austria* (1995).

fines would fall outside Articles 5 and 6. This may well be different, however, if the fine imposed has to be paid not to the State, but to the *creditor*, like under the French system of *astreinte*. In this case it can well be argued that the decision is a determination of civil rights and obligations and, hence, Article 6 should apply.

However, even in a traditional system where the fine has to be paid to the State, it can be argued that Article 6 should apply to the imposition of sanctions for failure to comply with a court order if some aspects have not yet been determined at the trial stage of the proceedings.[114] This concerns, mainly, the question whether there has in fact been a violation *after* the judgment had been entered. Therefore, if the issue is whether there actually has been a violation, this has to be resolved in a proceeding complying with the guarantees of Article 6. However, such a determination is arguably only necessary if the defendant contests that he violated the judgment. Thus, especially when—as in the case of fines—only pecuniary interests are at stake, it is probably compatible with the Convention to impose sanctions on the mere basis of allegations of the creditor in an ex parte proceeding, provided the defendant has access to a court proceeding where the question whether he in fact violated the judgment could be examined in full in case he wants to contest this issue.

It should be noted, however, that even if the guarantees of Article 6 were to apply to the imposition of sanctions for failure to obey a court order—as a matter of domestic law—the stricter rules of evidence and standard of proof normally required in criminal proceedings do not apply to these kind of proceedings. Thus, the German Constitutional Court has held that prima facie evidence may be sufficient under German constitutional law.[115]

12. Costs of proceedings

Enforcement proceedings often entail a decision awarding costs to the creditor. While the determination of the cost of proceedings was generally held by the Commission not to involve the civil rights of the individual,[116] this

---

[114] See, P Oberhammer, 'Verfassungsgesetzliche Schranken der Haft im zivilrechtlichen Erkenntnis-, Exekutions- und Insolvenzverfahren', Österreichische Juristenzeitung 1994, 265 (266)]; W Rechberger & P Oberhammer, `Die Anforderungen der EMRK an ein 'fair trial' und das österreichische Zwangsvollstreckungsverfahren' (1996) *Dike International* 287 (289 f).

[115] BVerfGE 84, 82, 87.

[116] See particularly Decision of 25 May 1995, No 21775/93, *Aires v Portugal*, 81 DR 48, where the Commission found the question of costs was a subsidiary issue to the main civil proceedings and did not concern civil rights and obligations. This view is similar to the accepted interpretation of the European Regulation of Jurisdiction and Recognition of Judgments according to which the requirement that the document instituting the procedure is served on the defendant does not apply to 'ancillary proceedings' (see J Kropholler, *Europäisches Zivilprozeßrecht* (7th edn Art 34 No 26, specifically mentioning, *inter alia*, deci-

view was overruled by the Court in *Robins v United Kingdom*.[117] It now appears established that, where the substantive proceedings involve civil rights and obligations, the costs proceedings, even if separately decided, must be seen as a continuation of the substantive litigation and fall within the scope of Article 6, paragraph 1.[118] In *Robins*, the Court applied the reasonable time requirement and held that four years taken in the costs proceedings disclosed a violation of Article 6, paragraph 1. More recently, the Court has applied the principle of 'equality of arms' to decisions on costs. Thus, in *Beer v Austria*,[119] the Court found a violation of Article 6 in a case where an award of costs was reduced on an ex parte appeal in which the other side was not afforded an opportunity to be heard. The Court now apparently takes the position that costs awarded to a successful litigant constitute 'civil rights' under Article 6. On the other hand, in *Stockholm Försäkrings-Och Skadestansjuridik AB v Sweden*,[120] the Court held that a decision on costs was not subject to the guarantees of Article 6 ECHR if no 'controversy' was possible because the obligation to pay costs was determined unequivocally by statute. Since, however, in many countries the costs of proceedings, even if regulated by a statute, require some determination not only as to quantum, but also as to the necessity or reasonableness of the underlying procedural steps for which an award of costs is sought, it seems that Article 6 applies to these kind of proceedings. However, considering the limited or technical nature of the issue arising in costs proceedings, it is doubtful that the guarantees of Article 6 will apply with full vigour, for example, as regards the requirement for public hearings or the public tender of the decision.[121]

13. Preliminary measures

It is well-established case law that preliminary measures fall outside the scope of Article 6 which applies only to final determinations of civil rights and liabilities.[122] However, a different result may be reached in exceptional

---

sions on costs). See also K Reid *A Practitioner's Guide to the European Convention on Human Rights* (1998) 76 (citing further authority).

[117] *Robins v United Kingdom*, judgment of 23 Sept 1997, ECHR Reports 1997-V.

[118] K Reid *A Practitioner's Guide to the European Convention on Human Rights* 76.

[119] *Beer v Austria*, judgment 6 Feb 2001.

[120] *Stockholm Försäkrings-Och Skadestansjuridik AB v Sweden*, judgment of 16 Sept 2003, No 38993/97. The case concerned the debtor's liability, under Swedish law, for the costs of bankruptcy proceedings even if the opening of proceedings was later declared unlawful on appeal.

[121] K Reid *A Practitioner's Guide to the European Convention on Human Rights* (1998) 76.

[122] Commission decision DR 24, 60; Commission decision of 12 Jan 1994, *FMZ Gesellschaft m.b.H. v Austria*, no 18,411/91.

cases depending on the kind of measure and the time it is (intended to be) in force.

14. Exequatur *proceedings*

While the Swiss Supreme Court (*Bundesgericht*) has already held more than 25 years ago that proceedings for obtaining a declaration of enforceability of a foreign decision fall under Article 6 ECHR,[123] the prevailing view seems to be to the contrary. This view is supported by a decision of the Commission[124] refusing to apply Article 6 to the enforcement of a sanction imposed by a foreign court on the ground that 'determination involves the full process of the examination of an individual's guilt or innocence of an offence, and not the mere process of determining whether a person can be extradited to another country'.[125] *Mutatis mutandis*, this reasoning also seems to apply to proceedings deciding on the recognition and enforcement of foreign civil judgments.

Some recent decisions of the Court, however, tend to support the view that closer scrutiny may be required in *exequatur* proceedings if the decision to be enforced emanates from the courts of a country which does not apply the Convention. In *Pellegrini v Italy,*[126] the Court had to decide on a recognition of an annulment of a marriage by the ecclesiastic courts of the Vatican. The Court noted at the outset that the Court's task was

> not to examine whether the proceedings before the ecclesiastical courts complied with Article 6, but whether the Italian Courts, before authorising enforcement of the decision annulling the marriage, duly satisfied themselves that the relevant proceedings fulfilled the guarantees of Article 6. A review of that kind is required where a decision in respect of which enforcement is requested emanates from the courts of a country which does not apply the Convention.

Conversely, if the judgment was rendered in a country respecting the requirements of the Convention, such scrutiny appears not to be required

---

[123] SJIR 34 [1978], 208.

[124] CD 13, 69.

[125] See P van Dijk and G J H van Hoof, T*heory and Practice of the European Convention on Human Rights* (1998) 408.

[126] *Pellegrini v Italy*, judgment of 20 July 2001, Reports 2001-VIII, §40, no 30882/96. See also *Drozd and Janousek v France and Spain*, judgment of 26 June 1992, series A no 240, no 12747/87, concerning enforcement of a decision in a criminal proceeding which emanated from Andorra where the Convention is not applied. In *M & Co v Germany*, decision of 9 Feb 1990, 13258/87, the Commission had to deal with a fine imposed by the European Commission. The Commission noted that the legal system of the European Communities not only secured fundamental rights, but also provided for control of their observance, which justified a lesser degree of scrutiny on part of the Member States before issuing a writ of execution for a judgment of the European Court of Human Rights.

under the Convention.[127] It should be noted, however, that this concerns the *intensity of review* of the decision of which recognition is sought rather than the *procedural guarantees* to be afforded in *exequatur* proceedings themselves.

On the other hand, the Court has held that the outcome of proceedings brought in the ordinary courts to have an *arbitration award* set aside is decisive for civil rights and so within the scope of Article 6 paragraph 1.[128] This decision, however, did not arise in the context of *exequatur* or enforcement proceedings per se, but on the occasion of a challenge of an arbitral award brought by the debtor.

15. Bankruptcy

While earlier decisions have taken the view that bankruptcy proceedings fall completely outside Article 6,[129] more recently the Court and the Commission have taken the position that the procedure leading to *the opening of bankruptcy* falls under Article 6 ECHR since the opening of bankruptcy proceedings involves civil rights of the debtor (but not of the creditor)![130]

Although the remainder of the proceedings normally is not concerned with a determination of civil rights and obligations (possible exceptions include composition proceedings), the Court has occasionally found a violation of the time requirement of Article 6.[131] The better view would probably be to focus on the underlying substantive rights affected by the pending bankruptcy proceeding.

16. Compensation

As in the case of other rights protected by the Convention, a violation of

---

[127] This aspect is important in the context of the Regulation on the European Enforcement Order which was adopted on 21 April 2004, which provides for ipso facto recognition and enforcement for all decisions in uncontested cases. In light of the case law cited above, the abolishment of *exequatur* proceedings in this context is not objectionable since all Member States of the European Union have adopted the Convention, which indeed is also incorporated in Art 6 para 2 of the European Constitution. See F Stein 'Der Europäische Vollstreckungstitel für unbestrittene Forderungen' (2004) IPRax 181, 186

[128] *Stran Greek Refineries and Stratis Andreadis v Greece*, Judgment of 9 Dec 1994, Series A, No 301-B.

[129] See, eg, Commission decision *X v Belgium*, DR 24, 198 (2002), noting that the function of bankruptcy proceedings 'was not to settle a dispute, but to provide a safeguard in the interests of the existing or potential creditors'.

[130] A discussion of the influence of the ECHR on bankruptcy proceedings is beyond the scope of this chapter. See G Kodek 'Gehörprobleme im Konkurs' in A Konecny (ed) Insolvenzforum (2003).

[131] See, eg, *Ceteroni v Italy*, judgment of 21 Oct 1996.

Article 6 paragraph 1 gives rise to a claim for *compensation* pursuant to Article 50.[132] This includes not only the costs incurred, but also pecuniary and non-pecuniary damages. The question of whether this compensation may also include non-pecuniary damages (for example as a result of anxiety) if the victim was a legal person, which had been left open by former decisions,[133] was recently answered in the affirmative.[134] While in many decisions the Court considered a finding of a violation in itself would constitute sufficient just satisfaction, particularly in case of a failure of adequate enforcement of rights of access and custody rights, the amounts awarded by the Court often are quite significant.[135]

IV. CONCLUSION

From a perspective of the creditor, the right to enforce a decision is protected by Article 1 of Protocol No. 1 and, in some cases, also by Article 8. The debtor, on the other hand, is generally not protected from enforcement of judgment rendered against him by Article 1 of Protocol No 1. However, in some cases Article 8 may afford some protection, particularly against overly intrusive searches and seizures without judicial authorization.

As to procedural guarantees, ordinarily enforcement proceedings following a civil court judgment do not come within the scope of Article 6. They do not themselves constitute a determination of a dispute relating to civil rights, but presuppose a prior determination of these rights by an independent court. Article 6, however, applies as to the duration of enforcement proceedings. In addition, enforcement proceedings are arguably subject to general 'fairness' requirement under Article 6. A full applicability of Article 6 is warranted if the enforcement proceedings also entail a determination of

---

[132] Art 50 provides: 'If the Court finds that a decision or measure taken by a legal authority or any other authority of a High Contracting Party is completely or partially in conflict with the obligations arising from … the Convention, and if the internal law of the said Party allows only partial reparation to be made for the consequences of this decision or measure, the decision of the Court shall, if necessary, afford just satisfaction for the injured party.'

[133] *Immobbiliare Saffi* v *Italy*, judgment of 28 July 1999, §79, ECHR 1999-V.

[134] *Comingersoll v Portugal*, judgment of 6 Apr 2000, §32.

[135] See, eg, *Sophia Gudrun Hansen v Turkey*, judgment of 23 Sept 2003 (€50,000 pecuniary damages and €15,000 non pecuniary damages); *Sylvester v Austria*, judgment of 3 Apr 2003 (€20,000 non-pecuniary damages). For an award in other cases see, eg, *Comingersoll v Portugal*, judgment of 6 Apr 2000 (PTE 1,500,000); *Walston (No 1) v Norway*, judgment of 13 May 2003 (€8,000 in non-pecuniary damage); see also the judgments of the Court concerning eviction proceedings, eg *Zappia v Italy*, judgment of 29 August 1996 (24 million ITL); *Immobiliare Saffi v Italy*, judgment of 28 July 1999 (28 million ITL); *Palumbo v Italy*, judgment of 30 Nov 2000 (30 million ITL); *Cvijetic v Croatia*, judgment of 26 Feb 2004 ((€5,000 in respect of pecuniary damage and another €5,000 in respect of non-pecuniary damage).

civil rights. Examples include the determination of quantum in an action for damages or how to partition property held jointly by the litigants. In proceedings involving the imposition of sanctions for failure to comply with a court decision, Article 6 is likely to apply if the fine imposed—like under the French system of *astreinte*—has to be paid to the creditor. Even if this is not the case, arguably the question of whether in fact a violation took place also has to be determined in a proceeding compatible with Article 6.

CHAPTER 18

THE IMPACT OF THE EUROPEAN CONVENTION ON ENFORCEMENT PRACTICES IN ENGLAND AND WALES[1]

John Kruse[2]

Besides my own personal interest, bailiffs' law within England and Wales is an appropriate topic in the sense that this it has been the particular focus of attention of the Lord Chancellor's Department (now the Department for Constitutional Affairs) in England for approximately the last 10 years. One may think that having heard the analogy of the jigsaw puzzle from Georg Kodek, that the jigsaw puzzle has been thrown up in the air and then the pieces kicked around the floor quite liberally when one examines the current state of enforcement law in England and Wales.

But this chapter is going to look at remedies specifically, and in particular the remedy of seizure of goods. One can say that there are obviously two levels at which we can examine the impact of the European Convention on Human Rights Convention within England and Wales. One level of study is the specific forms of enforcement to recover a judgment or an order or whatever it may be. Secondly, we may rise up from that and look at the broader structure within which those different remedies are operating. And to pre-empt one's conclusions, it is likely that on that second point that England and Wales will be found wanting.

In the first area, there are fewer problems. Given the international nature of this discussion, it might be appropriate to introduce the reader to the various terms used in England and Wales on this subject.

There is an important distinction within English law between the extra-judicial use of seizure of goods, which is typically called distraint or distress, and execution, the seizure of goods to enforce a civil court judgment. In

[1] This chapter based in part on proceedings from the final meeting for this project held at the British Institute of International and Comparative Law in London on 23 April 2004 and entitled *Enforcement Agency Practice in Europe: Cooperation or Harmonization?*
[2] Civil Enforcement Consultant, United Kingdom.

many details they are the same process and there is not much to choose between them, but clearly the presence or absence of a judgment by a court is a very significant difference. Much of the recent discussion centres on the activities of county court bailiffs and high court enforcement officers enforcing civil court judgments, but there is a considerable area of enforcement which does not go through the civil courts within England and Wales which probably accounts, in terms of volume and the amount of debt being recovered, for the very largest proportion of enforcement in this country. That is obviously a major concern when looking at the system from the point of view of the Convention and particularly from the point of view of Article 6. This is the first problem to identify. Secondly, much has been said about the privatization of enforcement. We are well advanced in that area in England and Wales because we divide enforcement between the public sector and the private sector, though without any clear separation between the enforcement of judgments and the enforcement of other debts. So, there may be bailiffs employed by the public sector (for example by the county court or by the tax authorities recovering income taxes) but again the substantial part of the debt is recovered by private sector bailiffs. We have talked about reform of the High Court in England and Wales: the High Court bailiff (the Sheriff's Officer as was) is a private bailiff. Then there are a range of other private sector bailiffs operating in this country, many of them holding a certificate permitting them to practice from a county court, a process to which I shall return. You can see the complexity of our situation already, in the sense that some bailiffs are operating in the court system, some outside, some in the private sector, and some in the public sector, there being no clear division between those areas.

Just to build on a few points, there was some discussion from Dr Hess about status and qualifications, and a remark, I believe, that German bailiffs were not highly qualified. You will see later that we could not, with the best will in the world, say that English bailiffs are highly qualified. You may say that most English bailiffs have no qualifications whatsoever and you would be correct.

Is there a need for qualifications? Indisputably there is, but we are starting from such a very low level that clearly it is going to take England and Wales a very long time to come up to the aspiration of degrees for all enforcement officers. When you see the complexity of the law with which we are dealing, you would think that everybody confronted with English enforcement law should have a degree. Another point that was raised by Burkhard Hess concerns the desirability of neutral and independent judicial officers. Many of our officers are not judicial and I think it is fair to say that that neutrality and independence is often wanting as well. The preferred term now is enforcement agent and obviously many of the private sector bailiffs are acting as agents for the creditor. It is fair to say that there has been an over-identification of interest between the bailiff and the creditor for a very long time in this country and that private bailiffs in particular do not consider themselves as being impartial between creditor and debtor in the same way as a county court bailiff or a high court enforcement officer would. They see themselves as solely representing the creditor for whom they are acting. You might say, if you were cynical, that they see themselves solely representing their employer with a desire to extract the maximum amount of fee income out of the hapless debtor that they are visiting, but certainly in terms of the protection of just treatment of both sides, there is a great deal wanting there.

Increased professionalism is desired within enforcement in England and Wales and it is important to recognize that this is one of the key themes to the reforms presently proposed by the Department of Constitutional Affairs. One way in which that could be expressed is by bailiffs occupying an enhanced role as public officers, guarding the interests of both parties rather than purely somebody out to get the maximum from the creditor and not emphasizing the needs of the debtor.

Turning now to whether the specific aims and principles of the Convention are satisfied in England and Wales, it does not seem to me that there is any real problem here. Most of the enforcement we are talking about is the collection of local or national taxes, the enforcement of criminal court orders for compensation, criminal penalties or for maintenance, or the enforcement of civil court judgments for debt and damages. There is no real question of violation of those particular points, and obviously the view of the European Court of Human Rights does seem to be fairly relaxed about the use of seizure of goods as a means of enforcement. There is the case of *K v Sweden*,[3] where in effect the court said that bailiffs are an unpleasant experience, but if one does not pay one's debts then you must expect to have an unpleasant experience. Equally, in *Lewandowski v Poland* bailiffs with machine guns arrived at the property, having mistakenly been sent out by the tax authorities. Some twelve months later, Mrs Lewandowski died and a claim was brought under Article 1 of the Convention, but again the court had no problem with the process of enforcement as such.

Turning to specific remedies, the dominant form of enforcement in England and Wales is undoubtedly execution upon goods. Again, access to information has been mentioned by Georg Kodek. The creditor must gather the necessary information in this country. Though they will already have the relevant address, acquiring any further information can be extremely difficult even if you are using the county court system, so most creditors will simply rely on the address and send the bailiff to that address. Although

---

[3] No 41/1996.

there are other choices available they are used far less, particularly when we are talking about enforcement outside the court system.

If we turn to look at the procedures themselves, again there are no particular problems here. There are, of course, means of appeal and challenge, both within the court system and special procedures available for different forms of seizure of goods. The English common law has already developed concepts along the lines of proportionality—the long standing idea of excessive seizure of goods. Georg Kodek has made reference to whether the price for which goods might be sold could fall within the concept of proportionality, and English common law has struggled towards some concept of proportionality in that respect, though expressed in the terms of 'the best price possible' at the auction sale that takes place. Perhaps the biggest criticism advanced against one form of seizure in particular, distress for rent (the recovery by a landlord of rent arrears by seizure of goods) was that the landlord has the power to seize any goods on the premises regardless of the ownership of those goods, and it was suggested that perhaps that would cause particular problems under the Convention. However, the case of *Gasus Dosier Gmbh v The Netherlands*,[4] shows a degree of flexibility about the power of the Dutch Inland Revenue to seize third party goods. Thus, it does not seem English landlords have cause to worry, yet there still may be scope for improvement.

Within the English criminal courts, and certainly within the extra judicial procedures, the provision of procedural safeguards still has some way to go to ensure that aggrieved individuals do have some accessible and quick means of challenge. In response to this, the DCA are filling those gaps which cannot yet be filled by legislation, by means of guidelines and the *National Standards for Enforcement Agents* which have been in force for some years now.[5] These address such issues as complaints procedures and proportionality and raise the point of avoiding discrimination that may be in breach of Article 14 of the convention. In terms of seizing goods, attachment of earnings, and attachment of wages, there are minor problems. However, there does not seem to be a real problem with breach of the ECHR overall. We are facing the greatest difficulties when we turn to structure.

Indeed, there are severe problems and the first is the principle of quality of law developed by the court in Strasbourg. Enforcement must be in accordance with the law, and that is relatively well covered, but is that law clear and accessible? The answer is no, it is not. We have 15 different general forms of seizures of goods operating within England and Wales with many different sub-forms, and often they have their own unique remedies, created

---

[4] 1995] 20 EHRR 403.
[5] Available from the Department for Constitutional Affairs at <http://www.dca.gov.uk>.

within the legislation that establishes the liability. Currently, there is a seemingly endless list such as distress for lighthouse fees and distress for non-payment of market tolls, simply because the government invents a new form of distraint whenever it devises a new form of liability. The most recently created form of distraint is that for the congestion charge operating in London. If one drives into the centre of the city, one must pay a charge. If one fails to pay, one faces the seizure of goods; thus we have yet another remedy together with its associated fees. On the one hand, the government may be striving to reform this, and on the other the government is making it more of a challenge for the Department for Constitutional Affairs.

With respect to legislation, we have at least 29 Acts of Parliament and at least 14 associated sets of rules and regulations many of which are, to say the least, antique. Professor Correa Delcasso has made reference to the fact that the law is out of date and not in line with the modern world. As can be seen, a statute is still in force from the reign of King Henry III.[6] For the legal historian it may give great joy that one can still employ the statutes and case law from the reign of Henry III. But from the point of view of a modern enforcement system intended to comply with the European Convention on Human Rights, there are clearly some problems. One of the great mental leaps that the government has prompted stems from the fact that the Act of Parliament which brought the Convention partially into force in English law, requires that one understands that all existing Acts of Parliament be read as if they were written in light of the European Convention on Human Rights. Given this, one must assume that Henry III and the council of the realm, when they met in Marlborough in 1267, were working with the 1954 Convention in their minds!

You may see how the statute law has accrued over the centuries. There was a particular flurry of legislation at the end of the 19th century. For example the Law of Distress Amendment Act 1888 provides us with almost the only form of regulation that touches private bailiffs enforcing distraint outside the courts. It is here that there is an acute need for reform because that process of certification requires no qualifications and no adequate test of the knowledge, training and probity of the bailiff. This is partly the fault of the English judiciary. I have recently been researching how the 1888 Act was applied when it was first introduced. Judges were very active in their use of the certification process to weed out undesirable bailiffs and to ensure that a more professional and responsible attitude was encouraged. Perhaps inevitably, those powers have over the course of a century slipped

---

[6] The Statute of Marlborough (1267); other examples include The Distress for Rent Act (1689); The Distress for Rent Act (1737); The Sale of Farming Stock Act (1816); The Law of Distress Amendment Act (1888); The Law of Distress Amendment Act (1895); and The Law of Distress Amendment Act (1908).

into obscurity; judges barely know about them today—and certainly no longer use them.

In addition there is case law. There are several pertinent cases, one of which dates from 1505;[7] another is *Semayne's Case*. One may wonder as to the relevance of a case dating from the 21st year of the reign of Henry VII. However, it is still alive and working in the English common law, determining bailiffs' powers to secure goods on premises.[8] *Semayne's Case*, from 1604, is still the leading case on bailiffs' rights of entry in this country. It is a summary of the case law dating back to the reign of Edward II, which establishes bailiffs' rights; one can still perfectly reasonably quote cases from the reign of Edward II in order to establish a case in the courts now. Is this clear and accessible? Hardly.

Turning to the structure of the system, many local authorities and government agencies in particular have published guidelines and codes of practice in an attempt to deal with some of the problems that arise when using a medieval system of law. However, they are not always made available to members of the public or to advice agencies. Again, accessibility is clearly the problem.

It may be argued, perhaps perversely, that there are too many procedural safeguards. As stated, each form of seizure brings with it its own remedy. They are often obscure and inaccessible. The remedy of replevin, again a good early medieval writ (still happily alive in English law, though almost never used) and the law of the Distress Amendment Acts of 1895 and 1908 provide statutory remedies for distress for rent, again obscure and hardly used, and the government has suggested that many of these are swept away. I agree with these proposals.

Finally on structure, there are some more general points which made be made, and again I cite in the notes the case law from which it has been suggested, with good reason, that the extrajudicial nature of much of English enforcement may well breach the principles of the Convention. The French cases that have been mentioned involve the recovery of customs duties. In these cases, even though the seizures were being conducted by customs officers, the court in Strasbourg criticised the procedure where you have entirely private sector agents going out, possibly without any prior court order, which raises considerable concern. However, at the same time, much of the enforcement under discussion is certainly outside the protection that may be provided by the first protocol of Article 1, because it concerns the recovery of state liabilities, taxes and contributions. In addition, the first protocol of Article 1 is particularly concerned with permanent

---

[7] 1505 M.21 Hen.VII fo.39b pl. 55.

[8] Although the only way to access this case is by becoming a member of the Institute of Historical Research and consulting the appropriate yearbook, in legal French and printed in near-illegible gothic type.

deprivations and it is rare in this country that bailiffs ever need to actually sell goods. Further, it may be rare for them to ever need to seize goods, because the mere threat of seizure is enough to prompt payment from individuals. Thus, it may be that we are never actually engaging articles of the Convention, simply because of the way that the enforcement works and the source of liabilities being recovered in this country.

The final point to be made concerns the attitude of creditors and again, perhaps for a newcomer to the Convention, this is one of the most fundamental points. The Convention has only formally been part of English law for the last four years and so it is fair to question whether public bodies in this country fully appreciate what the Convention means for them. Do private sector bailiffs really identify themselves as public bodies who have duties under the Convention? One strongly suspects not, but rather that many individuals working in the recovery of local taxes, and income taxes, value-added tax and the like, will seldom have any real conception of what the European Convention on Human Rights may mean in their day to day recovery work. That is most keenly felt when you apply the principle of proportionality to choices of enforcement. For instance, local authorities collecting local taxes in this country have a range of remedies supplied to them by the relevant legislation, and clearly proportionality would suggest that they choose what is going to be the least invasive means of recovering that debt. But what do they do in fact? They obtain a court order, send in the bailiffs, and if that fails, threaten imprisonment. There are other ways of getting the money from individuals which are almost never used, and I think there is much work to be done by English lawyers in taking cases to court to get English public authorities to really absorb those principles. In conclusion, there is a need for England and Wales to improve on the structure. Inevitably, there is, one is sorry to say, much to be done.

PART VI: APPENDIX

CASE STUDIES ON UNLAWFUL ENFORCEMENT

A. Comparative Analysis of the Case Studies on Unlawful Enforcement[1]

Paul Oberhammer

The reason why it was decided to do these case studies is simple and complicated at the same time. The participants of our previous meetings will remember that a lot of the questions asked started with 'What happens in your country if . . .' And quite frequently, the answer was something like 'I do not completely understand your question, but . . .' Even one of our case studies started like this in the first place: Juan Pablo Correa Delcasso's answer to case number 3 was: 'We cannot understand which answer is expected because of the way in which the question is formulated.'

The source of that kind of conversation is the complicated reason I mentioned: there is only very little knowledge of what really happens in foreign enforcement procedures, especially when problems of wrongful execution occur. In the course of our project, we mostly discussed the bare essentials of enforcement law—not only because of our individual lack of knowledge of foreign enforcement law, but also because of a general lack of research in this field. Enforcement has simply never been a favourite with comparative lawyers, and therefore we had to start with the basics. By the way, this is exactly what I do these days, when I prepare for my lectures in Swiss enforcement law. I can tell you from experience that teaching contract law and even litigation in different countries is much easier than going from one system of execution to another as a law professor.

Let me give you two examples of this 'I don't really understand your question' situation from our work. Case two deals with the following

---

[1] This chapter is based on proceedings from the final meeting for this project held at the British Institute of International and Comparative Law in London on 23 April 2004 and entitled *Enforcement Agency Practice in Europe: Cooperation or Harmonization?*

problem: Execution is levied upon the debtor's bank account; the debtor claims that the money in the account comes from his monthly salary as an employee and is therefore not (or not to the full extent) subject to execution. I have to admit that when I suggested this case to the British Institute of International and Comparative Law, in the first instance, they suggested an eviction case which, whilst it was very interesting, was unlikely to occur on an international level, because judgments for the eviction of a tenant always originate in the courts in the country where it is subsequently executed. This is provided for in Article 22 (1) of the Brussels Regulation.

As our research was intended to enhance the understanding of European enforcement systems in light of a European move towards becoming a single area of jurisdiction, beneficial for the enforcement of judgments yet lacking a uniform enforcement law (something that would not be realistically remedied in the near future), I suggested the new case number two. When I did so, I remembered a recent discussion with Burkhard Hess, who was working on his study on garnishment procedures for the European Commission at that time. We were talking about the intricate questions arising from the transnational attachment of earnings and came to the conclusion that it might be better to refrain from suggesting any kind of law-making in that field on the European level today and in the near future.

However, we also saw the problem that future European legislation on garnishment procedures could perhaps exclude salaries from its scope of application, but clearly would have to give directions for handling the problem of salaries on bank accounts. This is why case number 2 came to my mind.

You may not be surprised that I could easily solve the case I had suggested myself by applying the elaborate provisions of Austrian law designed especially for such circumstances. As these provisions are not an Austrian invention, but were copied from the German code of civil procedure in 1991, the same was true for the German case study by Burkhard Hess and Marcus Mack. The English case study could even deal with the case without referring to any elaborate provisions or case law—apparently, this was 'an easy one' from the English perspective.

However, the detailed analysis given by Torbjörn Andersson and Hugo Fridén on the basis of Swedish law tells us (in a very polite and informative way): 'We do not understand your question from the Swedish point of view.' In Sweden, it is the enforcement agencies' task to decide whether and to what extent enforcement is to be levied upon the salary or a bank account; cases like our case number 2 therefore should not occur, unless the enforcement agency has neglected the rules on property exempt from execution, which does not seem to be very likely; and even if it does happen, the enforcement agency will simply revise its decision. I understand from Juan Pablo Correa Delcasso's case study that the law is approximately the same in Spain.

The problem here comes from a significant difference between German and Swedish Law: in Germany, there is no enforcement agency to calculate the amount to which a bank account is to be seized before the claim against the bank is attached; the creditor just asks for the seizure order and the court issues a third party debt order to the bank and that is it. The same is true for the seizure of earnings under German (as well as under Austrian), but not under Swedish (and, as I have recently learned, also not under Swiss) law: in Austria and Germany, the employer only receives a court order on the seizure of the earnings in general. It is up to the employer to calculate the amount he has to pay to the enforcement creditor (and not to the enforcement agency, as is the case in Sweden). While the employer always knows that the employee's claim is partially protected from enforcement, this is not necessarily the case with the bank. Therefore in such countries, we absolutely need a system of remedies giving the debtor a chance to prevent the the the bank from paying the wrong amount to the creditor.

Let me give you another example for the 'I don't understand your question'-situation. I think this one is even more explicit than the one before. Case number three was drafted from an English perspective. When I asked Mads Andenas whether it ever occurs in practice that a judgment creditor first refuses to accept payment without good reason and then maliciously proceeds to the execution stage, he answered in the affirmative, and indeed, the elaborate English case study shows that there is even case law in this respect.

This is hard to understand from a Swedish, German and Austrian point of view (and you may remember Juan Pablo's confession in this context cited previously): in these countries, it is as simple as this: the debtor can deposit the money by making payment to a regional authority (in Sweden) or to a court (in Austria and Germany). Therefore, on the one hand, the creditor cannot prevent the debtor from discharging his claim. On the other hand, this is the reason why the debtor has no grounds for a remedy whatsoever in case the creditor does not accept payment. Finally, nothing prevents the debtor from simply paying the money to the bailiff, which leads to the termination of the enforcement proceedings. To be frank, I find it rather hard to imagine that all this is not possible under the law of England and Wales.

And this is also typical of our case studies: Although we have discussed the cases and the draft solutions before, hardly any of the answers will be really comprehensible to everybody. This would require further work. I like this idea: Real comparative law dealing with problems that occur in real life, not the 'principles' frequently compared in books that are preoccupied with ideas in general than with law in practice. Don´t get me wrong; as you see from my lecture, I am not against comparison on a general level. But there is a tendency especially in comparative civil procedure to skip the details and go directly to the general ideas without knowing the practical problems.

The subject of our project was 'agents and remedies' in enforcement procedures. Our case studies show that these two matters are connected in a specific way. This becomes clear in case number 2, where it made the relevant difference whether there was an enforcement agency with the competence of the Swedish one or garnishment in the German or Austrian fashion. The same is more accurate for case number 1, which is almost classical. A claim is enforced against the husband but unfortunately the goods that are seized belong to his spouse. Of course, all reported jurisdictions give the wife the right to claim back her property. What is more interesting in this context is the fact that according to the English case study, the English bailiff is not allowed to do any research on whether or not the judgment debtor is the owner of the goods to be seized.

It is clear—also from the Swedish, German or Austrian point of view—that the bailiff can never render a formal decision on the question of ownership. However, it seems rather practical that in all of these countries the bailiff has to draw a prima facie conclusion from possession. In case the assets are in the sole possession of the wife, seizure must not take place. In addition, for example under Austrian law, the nature of the goods is used as an indicator of ownership, for example typical items such as woman's jewellery must not be seized in the course of an execution against the husband. Moreover, the danger of a seizure of assets belonging to third persons is even bigger in a jurisdiction where it is—as in England—at least theoretically possible to seize all assets on the debtor's premises *uno actu*.

The function of the remedies in this context seems to be completely different in England on the one hand and Germany or Austria on the other hand. From what I learned from the English case study, an important function of the interpleader proceedings is to protect the Sheriff from the parties making claims arising from wrongful execution. Therefore, the enforcement agent can also be a party in proceedings arising from the wrongful attachment of a third party's property. The legal situation is completely different in Sweden, Germany and Austria: the German *Drittwiderspruchsprozess* and the Austrian *Exszindierungsprozess* is a mere procedure between the third party and the creditor; in Sweden, the judgment debtor will also be a defendant in the respective proceedings. But in no case does the bailiff act as an applicant or defendant with regard to the respective proceedings. The fact that the enforcement agent might be responsible for the wrongful attachment is completely irrelevant in these proceedings. From an Austrian or German point of view, such a procedural position of the Gerichtsvollzieher would be absurd.

All countries strive to find a quick solution for cases such as number one: In English interpleader proceedings, rather short time-limits have to be observed. Swedish law offers three alternative remedies, among them a simple request for self-correction by the enforcement agency. German and Austrian law also provide for a rather simple remedy in cases where the *Gerichtsvollzieher* acted against his duty to seize only goods in the possession of the debtor; in all other cases, ordinary (and therefore potentially lengthy) court proceedings have to be instituted.

It is a typical feature of enforcement law in most countries, that there is a combination of applications and remedies before the enforcement agent and therefore within enforcement proceedings on the one hand and on the other hand cases where it is necessary to commence ordinary proceedings before a regular court. It is also typical that the relation between these two 'branches' is hard to understand from an outsider's point of view. According to the Swedish case study, the third party can apply for the mentioned self-correction of the enforcement agency in case he or she can prove his or her ownership before the enforcement agency; in case this attempt fails, the third party still can commence ordinary proceedings against the judgment creditor and debtor.

A similar system applies in Austria in cases where the debtor wants to raise the objection that he has already discharged the debt; but there is actually no such system of an initial and perhaps summary look at the third party's entitlement in cases like our case one (except, of course, for the fact, that the parties will try to gather such information outside of court proceedings in order to reach a settlement). From my point of view it is highly effective to provide for such a possibility or at least—like in English interpleader proceedings—a formal way to find out whether there are objections against the third party's claim before commencing litigation. I know from my Austrian experience that in a large number of such cases—where regular court proceedings have to be commenced—the claim is immediately acknowledged by the creditor just in order to avoid additional costs. I think the same is true for the German situation.

Here again, the available remedies are closely linked with the acting enforcement agent: A German *Gerichtsvollzieher* is far from being qualified to render even a summary decision on the third party's claim, for example, based on documentary evidence; therefore only a court can render such a decision. If there is a well-organized enforcement agency—as is apparently the case in Sweden—it seems to be reasonable to also give this agency the power to decide on such issues in the first place and, therefore, perhaps keep a significant number of conflicts away from the courts.

These examples from our case studies may sufficiently demonstrate that you cannot discuss remedies in enforcement procedures without having a look at the structure of enforcement agencies. As you know, it is one of today's policies of the European Union for civil procedure to abolish all formal requirements for the enforcement of foreign decisions originating from Member States, especially the *exequatur* procedures set forth in Art 38 to 52 of the Brussels Regulation. No matter what one's point of view might be in this context, one has to admit the following: It is most likely that the abolishment of these recognition proceedings will save some time for the individual creditor seeking transnational enforcement of a judgment within the Union, but it is not likely to lead to a sensational breakthrough in the efficiency of transnational debt collection in enforcement proceedings. Still, a foreign creditor will face numerous opportunities for the debtor to object against enforcement and still, there will be the uneasy feeling of being unwelcome at the enforcement agencies at the debtor's domicile and that the local lawyer you hired for the purpose of enforcement tells you things that are hard to believe.

All jurisdictions have very complex, but very different, remedial systems for enforcement and there is a natural tendency to accept the system of one's own jurisdiction, but to the exclusion of a foreign counterpart, which one perceives as lacking transparency. And, indeed, foreign enforcement law is always a little bit opaque when it comes to remedies, because it is always only the local enforcement agent or lawyer who at least claims to understand it. So, for example, in our case studies I found a significant part of the English/Welsh report rather hard to understand; and I am afraid that an English reader of my case studies will get a similar impression.

Therefore, one might think it desirable to call for a unification of remedies in enforcement procedures in Europe as a second and consequent step after having abolished *exequatur* proceedings. On the other hand, nothing is less likely to become the subject of unification in the near future than the structure of national courts and enforcement authorities.

I may therefore draw the conclusion that it would be rather unrealistic to strive for such unification, as long as we cannot find a uniform structure of enforcement agencies in Europe—I cannot imagine that this is going to happen in the next few years. By the way: The practice of the *exequatur* proceedings mentioned before is an additional piece of evidence for this opinion: Although there are uniform rules in the Brussels regulation, the *exequatur* proceedings are quite different from country to country. There are provisions that implement the European standards in quite different ways, all claiming to be perfectly in accordance with European Law—and practice is different as well, although the differences between the relevant court systems are much smaller than (for example) the difference between a German *Gerichtsvollzieher* and a French *huissier de justice*.

Cases One and Two also give us examples of an important issue that might be (among others) an interesting subject of future research: The question of creditor autonomy in enforcement proceedings. This issue was intensely discussed in a number of jurisdictions in relation to insolvency proceedings, but is also interesting from the perspective of execution: In case number 1 the claimants 'start execution...against A's movable assets', and in case number 2, the 'judgment creditor decides to seize the bank account'.

Both cases are therefore based on the assumption that it is the creditor who decides what to seize. That is the case under German and Austrian law and also seems to be true for the law of England and Wales. Different from that, in Sweden—I cite the Swedish case study—'it is the enforcement inspector or the bailiff who forms an opinion of what kind of assets...can be seized in a given situation'. The same is true for example in Swiss law where, again, it is not the creditor but rather the bailiff who decides (according to statutory provisions) what assets are subject to attachment.

This difference of systems has a number of consequences: For example, in case it is up to the bailiff to decide what assets should be attached, it seems quite natural that asset research is among his duties, as is the case in Sweden. Under Swedish law (I cite the Swedish case study again), 'priority should be given to property which inflicts the lowest cost for the debtor, the least loss and the least of other inconveniences'. This seems to imply that there is something like a principle of proportionality under Swedish enforcement law.

Some of you may remember that this was an interesting part of our discussion in Heidelberg, where a number of participants stated that such a principle was part of their law while others—like me, for example—strongly opposed this view: Under Austrian law, you can levy execution upon immovable property because you have a claim for €10. From our point of view, the debtor is free to pay anyway, and if he does not, the creditor has the choice what he wants to attach for his claim, and perhaps will choose to 'hit the debtor where it hurts most'.

Our case studies were (naturally) restricted to some specific questions, although the Union now has 25 members. This is actually a rather small basis to draw conclusions from, but let me try the following: in the first place, all case studies show that the remedies in enforcement procedures cannot be understood without understanding the enforcement agency structure. Secondly, this context suggests that there is no way to unify the law of remedies without unification of the agency structures. Finally, not only our case studies, but also the whole project has shown fundamental differences between the enforcement agents acting in the different jurisdictions; while were used to calling these agents 'bailiffs' in English, we must never forget that a *Gerichtsvollzieher* in Germany or Austria is completely different from a *huissier de justice* in France. Therefore unification in that field is unlikely to happen in the near future.

However, this does not mean that there is nothing the European Union can do in the years to come. The present situation is far from perfect. The matters tackled by the European commission (which were also the focus of

Burkhard Hess's parallel project) cover a significant part of what should be done or at least thought about in the near future.

On the one hand, numerous typical questions of international enforcement law are still unsolved. One of these issues is the problem of transnational garnishment, another might be the coordination of the effects of judgments on an international level, for example, provisional enforceability or the question of which objections are estopped by a foreign judgment when it comes to enforcement abroad. These are typical questions of jurisdiction, of recognition and finally of the law of conflicts which could be subject to European legislation (but need a lot of consideration beforehand).

One the other hand, we need information: this means we need asset transparency, but we also require more information about enforcement law and practice. The case studies gave an insight into how different enforcement law works in practice. Enforcement abroad will continue to be something parties hand over to local lawyers for quite a long time. Thus, to understand and trust each other, but also to identify problems on the international level and in the single countries, we need more specific information. Discussing such cases would be an interesting approach for future work.

B. Questionnaires on Unlawful Enforcement

In this document three hypothetical cases of wrongful execution are presented with the legal evaluation in each of the seven jurisdictions. The first case deals with the involvement of third parties, the second focuses on garnishment and the third case is about a malicious creditor.

I. WRONGFUL EXECUTION: THIRD PARTIES

The claimants (A) obtain judgment against the defendant (B) for the sum of EUR15,000. Pursuant to the judgment, they start execution for recovery of the sum involved against A's movable assets. However, since execution has commenced, B's wife (C) gives notice that the assets, which are the subject of the execution process, belong to her. Execution nevertheless takes place.

(i) What are the remedies available to C in these circumstances?
How is the decision made as to what goods shall be seized?

What is the bailiff (agent, judge, whoever responsible) supposed to check before the seizure of the goods (ie does s/he have to positively know about the property situation, may he rely on the statement of the third person etc)?

How are joint and matrimonial goods treated?

Has C (in the case the wife) the opportunity to suggest alternative goods?

How burdensome is the recourse to remedies?

II. WRONGFUL EXECUTION: PROCEDURAL ISSUES

A, the judgment debtor, has a bank account with B (the bank). C, the judgment creditor, decides to seize the bank account to make good the value of the judgment. C therefore proceeds and seizes the bank account. A wants to object to the seizure on the basis that the bank account comes from his monthly salary as an employee and is therefore not (or not as a whole) subject to execution. What are the remedies available to A in these circumstances?

III. WRONGFUL EXECUTION: SUBSTANTIVE ISSUES

C obtains judgment against D for €20,000. D makes a genuine offer to pay the whole sum and the legal costs upfront in satisfaction of the debt. C however ignores D's offer for no good reason, and issues execution for the whole debt of €20,000. C then proceeds to the execution stage. Goods to a value far in excess of the debt owed and legal costs are then seized. What are the remedies available to D in these circumstances?

National Case Studies

C. Austria

Paul Oberhammer

I. WRONGFUL EXECUTION: THIRD PARTIES

The claimants (A) obtain judgment against the defendant (B) for the sum of €15,000. Pursuant to the judgment they start execution for recovery of the sum involved against A's movable assets. However, since execution has commenced, B's wife (C) gives notice that the assets, which are the subject of the execution process, belong to her. Execution nevertheless takes place. What are the remedies available to C in these circumstances?

Under Austrian law movable assets are attached by the *Gerichtsvollzieher* (court bailiff) listing and describing the goods in a record. Pursuant to section 253 (1) Execution Code (*Exekutionsordnung,* hereinafter referred to as *EO)* only assets which are in the debtor's '*Gewahrsame*' (a technical term which could be translated with 'custody') can be attached. This means the following: The court bailiff does not have to check whether the assets to be attached are owned by the debtor; instead the court bailiff only has to check whether it appears that the debtor has control over the assets according to a generally accepted view.[2]

If the court bailiff attaches assets which are not in the debtor's custody the third party thereby affected can defend himself in the execution proceedings by filing an appeal against execution *(Vollzugsbeschwerde)* pursuant to section 68 *EO*. However, if the asset was in the debtor's custody, but was not owned by the debtor, the attachment by the court bailiff was perfectly correct. The third-party owner of the asset cannot therefore file an appeal against execution under section 68 *EO*. Instead he has to try an ordinary action and file a suit: By filing a third-party action against execution *(Exszindierungsklage)* pursuant to section 37 *EO*, the third-party owner of the attached assets claims that he has a right to the attached assets which makes it unlawful to levy execution. If the third-party action against execution *(Exszindierungsklage)* succeeds, execution must be stopped pursuant to Section 37(4) *EO*.

In order for the attachment to be admissible it is sufficient if the debtor has 'co-custody' (*Mitgewahrsame*); this means that it is sufficient if he shares control over the asset together with one or more persons.[3] In this connection there are no special provisions which apply to spouses; instead the general principles apply: If more than one person lives in an apartment, one can generally assume that these people have joint custody. In practice spouses are particularly presumed to have joint custody.[4] This presumption of joint custody also applies to property which is used by the spouses but is not inside the matrimonial home, such as for example a car. Something different can apply only if, in the circumstances, it is clearly obvious that only one spouse had custody over an item (typical examples are, for instance, items of clothing or jewellery, when it is obvious that these items are only used by the wife).

In the case in question this means the following: The attachment by the court bailiff of the movable property owned by the wife was initially lawful from a mere procedural perspective, provided the items were not something over which clearly only the wife (and not also her husband) had control. If

---

[2] Oberster Gerichtshof (Supreme Court) , SZ 57/99.
[3] ibid SZ 57/99.
[4] Cf F Mohr in P Angst Exekutionsordnung (2000) §253 n 13.

items were attached, which were clearly only within the wife's actual sphere of control, the wife could defend herself against the attachment by filing an appeal against execution *(Vollzugsbeschwerde)* pursuant to section 68 *EO*. In any other case, the wife would have to file a third-party action against execution *(Exszindierungsklage)* against the creditor pursuant to section 37 *EO*. If in the proceedings on the third-party action against execution *(Exszindierungsklage)* the wife succeeds in proving that she owns the attached property, the execution would have to be stopped or restricted to those goods which are not owned by the wife.[5]

II. WRONGFUL EXECUTION: PROCEDURAL ISSUES

A, the judgment debtor, has a bank account with B (the bank). C, the judgment creditor, decides to seize the bank account to make good the value of the judgment. C therefore proceeds and seizes the bank account. A wants to object to the seizure on the basis that the bank account comes from his monthly salary as an employee and is therefore not (or not as a whole) subject to execution. What are the remedies available to A in these circumstances?

Sections 290 et seq Execution Code *(Exekutionsordnung,* hereinafter referred to as *EO)* contain detailed provisions about the protection of a debtor when execution is levied on money claims. Under section 290 *EO* certain receivables cannot be attached at all. Section 290 a *EO* contains a catalogue of receivables which can only be attached within limits; these include, in particular, wages. Receivables deriving from bank accounts are, as a general rule, neither non-attachable claims nor are they claims which can only be attached within limits. Instead they are subject to unlimited execution.

This has given rise to the problem presented in the case in hand that a debtor receives his wages—which can only be attached within limits—by way of a transfer to a bank account and the creditor then, by garnishing the debtor's bank account, has unlimited access to a sum which is actually non-attachable (ie the minimum subsistence level, which the debtor must be left with in any event). In order to overcome this problem the provision in section 292 i *EO* for the so-called protection of accounts was introduced in 1991. This provision is very much in line with the German Code of Civil Procedure,[6] which served as a model for the 1991 legislation.

---

[5] This case has been resolved under the presumption that the spouses lived under the statutory marital property regime of separation of goods, which nowadays is practically the case in Austria almost without exception.

[6] Cf §850 k and §835 Abs 3 of the German Code of Civil Procedure (Zivilprozessordnung).

If money claims, which can only be attached within limits (ie for instance wages), are transferred to a bank account of the debtor, the garnishment of the bank account must, upon the application of the debtor, be lifted by the execution court *(Exekutionsgericht)* for the period from garnishment to the next payment date to the extent that the credit balance corresponds to that part of the non-attachable wages (section 292 i (1) *EO*). In the case in hand the debtor can therefore file an application for the garnishment of his bank account to be restricted to that part of his wages which can be attached (so that he is thus left with the non-attachable minimum subsistence level on his bank account). Before making a decision about this application, the court must hear the creditor.

This protection is, of course, incomplete insofar as the debtor's application (or the court's decision about the application) will usually come too late, because the bank where the account is held, would have to follow the garnishment ordered by the court immediately and therefore pay out the garnished sum to the creditor. When the debtor files his application, his entire bank balance might therefore have already been paid out to the creditor.[7] Section 292 i (2) *EO* therefore stipulates that the bank may only pay the garnished sum 14 days after the garnishee order was served on it. The debtor is thereby supposed to have time to file an application under section 292 i (1) *EO*.

In this connection there is another problem: The debtor does not obtain any right to dispose of the amount which has been garnished for the benefit of the creditor merely by filing an application under section 292 i (1) *EO*; therefore, he could not access his account balance until the court has reached a final decision about his application. Section 292 i (3) therefore allows the garnishment to be subjected to a preliminary restriction *(Vorabeinschränkung der Pfändung)* in a simplified procedure.[8] If the debtor can establish prima facie that the preconditions of section 292 i (1) *EO* are met and if he urgently needs the garnished credit balance or part thereof for himself or to fulfil his ongoing statutory maintenance obligations, the execution court must preliminarily lift the garnishment of the balance to this extent.

The differences between this 'fast track' process under section 292 i (3) *EO* and the filing of an application under section 292 i (1) *EO* are the following: In the accelerated process under section 292 i (3) the debtor only has to establish the preconditions prima facie (ie demonstrate that they are likely on a balance of probabilities), he does not have to prove them. The preliminary restriction *(Vorabeinschränkung)* under subsection (3) will perhaps concern a smaller amount than the final restriction under subsec-

---

[7] Cf P Oberhammer in P Angst *Exekutionsordnung* (2000) §292 i n 5.
[8] Cf for details P Oberhammer in P Angst, *Exekutionsordnung* (2000) §292 i n 5.

tion (1). Most importantly, the restriction ordered under subsection (3) is effective immediately (while in the case of subsection (1) the court's decision first has to become final); finally, in the case of a preliminary restriction *(Vorabeinschränkung)* under subsection (3) the hearing of the creditor is only required if the associated delay is reasonable for the debtor.

In practice the above case is therefore resolved as follows: After the account has been garnished the bank, where the account is held, is not allowed to pay out the garnished amount to the creditor for 14 days. In this period the debtor will file an application for the garnishment to be subject to a preliminary restriction pursuant to section 292 i (3) and an application for the garnishment to be subject to a final restriction pursuant to section 292 i (1) *EO*. On the basis of the application pursuant to section 292 i (3) *EO* the court will immediately (maybe even without hearing the creditor) issue an order, pursuant to which the bank must pay out a certain partial amount of the garnished account to the debtor; the bank must comply with this order immediately. A decision on how much of the garnished account is to be finally paid out to the debtor will be made, on the basis of the application for the garnishment to be subject to a final restriction pursuant to section 292 i (1) *EO*, after the creditor has been heard. In the end therefore, with the order issued pursuant to section 292 i (3), the creditor is therefore usually faced with a fait accompli because also the cash already paid out to the debtor in advance has, for the time being, been removed from the levy of execution (section 250 (1) *EO*); it is usually of no help to the creditor if the application is later refused under section 292 i (1) because at that point in time the money is normally no longer available.[9] The practical significance of any decision about an application under section 292 i (1) *EO* ceases with the question of whether the debtor is to be paid out a higher amount than that which he has already received due to the preliminary restriction of the garnishment under section 292 i (3) *EO*.

III. WRONGFUL EXECUTION: SUBSTANTIVE ISSUES

C obtains judgment against D for €20,000. D makes a genuine offer to pay the whole sum and the legal costs upfront in satisfaction of the debt. C however ignores D's offer for no good reason, and issues execution for the whole debt of €20,000. C then proceeds to the execution stage. Goods to a value far in excess of the debt owed and legal costs are then seized. What are the remedies available to D in these circumstances?

---

[9] Cf ibid.

(a) Creditor's default in acceptance

By rejecting performance the creditor is in default in acceptance. Pursuant to section 1419 Austrian General Civil Code *(Allgemeines Bürgerliches Gesetzbuch,* hereinafter referred to as *ABGB)* the creditor in default therefore suffers the 'adverse consequences' *(die widrigen Folgen).*[10] The creditor's default does not, however, lead to the claim being lost.[11] If, in these circumstances, the debtor wishes to release himself from the obligation to pay, he would have to deposit the amount payable with the court (cf. section 1425 *ABGB).*

If, in this case, the debtor had chosen to deposit the amount with the court pursuant to section 1425 *ABGB,* he could use satisfaction of the claim as a defence against execution by his creditor. In this case the debtor could apply for the execution to be stopped pursuant to section 40 Execution Code *(Exekutionsordnung,* hereinafter referred to as *EO);*[12] such an application must usually be granted because the debtor can normally prove that he has made the deposit with an unobjectionable instrument within the meaning of section 40(1) *EO* (namely a receipt for the deposit with the court); if this were not the case the debtor would have to file an opposition action *(Oppositionsklage)* pursuant to section 35 *EO.*

In the present case there is, however, no indication that the sum owed has been deposited with the court; the default in acceptance therefore does not prevent the creditor from levying execution against the debtor. As far as can be seen, the problem in this case has never been decided by an Austrian court and has never been the subject of opinions in legal literature (which is probably because the facts are not very likely in practice). If such facts were ever to arise, one could examine whether execution by the creditor, which would be arbitrary, would give the debtor the defence that the execution was vexatious (which is, in my opinion, not the case) and one could ask whether in such cases the debtor would not have to pay the costs of execution.

(b) The attachment of assets whose greatly exceed the value of the creditor's claim

Pursuant to section 27 Execution Code *(Exekutionsordnung,* hereinafter referred to as *EO),* execution may not be levied to a greater extent than is necessary in order to realize the right described in the warrant of execution *(Exekutionsbewilligung);* here the costs incurred by the creditor must also

---

[10] Cf for the question of what these 'adverse consequences' (widrigen Folgen) P Rummel *Allgemeines Bürgerliches Gesetzbuch* (2002), §1419 nn 8 and 9.
[11] Cf Oberster Gerichtshof, SZ 39/223; SZ 45/11.
[12] Cf W Jakusch in P Angst *Exekutionsordnung* (2000) §40 n 9.

be taken into account. This provision applies to all types of execution; however, its main sphere of application is in the levy of execution upon movable property: Here the court bailiff already has to ensure (when property is attached) ex officio that the value of the property attached does not greatly exceed the sum required to satisfy the creditor (including the costs).

Pursuant to section 41(2) *EO* the execution must be restricted if it is levied to a greater extent than is necessary to fully satisfy the creditor. In this case the debtor can file an application for the execution to be restricted. The execution court will decide this after having heard the creditor. It is a precondition for the application of section 41(2) *EO* that execution has been levied upon several items; section 41(2) *EO* cannot therefore be invoked to counter execution if it has only been levied on a single asset, from which the proceeds are expected to be much higher than required to satisfy the creditor.[13] It is a precondition for the application of section 41(2) *EO* that it can be assumed with certainty that not all of the execution measures ordered or ruled are required to satisfy the creditor within a reasonable period, ie that the same degree of satisfaction can be achieved with restricted execution.[14]

For the sake of completeness various special provisions should be pointed out which also protect the debtor from execution being levied to a greater extent than necessary. In this connection, section 96 *EO* should first be pointed out: Pursuant to this provision the levy of execution by the creation of a compulsory mortgage *(Zwangshypothek)* can be restricted if the creditor has obtained too much security. Under section 201 *EO*, instead of auctioning a property, the property can be placed under receivership (compulsory administration) for the benefit of the creditor's enforceable claim if the average annual net earnings from managing the property to be auctioned are sufficient to satisfy the creditor's claim (in the course of one year). Under section 263 *EO* the attachment of movable property can be restricted if the creditor has movable property of the debtor in his sphere of control, over which he has a lien or right of retention; in this case the debtor can demand that the lien over this property be restricted provided the claim is covered by the value of the property.

---

[13] ibid §41 n 11.   [14] Oberster Gerichtshof, SZ 26/208.

D. England and Wales

Mads Andenas

I. THIRD PARTIES

The claimants (A) obtain judgment against the defendant (B) for the sum of EUR15,000. Pursuant to the judgment they start execution for recovery of the sum involved against A's movable assets. However, after execution has commenced, B's wife (C) gives notice that the assets, which are the subject of the execution process, belong to her. Execution nevertheless takes place. What are the remedies available to C in these circumstances?

(a) What are the remedies available to C in these circumstances?

(i) Legal situation

In answering this case study, it should be noted from the outset that it has been assumed that the goods did indeed belong to C, and were not jointly owned with A.[15]

Furthermore, should the third party (in this case the spouse) intentionally induce the enforcement agent to seize the goods, either by expressly or impliedly representing that the goods were the debtor's, then the spouse may be estopped from recovering damages.[16] However, as soon as notice of the true situation is given, the enforcement agent/bailiff becomes liable for any subsequent wrongful acts such as proceeding to sell the goods.[17]

(ii) Remedies

The remedies available are as follows:

- Interpleader
- Wrongful Interference with Goods
- Wrongful Execution
- Pay and Sue

---

[15] Age does not alter the position that a woman is capable of acquiring, holding, and disposing of any property and that she can do so in all respects as if she was a single woman. This is set out in section 1 (a) Law Reform (Married Women & Tortfeasors) Act 1935. All property belonging to women when they marry or which they acquire by or which devolve upon them after that date belong to them as if they were single, set out in s 2(1). Such goods cannot be seized. However, couples may jointly own goods (s 4 (2) (c). In fact, the courts generally assume that items bought after marriage are to be shared and allocate equal interest in such items; such items can be seized.

[16] *Pickard v Sears* (1837) 6 A&E 469.

[17] *Dunstan v Paterson* (1857) 2 CBNS 495.

(iii) Interpleader

This is a proceeding by which a person, from whom two or more persons claim the same property or debt, and who does not himself claim it, can protect himself from legal proceedings by calling upon the two claimants to interplead so that title to property may be decided. Thus one type of Interpleader proceeding is where the bailiff or Sheriff has seized (or intends to seize) goods and a person other than the judgment debtor (here the spouse) claims them. The bailiff or Sheriff initiates these proceedings after receiving notice from the third party; otherwise, since they are faced with competing claims for goods, they could be sued by different people in respect of those claims. It is a way of compelling claimants to pursue their claims, and offers protection to the Interpleader. Interpleader is not available however where the bailiff is no longer in possession of the disputed goods, for example because they have already been sold and the proceeds given to the creditor.

Procedure

The Interpleader claimant (here C) delivers notice of his claim to the bailiff holding the warrant of execution. Once notice is received the court sends notice to the execution creditor and, unless the Interpleader is claiming the proceeds or value of the goods, the court sends notice to the Interpleader claimant seeking security.[18]

In the High Court the third party must give notice of the claim to the Sheriff, including a full description of the goods and the Sheriff will notify the creditor. The creditor then has seven days to respond, to either admit or contest the third party claim. If the creditor admits the claim then the Sheriff withdraws. The goods then cease to be in legal custody and may not be distrained.[19] The claimant may not simply remove the goods as this would be contempt.[20]

If, on the other hand, the claim is disputed or the creditor fails to reply, the Sheriff can apply to the court for protection against any proceedings relating to the seizure of the goods. An application is made by the Sheriff's officer under RSC Order 17. The Sheriff should withdraw from possession of the goods claimed. Protection is usually granted unless there is a substantial grievance against the Sheriff.

Within 14 days of the Interpleader proceedings being issued, the Interpleader claimant must serve on the other parties an affidavit specifying

---

[18] The High Court may require security but the County Court must require this under O.33 r (1) (2)(b) and s 100 CCA.

[19] *Cropper v Warner* (1883) Cab & El 152.

[20] J Kruse *The Law of Seizure of Goods: Debtor's Rights and Remedies* (Barry Rose Chichester 2000) 177.

the goods claimed and the grounds for the claim. The claimant may also claim damages against the Sheriff.

In the County Court the Interpleader claimant files notice of his claim in the office of the court for the district in which the goods were seized if the levying bailiff will not accept the claim. The District Judge then notifies the creditor who has only four days to reply. If the claim is admitted, the bailiff withdraws and the creditor is only liable for fees incurred before the notice was served.[21] Furthermore, the District Judge may then seek an order from a Circuit Judge restraining the bringing of a claim against the District Judge in respect of his taking possession of the goods.[22]

If, on the other hand, the claim is disputed or the creditor fails to reply, the District Judge issues Interpleader proceedings, giving notice to the creditor and Interpleader claimant.[23] A hearing of the case is then arranged.[24]

By initiating these proceedings the bailiff and Sheriff gain protection from other court actions arising out of any real and substantial grievance caused by their wrongful acts.[25] An action brought against the bailiff can result only in the award of nominal damages.[26] In respect of the Sheriff, Interpleader will afford him protection even if he has entered premises and, through honest mistake, seized third party goods. The Sheriff will be deemed to have committed 'mere trivial trespass' and will be protected unless there is an aggravating factor, such as insolent or oppressive behaviour.[27]

The effect of the issue of Interpleader proceedings is to stay enforcement of the debt by any other means.[28]

Damages may be claimed in both the County Court and the High Court, though in the latter any such claim will form part of a separate action.[29] If a 'substantial grievance' is proved by the Interpleader claimant, or substantial injury suffered, damages should be awarded, as in these circumstances it is not just and reasonable to protect the bailiff.

Those factors taken into account to establish a 'substantial grievance' are where:

- there has been a sale at an undervalue;[30]
- the bailiff is guilty of a moral fault and substantial grievance is caused;[31] or where

---

[21] CCR Order 33 r 2.   [22] ibid r 3.
[23] ibid r 4.   [24] ibid.
[25] See n 20 above.
[26] *Cave v Capel* [1954] 1 QB 367. See J Kruse *The Law of Seizure of Goods: Debtor's Rights and Remedies* (2000) at 177.
[27] Above n 20. See also *Smith v Critchfield* [1885] 14 QBD 873.
[28] *Re: Ford* [1886] 18 QBD 369.   [29] Above 80 at 179.
[30] *New London, Chatham & Dover Railway Co Ltd v Cable* [1899] 80 LT 119.
[31] *De Coppet v Barnet* [1901] 17 TLR 273.

- the claim arises as a result of the bailiff's own wrongful actions, for example, forced entry, trespass against the person, or the goods were seized in the knowledge that they did not belong to the debtor.[32]

However, as previously stated, if the bailiff has acted with honest belief that the goods belonged to the debtor he may be protected from an action of trespass if no substantial grievance has been done.[33]

At the hearing, if the claimant only establishes title to some of the goods, they are entitled to payment of a sum representing the value of the goods, and the creditor will receive the balance.[34]

If the claimant fails, the bailiff can recover costs from the date of notice of the claim or from the sale, whichever is earlier. If the claimant succeeds, the bailiff can recover costs from the creditor from the time when the creditor authorised Interpleader proceedings. All costs are awarded at the judge's discretion.

(iv) Wrongful interference with goods

This action's legal basis comes from the Torts (Interference with Goods) Act 1977. Wrongful interference can be trespass, negligence or conversion,[35] and is often a mix of these.

A claim of wrongful interference may result in one of the following:

- an order for the delivery of the goods and the payment of any consequential damage;[36]
- an order for delivery with the alternative for the defendant to pay damages based on the value of the goods plus consequential damages in either case;[37]
- damages alone, based on the assessed value of the goods plus any consequential damages;[38] and
    (i) an interlocutory injunction for recovery of the goods.[39]
- An order for delivery on its own is rare unless the item of special significance or value to the claimant, or it would be impossible to replace the item. It is open to the claimant to sue both the bailiff who commits the act and any person responsible for the bailiff's actions, such as the creditor who has authorised the wrongful seizure.

(v) Wrongful execution

A wrongful execution occurs where it is authorized by neither the judgment

---

[32] *Tufton v Harding* (1859) 29 LJ Chapter 225. [33] Above 80 at 179.
[34] *Tellus Super Vacuum Cleaners v Ireland* (1938) LJNCCR 54.
[35] Conversion is appropriating or altering another's goods, or depriving that person of their use or possession.
[36] Section 3(2)(a) 1977 Act. [37] Section 3(2)(b).
[38] Section 3(2)(c). [39] Section 4.

nor the writ: for example the execution is at the wrong address or against the wrong person's goods.[40]

The remedy is to take an action for trespass,[41] but it is not trespass *ab initio* and the levy remains good. Such actions will be against the Sheriff or maybe against the creditor if they instructed the Sheriff to act in a wrongful manner.[42]

An action for damages might also be an option if there is evidence of bad faith, malice or actual damage which can be proved or if the goods have been sold.[43]

(vi) Pay and sue
It would also be open to the third party owner of the goods to pay the debt and then sue the debtor. This is because it is a legal principle that if one person's goods are taken to satisfy the debt of another, the owner shall have a remedy against the debtor for an indemnity.[44] The action would be for the sum paid to the bailiff or the value of the goods if they have been sold.[45]

(b) How is the decision made as to what goods shall be seized?

Distraint and execution require both 'the seizure of the goods and the subsequent securing of the goods (generally called impounding)'.[46] While the term 'seizure' is often used to encapsulate both 'seizure' properly understood and 'impounding', they constitute two of the three distinct phases of the execution process (the other phase being entry into the debtor's premises). Hence seizure is the process of identifying, selecting and securing the goods upon which the judgment will be executed; impounding places the goods in the 'custody of the law' and affords the Sheriff or bailiff possession and control over the goods seized.

High Court Sheriffs and County Court bailiffs, unlike other enforcement agents (such as landlords in distrainment, or private bailiffs), achieve impounding simultaneously to seizure. Strictly speaking, they do not need to perform a separate and distinct act to impound the goods. This special treatment is best explained by reference to their status as 'officers of the court'. Despite this anomaly, the Sheriff or bailiff will generally prefer to

---

[40] See *Hilliard v Hanson* [1882] 21 Chapter D 69; *Smith v Critchfield* [1885] 14 QBD 873.
[41] See *Hooper v Lane* (1857) 6 HL Cas 443.
[42] See *Morris v Salberg* [1889] 22 QBD 614.
[43] *Perkins v Plympton* (1831) 7 Bing 676.
[44] *In Re: Button ex Parte Haviside* [1907] 2 KB 180; *Edmunds v Wallingford* [1885] 14 QBD 811.
[45] *Groom v Bluck* (1841) 2 Man & G 567; *Lampleigh v Braithwaite* (1620) Hobart 106; *Dering v Winchelsea* (1787) Coa 318.
[46] Per Simon Brown J in *Evans v South Ribble Borough Council* [1992] 2 All ER 695.

carry out both phases in sequence, and in a manner that is clear to those involved[47]

The courts' officers' status also results in a very low juridical threshold to be met by them when seizing or impounding the goods. From a purely legal point of view, seizure can be effected by:

(i)   The Sheriff entering the premises under a warrant, not as a trespasser, with the intention of seizing, and an officer remains in the premises,[48] or

(ii) The Sheriff entering the premises (with or without a warrant) and making it verbally known that he has arrived to seize the goods,[49] or

(iii) Without entering the premises, the Sheriff looking through the window and making it known that he intends to seize the goods.[50]

In addition, the Sheriff is availed by a legal presumption that seizure of one part of the property is tantamount to seizure of the goods in the whole property.[51]

Hence, for the Sheriff to fail to seize the goods he must also fail entirely to make his intention clear, or fail to indicate the purpose of his entering the premises. Further, it seems that, at least in theory, the Sheriff is entitled to seize the contents of the premises in toto.[52]

Should the Sheriff proceed in this fashion, it could be very worrying for C, the wife, since she would not be in an easy position to immediately state her claim to any goods. Such indiscriminate seizure would also arguably conflict with the Sheriff's duties as discussed in (iii) below, and may render him vulnerable to court proceedings.

However, it seems that Sheriffs will rarely exercise their powers in this manner.[53] In practice it is likely that a Sheriff or bailiff will identify the goods he intends to seize, be it verbally, by touching them, or by producing an inventory ('actual seizure').[54] At the same time, or perhaps on a subsequent occasion, he will impound the goods by means of one of the following procedures:[55]

[47] J Kruse 127.
[48] *Bird v Bass* (1843) 6 Scotts NR 928.
[49] *Gladstone v Padwick* (1871) LR 6 Exch (without warrant), *Balls v Pink* (1845) 4 LTOS 356 (with warrant).
[50] *Giles v Grover* (1832) 1 Cl & Fin 72.
[51] *Balls v Pink* (1845) 4 LTOS 356.
[52] J Kruse 127.
[53] See also J Keith, W Podevin, and C Sandbrook *The Execution of Sheriffs' Warrants* (2nd edn Barry Rose Chichester 1995).
[54] See J Kruse 117; this may be contrasted with 'constructive seizure' where 'some act must be done to intimate that seizure has been made': *Noseworthy v Campbell* (1929) 1 DLR 964.
[55] J Kruse 121–2.

1. Immediate removal, where the goods are taken to a store room. This method is rarely employed because of the expense and the trouble involved.
2. Close possession, where a bailiff or official is left on the judgment debtor's premises guarding the goods as 'possession man'. The costs of this modality render it impracticable.
3. Walking possession, whereby the debtor agrees (usually in writing) that the goods will remain in his premises, subject to the bailiff/Sheriff's possession and right to return and remove them for sale (and also subject to the payment of a small daily fee to the bailiff). Walking possession agreements are the most common form of modern impounding.

The decision as to what goods will be seized must be examined in the context of the Sheriff's position vis-à-vis A, B and C. While he is A's agent, he is also a neutral party to any disputes arising between the trio.[56] His only indication of ownership or title will arise from the warrant issued by A, which may or may not include a list of goods allegedly belonging to the judgment debtor. Thus, the Sheriff can do little more that seize, or announce his intention to seize, the debtor's goods and await any third party claim by, say, C.

Hence, it is good practice[57] for Sheriffs to give the judgment debtor notice of the execution and require any third parties to formulate any claim to ownership in writing, consequently affording C the earliest possible opportunity to interpose a claim.

The Sheriff's position of neutrality requires him to permit A and C to resolve their conflicting claims to ownership of the goods; if A and C cannot agree, the Sheriff will then seek Interpleader relief. It is not up to the Sheriff to investigate the merits of the conflicting claims; indeed, by so doing he risks losing his right to protect himself through Interpleader.[58] Similarly, the Sheriff's status as agent of the judgment creditor disentitles him from simply choosing not to levy C's goods upon receipt of the third party claim. He should refer the claim to the execution creditor, seek further information from him, and decide whether he wishes to resort to Interpleader; it is then up to the creditor to determine whether or not he wishes to oppose the third party claim, and instruct the Sheriff accordingly.[59] Exceptionally, the Sheriff may have the discretion to return no goods at all. This will only occur where he suspects a claim by a third party may be made in respect of the majority of the goods. But unless he decides not to levy at all, he is not entitled to pick and choose, because that is the judgment creditor's prerogative.[60]

---

[56] J Keith and W Podevin 70.   [57] ibid 29.
[58] *Crump v Day* (1847) 4 CB 760.   [59] J Keith and W Podevin 73.
[60] J Kruse 176.

(c) What is the bailiff supposed to check before the seizure of the goods (ie does s/he have to positively know about the property situation, may he rely on the statement of the third party, etc.)?

As indicated above, the bailiff should give notice of execution and invite third parties to formulate their claims to ownership of the goods. Once on notice of third party ownership, the Sheriff or bailiff will be liable for any subsequent wrongful acts.[61] Yet it is not up to the Sheriff to determine the merits of a third party's claim. His sole duty in this respect is to determine the existence of any such claim. He should take all reasonable steps to ensure that the assets seized are those of the debtor. He must certainly ask the judgment debtor in this regard, or make enquiries of such authorities as the DVLA, HP Information Ltd and any other registers that record ownership of goods.[62] He can certainly rely on a third party's claim in writing in order to determine the existence of conflicting claims to ownership of any goods.

In order to become entitled to Interpleader relief the bailiff must obtain the third party's claim in writing. An oral claim will require full investigation; it is submitted that if upon receipt of the oral claim the Sheriff invites the claimant to issue a written claim, and the third party fails to do so, said third party may be estopped from proceeding against the Sheriff.[63]

It also seems that where the Sheriff comes across goods which he believes a third party may, unwittingly, have claim to, it would be good practice to raise with said party whether s/he wishes to raise a claim.[64]

In summary, Sheriffs/bailiffs are under an obligation to make reasonable enquiries as to the existence of third party claims to any goods they intend to seize. They are not expected—indeed, they are forbidden from—fully investigating ownership of the goods. That is the exclusive business of the courts in Interpleader proceedings.

(d) How are joint and matrimonial goods treated?

Jointly owned goods can be seized; the proceeds of such goods must however be divided among the owners *pro rata*.[65] The same regime applies to matrimonial goods.

Once again, it is not the Sheriff's duty to ascertain the merits of claims to joint property, but merely the existence of such a claim. Provided the judgment debtor has an interest in the property, the Sheriff or bailiff should

---

[61] *Dunstan v Paterson* (1857) 2 CBNS 495.
[62] J Keith and W Podevin 72.
[63] See 2 above; *Pickard v Sears* (1837) 6 A&E 469.
[64] ibid 37, by analogy.
[65] *Farrar v Beswick* (1836) 1 M&W 682; *The James W Elwell* [1921] P 351.

seize and seek a notice of claim to part from the other person(s) having an interest. It is open to the court to make an order for sale and for the allocation of the proceeds. Often said order will require the Sheriff to first invite the third party to purchase the share of the judgment debtor.[66]

(e) Has C (in the case of the wife) the opportunity to suggest alternative goods?

From a purely technical perspective, the answer to the above question must be in the negative. Interpleader is negative in nature i.e. it seeks to exclude the third party's goods from the ambit of the Sheriff's influence, and it refers exclusively to goods that allegedly pertain to the Interpleader claimant.

In practice, however, there is no reason why C should not be entitled to informally advise the creditor and/or the Sheriff of the existence, or suitability, of other goods, the seizure of which would preclude the inconvenience and expense of Interpleader proceedings.

(f) How burdensome is the recourse to remedies?

To the extent these remedies require the intervention of the courts, they are relatively burdensome. In the case of Interpleader, the claimant may be able to obtain swift redress (within 7 days) if the creditor agrees to his claim. A prudent creditor may well adopt this course, simply executing other alternative goods, so as to avoid the burden and costs risk of an Interpleader. Yet this will be the Interpleader claimant's only hope of fast relief. Should the creditor dispute the claim, or ignore it (hence obligating the Sheriff or bailiff to interplead himself) the wife will be subjected to a process that could last for months. She may have to provide a security deposit; should she lose, she may also be liable in costs.

Similar considerations apply to Interference with Goods, Wrongful Execution and Pay and Sue, all of which also require full court proceedings.

II. WRONGFUL EXECUTION: PROCEDURAL ISSUES

A, the judgment debtor, has a bank account with B (the bank). C, the judgment creditor, decides to seize the bank account to make good the value of the judgment. C therefore proceeds and seizes the bank account. A wants to object to the seizure on the basis that the bank account comes from his

---

[66] J Keith and W Podevin 51. This practice is particularly common in the case of matrimonial goods. See also *Farrar v Beswick* (1836) 1 M&W 682 and *Mayhew v Herrick* (1849) 7 CB 229.

monthly salary as an employee and is therefore not (or not as a whole) subject to execution. What are the remedies available to A in these circumstances?

Garnishment

A, the judgment debtor, has a bank account with B (the bank). C, the judgment creditor, decides to seize the bank account to make good the value of the judgment. C therefore proceeds and seizes the bank account. A wants to object the seizure on the basis that the bank account comes from his monthly salary as an employee and is therefore not (or not as a whole) subject to execution. What are the remedies available to A in these circumstances?

(a) Legal situation

Two versions of this situation are conceivable. Either the execution covers more that the deductible amount of salary, then the execution is excessive, or the execution is confined to the deductible amount, but the debtor cannot afford to pay.

(i) First version
The seizure of the bank account is a wrongful execution of a third party debt order (formerly: garnishee proceeding). Given, that the salary is seized as a whole,[67] this execution is an excessive distress.

(ii) Second Version
Under changes recently introduced by the Lord Chancellor's Department, a debtor subject to a 'third party debt order' may apply to court for a 'hardship payment order' if the effect of the execution against his or her account is that s/he cannot meet ordinary living expenses. Funds could be released

---

[67] A debtor's monthly salary generally constitutes attachable earnings (Attachment of Earnings Act 1971, s 24 para 1 (a)). So far, the protected earning rate (PER) is individually calculated for every debtor. The Enforcement Review suggests a system with fixed rates. The PER will depend on the amount of the salary and is 100 per cent with a monthly net pay of £220 and less. If the PER is not left untouched, the execution of the third party debt order is excessive. The salary needs to be:
- unconditional;
- owing or accruing to the debtor solely in his own right beneficially (Harrods Ltd v Tester (1937) 157 LT 7); and
- within the jurisdiction (Richardson v Richardson [1927] P 228).

The debt must be in existence as a debt in law, but need not necessarily be immediately payabl (*Dawson v Preston* [1955] 1 WLR 1219, applying *O'Driscoll v Manchester Insurance Committee* [1915] 3 KB 499). The debt must be for a minimum of £50 (both in High Court and in the County Court).

but the application would not be invalidated (Civil Procedure Rules Part 72.7).

(b) Remedy for the first version

The remedy is to take an 'action on the case' in form of a tort (trespass; rather than a tort per se) because of excessive distress, which also includes negligence.[68]

To sue for a tort is to sue for a civil wrong. This civil wrong is the trespass by the enforcement agent into the judgment debtor's bank account. The trespass lies in the fact that the bank account is seized beyond the protected amount of salary. The seizure itself is lawful as it is grounded on a lawful judgment (that is the reason why the seizure is not a tort per se but a tort based on excessive execution). Three general forms of trespass are recognized: trespass to land, goods or persons. The trespass into a bank account is strictly speaking a trespass into a claim of the bank account holder against the bank. This is, however, understood as a trespass into goods. To succeed in the remedy based on tort, the proof of the wrong done suffices (*Williams v Mosty* (1838) 4 M&W 145).

The remedy action is to be directed against the Sheriff (High Court) respectively the bailiff (County Court; *Gauntlett v King* (1857) CBNS 59).

(c) Remedy for the second version

If a judgment debtor is prevented from withdrawing money from his or her account due to a third debt order, the court may make an order permitting the bank to make a payment out of the account (hardship payment order). Precondition is that the JD or his or her family is suffering hardship in meeting ordinary living expenses (Civil Procedure Rules Part 72.2). The application for a hardship payment is to be made in High Court proceedings ate the Royal Court of Justice or to any district registry; and in County Court proceedings to any County Court. The application notice must be served on the judgment creditor at least 2 days before the hearing.

III. CASE III: EXECUTION ISSUED MALICIOUSLY

C obtains a judgment against D for EUR20,000. D makes a genuine offer to pay the whole sum and the legal costs upfront in satisfaction of the debt. C however ignores D's offer for no good reason and issues execution for the

---

[68] *Messing v Kemble* (1800) 2 Camp 116. Cf J Kruse *The Law of Seizure: Debtor's Rights and Remedies* at 71.

*whole debt of EUR20,000. C then proceeds to the execution stage. Goods
to a value far in excess of the debt owed and legal costs are then seized.
What are the remedies available to D in these circumstances?*

(a) Legal situation

The execution is illegal because 'it is authorised by neither the judgment nor
the writ', as the judgment debtor has made a proper tender.[69] The tender
was made before seizure and so would lead to satisfaction of the debt.[70]
The execution is 'issued maliciously', because the judgment creditor refuses
the tender and proceeds to execution.[71]

Side-aspect: If the judgment debtor had not actually tendered the money
and the creditor had not refused it, then the seizure would only be irregular and not illegal. Then the wrongful aspect of the seizure would be the
bailiff's 'excessive levy'. The remedy would be to sue for damage in tort.
The measure would be the difference in value between what should properly have been taken and what was actually seized. The seizure would be
irregular but the circumstances of the issue of the warrant would not render
it illegal.

(b) Remedies

Remedies, debtor may choose alternatively to:

- sue for a tort actionable per se (trespass to goods; *Williams v Mosty*
  (1838) 4 M&W 145)
- replevy.

(c) Trespass

Here, it is a tort of trespass to goods. The action of trespass is a remedy
affording compensation for injury to a chattel in the claimant's (here judgment debtor) possession.[72] The question is whether the trespasser has
directly interfered with the claimant's possession. Here, the judgment creditor as trespasser has authorized the seizure of goods despite the fact that he
refused the judgment debtor's tender. This counts as if he had perpetrated
the trespass himself.

---

[69] J Kruse 68, *Cubitt v Gamble* [1919] 3 TLR 223.
[70] *Wilson v South Kesteven DC* [2000] WL 877755.
[71] J Kruse 69, *Dilding v Eyre* (1861) 10 CBNS 592.
[72] A M Dugdale (gen ed) *Clerk & Lindsell on Torts* (18th edn Sweet & Maxwell London)
no 22-02.

(d) Replevy

Replevy is a process by which a person out of whose possession goods have been taken may obtain their return until the right to the goods can be determined by the court.[73] The procedure is regulated in the County Courts Act 1984, but can be neglected here as it is rarely in use

(e) Extent of the remedy

In addition to the restitution of the damage, the judge can decide on an exemplary damage against the malicious execution/judgment creditor (*Moore v Lambeth County Court Registrar and Others* [1970] QB 560).

(f) Whom to sue

In illegal distress the action is generally against the bailiff; here, however, the creditor may be sued as s/he authorized the illegal execution (*Gauntlett v King* (1857) CBNS 59; *Hurry v Rickman & Sutcliffe* [1831] 1 Mood & R 126). Precondition for the claim against the judgment creditor is the proof of malice (*Phillips v General Omnibus Co* (1880) 50 LJQB 112).

E. France

Marie-Laure Niboyet and Sabine Lacassagne[74]

I. CASE (1): WRONGFUL EXECUTION—THIRD PARTIES

The claimant (A) obtains judgment against the defendant (B) for the sum of EUR15,000. Pursuant to the judgment they start execution for recovery of the sum involved. However, since execution has commenced, B's wife (C) gives notice that the goods, which are the subject of the execution process, belong to her. Execution nevertheless takes place. What are the remedies available to C in these circumstances?

If B and C are married, and, in execution of the judgment against B assets belonging to C are seized, certain remedies are available to C.[75] The

---

[73] ibid no 22-128.

[74] Centre de Droit Civil des Affaires et du Contentieux Economique, Université Paris X-Nanterre.

[75] The jurisdiction of the JEX (execution judge) allows very simple and efficient remedies against irregular or illegal enforcement, provided the debtor or the third person respect the time limitations to contest the measure.

measure that takes place is the *saisie-vente* (seizure followed by judicial sale of the asset).

The JEX is competent to engage the civil responsibility of the huissier. His fault results from the violation of Article 1382 of the Civil Code. The execution of the judgment is irregular. The execution must concern the debtor's assets, even if the wife or husband is jointly liable provided he or she is not designated in the judgment then that individual's assets cannot be subject to the execution of the judgment.[76] The remedies depend on the gravity of the wrongful action.

It is worth noting that the judicial officer is the only person who has the power to determine the goods that shall be seized. His choice depends on whether or not it is in the creditor's interest to sell the goods, ie whether they will cover the debt. However, if the wife is present at home during the seizure, she can suggest alternative goods belonging to her husband. She can prove the property of her personal goods in order to contest their seizure.

The judicial officer has no positive duty to check the property of the goods before the seizure.

Rules relative to basic matrimonial status (Article 215 of the Civil Code) provide that husband and wife are both jointly responsible for the debt in housekeeping and educational matters (Article 220 of the Civil Code). Creditors can seize the property of every personal good of the debtors. If the debt exceeds clearly the family standard of living, the seizure can be executed only against the property of one of the debtors who incurred the debt, except if the other gave his or her consent. The things which are necessary for the life or for the job of the debtor or his family cannot be seized.

In cases of separation of matrimonial status, personal creditors can seize the sole personal goods of the debtor, whichever spouse that may be. In case of community matrimonial status, creditors can seize all common goods during the time of the communion, except in cases of fraud. These are the goods which are bought during the period of marriage by both spouses or by one of them. However, creditors cannot seize 'personal' goods of the spouse which belonged to him or her before his or her union through purchase, inheritance or deed of gift.

C can obtain the *distraction* (abstraction) of the seizure (Article R.128) on proof of her property title, but only before the judicial sale. The *distraction* stays the execution until the JEX decides who owns the assets.

After the sale, the owner can protest in civil court (action en revendication) but the buyer is still able to contest the *revendication* if he invokes 'possession amounts to title' (Art 2279 of the civil code). In such a situation, the owner can only obtain the amount of the sale before it is distributed to

---

[76] Civ. 2ème, 28 octobre 1999, RTD Civ 2000, obs. P Vareilles Personnes et droits de la famille, January 2000, 14, note S Valory.

the creditor. If the amount is already distributed, it is possible to pursue the debtor because of an 'enrichment without cause' (Art 1371 s of the civil code).

II. CASE (2): PROCEDURAL ISSUES

A can contest before the JEX the enforcement of the measure (saisie-attribution) during the month after he has been informed about it (Art R. 66 al. 1er). The judge can order the *mainlevée* of the part of the seizure that exceeds the amount that is not liable to seizure and order the seizure for the remainder (Art R.67 al. 1er).

III. CASE (3): SUBSTANTIVE ISSUES

The creditor and the *huissier de justice* are both responsible for the enforcement of an unjustified measure. The debtor can obtain remedies by invoking Article 1382 of the Civil Code. The JEX is competent to order the 'mainlevée' of the seizure and to assess damages.[77]

Following the Decree of 11 September 2002, the debtor has the possibility of keeping back a minimum sum on which to live. So, for instance, the *RMI* (income support) cannot be seized by the creditor. Before this decree, a person could not have access to his bank account for one month. This is no longer the case.

F. Germany

Burkhard Hess

I. CASE (1): WRONGFUL EXECUTION—THIRD PARTIES

The claimant (A) obtains judgment against the defendant (B) for the sum of EUR15,000. Pursuant to the judgment they start execution for recovery of the sum involved. However, since execution has commenced, B's wife (C) gives notice that the goods, which are the subject of the execution process, belong to her. Execution nevertheless takes place. What are the remedies available to C in these circumstances?

---

[77] Civ. 2ème 24 juin 1998, GP 1999, 14/01, pan jurisp 9.

(a) General Points

A German bailiff is not empowered to check the validity of the title, but must ensure that the general conditions of enforcement are met. In the case of execution in movable assets, section 808 ZPO adds the further condition that the asset must be in possession of the debtor.[78]

As section 808 ZPO reflects the assumption that the possessor of a movable good is also its owner (section 1006 BGB), the bailiff does not investigate the ownership of such objects.[79] Such potentially difficult and time-consuming legal questions are to be dealt with by the court under section 771 ZPO on application of the third party (above 7.1.2.2.). If the bailiff were to stop the attachment solely on the basis of the debtor's or a third party's objection, the creditor's right to enforcement would be infringed and the bailiff may incur liability under the rules of state responsibility.[80]

First exception to the rule: if, from the bailiff's perspective, there is no doubt that the asset in question belongs to a third person, the bailiff will refrain from seizing it (GVGA section 119 n°2).[81]

Second exception: as it is basically left to the bailiff's discretion which objects in A's possession to choose for execution purposes,[82] he is free not to attach assets that probably belong to a third party, if there is a sufficient number of other valuable goods that can be attached (section 136 (2) GVGA).

It should be noted at this point that, under section 808 (2) ZPO, attached goods other than money, security papers or treasuries are left in the debtor's

---

[78] Objects in possession of a third party can be attached, if the third party agrees; s 809 ZPO.

[79] With the evident exception of cases of s 809 ZPO (see previous footnote), H Brox and W Walker *Zwangsvollstreckungsrecht* para 260.

[80] F Baur and R Stürner *Zwangsvollstreckungsrecht* §28 para 28.8.

[81] The GVGA provides, as an example, defective goods at a repair shop which do not belong to the owner of that shop. This rule does not apply if the possessor has an Anwartschaftsrecht in the object, that is, a right (quasi) in rem to acquire full title, eg, in case of sale with reservation of title. In this case, according to dominant opinion, the judgment creditor has to apply (1) for the attachment of the Anwartschaftsrecht by the Rechtspfleger (ss 829, 857 ZPO) and (2) the seizure of the object by the bailiff. The creditor will pay the outstanding price to seller, thereby transforming debtor into the owner of the object. Then the bailiff can sell the object. Of course, this is only an economically viable solution if the outstanding part of the price is small.

[82] Concerning the choice of the goods to be seized, the bailiffs' discretion is limited in two other ways: First, s 811 ZPO contains a list of objects that can not be attached (eg radios; everyday clothing; tools the debtor needs for trade). Secondly, the choice is influenced by the principle of proportionality which demands taking into account both the interests of the creditor and of the debtor. Following s 131 GVGA, the bailiff is held to choose the objects which promise to allow most rapid satisfaction of the creditor while being expendable to the debtor's household. Accordingly, the bailiff first tries to attach monies and security papers. If the debtor suggests alternative goods, this normally makes them 'expendable', but the bailiff still has to check whether they allow for rapid satisfaction of the creditor.

possession for continued use, as long as this situation does not jeopardize the satisfaction of the creditor's claim. For the time being, such goods are simply marked with a seal. The bailiff takes them into possession shortly before he proceeds to public auction (section 814 ZPO).[83]

(b) Creditors' Orders

It is disputed to what extent the bailiff is bound by orders of the creditor regarding the object of the seizure, if these orders do not contravene the legal provisions or his duties according to the GVGA as described above. According to some authors, the bailiff only has to 'take into account the wishes' of the creditor (and the debtor),[84] while others argue that the creditor can order the bailiff to seize specific objects, to the extent that this does not infringe protected interests of the debtor.[85] It seems to be clear at least, that the creditor can exclude objects he owns himself or order the bailiff to seize his (the creditor's) own property (cf. note 94).[86] If creditor and debtor agree on an object, the bailiff is bound by this agreement.[87]

(c) Spouses

Special legal provisions apply to spouses. In Germany, the normal matrimonial regime is the *Zugewinngemeinschaft* (section 1363 BGB), which in principle provides for separated estates of the two spouses.[88] Nevertheless, section 1362 BGB creates an assumption in favour of a creditor of one of the spouses stating that assets, which are in common possession of both spouses or even in possession of the other spouse, shall be regarded as to be (solely) owned by the debtor.

Referring to this assumption, section 739 ZPO creates the legal assumption that assets, which are in common possession of both spouses or in possession of the other spouse, shall be regarded as being only in the possession of the spouse who is subject to enforcement. However, this provision does not apply if the spouses have separated (section 1362 (1) BGB) or if

---

[83] F Stein, M Jonas, and W Münzberg, *ZPO* §808 para 35.

[84] Schilken in *Münchener Kommentar ZPO* §808 Rz 14, LG Berlin MDR 1977, 146. This is also the position of s 104 GVGA (which however does not have the force of law, see above n 31).

[85] H Brox and W Walker, *Zwangsvollstreckungsrecht* para 213, F Baur and R Stürner *Zwangsvollstreckungsrecht* §8 para 8.5.

[86] H Brox and W Walker, *Zwangsvollstreckungsrecht* para 213.

[87] ibid para 213. Exception: if the object evidently belongs to a third party and the debtor does not have an Anwartschaftsrecht.

[88] In case of joint property, the partial property of a co-owner must be attached by the enforcement court under §749 ZPO. The creditor can then demand from the other co-owner(s) to end the co-ownership (sale at auction).

the asset is for the exclusive personal use of one of the spouses (for example perfume for women etc), section 1362 (2) BGB.

In this respect, the bailiff must investigate whether (1) the asset is in possession of (at least) one of the spouses, (2) the spouses have not separated and (3) the asset is not for the exclusive personal use of one of the spouses.

(d) Remedies

(i) Drittwiderspruchsklage

The basic remedy for a third party whose assets which are (unlawfully) seized, is the *Drittwiderspruchsklage* (third party complaint in opposition, above 7.1.2.2). The execution court (*Vollstreckungsgericht*) at the place where the execution took place is competent to decide on the opposition. C must sue A as defendant. The bailiff is not involved in the proceedings.

C as the third party must prove ownership of the affected good and refute the presumption of section 1362 BGB.[89] Once the complaint is filed, the court can order a stay of the execution proceeding regarding this asset until the final decision on the complaint is made, section 771 (3) ZPO. If the court finds that the asset belongs to C, the court will declare the execution in the assets to be inadmissible (*unzulässig*). This decision will be declared provisionally enforceable, section 708 ZPO.

Under section 775 (1) and (2), 776 ZPO, the decision's legal effects are as follows:

1. If movable assets are still in possession of the bailiff, C can get them back at the premises of the bailiff, section 171 (3) GVGA. If the assets are on the way to being publicly sold, the bailiff has to stop the auction and keep them in his possession (exception: perishable goods). Section 171 GVGA states—without any legal force—that the creditor has to pay for the costs of the transport back to the place where attachment took place. Whether such a claim really exists, is however a question of private law, and debatable.[90]
2. If movable assets were left in the possession of B and C, the bailiff has to remove the seals from the attached assets or allow B and C to do so.
3. In the case of garnishment, a positive decision of *Vollstreckungsgericht* on the complaint normally comprises the abrogation of the attachment.[91]

---

[89] According to a Supreme Court ruling, the third party only has to prove having once acquired property of the object; proof of never having lost the property afterwards is not required; BGH NJW 1976,238 .

[90] See F Stein, M Jonas & W Münzberg ZPO § 771 para 56; H Brox & W Walker, *Zwangsvollstreckungsrecht*, para 1448.

[91] Imperial Supreme Court 84 RGZ 200.

(ii) Vollstreckungserinnerung

An additional remedy, the *Vollstreckungserinnerung* (section 766 ZPO, infra 7.1.1.1.) can successfully be filed by C, if the bailiff violated procedural rules. Section 808 I, 739 ZPO would be violated, if the bailiff seized assets that were for C's exclusive personal use, or if the spouses separated before the execution took place (infra 12.1.1.). The legal consequences of a successful complaint would be the same as described above.

II. CASE (2): WRONGFUL EXECUTION—PROCEDURAL ISSUES

A landlord (L) leases a flat to a tenant (T). L subsequently obtains a judgment against T for possession of the flat and recovery of arrears. T does not comply with any part of the judgment and execution proceedings are issued for possession and the levy of the outstanding sum. T applies for a stay of execution, which is granted on the basis that T pays a certain sum each month. T complies with this condition. In the meantime, the enforcement agent arranges for the premises to be delivered back to L and seizes goods to the value outstanding. What are the remedies available to T under these circumstances?

Eviction proceedings are dealt with by section 885 ZPO. The bailiff dispossesses the debtor and confers possession on the creditor. The recovery of outstanding rent, on the other hand, is normally effected though garnishment of claims or the attachment of movable goods.

This case can be interpreted in two ways:

(a) T applied for a stay of execution under section 765a ZPO (infra 7.1.5.). Such a stay can be granted subject to the condition of payments of the debtor, if the weighing of interests would have lead to a denial of T's motion without this payment.[92] Such a decision constitutes an obstacle to execution the bailiff has to respect. Else, T may raise a *Vollstreckungserinnerung* (section 766 ZPO) to the execution court (*Vollstreckungsgericht*).

(b) L and T also could have concluded an agreement providing for a provisional stay of enforcement proceedings. This agreement is qualified as a procedural contract and must be respected by the bailiff. Otherwise, T may institute proceedings under section 766 ZPO, including the option of a provisional stay of enforcement (section 766 (1) S.2, 732 ZPO).

---

[92] F Stein, M Jonas, and W Münzberg, *ZPO* § 765a para 15.

(a) Protection of earnings in Germany

In German law, salary income is protected by the sections 850 et seq. ZPO.[93] The law defines minimum amounts that can not be attached or only be attached in special cases (for example for alimony claims). These limits are normally calculated by the employer, who will transfer the protected remainder of the income to his employee.

After transfer of the protected funds to a bank account, the same limits apply. However, the attachment of the account can freeze the whole account (depending on the amount to be enforced) and it is up to the employee to apply to the court for release of the protected funds. When the bank account of a natural person is attached, section 835 (2) ZPO therefore provides for a delay of 2 weeks during which the bank is not allowed to pay the attached monies to the creditor. This delay can be extended by the court, if it is not able to decide on the application in time.[94]

(b) The basic remedy: section 850k (1) ZPO

After attachment took place, the debtor can apply to the enforcement court for release of the protected part of the income. However, the date of the attachment has to be taken into account. If the attachment took place for example at the 15th day of the month, the law assumes that half of the monthly expenses have already occurred. Only 50 per cent of the protected income will therefore be released. The debtor bears full burden of proof in these proceedings. [95]

(c) Provisional protection (Vorabschutz): Section 850k (2) ZPO

In practical terms, the more important remedy is sec. 850 k (2) ZPO. After an application under section 850 k (1) ZPO has been filed, the enforcement court can—ex officio or on application—avoid any hardship for the debtor and his family by releasing the funds necessary to bear the current necessary maintenance costs. The sum so released may not exceed the amount that will probably be released in the end under paragraph (1). This provisional procedure is faster than the normal procedure because the debtor only has to show a prima facie case and because the creditor will not be heard if the delay caused by the hearing would harm the debtor.

---

[93] Special rules apply to social benefits (ss 54 and 55 Sozialgesetzbuch) .
[94] F Stein, M Jonas, and W Brehm, *ZPO* § 850k para 26 .
[95] ibid para 16.

*(d) Protection against enforcement (Vollstreckungsschutz): Section 765a
    ZPO*

It is debated to which extent this remedy can be used in cases where the
creditor positively knows that the attachment of an account can not
amount to any positive result. This might be the case, if for example the
creditor already attached the income as such, and afterwards attaches the
debtor's bank account where only the protected part of the salary comes
in.[96]

III. CASE (3) WRONGFUL EXECUTION—SUBSTANTIVE ISSUES

*C obtains judgment against D for €20,000. D makes a genuine offer to pay
the whole sum and the legal costs upfront in satisfaction of the debt. C
however ignores D's offer for no good reason, and issues execution for the
whole debt of €20,000. C then proceeds to the execution stage. Goods to a
value far in excess of the debt owed and legal costs are then seized. What
are the remedies available to D in these circumstances?*

D would have been able to *avoid* the seizure of movable assets by
payment of the whole sum (including costs of execution)[97] to the bailiff,
section 754 ZPO, or by transferring the money via a bank to C and presenting a document from the bank proving this fact to the bailiff, section 775
n°5 ZPO.

If D presents such a document after the attachment, the bailiff will take
no further steps to sell the goods or to attach any other goods, section 775
n°5 ZPO. However, D does not get his goods back on this basis alone,
section 776 ZPO.

Rather, D has to bring an action against C under section 767
(*Vollstreckungsabwehrklage*) before the court of first instance that decided
on the merits of the case. D has to show that the debt was extinguished by
payment. The court will declare the execution in the assets to be inadmissible (*unzulässig*). This decision will be declared provisionally enforceable.
The effects are as described in case (1).

As C ignored D's offer, the execution was not 'necessary' in the sense of
section 788, 91 ZPO (above 9.5). He is therefore obliged to pay the costs
of the execution proceedings.[98] He is also liable for the costs of the
Vollstreckungsabwehrklage (section 91 ZPO).

---

[96] See LG Rostock, *Rechtspfleger* 2003, 37 (37) and LG Traunstein *Rechtspfleger* 2003,
309 (309).
[97] H Brox and W Walker, *Zwangsvollstreckungsrecht*, para 311.
[98] Cf ibid para 316.

G. The Netherlands

Ton Jongbloed

I. WRONGFUL EXECUTION: THIRD PARTIES

The claimants (A) obtain judgment against the defendant (B) for the sum of €15,000. Pursuant to the judgment, they start execution for recovery of the sum involved against A's movable assets. However, since execution has commenced, B's wife (C) gives notice that the assets, which are the subject of the execution process, belong to her. Execution nevertheless takes place.

(a) What are the remedies available to C in these circumstances?

In such a case B's wife C has some remedies. First of all, it is important to understand the matrimonial regime of The Netherlands. Most Dutch couples (approximately 75 per cent) are married. In the absence of an ante nuptial settlement, under the legal system of the Netherlands the joint estate of the husband and wife comprises all property, present and future, rendering all assets to be in common between them. In a scenario such as the one above, C must accept that A will execute her assets, because in such a case C's belongings are also B's.

Suppose, however, that B and C have made an ante nuptial contract, stating that *no* assets will be in common. In that case, A cannot execute C's assets as such an action would give rise to a tortuous claim.

Alternatively, husband and wife (B and C) may have made an ante nuptial contract declaring *some* assets as being in common. If the execution takes place and the assets of C—who has given notice that these assets belong to her—are sold, the execution will be illegal and C can commence a claim against A for damages.

(b) How is the decision made as to what goods shall be seized?

The decision as to what goods shall be seized is made jointly between the claimants and the bailiff. The bailiff will advise them, having regard to his professional knowledge, the value of the goods, and likelihood of a successful sale and other relevant factors.

(c) What is the bailiff (agent, judge, whoever responsible) supposed to check before the seizure of the goods (ie does s/he have to positively know about the property situation, may he rely on the statement of the third person etc)?

The bailiff does not have to have positive knowledge of the property situation.

According to Dutch law, most spouses are married with the joint estate between husband and wife comprising all property present and future meaning that *all* assets are common unless proved otherwise. C must show that there is joint estate by producing a copy of the ante nuptial agreement drafted by a notary-public or the postnuptial agreement given by the district court. The bailiff may not rely on a statement given by a witness, as such an agreement can only be evidenced by a statement drafted by the notary-public or the district court (compare article 61 Bankruptcy Code).

(d) How are joint and matrimonial goods treated?

See above

(e) Has C (in the case the wife) the opportunity to suggest alternative goods?

Yes, C has the opportunity to suggest alternative goods provided the claimants receive their money. So, for example, C could reasonably suggest the sale of her husband's car, or 'his' personal computer rather than the sale of 'her' jewels.

(f) How burdensome is the recourse to remedies?

The recourse to remedies is not unduly burdensome. Sometimes the wife can point out goods that can be sold easily and will bring in enough money for the claimants. In other cases the claimants will not get their money because the wife can not point to alternative goods or they fail to be of the requisite value to satisfy the judgment. In such cases the claimants are entitled to goods used by the wife.

II. WRONGFUL EXECUTION: PROCEDURAL ISSUES

A, the judgment debtor, has a bank account with B (the bank). C, the judgment creditor, decides to seize the bank account to make good the value of the judgment. C therefore proceeds and seizes the bank account. A wants to object to the seizure on the basis that the bank account comes from his monthly salary as an employee and is therefore not (or not as a whole) subject to execution. What are the remedies available to A in these circumstances?

In the Netherlands, there are no special rules stating that the bailiff has to find out where the money is coming from when seizing a bank account. Seizing the bank account means that the bank has to tell the bailiff within four weeks what the amount is (for example minus €100 or plus €234), and then, if the amount is positive, the bank must pay the requisite amount to the debtor. The bailiff has to divide the total amount between all the creditors.

However, in order to conform with Dutch law (Art 475a ff CCP), *a salary can only be partly seized*. First, there is a minimum amount that can be seized. For married persons, this is currently fixed at €1023,27 together for both, yet the figure changes every half year when social security payments are changed. For single people the amount is dependent on the income of the individual. It varies from between €511,64 (with an income of €568,49) to €716,29 (relative to an income of €795,88). As can be seen, the seized figure is 90 per cent of the individual's income. For single people living with children, there are special rules. In those circumstances, the bailiff will only seize a part of the income and the employer has to pay the sum of €511,64–€1023,27.

III. WRONGFUL EXECUTION: SUBSTANTIVE ISSUES

C obtains judgment against D for €20,000. D makes a genuine offer to pay the whole sum and the legal costs upfront in satisfaction of the debt. C however ignores D's offer for no good reason, and issues execution for the whole debt of €20,000. C then proceeds to the execution stage. Goods to a value far in excess of the debt owed and legal costs are then seized. What are the remedies available to D in these circumstances?

In such a situation there will be abuse of seizure, which will lead to a claim in tort. The result, is that C will be held liable in damages for the wrongful seizure suffered by D. In CCP there are no rules regarding this specific issue. Article 13 of Book 3 Civil Code concerns an abuse of rights, and that will be the basis for a legal claim by D.

In most instances of this sort, there will be a summary proceeding and the president of the district court will forbid C to continue with the execution.

H. Spain

Juan Pablo Correa Delcasso

I. WRONGFUL EXECUTION: THIRD PARTIES

The claimants (A) obtain judgment against the defendant (B) for the sum of

€15,000. Pursuant to the judgment, they start execution for recovery of the sum involved against A's movable assets. However, since execution has commenced, B's wife (C) gives notice that the assets, which are the subject of the execution process, belong to her. Execution nevertheless takes place.

(a) What are the remedies available to C in these circumstances?

It is vital to distinguish whether C's assets are private or joint. If the former, C will have every right to claim against the seizure as explained below. If the latter, it must be ascertained whether the joint assets are eligible to be realized to pay off a debtor of B.

Article 1347 of the Spanish Civil Code (hereinafter the CC) lists the different classes of joint assets, namely:

(1) Assets derived from the work of any of the partners.
(2) Rents or interests from both private and joint assets.
(3) Assets acquired by purchase.
(4) Assets acquired by redemption right.
(5) Companies.

Those assets may be executed in some circumstances. In fact, the Civil Code suggests that in principle joint assets will be realized to pay off any partner's debt where:

(1) Debts arising from household matters. (Art 1365 CC)
(2) Debts arising from the partner's job. (Art 1365 CC)
(3) Debts arising from extracontractual obligations for the benefit of the joint assets regimes as far as they are not owed by reason of B's negligence. (Art 1366 CC)
(4) There was agreement between the partners as to which assets must be realized. (Art 1367CC)

If the assets are realisable, it will be seen below that C has no right to oppose. Beyond those cases, the joint assets are not realisable and thus C has a right of opposition.

Bearing the above in mind, Article 556 of the Spanish Civil Litigation Act 2000 (hereinafter the SCLA) entitles C to claim against the execution of her assets within 10 days after receipt of the execution notice. The legal action is called *terceria de mejor dominio* (the better right of a third party over property) and C is fully entitled to stand against the seizure of the joint assets which are not meant to be realized for the payment of debts.

Article 541 of the SLA expressly recognizes the right of the non-debtor partner to oppose the seizure of the above assets where they are not meant to be realized. C should claim lack of legal title of the seizure as stated in Article 563 of the SCLA

It is critical to distinguish that while C has a right to oppose the seizure of the joint assets if they are not eligible for realization, the situation is rather different where the seizure is undertaken due to the lack of private assets of B. In that case, there is no right of opposition to the seizure. Where the joint assets are seized due to lack of enough private assets, C may only ask for the dissolution of the joint assets regime (*sociedad de gananciales*) and the court therefore will divide the goods. The SCLA is silent on the period of time for asking for the dissolution so it is sensible to think that it is for the Court to do so.

According to Article 541 (2) it is for A to show that the joint assets should be seized.

Besides the above, C may also oppose the execution on the more general grounds put forward in Article 556 (1), such as the existence of a written agreement opposing execution or the prescription of the right to execution.

(b) How is the decision made as to what goods shall be seized?

In principle, the court will decide to seize those goods that are easier to liquidate and are less onerous for the debtor. In addition, the above mentioned Article 1365 is critical to ascertain the eligibility of the assets when it comes to execute goods because of a partner's debts.

(c) What is the bailiff (agent, judge, whoever responsible) supposed to check before the seizure of the goods (ie does s/he have to positively know about the property situation, may he rely on the statement of the third person etc)?

The wording of Article 593 (1) of SCLA suggests a rather subjective approach, based on appearances and evidence of title. In addition, the Court will ascertain the goods by reviewing the copies of the Land Registry, as foreseen in Article 593 (3)

(d) How are joint and matrimonial goods treated?

It greatly depends on the matrimonial economic regime adopted by the couple. If they agreed on a separated regime (*separación de bienes*) the goods are held separately. It follows that C's goods will not be affected by B's debts at all. However, if the goods are held jointly, some goods may be affected, that is, the joint ones, in opposition to the private ones.

The core principle is set forth in Article 1373 of the Spanish Civil Code (hereinafter the CC) whereby assets held jointly by the couple are eligible for seizure, in particular where there are debts arising from household deals and professional matters. If so, the other partner must be notified. It is worth dwelling on the fact that, as explained above, not all joint assets are necessary capable of being seized.

(e) Has C (in the case the wife) the opportunity to suggest alternative goods?

Article 541 (2) of the SCLA states that C may suggest to substitute the debtor's private share of the joint assets for the common share of the joint ones. In that case, the joint economic regime of the couple will come to an end.

(f) How burdensome is the recourse to remedies?

Although it is fair to admit that the process may take some time, on the other hand the fact that most goods are normally registered eases the execution since checking to whom the goods belong is quite straightforward. In addition, it must be borne in mind that the Court may ask C to deposit some money before filing its claim. Yet, this is not always the case and is a power that only the Courts hold. The SCLA is silent about the amount of the deposit but is is submitted that it heavily depends on the potential damages C's claim may cause. In most of the cases it is necessary to be represented by a lawyer. In addition, according to Article 541 (4) if the court rejects C's claim, C still has right to appeal the court's decision.

II. WRONGFUL EXECUTION: PROCEDURAL ISSUES

A, the judgment debtor, has a bank account with B (the bank). C, the judgment creditor, decides to seize the bank account to make good the value of the judgment. C therefore proceeds and seizes the bank account. A wants to object to the seizure on the basis that the bank account comes from his monthly salary as an employee and is therefore not (or not as a whole) subject to execution. What are the remedies available to A in these circumstances?

Article 607 of the SCLA expressly states that the Minimum Salary is not subject to seizure. Yet, the rest of the salary which surpasses that amount is subject to some rules put forward in Article 607 (2). If the seizure covers part of the salary which falls within the Minimum Salary, the seizure will be void and thus A will have a right to oppose the seizure of that part of the salary.

III. WRONGFUL EXECUTION: SUBSTANTIVE ISSUES

C obtains judgment against D for €20,000. D makes a genuine offer to pay the whole sum and the legal costs upfront in satisfaction of the debt. C however ignores D's offer for no good reason, and issues execution for the whole debt of €20,000. C then proceeds to the execution stage. Goods to a value far in excess of the debt owed and legal costs are then seized. What are the remedies available to D in these circumstances?

In virtue of Article 585 of SCLA the seizure is avoided or (stopped) where the debtor pays the courts the amount due plus the interests and the seizure costs.

I. Sweden

Torbjörn Andersson and Hugo Fridén

I. WRONGFUL EXECUTION: THIRD PARTIES

The claimant (A) obtain judgment against the defendant (B) for the sum of 15,000 euros. Pursuant to the judgment they start execution for recovery of the sum involved against B's movable assets. However, since execution has commenced, B's wife (C) gives notice that the assets, which are the subject of the execution process, belong to her. Execution nevertheless takes place. What are the remedies available to C in these circumstances?

(a) Comments

As a first alternative, C may contact the Enforcement Agency and the Crown Inspector who has decided on distress and make a request for self correction by the agency. Then, the chief of departement, generally a lawyer with the title bailiff (*kronofogde*), will have to scrutinize the seizure decision and the basis upon which it is founded. Should the chief find that the wife has proved her right of property, the agency will cancel the seizure order under the Code of Execution Chapter 4 section 33. In case it turns out possible that the wife co-owns the assets, the order may be altered to encompass only part of them. Where it is found that the wife makes her claim only probable, but not certain—that is, where she has not proven a right of property, nor co-ownership—the agency may submit her to, within a month, bring court proceedings against the claimant (A) and the debtor (B). Should C refrain from bringing court proceedings within a month, she will have lost her right against A.

A second alternative for C is to appeal against the seizure order before a County court. This possibility is provided for by the Code of Execution Chapter 18 sections 1–2. This kind of appeal is not subject to time limits (Code of Execution Chapter 18 section 7). To some extent, the decision by the County Court may be appealed to the Court of Appeal and further on to the Supreme Court. When C appeals against the distress order, the executive procedure is not stayed. To bring about a stay of execution, C has to obtain an order of interim relief by the court.

A third alternative would be for C to use the ordinary civil procedure. She could bring a direct claim before a County court for a declaration of her right of property to the contested assets, against B (and A). Before or after bringing such a claim, she may also apply for interim relief in order to bring about a stay of execution.

II. WRONGFUL EXECUTION: PROCEDURAL ISSUES

A, the judgment debtor, has a bank account with B (the bank). C, the judgment creditor, decides to seize the bank account to make good value of the judgment. C therefore proceeds and seizes the bank account. A wants to object to the seizure on the basis that the bank account comes from his monthly salary as an employee and is therefore not (or not as a whole) subject to execution. What are the remedies available to A in these circumstances?

(a) Comments

In Swedish law of execution, there is a distinction between seizure and attachment of earnings. The latter form of enforcement means that generally the employer of the debtor is ordered to separate a certain amount of the debtor's salary, regularly once a month. The money is periodically transferred directly to the account of the Enforcement Agency. Thus, the periodically seized sums are out of the debtor's reach. Attachment of earnings, therefore, provides for the Enforcement Agency to notify both employer and employee that part of the latter's earnings must be seized. This notification generally takes place before the income is earned and always before payment.

When deciding on attachment of earnings, the Enforcement Agency also estimates a sum reserved for the living expenses of the debtor and his or her family. This sum includes expected costs for lodging, food and clothes. One of the requirements for deciding on attachment of earnings is that the income of the employee covers the sum reserved for living expenses.

When commenting on case 2 from a Swedish perspective, first one has to decide whether the requirements of attachment of earnings are met. Assuming therefore, in the context of the case, that there has been a decision on attachment of earnings, A may raise a number of objections. For instance, the employer may have reserved a too scarce an amount for the benefit of A and his or her family, in comparison to the notification delivered by the Enforcement Agency. In case the sum withheld by the employer still has not been transferred to the Enforcement Agency, the employer must hand over the missing money to A. Should the sum have been transferred to the Enforcement Agency, the agency must pay it to A directly.

Another possibility would be that the Enforcement Agency has notified a too small amount for the benefit of A. In that case, the Enforcement Agency must recalculate the sum reserved for the debtor and notify the employer and the debtor that a smaller amount will be withheld from future income payments (Code of Execution Chapter 7 section 10). The money wrongly withheld will be repaid to the debtor.

Yet another objection would be that attachment of earnings is not the proper form of execution. That form of execution presupposes that the assets in the bank account are considered to be income of employment (Code of Execution Chapter 7 section 1). Such an objection is probably unlikely, given the argument purported by A in the context of the case. Furthermore though, attachment of earnings requires that the money was not transferred to the bank before the moment the attachment was carried out (Code of Execution Chapter 7 section 24). Thus, if there is a decision on attachment of earnings and the money have been transferred by the employer to the bank beforehand, the decision cannot be used to seize the money from the bank. Such an objection meets with the circumstances of the hypothetical case and is likely to succeed. If this turns out to be the case, the attachment of earnings must be cancelled after re-evaluation and self correction by the Enforcement Agency or after appeal and review decision by court.

Now, it is an alternative possibility that A's bank account was not seized by way of attachment of earnings, but by way of ordinary seizure. For the circumstances of the case to occur in the context of ordinary seizure, it is likely that the Enforcement Agency has neglected the rules on property exempt from execution ('beneficiary rules').

Under the Code of Execution Chapter 5 section 1 the following are exempted: money, bank accounts, other claims and needs, insofar as these assets are required for the maintenance of the debtor, until the need is fulfilled by expected income. Unless extraordinary reasons are at hand, assets may not remain unconsummated and be exempted for more than a month.

This means that it is possible to seize a bank account containing 'salary money', but only insofar as the assets are not needed for the maintenance of the debtor. Seizure of a bank account containing the complete salary of a debtor is most likely in breach of the Code of Execution Chapter 5 section 1.

A procedural error of this kind may be remedied by the Enforcement Agency correcting itself, something that will be possible after application by the debtor. Under Code of Execution Chapter 4 section 34 the Enforcement Agency may correct its decisions within two weeks time from the seizure, when seizure has been decided in respect of property that should not have been made subject of seizure. Alternatively, the debtor may, within three weeks, make an appeal against the seizure decision. Appeal is made before a County Court under the Code of Execution Chapter 18 sections 1–2. Irrespective of whether the procedure of self correction or appeal is used, the finding that the whole or part of the bank account should be reserved for the debtor, the seizure may be cancelled in whole or in part accordingly.

III. WRONGFUL EXECUTION: SUBSTANTIVE ISSUES

C obtains judgment against D for €20,000. D makes a genuine offer to pay the whole sum and the legal costs upfront in satisfaction of the debt. C however ignores D's offer for no good reason, and issues execution for the whole debt of €20,000. C then proceeds to the execution stage. Goods to a value far in excess of the debt owed and legal costs are then seized. What are the remedies available to D in these circumstances?

(a) Comments

Under Swedish private law a debtor is entitled to pay his debt when it is due for payment. A creditor cannot refuse to accept payment. Would a creditor still try to escape payment, the debtor may deposit a sum of money corresponding to the amount of the debt. Under an old act (1927:56 on Deposition of Payments) such a deposition may be made to a public body picked or appointed. According to section 1, a debtor hindered to satisfy a debt due to circumstances on the side of the creditor, may make payment to the Regional Board, which is the public body designated as competent. A deposit bars execution of the claim which the payment concerns (Code of Execution Chapter 3 section 21). Furthermore, deposition results in cancellation of the enforcement.

Alternatively, the debtor may satisfy the debt to the Enforcement Agency. Under the Code of Execution Chapter 4 section 28 this kind of payments is considered to be immediately seized. When the money has been transferred to the Enforcement Agency, execution is terminated (Code of Execution Chapter 8 section 17). The prior seizure does not in any way hinder a voluntary payment to the Enforcement Agency; on the contrary, the prior seizure will be cancelled by the Enforcement Agency.

This solution is completely in line with the so called 'order of execution'. According to this order, the Enforcement Agency should make its pick among the assets of the debtor, giving priority to property the seizure of which will inflict the lowest cost on the debtor, the least loss and least of other inconveniences.

Thus, this way the debtor may satisfy his or her debt to a creditor, although the debt is subject to enforcement. This illustrates that the system leaves little room for collusive creditors, trying to get hold of more than the value of their claims.

Bibliography

Andenas, M (ed), *English Public Law and the Common Law of Europe* (Key Haven Publishing London 1998)

Andenas, M and Sanders, G (eds) *Enforcing Contracts in Transition Economies: Contractual Rights and Obligations in Central Europe and the Commonwealth of States* (BIICL/EBRD London 2005).

Andrews, N, 'Towards an European protective order in civil matters' in M Storm (ed) *Procedural Laws in Europe towards Harmonization* (Maklu-Uitgevers Antwerp 2003)

Angst, P (ed), *Kommentar zur Exekutionsordnug* (Manz Verlag Vienna 2000)

Angst, P, W Jakusch and H Pimmer, *Exekutionsordnung samt Einführungsgesetz, Nebengesetzen und sonstigen einschlägigen Vorschriften* (Manz Verlag Vienna 1995)

Anquetil, *Compétence d'attribution du juge de l'exécution* in S Guinchard and G Moussa (eds) *Droit et Pratique des Voies d'Exécution* (2004/05) 212.60

Asser, WDH, HA Groen and JBV Vranken, *Een niuwe balans; Interimrapport Fundamentele herbezinning Nederlands burgerlijk procesrecht* (Boom Juridische uitgevers uitgevers Den Haag 2003)

Bauer, F, *Studien zum einstweiligen Rechtsschutz* (Mohr Siebeck Tübingen 1967)

Baur, F and R Stürner, *Zwangsvollstreckungsrecht* (UTB Heidelberg 1995)

Blomeyer, J, *Die Erinnerungsbefugnis Dritter in der Mobiliarvollstreckung* (Duncker & Humblot Berlin 1966)

Bosina, J and M Schneider, Mahnverfahren und die ADV-Drittschuldneranfrage (Manzsche Verlag Vienna 1987)

Briggs, A, [2003] Lloyds' MCLQ 418

Briggs, A and P Rees, Civil Jurisdiction and Judgments (3rd edn Informa Books London 2002)

Brooke, H (ed), *Civil Procedure* ('The White Book') (Sweet & Maxwell London 2004)

Brox, H and W-D. Walker, *Zwangsvollstreckungsrecht* (Heymanns Cologne 2003)

Bruns, R, 'Die Collstreckung in küntftige Vermögensstücke des Schuldners' 171 *AcP* 358

Bülow, O and J Braun, *Gemeines deutsches Ziovilprozessrecht* (Mohr Siebeck Tübingen 2003)

Bundesministerium für Justiz (ed)
—*ADV-Exekutionsverfahren* (1995)

—*Die Organization der Rechtsberufe in Österreich* (.2002)

Burgstaller, A and A Deixler-Hübner, *Exekutionsordnug*

Caliebe, G, in *NJW* (2002) 285

Callewaert, J, 'The Judgments of the Court: Background and Content' in R MacDonald, F Matscher and H Petzold (eds) *The European System for the Protection of Human Rights* (Martinus Nijhoff Leiden 1993)

Canstein, R von, *Lehrbuch des österreichischen Civilprocessrechts* (2nd edn Carl Heymanns Verlag Berlin 1880)

Caupain, M and G de Leval (eds) *L'efficacité de la justice civile en Europe* (Larcier Brussels 1999)

Claassen, RD, Dictionary of legal words and phrases (2nd edn Durban LexisNexis Butterworths 1997)

Cleveringa Jzn, RP, 'De ontwerpen-1816 en-1820' in Scholten, Meijers and Zwolle *Gedenkboek Burgerlijk Wetboek 1838-1938* (Zwolle 1938)

Collins, L, *Provisional and Protective Measures in International Litigation* 234 *RdC* (1992)

Cuniberti, G, *Les mesures conservatoires portant sur des biens situés à l'étranger* (LGD Paris 2000)

Däumichen, F, 'Hat die Übertragung des Verfahrens zur Abgabe der eidesstattlichen Versicherung auf den Gerichtsvollzieher einen positiven Effekt erzielt?' *DGVZ* 2000, 183

Deakin, S, 'Regulatory Competition Versus Harmonization in European Company Law' in D Esty and D Gerardin (eds) *Regulatory Competition and Economic Integration: Comparative Perpectives* (OUP Oxford 2001)

Dicey, C and AV Morris, *The Conflict of Laws* (Sweet & Maxwell London 2003)

Dougan, M, *National Remedies Before The Court of Justice* (Hart Publishing Oxford 2004)

Edenfeld, S, 'Der Schuldner am Pranger-Grenzen zivilrechtlicher Schuldenbeitreibung' *JZ* 1998, 645

Fallon, M, 'Private International Law in the European Union and the Exception of Mutual Recognition' (2000) 4 Yearbook of Private International Law 37

Fallon, M und eussen, 'Private International Law in the European Union and the Exception of Mutual Recognition' [2003] YB Private International Law 38

Feil, E, Exekutionsordnung (Linde Vienna 1997)

Fink, H and A Schmidt, *Handbuch zure Lohnpfändung* (Vienna/Eisenstadt 1995)

Freudenthal, M and FJA van der Velden, 'Europees procesrecht van het Verdrag van Amsterdam' in EH Hondius et al (eds) *Van Nederlands naar Europees Procesrecht? Liber Amicorum Paul Meijknecht* (Kluwer Dordrecht 2000) 81–98

Freudenthal 'The Future of European Civil Procedure' (2003) 7/5 Electronic Journal of Comparative Law <http://www.ejcl.org/ejcl/75/art75–6.html>

Fricéro, N
—'La libre exécution des jugements dans l'espace judiciaire européen, un principe émergent?' (2003) Mél Normand
—'Le droit européen à l'exécution des jugments' (2002) Revue des Husissiers de Justice 6

Frowein, J, 'The Protection of Property' in R MacDonald, F Matscher and H Petzold (eds) *The European System for the Protection of Human Rights* (Martinus Nijhoff Leiden 1993)

Gaudemet-Tallon, H, *Compétence et reconnaisance* no 312

Gaul, HF
—*Das Rechtsbehelfssystem der Zwangsvollstreckung* ZZP 85 (1972) 251
—'Das Rechtsbehelfssystem der Zwangsvollstreckung—Möglichkeiten und Grenzen einer Vereinfachung' ZZP 85 (1972)
—*Neukonzeption der Sachaufklärung in der Zwangsvollstreckung* 108 ZZP 1, 8 [1955]
—*Zeitschrift für den Zivilprozess* 85 (1972) 251
—'Zur Struktur der Zwangsvollstreckung' *Der Deutsche Rechtspfleger (1971) 81*

Goldstein, S, *Commercial Litigation—Pre-emptive Remedies*

Guinchard, E Les procédures civiles d'exécution en droit international privé' in *Droit et Pratique des Voies d'Exécution* 2004/2005

Hagen, O, 'Zur Reform der Lohnpfändung' DRdA 1991, 329

Hendrikse, ML and AW Jongbloed (eds), *De toekomst van het Nederlands burgerlijk procesrecht* (Kluwer Deventer 2004)

Hess, B
—'Aktuelle Perspektiven der europäischen Prozessrechtsangleichung' *Juristenzeitung* 2001
—'Der Binnenmarktprozess' *Juristenzeitung* 1998 1021–32
—'EMRK, Grundrechte-Charta und Europäisches Zivilverfahrensrecht' *liber amicorum Eric Jayme* vol I (2004)
—IPRax 2001
—'Menschenrechtsschutz im europäischen Zivilprozessrecht' *Juristenzeitung* 2003
—'National Report: Germany' in A Verbeke and M Caupain (eds) *La transparence patrimoniale* (France Quercy Paris, 1999)
—Study JAI A3 02/2002 *Making More Efficient the Enforcement of Judicial Decisions within the European Union*
—Study JAI A3/02/2002 *Transparency of a Debtor's Assets, Attachment of Bank Accounts, Provisional Enforcement and Protective Measures* in Wiezcorek & Schütze *Kommentar zur Zivilprozessordnung* (3rd edn Munich 1999)

Hess, B and C Michailidou, 'Die Kollektive Durchsetzung von Schadensersatzansprüchen im Kapitalmarktrecht' in *Wertpapier Mitteilungen* (2003)

Hoeren, T, 'Der Pfändungs- unde Überweisungsbeschlub: Praktikabilitaät' *NJW* (1991) 410

Holzhammer, R, *Österreichisches Zwangsvollstreckungsrecht* (Springer Vienna 1993)

Ingenhoven, T, Grenzüberschreitender Rechtsschutz durch englische Gerichte (Nomos Verlag Gesellschaft Baden Baden 2001)

Isnard, J and J Normand (ed)
—*L'aménagement du droit de l'exécution dans l'espace communautaire— bientôt les premiers instruments* (Éditions Juridiques et techniques Paris 2003)
—*Nouveaux droits dans un nouvel espace europen de justice : Le droit processuel et le droit de l'exécution* (Éditions Juridiques et techniques Paris 2002)

Jakusch, W
—'Die EO-Novelle 2003' *Österreichiche Juristenzeitung* (2004) 201 in P Angst (ed) *Kommentar sur Exekutionsordnung* (Manz Verlag Vienna 2000)

Jungbauer, S, 'Die Zwangsvollstreckungsklausel-Rechtsmittel und Rechtsbehelfe nach der ZPO Reform', *JurBüro 2002*, 285

Kahlke, W, in *NJW* (1991) 2688

Kaye, P (ed) Methods of Execution of Orders and Judgments in Europe (Chancery Wiley Law Publications 1996)

Keith, J, W Podevin and C Sandbrook, *The Execution of Sheriffs' Warrants* (2nd edn Barry Rose Law Publications Chichester 1997)

Kennett, W
—'General Report: Enforcement' in M Storme (ed) *Procedural Laws in Europe towards Harmonization* (Maklu-Uitgevers Antwerp 2003)
—*The Enforcement of Judgments in Europe* (OUP Oxford 2000)
—*The Regulation of Civil Enforcement Agents in Europe* (published at www. cf.ac.uk/claws/staff/kennett 2001)

Kerameus, KD
—'Angleichung des Zivilprozessrechts in Europa' (2002) 66 RabelsZ 5
—*Enforcement in the International Context* 264 RdC (1997)
—'Enforcement Proceedings' *International Encyclopedia of Comparative Law* XVI K. Zweigert and U. Drobnig (eds) (Tübingen/Martinus Nijhoff Leiden Boston) (2002)

Klicka, T and I Albrecht, *Die EO-Novelle 1995—Änderungen im allge- meinen Teil*, ecolex 1995, 707

Kloiber, B
—'Das Auffindungs- und Zugriffsverfahren' *ZIK* 1996, 80

—'Die Exekutionsordnung-Novelle 1995. Ein Überblick über die mit 1.10.1995 in Kraft getretenen Änderungen' *ÖA* 1996, 2

Kodek, G, 'Gehörprobleme im Konkurs' in A Konecny (ed) *Insolvenzforum* (2003)

Köhler, K, 'Götterdämmerung des Gerichtsvollziehersystems?' DGVZ 2002, 19

Kollrob, H, 'Zure mandelnden Wirksamkeit der Fahnizexekution' *GZ* 1929, 137

Konecny, A

—'Automationsunterstützte Datenverarbeitung im Exekutionsverfahren' in Bundesministerium für Justiz (ed) *ADV-Exekutionsverfahren* (1995) 65

—'Die *Exekutionsordnung* nach 100 Jahren' in G Mayr (ed) *100 Jahre österreichische Zivilprozebgesetze* (Manz Verlag Vienna 1988)

Kropholler, J, *Europäisches Zivilprozebrecht* (7th edn Verlag Recht und Wirtschaft Heidelberg 2002)

Kruse, J, *The Law of Seizure of Goods, Debtor's Rights and Remedies* (Barry Rose Law Publications Chichester 2000)

Lenken, Zeitschrift für den Zivilprozess 106 (1966)

Leval, G, 'Le rôle sociale de l'huissiers de justice' in Chambre Nationale de *Huissiers* de Justice (eds), *Le rôle social et économique de l'huissier de justice* (Brussels 2000), 199

Maher, G and B Rodger, 'Provisional and Protective Remedies, The British Experience of the Brussels' Convention' (1999) 48 ICLQ 302

Mance, J in M Andenas, N Andrews and R Nazzini (eds) *The Future of Trans-National Commercial Litigation: English Responses to the ALI/UNIDROIT Principles and Rules of Trans-National Civil Procedure* (BIICL London 2004)

Matscher, F, 'Methods of Interpretation of the Convention' in R MacDonald, F Matscher and H Petzold (eds) *The European System for the Protection of Human Rights* (Martinus Nijhoff Leiden 1993)

Mayr, Peter G

—*Die Exekutionsordnungs-Novelle 1991* (WUV Vienna 1992)

—*Die österreichische Juristenausbildung* (WUV Vienna 1998)

—'Stellung und Aufgaben des Rechtsflegers in Österreich' *DRpfl* 1991, 397

Mohr, F

—'Anfrage an den Hauptverband bei Gehaltsexekution' *RdW* 1988, 91

—'Die neue Lohnpfändung' *EO-Novelle* 1991

—*Die neue Zwangsversteigerung. EO-Novelle 2000* (Manz Verlag Vienna 2000)

—'Die Zwamgsversteigerung einer Liegenschaft nach der *Exekutionsordnung-Novelle 2000*', Immolex 2000, 275

—*Executionsordnungs-Novelle 2000*, ecolex 2000, 641

—in P Angst (ed) *Kommentar sur Exekutionsordnung* (Manz Verlag Vienna 2000)

—'Vereinfachtes Bewillingungsverfahren und andere am 1.10.1995 in Kraft getretene Bestimmungen der EO-Novelle 1995', *ÖJZ* 1995, 889

—'Zwangensversteigerung einer Liegenschaft' in *Festschrift für Robert Dittrich* (Vienna 1000)

Moussa, T and S Guinchard, *Droit et Pratique des Voies d'Exécution* (2004/2005) 125.11

Muzielak, H and W Voit, *Zivilprozessordnung- Kommentar* (3rd edn Verlag CH Beck Munich 2002)

Nelle, A, *Anspruch, Titel und Vollstreckung im internationalen Rechtsverkehr: Einwendungen gegen einen titulierten Anspruch im deutschen und europäischen Zivilprozessrecht* (Mohr Siebeck Tübingen 2001)

Neumayr, M, *Exekutionsrecht* (Manz Verlag Vienna 2004)

Oberhammer, P

—'Fahrnisverwertung nach der EO-Novelle 1995: Grundsätzliche Neuerungen im Verwertungsverfahren' *ZIK* 1996, 84 in P Angst (ed) *Kommentar zur Exekutionsordnung* (Manz Verlag Vienna 2000)

—'Unternehmen, Gesamtsache, Unternehmenszubehör- und Pfändung *in* Festschrit für Heinz Krejci (Verlag Österreich Vienna 2001)

Oberto, G, Recrutement et formation des magistrats en Europe (Council of Europe 2003)

Ormanschick, H and O Rieke

—'Aufträge zur Abnahme der eidesstattlichen Versicherung durch Inkassounternehmen' *DGVZ* 2000, 181

—'Viertelshausen, Tätigkeitsgrenzen der Inkassounternehmen in der Zwansvollstreckung' *DGVZ* 181

Perrot, R, 'Le rôle économique et sociale des huissiers de justice' in Chambre Nationale de *Huissiers* de Justice (eds), *Le rôle social et économique de l'huissier de justice* (Brussels 2000), 199

Perrot, R and P Thery, *Procédures civiles d'execution* (Dalloz 2000)

Prütting, H and W Weth, 'Die Drittwiderspruchsklage gemäb §771 ZPO' *Juristische Schulung* 1988, 505

Rauscher, T and S Leible, *Commentary on Brussels Regulation [2003], no 20*

Rechberger, W, 'Franz Klein und das Exekutionsrecht' in H Hofmeister (ed) *Forschungsband Franz Klein* (Manz Verlag Vienna 1988)

Rechberger, W and D Simotta, *Execkutionsverfahren* (WUV Vienna 1993)

Rechberger, W and P Oberhammer, *Exekutionsrecht* (WUV Vienna 2002)

Reid, K, *A Practitioner's Guide to the European Convention on Human Rights* (Sweet & Maxwell London 1998)

Rennen, G and G Caliebe, Rechtsberatungsgesetz (RBerG) (CH Beck Munich 2000)

Rosenberg, L, HF Gaul, and E Schilken

—*Zwangsvollstreckungsrecht* (10th edn Munich 1987)

—*Zwangsvollstreckungsrecht* (11th edn CE Beck Verlag Munich 1987)

Rummel, P, *Kommentar: Allgemeines Bürgerliches Gesetzbuch* (Manz Verlag Vienna 2002)

Schilken, E, 'Stellungnahme zu den Vorschlägen der Kommission "Strukturelle Änderungen in der Justiz" des Deutschen Gerichtsvollzieher Bundes e.V.' *DGVZ* 2003, 65

Schiller, J, 'Auswahl des richterlichen Nachwuchses' *RZ* 1994, 156

Schlosser, P

—'Judicial and Administrative Cooperation' 284 *RdC* 284 (2000)

—'Protective Measures in Various European Countries' in J Goldsmith (ed) *International Dispute Resolution* (Fourteenth Sokol Colloquium Transnational Publishers Irvington NY 1997)

Schneider, E and H Roth, 'Eine Leistungsschau des österreichischen Zivilprozesses anhand der Zahlen des Jahres 1996' in Bundesministerium für Justiz, P Lewisch and W Rechberger (eds) *100 Jahre ZPO. Ökonomische Analyse des Zivilprozesses* (Manz Verlag Vienna 1998)

Schulz, [D], 'Einstweilige Mabnahmen nach dem Brüsseler Gerichtsstands- und Vollstreckungsübereinkommen in der Rechtssprechung des Gerichtshofs der Europäischen Gemeinschaften' *ZEuP* 2001

Scohlten, P, EM Meijers and WEJ Tjeenk Willink Zwolle (eds), *Gedenkboek Burgerlijk Wetboek 1838–1938* (Zwolle 1938)

Seip, D, 'Die Zukunft des Gerichtsvollziehers' *DGVZ* 1999, 113

Simotta, D, 'Einige Probleme des Datenschutzes im Zivilverfahrensrecht' *ÖJZ* 1993, 842

Snijders, HJ, 'Netherlands Civil Procedure' in *Access to civil procedure abroad* (CH Beck Verlag Munich 1996)

Stadler, A, Erlab und Freizügigkeit einstweiliger Mabnahmen im Anwendungsbereich des EuGVÜ *JZ* 1999

Stein, F, 'Der Europäische Vollstreckungstitel für unbestrittene Forderungen' (2004) IPRax 181

Stein, F, M Jonas and W Münzberg, *ZPO—Kommentar zur Zivilprozessordnung* (22nd edn Tübingen Verlag Mohr Siebeck 2002)

Storme, M (ed)

—*L'approchement du Droit Judiciaire de l'Union Européenne / Approximation of Judiciary Law in the European Union* (Nijhoff Dordrecht 1994)

—Procedural Laws in Europe (Maklu-Uitgevers Antwerp 2003)

Storme, M and G Tarzia (eds), *Rapprochement du Droit Judiciaire de l'Union européenne/Approximation of Judiciary Law in the European Union* (Dordrecht etc. 1994)

Stürner, R, *Generalbericht* in M Storme (ed) Procedural Laws in Europe (Maklu Uitgevers Antwerp 2003)

Thomas, H and H Putzo, *Zivilprozessordnung (ZPO), Kommentar* (CH Beck Verlag Munich 2003)

Tombe-Grootenhuis, M de, 'Relationships between Parties, Lawyers and Judges in Civil Contentious Proceedings' in M Elizondo Gasperín *Relaciones entre las Partes, los Jueces y los y los Abogados* (Instituto Nacional de Estudios Superiores en Derecho Penal, AC División Editorial Mexico 2003)

United Kingdom for Constitutional Affairs, *White Paper on Effective Enforcement* March 2003, Cm 5744 HMSO

van Boneval Faure, R, *Het Nederlandsche Burgerlijk Procesrecht* part 1 (3rd edn EJ Brill Leiden 1893)

van Brakel, S, 'De geschiedenis van de totstandkoming van het Burgerlijk Wetboek van 1820 tot 1838' in Scholten, Meijers and Zwolle *Gedenkboek Burgerlijk Wetboek, 1838–1938* (Zwolle 1938)

van Compernolle, J and G Tarzia, *Les mesures provisoires en droit belge, frantais et italien* (Bruylant Louvain-la-Neuve 1998)

van Dijk, P, in R MacDonald, F Matscher and H Petzold (eds) *The European System for the Protection of Human Rights* (Martinus Nijhoff Leiden 1993)

van Dijk, P and GJH van Hoof, *Theory and Practice of the European Convention on Human Rights* (Kluwer Law and Taxation Publishers The Hague 1998)

van Ingen, MJW and AW Jongbloed, 'Executoriale verkoop uit de hand' ex Art 3:251 lid 1 BW en met name Art 3:268 lid 2 BW (Kluwer Deventer 1998)

van Kan, J, 'Het BW en de Code Civil' in Scholten, Meijers and Zwolle *Gedenkboek Burgerlijk Wetboek 1838–1938* (Zwolle 1938)

van Koppen, PJ and M Malsch, 'De waarde van civiele vonnissen' in PJ van Koppen (ed) *Het recht van binnen; psychologie van het recht* (Kluwer Deventer 2002)

van Rhee, CH 'Civil Procedure: A European Ius Commune?' ERPL, 2000 589–611 589–611

van Rossem, W and Cleveringa Jzn, RP, Mr W van Rossem's Verklaring van het Nederlands Wetboek van burgerlijke rechtsvordering (Zwolle 1972)

Verbeke, A

—'Execution Officers as a Balance Wheel in Insolvency Cases' [2001] 9 Tilburg Foreign Law Review 7

—'L'information sur le patrimoine. Nécessité d'un droit d'exécution équilibré' in Chambre Nationale de *Huissiers* de Justice (eds) *Le rôle social et économique de l'huissier de justice* (Brussels 2000), 165

Verbeke, A and M Caupain (ed), *La Transparence patrimonial - Condition nécessaire et insuffisante du titre conservatoire européen?* (France Quercy Paris 1999)

Viertelhausen, A, 'Volstreckung in Werpapeier' *Deutsche Gerichtsvollzieherzeitschrift (DGVZ)* 2000 129

Wacke, A, '*Audiatur et altera pars* Zum rechtlichen Gehör im römischen Zivil- und Stafprozess' in *Festchrift Waldstein* (Stuttgart 1993)

Weibmann, H and E Riedel *Handbuch der internationalen Zwangsvollstreckung* (looseleaf edition Verlag Recht und Praxis Cologne)

Wetzell, GW, *System des ordentlichen Civilprozesses* (3rd edn Leipzig 1878)

Winterstein, B and R Hippler, 'Dienstleistungsunternehmen Gerichtsvollzieher' *DGVZ* 1999, 108

Wolf, in *Europäisches Wirtschafts- und Steuerrecht* 2000, 11

Yessiou-Faltsi, P

—'Der Europäische Vollstreckungstitel und die Folgen für das Vollstreckungsrecht in Europa *in Tübinger Tagung der Wissenschaftlichen Vereinigung für Internationales Verfahrensrecht*, Part III 3

—'Le droit de l'exécution selon la jurisprudence de la Cour Européenne des Droits de l'Homme: Analyse et Prospective' in J Normand and J Isnard *Le droit processuel et le droit de l'exécution* Editions Juridiques et techniques Paris 2002

Zöller, R and MG Vollkommer, *Kommentar zur Zivilprozessordnung (ZPO)* (Schmidt Cologne 2003)